A
PROPHETIC
ANALYST

A
PROPHETIC
ANALYST
Erich Fromm's Contribution to Psychoanalysis

Edited by
Mauricio Cortina, M.D.
and
Michael Maccoby Ph.D.

JASON ARONSON INC.
Northvale, New Jersey
London

The editors gratefully ackowledge permission to reprint material from the following sources:

Erich Fromm's *The Forgotten Language* (1951), *The Sane Society* (1955), *The Heart of Man* (1964), and *The Anatomy of Human Destructiveness* (1973) by permission of the Erich Fromm Literary Estate, Dr. Rainer Funk, executor. "Two Tramps in Mud Time" from *The Poetry of Robert Frost* edited by Edward Connery Lathem. Copyright © 1936 by Robert Frost. Copyright © 1964 by Lesley Frost Ballantine. Copyright © 1969 by Henry Holt and Co., Inc. Reprinted by permission of Henry Holt and Co., Inc.

This book is set in 11 point Palacio by TechType of Upper Saddle River, New Jersey, and printed and bound by Book-mart Press of North Bergen, New Jersey.

Library of Congress Cataloging-in-Publication Data
A prophetic analyst : Erich Fromm's contribution to psychoanalysis /
    edited by Mauricio Cortina and Michael Maccoby.
        p. cm.
    Papers originally presented at the Erich Fromm International
Symposium held at the Washington School of Psychiatry, May 6–8,
1994.
    Includes bibliographical references and index.
    ISBN 1-56821-621-1 (alk, paper)
    1. Fromm, Erich, 1900–Congresses. 2. Psychoanalysis–
Congresses. I. Cortina, Mauricio, 1945– II. Maccoby, Michael, 1933–
    III. Erich Fromm International Symposium (1994 : Washington
School of Psychiatry)
BF109.F76P76   1995
150.19'57'092–dc20   95-16850

Manufactured in the United States of America. Jason Aronson Inc. offers books and cassettes. For information and catalog write to Jason Aronson Inc., 230 Livingston Street, Northvale, New Jersey 07647.

The prophet sees reality and speaks what he sees. He sees the inseparable connection between spiritual strength and historical fate. He sees the moral reality underlying social and political reality—the consequence that will necessarily result from it. He sees the possibilities of change and the direction the people must take, and he announces what he sees.

E. Fromm, *You Shall Be As Gods*

He has showed you, O man, what is good; and what does the Lord require of you but to do justice, and to love kindness, and to walk humbly with your God?

Micah 6:8

The idea of the One who loves truth and justice but whose love is greater than his justice, the idea that man must find his goal by becoming fully human, was carried by men of vision—The prophets.

E. Fromm, *You Shall Be As Gods*

For I have set before you life and death; blessing and curse; choose life, that you and your children may live.

Deuteronomy 30:19

[The prophets] do not think in terms of individual salvation only, but believe that individual salvation is bound up with the salvation of society. Their concern is the establishment of a society governed by love, justice, and truth; they insist that politics must be judged by moral values, and that the function of policital life is the realization of these values.

E. Fromm, *You Shall Be As Gods*

Contents

PART III THE INTERSECTION BETWEEN SOCIAL CHARACTER AND CLINICAL WORK

PART IV ERICH FROMM'S PLACE IN THE PSYCHOANALYTIC MOVEMENT

Acknowledgments

This book is the culmination of the Erich Fromm International Symposium that took place May 6–8,1994 at the Washington School of Psychiatry. The event was cosponsored by the Washington School of Psychiatry, the William Alanson White Institute, the Instituto Mexicano de Psicoanálisis, and the International Erich Fromm Society. Without the collaborative support of these institutions the symposium would not have been successful and this book would not have had such a distinguished cast of international contributors.

We want to thank David Scharff, M.D., then director of the Washington School of Psychiatry, for his unstinting and enthusiastic support for the effort and for directing us to Jason Aronson to publish this book based on the international meeting. Neil MacLaughlin, David Scharff, M.D., Alan Grey, Ph.D., and Daniel Burston, Ph.D. all made useful and encouraging comments on the introduction. Dale Ortmeyer, Ph.D., Gerard Chrzanowski, M.D., Klauss Hoffmann, M.D., Alejandro Cordoba, M.D., Guadalupe Sanchez, Ph.D., Stanley Palombo, M.D., Jill Scharff, M.D., and Ann-Louise Silver, M.D. participated in the symposium, enriching the discussion. We hope some of this discussion is reflected in the book. The comments of Jorge Silva, M.D., in the symposium were also very helpful. Many thanks to Debby Ziff for typing many of the chapters in the book and correcting mistakes and to Lynn Starbird and Maria Stroffolino for technical assistance with computer documents. Barbara Lenkerd, Ph.D., in her dual role as colleague and wife of Mauricio Cortina, helped greatly with the editing and lovingly supported his work.

Contributors

Marco Bacciagaluppi, M.D. Milano, Italy. Fellow of the American Academy of Psychoanalysis. Training and supervising psychoanalyst, Instituto Erich Fromm (Bologna).

Ana Maria Barroso, M.D. Mexico City. Psychoanalyst, Instituto Mexicano de Psicoanálisis.

Romano Biancoli, Ph.D. Ravenna, Italy. Training and supervising psychoanalyst and Director, Instituto Erich Fromm (Bologna).

Sandra Buechler, Ph.D. New York. Supervision psychoanalyst, William Alanson White Institute. Faculty, Institute For Contemporary Psychotherapy (New York). Clinical supervisor, New York State Psychiatric Institute, Columbia-Presbyterian Medical Center.

Daniel Burston, Ph.D. Pittsburgh. Assistant Professor,

Department of Psychology, Duquesne University, Pitts-
burgh, Pennsylvania.
Mauricio Cortina, M.D. Washington, D.C. Clinical
Director, Eugene Meyer III Treatment Center, and faculty,
Washington School of Psychiatry. Honorary member,
Instituto Mexicano de Psicoanálisis, Clinical Assistant Pro-
fessor, Department of Psychiatry and Behavioral Sciences,
George Washington University.
Sonia Gojman, Ph.D. Mexico City. Training and super-
vising psychoanalyst, Instituto Mexicano de Psicoanálisis.
Codirector Seminario de Socio-psicoanálisis.
Carl Goldberg, Ph.D. New York. Associate Clinical
Professor, Department of Psychiatry, Albert Einstein Col-
lege of Medicine. Adjunctive Associate Professor of Social
Science, New York University.
Alan Grey, Ph.D. New York. Professor Emeritus of
Psychology, Fordham University. Faculty and supervising
psychoanalyst, William Alanson White Institute, West-
chester Center for the Study of Psychoanalysis and Psy-
chotherapy and Manhattan Institute for Psychoanalysis.
Marianne Horney Eckardt, M.D. New York. Associate
Professor of Psychiatry, New York Medical College. Fac-
ulty, Institute of Psychoanalysis (New York). Former
president, American Academy of Psychoanalysis.
Douglas LaBier, Ph.D. Washington, D.C. Director,
Center for Adult Development, Washington, D.C. Fac-
ulty, Washington School of Psychiatry. Private practice of
psychoanalytic psychotherapy.
Paul Lippmann, Ph.D. Stockbridge, Massachusetts.
Training and supervising psychoanalyst, William Alanson
White Institute. Clinical Associate Professor of Psychol-
ogy, Postdoctoral program in psychotherapy and psycho-
analysis, New York University.
Michael Maccoby, Ph.D. Washington, D.C. President,
The Maccoby Group. Director, Project on Technology,
Work, and Character. Member, Instituto Mexicano de

Psicoanálisis, former faculty member Washington School of Psychiatry and Kennedy School of Government, Harvard University.
Richard Margolies, Ph.D. Washington, D.C. Vice President, The Maccoby Group. Private practice in psychoanalytic psychotherapy, Washington, D.C.
Salvador Millán, M.D. Mexico City. Training and supervising psychoanalyst, Instituto Mexicano de Psicoanálisis. Codirector, Seminario de Socio-psicoanálisis.
Sharna Olfman, Ph.D. Pittsburgh. Assistant Professor, Department of Humanities and Human Sciences, Point Park College, Pittsburgh, Pennsylvania.
Paul Roazen, Ph.D. Menemsha, Massachusetts. Professor Emeritus, Department of Political Science, York University, Ontario, Canada. Member of Royal Society of Canada.

Introduction: Erich Fromm's Contributions to Psychoanalysis

Mauricio Cortina and
Michael Maccoby

THE NEGLECT OF FROMM'S CONTRIBUTIONS TO PSYCHOANALYSIS

Fromm's work suffered a strange fate. A well-known and respected writer whose ideas influenced the intellectual debate in the 1940s and '50s, his fame began to fade by the middle 1960s despite the fact that he continued to publish actively until the time of his death in 1980. Consider the following. Two of his important and original books, came out in the early 1970s, one on human aggression (Fromm 1973), *The Anatomy of Human Destructiveness*, and an ambitious study of peasant character and development, *Social Character in a Mexican Village* (1970, coauthored with Michael Maccoby). Neither of these major works received much attention. Even at the height of his popularity, the psychoanalytic establishment ignored or dismissed

Fromm, so its later silence was hardly a surprise. Fromm's ability to integrate sociological analysis with depth psychology in a clear, jargon-free style, threatened academicians entrenched in their own insular worlds. The scholarship and methodological rigor of these books could not be appreciated as it threatened the rigidity of departmental boundaries (McLaughlin 1995). The political left, another possible audience for Fromm's work, became in the 1960s infused with revolutionary fervor, a mixture of idealism and youthful zest. Fromm's message of emotional maturity and rational discourse was just not "hip" enough to engage the imagination of the flower children nor angry enough to influence the black power movement. The famous Fromm-Marcuse 1955–56 debate in *Dissent* magazine unjustly hurt Fromm's reputation with the left. Marcuse grossly misrepresented Fromm by grouping him as a neo-Freudian with a superficial culturalist outlook and distorted Freud by describing him as a radical philosopher (Burston 1994, Rickert 1986). However, the critique stuck, and reinforced the dismissal of Fromm by the psychoanalytic mainstream as being shallow.

The humanistic "third force" in psychology seemed another natural audience, given Fromm's commitment to humanistic principles. However, Fromm's efforts to grapple with the nature of destructive passions and his trenchant critique of consumerism was not in synchrony with humanistic psychology's appeal to the segment of the baby-boom generation interested in finding a less rigid alternative to the Protestant ethic. Fromm in turn found the message of humanistic psychology superficial and misleading.

Other ironies dogged Fromm's career. Within the psychoanalytic establishment, he had been branded a heretic. But as any careful reading of Fromm demonstrates, of all the independent-minded dissidents, he was most closely aligned to the spirit of Freud (Burston 1991). Fromm does not fit neatly into the drive-relational dichotomy (Greenberg and Mitchell 1983). In many ways Fromm was a drive theorist, albeit his conception of drives differed markedly from Freud's tension-reduction and mechanistic views that he so effectively criticized. Fromm revised Freud with an elegant existential and humanistic theory of human motivation, but this revision did not jettison Freud's vision of human nature as a continual conflict between opposing tendencies. Indeed, as Fromm indicated in *The Anatomy of Human Destructiveness* (1973), Freud's mature and vitalistic view of motivation, eros, and the death instinct, did not square with his mechanistic paradigm and called for a major revision.[1] What is surprising is that so few commentators, either critical or sympathetic to Fromm, have noticed his close affinity (for better or for worse) to Freud's intellectual legacy (Burston 1991, Cortina 1992).

From the start, psychoanalysis has been beset by political feuds and fractious attacks that carried over to the United States, creating many bitter schisms (Eckardt 1978, Frosh 1991, see also Roazen, Chapter 17 in this volume). Among other negative consequences, this divisiveness has produced a Tower of Babel, with jargon proliferating from different psychoanalytic schools. This curse has impeded scholarship while promoting insular smugness and sloppy thinking. Many of the wounds to psychoanalysis have been self-inflicted.

While it has become fashionable to announce the demise of psychoanalysis (Crews 1993), the last two decades have produced exciting new developments that demonstrate that the news of its death is exaggerated. There is enough intellectual vigor to support a belief that psychoanalysis as a theory of human development and as a treatment in the form of dynamic psychotherapies will prosper in its next hundred years. Some of the promising developments have taken the form of integrating psychoanalysis with developmental psychology (Ainsworth et al. 1978, Bowlby 1969, 1980, 1988a, Bretherton 1990, Emde 1988, 1991, 1994, Lichtenberg 1983, 1989, Main 1993, Main et al. 1985, Sandler 1994, Sroufe 1989, Stern 1985, 1994), developmental psychopathology (Cicchetti 1989, Crittenden 1992, 1994, Fonagy 1993, Sroufe and Rutter 1984), cognitive theories and the neuroscience (Clyman 1991, Erdelyi 1985, Horowitz 1989, Peterfreund 1980, Rosenblatt and Thikstun 1978). There are current efforts to validate clinical hypotheses derived from psychoanalytic work with patients using sophisticated methodologies (Caston 1993, Caston and Martin 1993, Weiss and Sampson 1986).

Another promising development has been the growing dialogue between schools of psychoanalysis. An early effort in this direction was taken by Harry Guntrip, a member of the "middle group" (currently known as the independent group) of the British Psychoanalytic Society. Greatly influenced by the two independent voices of Fairbairn and Winnicott, Guntrip (1969, 1971) tried to establish a transatlantic dialogue, by comparing and contrasting the object relations approach with the work of the interpersonalists in the United States (Horney, Sullivan, Fromm) as well as the ego psychologists (Erikson and Hartmann). The effort was carried on by Greenberg and Mitchell (1983), whose book *Object Relations in Psychoanalytic Theory* became a landmark effort that facilitated efforts to establish a "comparative psychoanalysis." At least one major journal (*Psychoanalytic Dialogues*) and several books have continued this effort (Mitchell 1988, Pine 1990, Tyson and Tyson 1992).

Here we encounter another irony. Fromm's work is rarely mentioned in current efforts to build bridges between different schools of psychoanalysis. Yet no one can seriously dispute that Fromm's was one of the earliest critiques of libido theory. Fromm broadened the purview of psychoanalysis from the narrow confines of oedipal theory to encompass a wide range of social and cultural factors that influence human development. Like Fairbairn and later Bowlby, Fromm reformulated Freud's belief that the infant's primary drive was to minimize tension and seek pleasure, insisting that the infant's (and the adult's) primary need is to establish affectional ties that provide a sense of security and belonging (see below).

It would seem that for several reasons and different circumstances Fromm's contribution was fated to be unappreciated or misunderstood. To what extent did Fromm contribute to this situation? We think several factors have played a role. Fromm believed that if psychoanalysis was to have any relevance for the problems of his day, he had to reach a large educated public. His instant success with *Escape from Freedom* (1941), a brilliant combination of depth psychology and historical and sociological analysis, set the tone for the rest of his career. Fromm discovered that he could bypass the psychoanalytic community and did not need its approval. He continued to write for a broad audience. His contributions to psychoanalysis are interspersed with a radical critique of society and with a commitment to and analysis of humanistic values and ideals. Had Fromm written a straightforward account of his views on psychoanalysis, emphasizing the clinical implications of his theoretical revisions, his work might not have been so easily ignored. In today's more pluralistic environment it would have been easier to identify Fromm as one of the pioneers of current psychoanalytic trends. As it is, clinicians have to make a sustained effort to sift through Fromm's many books (he was a prolific writer) in order to get an idea of Fromm the clinician. Many are put off in the process by Fromm's prophetic message, as was

Erik Erikson, whose work otherwise shows striking similarities to Fromm's.[2]

THE CONTRADICTIONS BETWEEN FROMM'S PROPHETIC AND ANALYTIC VOICES

Fromm's promised volume on clinical psychoanalysis was never completed.[3] Maccoby (Chapter 2 in this volume) analyzes the contradictions in Fromm's work that contributed to his difficulty in delivering on this promise. Two distinct voices can be discerned in Fromm's work. The analytic voice describes what *is* and how it came to be. It provides an analysis of the thoughts, emotions, and behavior patterns that may be conscious or unconscious. While the analytic voice helps us understand what *can* be, the prophetic voice states what *should* be. The prophetic voice looks to the future and rekindles hope. Fromm's messianic view of hope is central to the prophetic vision. As the Swedish neurophysiologist David Ingvar (1985) has shown, the human brain cannot function without hope. At its best, the prophetic voice gives expression to this basic human need.

When these two voices sing in harmony, as they do in Fromm's (1941) study of fascism, his theory of existential needs (1947, 1955, 1973) or his analysis of biblical images of God in the Old Testament (1966), the result is a penetrating and enormously helpful vision. At other times the two voices are discordant. In the midst of a keen observation, you may encounter a dogmatic statement, as Lippmann observes (Chapter 4 in this volume) in regard to Fromm's contribution to the understanding of dreams. Or Fromm may call for loving relatedness while at the same time urging us to break our primary ties, as if all forms of dependency (or attachment, to use Bowlby's apt term) are unhealthy and need to be jettisoned (see Cortina, Chapter 3 in this volume). Marianne Eckardt (Chapter 5 in this volume) reminds us that we need to read Fromm with caution and not get caught up in trying to turn Fromm's critique of orthodoxy into another dogma.

At times, Fromm's prophetic voice overwhelms the analytic voice, and high-minded moralism, but moralism nonetheless, substitutes for analytical discourse. We hasten to add that Fromm's moral imperatives were tempered by his focus on social and economic forces that limit the possibilities for freedom and happiness. This was not so true when his moral imperatives were disconnected from socioeconomic analysis.

The issues of how to integrate a normative approach to the social sciences and psychotherapy are too complex to be addressed here (see Burston and Olfman, Chapter 12 and Eckardt, Chapter 5). But whatever its strengths and limitations, Fromm's attempt to develop a normative approach to psychoanalysis and the social sciences was bold and courageous. Moreover, its weaknesses are instructive, alerting us to the importance of keeping principled approaches to patient care and the social sciences grounded in historical and empirical research.

It was more in Fromm's clinical practice that the conflict between the analytic and the prophetic voice became evident. Fromm struggled with this conflict, and he experimented with analytic technique in an attempt to integrate these two voices. For ten years he practiced as a strict Freudian, then abandoned the couch to establish a more direct connection with the analysand. In the 1960s, he immersed himself in Zen Buddhism and became at times like the Zen master, who as Maccoby points out, figuratively hit you on the head to wake you up.

Fromm expressed some reluctance to write a book on

psychoanalytic technique that would codify his approach
to psychoanalysis. But perhaps the most important factor
that obliged him to continually postpone his book on
clinical psychoanalysis was his difficulty in reconciling
these two voices. Another analysis of why Fromm could
not deliver on his promise to write a book on clinical
psychoanalysis is developed in Victor Saavedra's recent
book, *La Promesa Incumplida de Erich Fromm* (Erich Fromm's
Unfulfilled Promise) (1994). Saavedra, who was a student
of Fromm's at the Mexican Psychoanalytic Institute, argues that Fromm's approach to clinical psychoanalysis
was seriously flawed and not "psychoanalytic." According
to Saavedra, Fromm lacked a sound developmental approach; he ignored or minimized oedipal strivings and the
phenomena of repetition compulsion and regression. Saavedra also thinks Fromm replaced the analysis of transference with a humanistic ideology and assumed an omniscient position toward the patient. While we concur with
part of Saavedra's criticisms, particularly in regard to
Fromm's approach to transference in psychoanalysis (see
below), we also have major disagreements.[4]

Saavedra believes that Fromm's critique of orthodoxy
ended up throwing the baby away with the bathwater. We
think this is what Saavedra has done in his critique of
Fromm. Fromm's contribution to psychoanalysis is rich,
complex, and checkered. A balanced evaluation of
Fromm's legacy depends on an explicit understanding of
his contribution to psychoanalysis. It is to this assessment
that we now turn. Our main purpose is not to be comprehensive, but to correct a historical injustice, observing
where Fromm anticipated contemporary trends and
where his contribution still awaits full understanding and
further development. By lifting Fromm's contribution to
psychoanalysis from obscurity, we hope to demonstrate

the relevance of Fromm's distinctive voice to the ongoing psychoanalytic dialogue.

FROMM'S MAIN CONTRIBUTIONS TO PSYCHOANALYSIS

Fromm: An Early Precursor of the "Relational" Model in Psychoanalysis

Fromm was one of the earliest and most radical proponents of a relational model in psychoanalysis (see LaBier, Chapter 7 in this volume). In a manner very similar to Fairbairn's (1952) radical object relations theory in which libido is primarily object seeking, not pleasure seeking, Fromm (1941) postulated that the "key problem in psychology is that of the specific kind of relatedness of the individual towards the world and not the satisfaction or frustration of this or that instinctual need per se" (p. 12).[5] Fromm (1970) expressed the same idea stating that the "dynamism of human nature is primarily rooted in this need of man to express his faculties toward the world, rather than his need to use the world as a means for satisfaction of his physiological necessities" (p. 49). Of course, the satisfaction of physiological needs is essential. However, the point Fromm emphasized repeatedly is that the satisfaction of specific human needs for self-expression and relatedness was just as important as satisfying physiological needs. Fromm distinguished productive and unproductive orientations based on the degree of relatedness, activeness, aliveness, and realism present in character structure (Fromm 1947, 1964, 1973). Fromm used to say that just as we need to survive physically by assimilating the material

world, so we need to survive emotionally by our relatedness to others. He considered human relatedness to be an
overarching motivation that could not be reduced to
Freud's pleasure/unpleasure principle.[6]
    Fromm went beyond the narrow dyadic focus of object
relations theories such as Fairbairn's. He developed a relational theory that saw the impact of society and culture
as becoming embodied in character structures, limiting the
range and depth of conscious experience and not simply as
affecting the surface of personality development (see our
discussion of social character theory, below). According to
Fromm this was accomplished by means of "socially conditioned filters" that permit certain experiences "to be filtered through, while others are stopped from entering
awareness" (Fromm et al. 1960, p. 99).[7]
    In addition, Fromm insisted that certain developmental
issues like security were not limited to infancy and childhood but were part of the human condition and compelled
us to adapt to historical contingency and necessity with no
less passion or fright than an infant's longing for the
security of mother (Fromm 1964). A life span approach is
now integral to many developmental and psychoanalytic
models of development (Ainsworth 1985, Bowlby 1969,
1988a, Connell 1990, Parkes et al. 1991, Sperling and
Berman 1994, Stern 1985).

The Role of Activity, Alienation, and Passivity in Human Development

Fromm's views of human nature are derived from thinkers
such as Aristotle, Spinoza, Hegel, Goethe, Feuerbach,
and Marx. From this tradition Fromm incorporated the
fundamental premise that human adaptation is not passive, but involves an active, dynamic process. Fromm's

views of individuality and identity were based on the belief that self was embodied in action or "activeness" (1947, 1962, 1968). In interaction with the cultural and material world, humans are cocreators of their own collective and individual histories. The concept of alienation (or estrangement) is a corollary of this position (Fromm 1961, 1962).

Alienation or estrangement are failed attempts to gain mastery over the world at the expense of losing touch with our most creative values and needs that stimulate consciousness and freedom. Derailed attempts at mastery become experienced as alien and oppressive forces.[8]

The concept of activity in the construction of models of the world and of self-other representations was central to Piaget's epistemology and is a dominant theme in contemporary views of development (Emde 1988, Kagan 1982, Sandler 1994, Sroufe 1990, Stern 1985). In clinical work, David Shapiro (1989) has come to see self-estrangement as the most important feature of neurotic character formation. Roy Schafer's (1976) action language is another brilliant extension of these principles.

Fromm's lifelong dialogue with Freud was an attempt to highlight the significance of the humanistic principles for psychoanalysis and the social sciences that were obscured by Freud's commitment to a physicalistic metapsychology and by the cultural trappings of his era (Fromm 1947, 1955, 1970). Holt (1972, 1973) also makes a distinction between Freud's mechanistic and humanistic images of man but never credits Fromm, who, more than anybody else, championed these ideas.

Fromm's Existential-Evolutionary Approach to the Understanding of Human Nature and Motivation

Freud saw the most primitive human drives as being rooted in our phylogenetic history. Fromm acknowledged our biological ancestry, but pointed out that some of our strongest passions are derived from the emergence of completely new characteristics that define the human condition. Fromm asked a basic question: What are the new characteristics that define the human animal that are not part of our shared biological ancestry with other animals? This was a completely new approach in psychoanalysis to the study of human nature, an approach that has found support in distinguished evolutionary thinkers such as the late George Gaylord Simpson (1949), Theodosius Dobzhansky (1962) and more recently, Stephen Jay Gould (1982).

According to Fromm (1947, 1955, 1973), two evolutionary trends define the human condition: the weakening of instinctual endowment in primates and the expansion of the brain's neocortex. This combination of trends produces new (emergent) phenomena; the capacity for self-awareness and foresight, the gradual recognition of our mortality, and needs for self-expression and creativity.

Fromm's approach to human nature led him to derive a list of specific human needs that result from this basic existential condition:

A need for a frame of orientation and devotion.
A need for roots.
A need for unity.
A need to be effective.
A need for excitation and stimulation.

While this list may be incomplete or flawed (Grey 1993; also see Grey, Chapter 11 in this volume), it has the great merit of drawing attention to a variety of human motivations that are primary and not always reducible to "deeper" atavistic inclinations. Fromm's motivational theory went far beyond Freud's concept of dualistic drives and set a new precedent with a multi-motivational model that has been followed by contemporary theorists of motivation such as Daniel Stern (1985), Robert Emde (1988, 1992), Michael Maccoby (1988), and Joseph Lichtenberg (1989).

Examples of the Application of Fromm's Evolutionary/Existential Approach to Understanding Religion and Human Destructiveness

Based on this view of the human condition, Fromm believed that the need for a "frame of orientation and devotion" (a cognitive and spiritual map) was universal. The important question for Fromm is not whether people considered themselves religious or not. Quoting Abbe Pire, Fromm thought what matters is the difference not between believers and unbelievers, but between those who care and those who don't. Fromm asked us to evaluate religious belief in terms of whether our practice of life affirms human solidarity or whether it is divisive and hateful. Do religious practices support a reverence for life or do they promote destruction? For Fromm (1950) neurosis could be seen as a "private religion" that requires devotion to power over others or to different forms of human bondage.

This view of motivation also led Fromm (1964, 1973) to make an important distinction between defensive aggression, which is biologically rooted and serves an important evolutionary function (and in this sense is in the service of life), and malignant aggression, rooted in the existential need to overcome a sense of impotence and aloneness by sadistic control or by destructiveness[9] (see Goldberg, Chapter 6, for an elaboration of these ideas).

Fromm's Revision of Oedipal Theory

The Oedipus complex was central to Freud's understanding of human development (Freud 1916) and history
(Freud 1912, 1938). No other aspect of psychoanalytic
theory—perhaps with the exception of his work on
dreams—was so passionately held by Freud. In questioning so directly Freud's interpretation of *Oedipus Rex*
and the importance of children's sexual strivings toward
parents in human development Fromm sealed his fate as a
psychoanalytic apostate. In questioning Freud's interpretation of Sophocles' tragedy, Fromm (1951) observed that
if one takes into account the other two parts of the trilogy,
Oedipus at Colonus and *Antigone*, an alternative interpretation is possible:

> the myth can be understood as a symbol not of the
> incestuous love between mother and son but of the rebellion
> of the son against the authority of the father and the
> patriarchal family; the marriage of Oedipus and Jocasta is
> only a secondary element, only one of the symbols of the
> victory of the son, who takes his father's place and with it all
> his privileges. [p. 202]

In Fromm's analysis of the trilogy, Antigone, Haemon,
and Oedipus (as becomes evident in *Oedipus at Colonus*)
are the voices of the matriarchal principle representing
unconditional acceptance and equality. Creon and Laius
are the voices of patriarchy representing the principle of
obedience and domination. The conflict between fathers,
sons, and daughters, so evident in the plays, is an
inevitable consequence of the clash between these two
principles.

Fromm (1980) believed that the oedipal striving toward
the mother was based on a "non-sexual desire for protec-

tion or safety" (p. 31). Fromm (1955) observed that normally, the emergence of sexuality serves as an impetus to
separate from mother, not as a source of fixation. Nonetheless, in Fromm's estimate, Freud's discovery of the
Oedipus complex could still be considered as one of his
most important contributions as long as the tie was
reconceptualized as a passionate need to maintain an
emotional unity with the mother. However, by Freud
giving the incestuous striving paramount significance,
"the importance of the tie with the mother is recognized;
by explaining it as sexual, the emotional—and true—
meaning of the tie is denied" (Fromm 1955, p. 45).

Indeed, Fromm considered this emotional tie as the most
important and intense of all strivings in humans. He redefined incest to mean the regressive desire to maintain a
symbiotic tie with mother, "nature, blood, and soil" (see
Cortina, Chapter 3 in this volume, for a critique of Fromm's
tendency to see the tie with the mother as primarily regressive in nature). Psychoanalytic revisions in general followed Fromm's lead in emphasizing the importance of the
tie with the mother as primary and nonsexual. Unlike
Fromm, most revisions were careful not to question the
importance of oedipal strivings (with a few exceptions, as
in Jung's, Horney's, Fairbairn's, Sullivan's and Bowlby's
work). A sophisticated version of this revisionist strategy
was Mahler and colleagues' (1975) seminal work on the
phases of separation and individuation based on the
premise of an early symbiotic infant–mother bond. Loewald (1979) is yet another example of this strategy. To our
knowledge, Fromm has never been credited for having
introduced the concept of symbiosis in psychoanalysis.

There is converging evidence from many fields such as
ethology, anthropology, and developmental psychology to
indicate that, in fact, incest avoidance is natural (not repressed) within the nuclear family or in people growing up

together in an intimate environment. Furthermore, this natural avoidance of incest serves a vital biological function (M. T. Erickson 1993).[10] Incestuous fantasies, frank incest, and seductive behavior of parents toward children (or vice versa) develop only when there is a history of pathologically disturbed attachments or when emotional attachments are absent (Sroufe and Wards 1980, Williams and Finkelhor 1995). Sexuality and attachment are distinct motivational systems that become blended developmentally in complex ways. Fromm was prescient in having seen that the primary tie with the mother was based on the nonsexual need for security and protection and helped pave the way for a better understanding of psychosexual development.

The Theory of Social Character

According to Fromm (1941), "man develops those traits that make him *desire* to act as he *has* to act" (Fromm's italics, p. 283) in order to adapt to prevailing social, cultural, and economic conditions. Fromm used the term *social character* for the syndrome of adaptive character traits that are shared by a large class or group within a given society. While individual character is a result of adaptation to the immediate environment of the family, social character is an adaptation to the broader sociocultural environment. Since the family, according to Fromm (1947), functions as "the psychic agent of society" (p. 68) much of individual character is channeled to meet social and cultural requirements. Consequently, Fromm believed that human development cannot be understood fully without considering what social, economic, and cultural factors impinge on individuals and families (see Chapters 13 through 15 by Millán, Funk, and Margolies, for an extended discussion of the relevance of these ideas for clinical practice).

The concept of social character is useful as a holistic view of development. It is also important in understanding social change. Much of human history can be seen as a struggle to find an equilibrium between human needs for freedom and self-expression and social and economic factors that demand adaptation. Many cultural and social beliefs born of necessity, become embodied as social character traits that provide cement to hold society together. When there is rapid social change and significant discrepancies develop between new social conditions and old social character types—adapted to previous conditions—the result can be social dynamite.[11]

Fromm's Contribution to the Understanding of Dreams: The Unconscious as a Repository of the Best and the Worst in Humans

Fromm shared with Jung a belief that unconscious processes could give expression through dreams to sophisticated intellectual and spiritual insights. Fromm's experiential approach to dreams (1951) took the manifest content of dreams as a coded symbol that could deliver a powerful message without the need of endless associations (see Lippmann, Chapter 4 in this volume). Overintellectualization deprives the dream of its creativity. This view of dreams is consistent with modern interpretations (Palombo 1978).

Fromm also expanded Freud's view of the content of the unconscious. Not only can individual thoughts, feelings, or motives be repressed, Fromm believed that every society excludes certain thoughts and feelings from being experienced. This lack of awareness is a consequence of the need to adapt to social and economic realities that *may* be in conflict with an individual's legitimate needs and aspirations. In addition, Fromm saw society as having a powerful facilitating function when there is greater harmony between human aspirations and social goals. For Fromm, the lifting of socially repressed thoughts and feelings required a commitment to improve society by overcoming oppression and expanding the sphere of freedom.

Fromm's Clinical Contributions: Strength and Weaknesses

Although Fromm's clinical approach to psychoanalysis was less developed than his other contributions, it is clear that he tried to bring to the clinical encounter the same humanistic beliefs that infused his theoretical work. Central among these beliefs was the famous aphorism of Terence that "nothing human is alien to me" (which was also the motto of Freud). While Fromm recognized that skill and competence are important factors in therapeutic success, he believed that analysts could only go as far with their patient as their ability to discover in themselves what their patients were experiencing. Fromm believed that we all have the capacity to be murderous, to experience madness, or to be saintly. Even though developmental paths and existential choices can take each of us closer to or farther from each of these possibilities, being human means accepting that "there, but for the grace of God, go I." Having identified the patients' humanity as their own, analysts cease to see patients simply as objects of study and engage with them directly, in what Fromm called a "center to center" relationship.

As Maccoby and Bacciagaluppi write in Chapters 2 and

8, Fromm did not fully follow the path that Ferenczi took of empathic immersion into patients' experiences, nor did he follow Freud's prescription of neutrality and detachment. Like Freud, he maintained a degree of skepticism about the patients' distortions and unconscious manipulations, but he believed that a purely intellectual approach was inadequate for understanding another person. The analyst had to be open to his own feelings in order to grasp the patient as a full human being. This is not a simple position. At his best, Fromm's interpretations were penetrating and encouraged the analysand's life affirming tendencies. At his worst, his prophetic voice could be overbearing and intimidating, ironically reproducing in the transference the type of idolatry that he passionately opposed.

As Saavedra (1994) points out, perhaps the most damaging aspect of this attitude is that Fromm acted at times as if he had clairvoyant knowledge and could see through patient's defenses and rationalizations (it is not surprising that some of his patients felt so threatened that they would have paranoid fantasies). Yet in other instances he could be warm, jovial, and generous. When he thought his students were serious and honest, he could be a tough critic, but enormously helpful and supportive. Due to these contradictions, Fromm's position can be seen as consistent with the contemporary emphasis on countertransference and the use of the analyst's emotional responsiveness as a vehicle for understanding and change — an empathic mode (see Chapters 9, 11, and 13 by Gojman, Grey, and Millán). He also can be interpreted as following a more traditional emphasis on insight and the analysis of resistance — an analytical mode (see Bacciagaluppi's discussion) — or he can be seen as bullying and arrogant — a prophetic-grandiose mode (Saavedra 1994).

Many therapists who have been influenced or trained in

psychoanalytic psychotherapy do not use a couch or see patients four or five times a week. For these therapists, Fromm's practice of psychoanalysis consisting of face-to-face meetings on a once or twice weekly basis (occasionally he saw patients three times a week) offers an alternative psychoanalytic model of treatment based on the premise that in-depth work does not require the use of the couch or four or five sessions a week. Fromm thought that the depth of analysis depended on the analysts' grasp of unconscious forces and the patients' active participation, in and out of sessions—practicing free associating and becoming alert to and vigilant about their own experience. There are now other analysts who believe that the use of the couch or number of sessions a week are factors extrinsic to the analytic process that should not be used as criteria to distinguish between psychoanalysis proper and other face-to-face psychoanalytic therapies (Gill 1982, 1988, 1994, Weiss 1993). The main differences between Gill's revisionist view of clinical psychoanalysis and Fromm's have more to do with the extent to which transference should be brought into the treatment (see our comments below).

Clearly, Fromm was ahead of his time. In current psychoanalytic debates between drive and relational models, one- versus two-person psychologies, intrapsychic versus interpersonal foci, and innate versus experiential factors, Fromm's work offers an interesting position that transcends some of these dichotomies. A case in point is his theory of social character that integrates individual and society from a psychoanalytic point of view. One common distortion of Fromm's work is that his approach was sociological or culturalist and neglected intrapsychic motivation (Rapaport 1967). In fact, the theory of social character is a bridge that helps explain how social norms and expectations become internalized. Individuals come to incorporate social values and norms as part of their psychic structure, even though some of these social norms are inimical to their well-being. If Fromm did not use intrapsychic language to explain this process, it was because the intrapsychic had become identified by orthodoxy with the Oedipus complex and with a mechanistic concept of energy. His interest, free from jargon and orthodoxy, was to understand how social norms became internalized as character syndromes.

Those of us who have been inspired and guided by Fromm's efforts to gain a deeper understanding of ourselves and the world around us have a special responsibility to build on his legacy. This challenge demands much of us. Fromm was a first-rate thinker and wore the mantle of a critical tradition well. His prophetic voice was at times visionary. Efforts to use reason in the service of furthering human needs and values is as daunting as it is necessary. Some of Fromm's efforts may have miscarried, but he can never be accused of shrinking from the task. The contributors to this volume have all tried to meet the challenge, stating his views clearly, presenting critical appraisals, and developing his views in the context of contemporary theory and practice.

Although the reader may not agree with one or another assertion, Fromm's work is especially valuable for clinicians and scholars who are attracted to a humanistic approach to psychoanalysis that integrates individual psychology with historical, social, economic, ideological, and religious factors influencing human development.

A SUMMARY AND BRIEF COMMENTARY OF THE CONTRIBUTIONS TO THIS BOOK

Part I: Contributions and Contradictions of Fromm's Thought

In Chapter 2, Michael Maccoby offers an assessment of Fromm from the perspective of a former analysand, coauthor, and colleague. Maccoby describes the two voices, the analytic and the prophetic, as they become expressed in Fromm's role as a social scientist, psychoanalyst, and religious thinker. Maccoby analyzes Fromm's contribution and shows how these two voices can be discerned in each of these different roles. As we observed earlier, sometimes the two voices are congruent and at other times incongruent and contradictory. Maccoby provides useful conceptual tools from which to make better use of Fromm's contributions.

In Chapter 3, Mauricio Cortina evaluates the strengths and weaknesses of Fromm's model of human nature and motivation by contrasting Freud's and Fromm's approach to the problem. Fromm provided a nonreductionistic model of motivation by exploring emergent (new) evolutionary properties that characterize the human species. This emphasis on what is evolutionarily new is the greatest strength of the model. However, the strength is associated with a significant weakness. While recognizing specifically new motivational structures, Fromm underestimates the importance of evolutionary and developmental continuity and transformation. The "eviction from paradise" biblical metaphor captures the essence of Fromm's view of the human condition. Fromm thought that a key factor in development was the struggle to overcome a regressive pull to return to the lost security provided by the mother figure or its symbolic equivalents such as blood ties, tribalism, and nationalism.

Cortina presents an alternative evolutionary and developmental model that is in keeping with Fromm's emphasis on the importance of evolutionary transformations in humans, but does not accept Fromm's premise that as a species we are uprooted from nature. The evolutionary perspective accounts for the plasticity of human adaptation— that Fromm attributed to a combination of a relatively weak instinctive endowment and the development of the neocortex—as the result of a neotenic process (the retention of juvenile characteristics into adult life). This neotenic interpretation, together with a developmental perspective derived from attachment theory, questions the paradigm of symbiotic unity that informed Fromm's view of development and still remains an influential model of development in many other psychoanalytic schools of thought. Research based on attachment theory shows that under normal conditions security is never "lost" but rather it is found, or more precisely it is constructed (Sroufe 1986). This construction between the infant and its primary caregivers continues over a very protracted period of human development when it gradually becomes internalized, providing a sense of continuity in human development. Under favorable conditions ties with parents are never relinquished but become transformed as new intimate relationships to peers and lovers develop, supplying a new source of emotional security. The chapter concludes with some clinical implications of this "secure base" model of development.

In Chapter 4, Paul Lippmann continues exploring the strengths and weaknesses of Fromm's work and directs our attention to Fromm's contribution to the understanding of dreams. As Lippmann observes, at times "the adventure down the royal road had become a lockstep for the faithful on a narrow and rigid path." Fromm reawakened an interest in exploring the richness and insight potential of dreams by focusing on the experiential approach to dream interpretation. To his credit, Fromm seriously engaged Jung's fundamental contribution. Although Fromm steered away from the stereotype of fixed universal archetypes, he agreed that dreams could give expression to the very best in us. He tried to reconcile Jung's contribution of the dream's expression of intellectual and spiritual insight with Freud's emphasis on the irrational motives expressed in dreams. The result was a more complex, balanced, and clinically useful approach to dreams that anticipated many creative efforts to expand our understanding of these mysterious nighttime visions. Yet, as Lippmann observes, dreams have the Rorschach-like capacity to elicit in would-be interpreters the reflection of their own interests and motivations, and are influenced by the analyst's theories. Fromm's dream interpretations were often the expression of his own beliefs, the voice of humanistic conscience, the expression of an irrational mother fixation, or the rebellion against the dehumanizing effect of modern society. In short, he introduced his own creed to dream interpretation.

In Chapter 5, Marianne Horney Eckardt offers a thoughtful meditation on the issue of normative principles in development and the practice of psychotherapy. She discerns three possible positions. The classical position as articulated by Heinz Hartmann would advise the analyst to stay clear of any moral position and hope for the best. In the position taken by Karen Horney, the issue of ethics lies at the center of neurotic development. The analyst's role, to use a metaphor, is to be a good gardener who will restore healthy development by providing the right conditions for further growth. We should mention in passing, that the belief in a self-righting tendency is central to many contemporary views such as Lichtenberg and colleagues' (1992) and Weiss's (1993). A third position, taken by Fromm and Stephen Jay Gould, claims that nature does not provide us with answers to the problem of living. Quoting Gould (1977), Eckardt believes that the complexity of human existence requires "humanists of every stripe" (p. 146) to provide us with moral guidelines by which we can live. She interprets Fromm as believing that humans are not inherently good or evil, but that life presents us with choices that can incline us in one direction or another. The role of the analyst in this position is much like the old biblical prophet or a Greek chorus. As therapists we can describe the alternatives provided by life choices and can urge patients to consider the possible consequences of different paths, some of them dire, others promising and hopeful, but we cannot tell patients which road to take.

Fromm's position was dialectical and incorporated elements of the second and third positions. Fromm thought that the main tendency in humans was toward goodness. The path to love and brotherliness also offered the best "solution" toward happiness. Evil was a second, ever-present potential, a capacity for cruelty and destructiveness that far exceeded anything observable in the animal kingdom. At its best, Fromm's approach to a humanistic ethics was historical. Any discussion of real possibilities—in a Hegelian sense—for good and evil had to be inserted within the context of a specific historical period and a particular life history. Without this contextualization, any discussion of ethics results in, by omission or by commission, simply supporting an ideology.

Eckardt's distinctions are valuable and help frame some of the issues of a humanistic ethics. We think her discussion of Fromm's belief in a negative theology also has implications for our position as therapists. Just as we cannot know what God *is*, we are also unable to predict, nor should we prescribe, formulas that lead to the good life. And just as a negative theology is defined by what God is *not*, so we can and do know about negative consequences for development when favorable conditions are lacking. Furthermore, we should not hide our values as therapists. A central paradox of human development is that while development is lawful, it is not predictable on an individual basis.

In Chapter 6, Carl Goldberg asks how malevolent transformation of personality takes place. Inspired by Fromm's work on the origin of destructiveness, Goldberg builds on Fromm's observation that an evil character tends to develop gradually by a succession of innumerable acts of inhumanity that are often rationalized and dismissed. Goldberg has found that the road that leads to sadism and cruelty is often paved by a history of shame and humiliation. Goldberg proposes stages of the sequential transformations of shame, humiliation, and rage that eventually lead to malevolence. He illustrates the theory with a very interesting case study. Goldberg's stages provide the basis for rich clinical exploration that could lead to a research agenda into the various possible pathways for the development of the malevolent personality.

In the final chapter of Part I Douglas LaBier explores the relational paradigm in psychoanalysis in Fromm's work. LaBier believes that the Stone Center's variant of the relational paradigm comes close to Fromm in maintaining a critical attitude toward society. The Stone Center's work is also consistent with Fromm's critique of patriarchy and calls into question patriarchal values of domination and independence over the need for intimacy and connection. Implicit but not stated in LaBier's chapter is the question of why the Stone Center has not cited Fromm's work.

An interesting comparison to LaBier's chapter is Margolies's chapter (in Part III). Margolies emphasizes the importance Fromm attributed to Bachofen's theory of Mother Right and the historical analysis of matriarchal and patriarchal principles (Fromm 1951, 1970). Like Bachofen and Fromm, Margolies believes that human development should ideally integrate the best of the patriarchal and matriarchal values and principles.

Part II. The Clinical Encounter

In Chapter 8, Marco Bacciagaluppi attempts to place Fromm's clinical approach within the spectrum of current psychoanalytic models of therapy. Based on Goldberg, Hoffman, and Hirsch, among others, Bacciagaluppi distinguishes three therapeutic stances: the observational-interpretative stance, in which the analyst observes conflict and limits his participation to providing insight; the "participation with" stance of empathic immersion into the patient's experience; and the "participation in" stance, which recognizes the analyst's inevitable involvement in (and likely reenactment of) the patient's problems. Bacciagaluppi notes several discrepancies in Fromm's approach, including the discrepancy between Fromm's advanced theoretical position, which places him in the "participation in" position, and his emphasis on insight, which places him in the observational-interpretative position. A second discrepancy is that between Fromm's emphasis on providing insight and the importance he attributed to providing a new experience for the patient. Bacciagaluppi concentrates primarily on the second discrepancy and illustrates Fromm's approach using a published case he supervised.

In the clinical case, Fromm is empathic and respectful toward the young woman's traumatic history and emphasizes, like Ferenczi and Bowlby, the importance of real-life experience. At the same time, Fromm states that the essence of analytical cure resides in the conflict engendered by the meeting of the rational and irrational parts of the personality. Bacciagaluppi points out that Fromm at times seems to downplay the importance of the analyst, and lists the personality of the analyst as just one of seven other factors that are important in clinical work.

In discussing the importance of new experience in therapeutic change, Bacciagaluppi points out that new experience is seldom new, and that we often find the existence of "weak precursors" (Hoffman 1983) that provided in childhood a supportive and positive experience for the patient. Bacciagaluppi points out that we should be grateful for these weak precursors, and need to be modest in our claims to success as healers, as we are often building on the positive contributions of others who preceded us. Bacciagaluppi offers two clinical examples that illustrate the weak precursor concept. The first example exemplifies a case in which the history of a weak precursor was present from the onset of the therapy. In the second example the existence of a positive figure in the patient's life emerged only much later in the therapy.

We agree with Bacciagaluppi that Fromm would have considered a patient's new experience in therapy as important. Fromm believed the psychoanalytic dialogue should be free of any sham or deceit. Fromm also valued the aliveness and vitality of the therapist and his capacity to experience within himself the repressed part of the patient's personality. Fromm summarized these beliefs by saying that analysis should aspire to provide "a few rich hours," an experience that in itself could become the basis for a significant transformation in a patient's life (Lesser 1992; also see, Chapter 9 in this volume). Fromm would have disagreed with Alexander and French's (1946) goal of providing a "corrective emotional experience" if this meant any attempt of manipulation, even when done for the patients "good." Fromm believed the patient should be respected as someone who seeks the truth and the analyst should not try re-create the role of the good parent.

In Chapter 9, Sonia Gojman traces many contemporary innovations in psychoanalytic technique to Fromm's explicit humanistic approach to psychoanalysis. As Gojman notes, Fromm emphasized the need to know the patient from within (from "center to center"). This requires from the analyst an openness to use his own experience as a vehicle for understanding the patient. Fromm legitimized the patient's observer role in the analytic process, and he supported efforts to abandon a mythical neutrality in favor of adopting a role as an observant participant who affirms not only unconscious truths but also steps toward health.

Gojman notes that these changes in *technique*—a term Fromm was reluctant to use since the stance he advocated was not simply a matter of the head but of the heart—are consistent with contemporary intersubjective approaches and with some of the positions advanced by Casement, Gill, and Mitchell, among others. Gojman also points out that in Fromm's discussion of technique in the Cuernavaca seminars, he repeatedly emphasized the analyst's unconventional attitude, his aliveness, his honesty, a profound interest in patients and their well-being. According to Fromm, these were all key ingredients to diminish the patient's resistance within the psychoanalytic process and increase the patient's confidence in the analyst.

Gojman courageously looks into the realities of psychoanalytic institutes, where analysands are exposed to their therapist as teachers and colleagues in a variety of situations. This leaves training analysts in an extremely difficult position, "surrounded by analysands and former analysands as junior colleagues, creating situations of high-risk professional communication in groups ridden by all kinds of secrets and nonusable information." Gojman proposes that rather than treat issues such as prestige and power in psychoanalytic institutes as nonexistent or useless sources of information, that the process be analyzed from the perspectives of the analyst and the analysand, each with different positions in the group structure. Needless to say, this effort is demanding for analyst and analysand alike, but may come as a relief "acknowledging our real participation and not struggling to conceal it."

Gojman takes issue with some of the critiques of Fromm's work such as Maccoby's (1982), who points out that Fromm's clinical practice was, paradoxically, not very participative. Gojman argues that the critique does not fully recognize the strength of Fromm's approach that built on Ferenczi's work and has been further developed by contemporary intersubjective and relational approaches.

We agree with Gojman that Fromm anticipated many contemporary clinical innovations and that the thrust of his contributions could be developed to reach a more profound understanding and appreciation of the intersubjective nature of clinical work. Nonetheless, Fromm's clinical practice differed significantly from some modern approaches, such as Gill's, that redirect the attention of the analyst to systematic examination of the therapeutic interaction. This approach recognizes that any intervention on the part of the analyst is embedded in the intersubjective nature of the interaction. Fromm did not systematically analyze the transference.[12]

We believe that the differences between what we described earlier and Gojman's own appreciation of Fromm's clinical contribution has to do with a contradiction within Fromm himself. A perceptive and intuitive thinker, Fromm could see where psychoanalysis should go, anticipating many contemporary approaches. However, his character did not allow him to follow some of his innovative clinical ideas or take them to their logical conclusion (as Gojman points out). Fromm was deeply identified with the prophetic tradition and visionary figures such as Meister Eckhart, Marx, and Freud. He saw his clinical role in the tradition of dissolving illusions and awakening the patient to his/her inner demons and spiritual aspirations, experimenting late in his career with a Zen-Buddhist approach to psychoanalysis. The process of change Fromm envisioned was closer to producing an epiphany than to the laborious work required by the careful analysis of the therapeutic interaction, which in any case may or may not produce such a radical transformation of consciousness. We think Fromm did not have the temperament or patience for this methodical and careful type of work.

In Chapter 10, Romano Biancoli presents a case study illustrating an application of Fromm's theoretical concepts to clinical work. Biancoli is intrigued by Fromm's theory of human freedom — which Fromm called alternativism — that bridges a position of "hard determinism" on one hand and the doctrine of "free will" on the other. Fromm recognized that the domain of human freedom lies between these two positions. Biancoli points out that Fromm saw the role of social science or psychoanalysis as articulating "real possibilities" for progressive change. This discovery of alternatives in the consulting room requires from analyst and analysand alike a realistic assessment of internal or external constraints — inherent in any specific situation — and a willingness to forgo illusory or unrealistic plans for change.

The case Biancoli presents is of a young woman torn between an unstable, aggressive, and impulsive attitude and a desire to form lasting and loving relationships. Biancoli takes us through the difficult steps that gradually lead the patient to a better understanding of the origin of this conflict and the transferential testing of the analyst.

We include in the chapter a discussion by Ana Maria Barroso of Biancoli's paper presented at the 1994 International Erich Fromm symposium. Drawing from the literature on countertransference and on the work of Casement and Weiss, Barroso presents another possible response to the transferential test based on a close analysis of the therapeutic interaction. The two approaches present interesting contrasts and show that there is no single, correct Frommian approach to clinical work. What is important to

keep in mind is the distinction Peterfreund (1983) makes
between stereotyped approaches to psychoanalysis that
shoehorn patients into a Procrustean bed of theory and a
heuristic approach based on the rediscovery and exploration of the patients' stories as they unfold within the
clinical setting.

We conclude the section on the clinical encounter with
Alan Grey's chapter. Grey makes a claim for countertransference similar to one Millán (see below) makes for transference, namely that Fromm's work can be seen as providing a more inclusive view of countertransference. Grey
builds his case examining Fromm's views in regard to the
unconscious, the motivational structure of character and
countertransference. Grey points out that Fromm's view
of the unconscious differed in several ways from Freud's.
Fromm saw the unconscious as containing primitive and
irrational elements, but also as the source of penetrating
insights that transcend the strictures of society. Moreover,
Grey sees Fromm as a modern thinker.[13] Fromm had little
use for Freud's energetic metapsychology. Fromm conceived of the unconscious in terms of processes, avoiding
the danger of reification. Grey notes that Fromm explicitly
discussed the "filtering" role imposed by language and
social norms that limit the range of human experience.

Grey notes that Fromm's theoretical views are more
consistent with contemporary models of the mind such as
that of Lazarus (1991).[14] According to Grey, Lazarus's
work (1991) describing the importance of the appraisal
function of emotions legitimizes the role of intuition as a
valid and important component of the analyst's repertoire
in understanding and responding to patients.

Grey argues that Fromm's revision of Freud's dualistic
drive model also contributed to the analyst's use of self in
work with patients by calling attention to the importance
of social and constructive motives. Fromm's model of

human nature was an important corrective over Freud's view of man as essentially evil. Fromm's motivational theory supports the analyst's intuitive responses as trustworthy guides in the therapeutic process without having to debunk altruistic motives as sublimations or reaction formations. According to Grey, what this all adds up to is that the use of self advocated by Fromm differs markedly from earlier views of countertransference. This is another aspect of Fromm's contribution that has not yet received the recognition it deserves in current efforts to examine the intersubjective nature of the psychoanalytic dialogue (Stolorow et al. 1987)

Despite the enormous advantages over the Freudian model, Fromm's ideal of development, the "productive character," is in Grey's estimate, misleading. Actual studies of productive personalities show, according to Grey, that "the very circumstances that favor one particular productive attribute tend to discourage another." A similar point is made by Maccoby in Chapter 2 (see also Maccoby 1982).

Part III. The Intersection between Social Character and Clinical Work

The theory of social character is useful in understanding what holds people together—or separates them—in natural social groups or nations, but is it relevant to the day-to-day clinical practice, and if so how?

The four chapters in Part III explore this question beginning with Daniel Burston and Sharna Olfman's provocative discussion of the pathology of normalcy. They note that early in his career Fromm had begun to question Freud's historical perspective that assumed that the advancement of society would necessarily create a stronger

repression of instinctual drives. According to Freud, there
were no free rides on the route to progress, and any
cultural advancement would leave in its wake a legacy of
common unhappiness. Regardless of the merits of this
position, Freud's sober outlook had the virtue of challenging the belief that reason would bring gradual and
inexorable progress. Fromm also thought that society had
a repressive function, but as Burston and Olfman point
out, Fromm's approach was qualitative rather than quantitative. Social demands based on economic modes of
production and unequal distribution of goods would conflict with human demands for freedom and happiness.
The conflict between social demands and human aspirations had to be analyzed for each particular case and could
not be generalized into false historical categories as
Freud's theory did.

Burston and Olfman show how this perspective led
Fromm to analyze how social demands create "socially
patterned defects" in people required to adapt to prevailing social conditions. The same concept appeared in
Fromm's later work as the "pathology of normalcy."
Speaking as a representative for human aspirations over
the social demand for conformity, Fromm raised the
question, Who is sick? Is the individual who rebels against
social pressures but is symptomatic, sick? Is the individual
who conforms but shows no symptoms, normal? As
radical as these questions may seem, Burston and Olfman
demonstrate that in fact they are not new, and can be
traced as far back as Greek philosophy. Moreover, they
were shared by Freud, who valued a neurotic with a
capacity for insight more than a normal person who
showed no signs of spiritual upheaval.

Where does all this leave us as clinicians? Not in any
morally or socially comfortable position, according to
Burston and Olfman. Fromm does not let us evade ques-

tions of our role as healers in a troubled society with troubled patients. He asks us to scrutinize our well-meaning therapeutic zeal. Where we practice, with whom we practice, the population we work with, and the goals of our institutional affiliations are becoming more relevant issues as we witness the corporate takeover of American medicine. With global changes of the economy and down-sizing trends in organizations, we are faced with the disappearance of the leisurely and secure middle class as we have known it. With corporate globalization and the erosion of the middle class, there is ample reason to be anxious about the future of psychotherapy and its remu-neration, particularly psychotherapies that are based on the intensive study of people's lives.

Burston and Olfman say that perhaps the real reason Fromm is ignored nowadays is that at his best he was "too provocative and disturbing to be readily assimilated into the analytic mainstream." We would add that because we live in disturbing times that have rekindled the strength of right-wing ideologies and tribal identities, Fromm's pro-vocative message just might be heard by those who seek understanding of the psychic roots of ideologies.

Salvador Millán's main thesis in Chapter 13, is that social character—the way patients and therapists inter-nalize the values, cultural beliefs, and class structure of their society—is always present in the consulting room and often becomes manifest as transference and counter-transference reactions. Indeed, according to Millán, trans-ference and countertransference are just another name for developmental processes of social adaptation as it be-comes expressed in a particular relationship between an analyst and his/her patient.

Millán takes us through the origin of the concept of transference in Freud, with its patriarchal and authori-tarian overtones, to its classical definition in Fenichel's work. With its surgical metaphors, Fenichel crystallized an approach to technique and the handling of the transference. Analytical technique required a neutral and detached observant role, with precise interpretations directed at the psyche, similar to a surgeon's skilled incisions into the patient's body.

Millán compares this approach with the guidance Fromm offered to the students of the Mexican Psychoanalytic Institute during supervision and in his seminars in Cuernavaca during the 1960s. Fromm's point of departure was like Freud's. Transference has to do with the experience of infancy that is repeated in the presence of the analyst. Fromm (1968) thought that this definition of transference, while true, was limited, since it took into account only one source of irrational strivings based on infantile longings. However, if one looked at transference as an experience in which the patient deposits in the person of the analyst the origin of "all of his expectations and fears," (p. 2) a much broader range of transferential reactions is taken into consideration. Some of these reactions may be traced to parental influence. Others may have origins that are broadly social, in which the parents' influence is based on being representatives of societal norms, or parental roles may even be irrelevant. In this definition, transference is not just based on childhood experience, but represents the whole experience of the patient's life.

Millán points out that one of the limitations of psychoanalysis is that it is primarily based on the experience of working with clinical populations. Millán briefly reviews a series of social character studies that have been conducted in the last two decades in factories, in corporate environments, and in rural communities with normal populations, and that have broadened our understanding of the process of social adaptation beyond the consulting room.

According to Millán, these studies provide support for Fromm's more inclusive concept of transference.

While we think Millán may be underestimating the importance Freud gave to the development of a negative transference in treatment (which he thought was inevitable and the major source of resistance), Millán's ideas in regard to transference and countertransference are refreshing. They will be welcomed by clinicians who would like to include a social dimension in their clinical work but have not had the conceptual tools that would help them consider the influences of cultural and economic factors in development and the role they play in therapy.

In Chapter 14, Rainer Funk offers another perspective on social character and clinical work. His main thesis is that the analysis of social character, understood as the syndrome of common traits shared by a class or group within society, is as important for understanding any given person as is his or her particular history and idiosyncracies. According to Funk, most clinical work starts and often ends with the analysis of what makes a particular individual unique and focuses almost exclusively on a patient's childhood. This approach runs the risk of overlooking assumptions shared by analyst and analysand alike that may be pathogenic or limiting, but are not recognized as such by virtue of their being shared social and cultural premises. Funk goes further by saying that contemporary social character, described by Fromm as the marketing orientation, has a pervasive alienating influence that corrupts efforts to build loving relationships or develop creative talents. This corrosive influence will infect the therapeutic effort unless the analyst is aware of social influences that have molded his or her own character and has a vision of human growth that is not distorted by this influence. Funk distinguishes self-alienation rooted in authoritarian structures or symbiotic

dependency from self-alienation of the marketing orientation. Following Fromm's analysis, he believes that the
marketing character's pervasiveness is due to its being
part of a "socially patterned defect." Funk puts on center
stage the analysis of alienating social character that affects
the analyst and patient alike. Any stance that deviates
from this position would be suspect if not collusive in
Funk's view.

Another approach to the analysis of contemporary
social character and its use in psychotherapy is provided
by Maccoby (Chapter 2) and Margolies (Chapter 15).
Maccoby argues that the marketing character described by
Fromm (1955b) and Whyte (1956) in the 1950s was heavily
influenced by the post–Second World War economic
boom, producing large corporate and governmental bureaucracies populated by middle managers with margin-
ally productive roles. To get ahead, middle managers had
to market their personalities rather than their talents.
However, Fromm did not consider the modern social
character as exclusively marketing. Indeed, in *Social Character in a Mexican Village*, Fromm and Maccoby (1970)
contrast the semi-feudal peasant society where "being
liked or pleasing the authority is a primary factor of
success" with an industrial society where "success depends primarily on achievement or competence, and
being liked is only a secondary factor" (pp. 110–111).
Today there is an accelerating collapse of industrial-
bureaucratic organizations. As corporations become
"leaner and meaner," secure employment is no longer
guaranteed. To get ahead or to compete for good jobs in
this new environment, people have to market their skills
and develop their competencies. This situation leads to
variations in social character with positive potentials for
self-development as well as negative marketing tendencies (Maccoby 1988).

Perhaps the difference in perspective between Funk and Maccoby toward the analysis of the marketing character can be attributed to the fact that Maccoby (1976, 1981, 1988) has been studying the social character of normal people. He finds weaknesses not only in the marketing character but also in other social character types such as bureaucratic "experts" who are addicted to controlling others.[15]

Nonetheless, we agree with Funk that analysts need to become aware of their own "social character" to maintain an unconventional attitude toward patients that does not accept social adaptation as an unqualified good or sees a rejection of social norms as necessarily pathological. We also concur with Funk that dynamic psychotherapists are too focused on the individual, reflecting an individualistic bias in psychoanalysis (Kirschner 1988) that overlooks pressing social realities that continue to mold personality, for better or for worse, into adulthood.

In Chapter 15, Richard Margolies observes that with the fast-paced expansion of global markets and the shift from electro-mechanical manufacturing to an information-based techno-service economy (Maccoby 1988), the last two decades have brought enormous changes that are reflected in society at many levels. Margolies argues that it is important and helpful to understand how social changes at the workplace affect people by enhancing or constraining adult development. Social character research within the last two decades bears testimony to these dramatic shifts. According to Margolies, from surveys of several thousand managers and employees and 300 in-depth sociopsychoanalytic interviews, five social character types emerge (Maccoby 1988): the expert, the helper, the defender, the innovator, and the self-developer. In concurring with Maccoby's analysis, Margolies notes that the main social character shift in our time has been from the

expert, adapted to industrial hierarchies and bureaucracies, to the self-developer, adapted to the uncertainty and
challenges of today's economy. While experts value autonomy, mastery, and hard work, and achieve self-esteem
based on excellence of their performance, self-developers
approach life and work as a continuous process "to learn,
grow, and develop themselves" while adding value to
their clients and customers. They maintain their self-
esteem and marketability by upgrading their skills. Self-
developers are more flexible, work well in teams, and
dislike hierarchies. However, they often have difficulty
with intimate relationships. Experts are less flexible and
more controlling, but they value and seek strong family
ties. Most self-developers come from two-career, divorced, or mobile families. Their expectations for work
mirror the uncertainty of their family life. Experts grew up
in an age of greater stability and upward mobility. They
are less able to adapt to the constant change and flat
hierarchies of the modern workplace.

To illustrate the usefulness of understanding social
character with patients, Margolies presents a case of a
talented and creative self-developer. According to Margolies, an important therapeutic aspect of the treatment was
understanding the patient's legitimate need to further his
own development that had not been particularly supported by a father who had forgone his own development
for the sake of the family. This meant making unconventional choices and resolving his ambivalence toward two
women he loved. Margolies believes that had he only
focused on the pathology without a clear understanding
and support for his patient's real-life choices, the therapy
would not have been as effective.

Sandra Buechler's commentary provides an interesting
counterpoint to Margolies's chapter. She observes that
Fromm believed work should be an expression and a

vehicle for self-development and that this urge transcends historical circumstance. She questions whether the categories we create hinder or enhance our understanding. She believes the self-developer category may have blinded the therapist to other aspects of the treatment. Her own reading of the clinical material would have led her to focus on different aspects of the patient, such as his narcissism and his sadistic sexual fantasies. Margolies would argue that these pathological elements were declining as he worked through old compromise solutions and developed life-affirming passions in work and love—particularly as he strengthened the positive strivings of his social character orientation.

Part IV: Erich Fromm's Place within the
Psychoanalytic Movement

We begin Part IV with a brief biography of Erich Fromm by Daniel Burston (Chapter 16). Burston calls attention to the importance of Fromm's Jewish roots and the influence that some of Fromm's early religious teachers had on his career. Burston emphasizes the importance of understanding Fromm's contribution within the context of a rich philosophic and spiritual tradition and his evolving interest in religious ideas such as Zen Buddhism.

In Chapter 17, Paul Roazen points out that Fromm was enormously courageous to have sustained a lifelong effort to revise Freud in the face of rejection from the psychoanalytic community. As an example Roazen points to one of Fromm's neglected contributions, *Sigmund Freud's Mission* (1959), which was the first challenge to Jones's uncritical biography of Freud. In it Fromm called attention to Freud's complex relationship to his mother, who stimu-

lated his ambition of becoming a great leader. This narcissistic investment in her son also had negative consequences. The ambivalence of Freud's relationship to his
mother did not escape Fromm's observations even before
it was known that Freud did not attend his mother's
funeral. (Instead Freud sent his daughter, Anna, as an
emissary.) Roazen also reminds us how ferocious—and
childish—attacks could be on those who dared to deviate
from the Freudian party line.

Paul Roazen's final remarks, express well the spirit of
this book.

> In keeping with Freud's original standing as an outsider, it
> is striking how much of an uphill struggle it has been to
> establish the legitimate role Erich Fromm has played in the
> history of psychoanalysis; but that only makes me think that
> rectifying the situation, and paying him his due honor, is
> especially incumbent upon us. Whatever legitimate disagree-
> ments there ought to be about what Fromm's legacy adds up
> to, I think few can deny that his responsible outspokenness,
> which I have called courage, should be a special beacon to us
> all.

CONCLUSION

We believe psychoanalysis will become more vital and
relevant to grappling with clinical and social problems by
integrating Fromm's contributions. As we have argued,
some of these contributions, such as a relational perspective, Fromm's focus on self, activeness, and alienation, his
multi-motivational approach to human needs, and his
experiential approach to dreams, have already become
part of the psychoanalytic mainstream.

Fromm's relational perspective went beyond contemporary concern with dyadic and two-person psychologies by emphasizing the importance of socioeconomic conditions in human development. Other contributions, such as his revision of oedipal theory (1951), his evolutionary-existential approach to human nature (1955b), his concept of the unconscious and social filters (Fromm et al. 1960), and his theories on human destructiveness (1964, 1973), still need to be recognized and further developed.

By ignoring some of Fromm's most original offerings such as social character theory (1941, 1947, 1962, 1970), psychotherapists remain disconnected form a conceptual tool that can explain how social influences become internalized in the psyche. By ignoring Fromm's analysis of human motivation and the need for a frame of orientation and devotion (1950, 1955b, 1976) psychotherapists are less able to help patients who struggle with spiritual and religious aspirations. By not taking advantage of Fromm's analysis of human destructiveness (1964, 1973), psychotherapists lose understanding of the passion for sadistic control and murderous rage.

Today many intellectuals believe psychoanalysis has nothing to offer society in terms of increasing our understanding of social problems. Moreover, Bellah et al. (1985) and Lasch (1995) see psychoanalysis as part of the "culture of therapy" that supports a weakening of personal responsibility and the decline in morality and religion. In contrast, Fromm shows clearly that psychoanalysis can both deepen our understanding of social factors and strengthen a sense of responsibility (ability to respond). For those who now call for a return to traditional values, Fromm shows that religion and morality can support either the development of solidarity, love, and reason or the development of authoritarian control and fanatical movements.

Using Fromm's powerful conceptual tools to explore the individual and social unconscious, psychotherapists can also expand their role at a time of profound social change, when the understanding of social pathologies as well as paths to productive development are desperately needed.

ENDNOTES

1. Fromm attempted this revision with his theory of biophilia (a syndrome of growth) as opposed to necrophilia (a syndrome of decay). The merit of this revision, about which some of us have reservations, is not an issue we will take up in this book.

2. Personal communication with Michael Maccoby. Roazen observes (in Chapter 17, this volume), that Erikson's cautiousness would not allow him to emphasize the similarities with Fromm and risk alienation from his psychoanalytic peers. We think this is particularly true with Fromm's concept of social character that was implied in Erikson's descriptions of character formation in the Sioux and the Yurok (Erikson 1950).

3. Posthumously an outline of this project has been published as *The Revision of Psychoanalysis* (Fromm 1992).

4. Perhaps our main differences with Saavedra is that he has launched his critique from a Lacanian and neo-Kleinian perspective (Meltzer, Etchegoyen). Some of the Lacanian language strikes us as metaphysical and speculative, hardly an improvement over Fromm, a clear writer who did not use jargon. Our position is grounded in contemporary life span (Ainsworth 1985, Parkes et al. 1991, Sperling and Berman 1994, Stern 1985) and developmental line perspectives (Bowlby 1988a, Sroufe 1989), which we think are consistent with Fromm's insistence that issues like security are salient existential realities through life. This perspective offers a corrective to an almost exclusive emphasis on early development stages that permeates psychoanalytic theorizing (Mitchell 1988). Our clinical position builds on Fromm's dialectic approach, is loosely based on a "relational-conflict model" (Mitchell 1988), and has been influenced by and

shares affinities with authors like Basch (1988), Bowlby (1988a), Casement (1991), Gill (1982, 1994), Lichtenberg et al. (1992) Peterfreund (1983) and Weiss (1993). Given these differences, we arrive at different conclusions in regard to Fromm's strengths and weaknesses on issues such as the role of oedipal theory, regression, transference, and countertransference in psychopathology and in therapy. To spell out these differences would require a separate essay, beyond the scope of this introduction (for a critique of Saavedra's position see Cortina 1995).

5. Saavedra (1994) takes Fromm to task for never having acknowledged the affinity of his work to Fairbairn and other members of the British middle school. In fact, Fromm did make a brief mention of this affinity in *The Anatomy of Human Destructiveness* (1973). For that matter, we would like to ask, where does Fromm ever get mentioned in the Kleinian or British object relations literature? It seems untoward to single out Fromm when he was just as much a victim of the narrow and partisan scholarship that Saavedra complains about.

6. Borrowing from Marx, Fromm expressed this idea poetically (1970, pp. 49–50) "because I have eyes I have the need to see; because I have ears I need to hear; because I have a brain I need to think; because I have a heart I need to feel. In short, because I am a man I am in need of man and of the world."

7. As Fromm et al. (1960) put it, experience can only enter into awareness under the condition that it can be "perceived, related and ordered in terms of a conceptual system and its categories. The system is in itself the result of social evolution" (p. 99). This view is consistent with contemporary models of the mind and emotions. For instance (Lazarus 1991) insists that a person's appraisal and evaluation of the environment is a key to the experience of emotion. Elkman (1971, 1977) has shown how culture constrains and facilitates the expression of emotions.

8. As Schecter (1971) observed, Fromm's contribution to understanding the principles of activity and passivity in devel-

opment were enthusiastically endorsed by Rapaport, the great systematizer of psychoanalytic theory, in a series of lectures delivered at the William Alanson White Institute. However, nowhere in Rapaport's published papers was Fromm's contribution acknowledged.

9. Some of Fromm's "existential needs" are examples of what Gould (1982) calls "exaptations." Exaptations are side consequences of Darwinian adaptations. Possessing bigger brains, an essential part of hominid evolution, is an adaptation in the Darwinian sense, since having a larger brain clearly confers greater survival and reproductive success. However, few would argue that becoming aware of our mortality serves any evolutionary purpose. This fortuitous consequence of possessing larger brains is an exaptation. The emergence of the religious motive (a need for a frame of reference and devotion in Fromm's terms), is another related consequence of possessing a bigger brain. While some exaptations end up being co-opted to serve a useful end, like the example of the panda's thumb (Gould 1980), other exaptations are of dubious benefit (awareness of our mortality) and are "tolerated" as long as the net Darwinian effect is useful or neutral. Fromm may not be off the mark when he describes humans as "freaks of nature."

10. This alternative view of incest avoidance originates with the Westermarck hypothesis (1891) that assumes that innate aversion to sexual intercourse develops among individuals who live in very close contact during childhood. Mark T. Erickson's excellent article marshals evidence for an alternative theory that builds on the Westermarck hypothesis. This biosocial model does not deny sexuality in children, but maintains that sexual activity at this stage of development is primarily autoerotic and/or is characterized normally by curiosity and wonder (sometimes directed toward peers). Cross generational transgressions of the incest barrier are pathological and have severe consequences on development (both Freud and the biosocial model of incest avoidance agree on this point).

Freud (1940) considered the diphasic onset of sexuality— emerging at age 4 or 5 as an incestuous wish toward the parent of the opposite sex, becoming repressed in latency, and re-emerging in puberty—as a hallmark of the process of hominiza-tion. He believed we had evolved from species that had an early efflorescence of sexuality in childhood and resorted to phyloge-netic arguments based on Lamarckism (the inheritance of ac-quired characteristics) to explain why this development was arrested in latency (Sulloway 1979). He hoped that primate investigations would confirm his view that incestuous proclivi-ties are common in closely related species (in fact these investi-gations have not confirmed Freud's hypothesis as M. T. Erickson shows). The diphasic hypothesis runs counter to modern evolutionary concepts. Human sexual maturation is not only not *accelerated*—as required by Freud's diphasic hypothesis of an early emergence of sexuality—but is in fact *retarded*. What is characteristic of primate evolution is the extraordinarily late development of sexual maturation. This retardation of develop-ment in primates is general, a phenomenon known in biology as neoteny (Gould 1977). Retardation, not acceleration, of devel-opment is the hallmark of hominid evolution.

11. This is what we see in modern postindustrial societies where global economic changes are producing enormous shifts in social structures and institutions. The painful transition is expressed as anger, cynicism, and disillusion with social insti-tutions and with political and civic leaders. A retreat to "family values" and the politics of self-interest are part of the backlash against society. A similar phenomenon is happening in Eastern European countries and the former Soviet Union. Social char-acters adapted to a command and control economy are strug-gling to take advantage of new market conditions. A large segment of the population that is left out or cannot take advantage of the new conditions retreats to tribal and national-istic identities and to the politics of hatred.

12. This point was made clear by Michael Maccoby and Jorge Silva—who were both analyzed by Erich Fromm—during the discussions that took place at the May 1994 International Erich Fromm Symposium at the Washington School of Psychiatry. We would like to clarify that we do not believe that a systematic

attention to the therapeutic interaction is the same as a systematic interpretation of the transference. It's a mistake to think that most of what patients tell us are veiled transferential communications that should always be interpreted. This position leads patients to assume that their therapists are interested only in material that is connected with the analyst, undermining the importance of external events in their lives or of taking courageous steps inside and outside of the consulting room. On this point we are in agreement with Fromm. As we see it, the importance of Gill's or Casement's approach is not just to alert us to the ubiquity of transferential meanings, but more importantly to recognize that any intervention we make must be explored in terms of what it means to the patient. We should not assume we know how patients will respond to even our most benign intentions. This attitude of modesty was sometimes lacking in Fromm's work with patients.

13. Fromm saw himself as a systems thinker who understood the psyche as a self-system in a dynamic relation with the social system in which it functioned (Fromm and Maccoby 1970).

14. Bowlby (1969) has also discussed the appraisal function of emotions in terms that are almost identical to those of Lazarus. The recent work of Antonio Damasio (1994) offers a brilliant integration of the neurobiological basis of emotions, supporting the view that emotion and cognition cannot be separated.

15. In another respect we think Funk's characterization of psychotherapists as expressing the values of the marketing orientation is too extreme. Increasingly, psychotherapy is being practiced by psychologists and social workers, most of whom are women (Philipson 1993). There is less prestige attached to the role of psychotherapy than when Fromm wrote. People who are attracted to the profession value the opportunity to be of help to others, to be able to set flexible hours, balancing demands between family and work. At its best, clinical work stimulates emotional growth and provides intellectual challenge. None of these conditions is particularly alienating or glamorous. Nor do we think that most therapists with a psy-

chodynamic orientation would react to the vignette presented by Funk of a young man who feels cut off and empty, by thinking that this presenting problem is "normal." Such a case may raise questions of a schizoid or anxiously detached personality (Fairbairn, Guntrip, Bowlby) or perhaps a false self development (Winnicott). The incapacity to form intimate relationships and lack of authenticity would become a focus of concern for many psychotherapists.

REFERENCES

Ainsworth, M. D. S. (1985). Attachments across the life span. *Bulletin of the New York Academy of Science* 61:792–812.

Ainsworth, M. D. S., Blehar, M. C., Waters, E., and Wall, S. (1978). *Patterns of Attachment: A Psychological Study of the Strange Situation*. Hillsdale, NJ: Lawrence Erlbaum.

Alexander, F., and French, T. (1946). *Psychoanalytic Therapy*. New York: Ronald Press.

Basch, F. M. (1988). *Understanding Psychotherapy. The Science Behind the Art*. New York: Basic Books.

Bellah, R. N., Madsen, R., Sullivan, W. M., et al. (1985). *Habits of the Heart*. Berkeley: University of California.

Bowlby, J. (1969). *Attachment and Loss. Vol. 1. Attachment*. New York: Basic Books.

_____ (1980). *Attachment and Loss. Vol. 3. Loss, Sadness, and Depression*. New York: Basic Books.

_____ (1988a). Developmental psychiatry comes of age. *American Journal of Psychiatry* 145:1–10.

_____ (1988b). *A Secure Base*. New York: Basic Books.

Bretherton, I. (1990). Communication patterns, internal working models and the intergenerational transmission of attachment relationships. *Infant Mental Health Journal* 11:237–252.

Burston, D. (1991). *The Legacy of Erich Fromm*. Cambridge, MA: Harvard University Press.

_____ (1994). *Repression, Reality, and Fidelity to Freud in the Fromm/Marcuse Debate*. Unpublished manuscript.

Casement, J. P. (1991). *Learning from the Patient*. New York: Guilford.

Caston, J. (1993). Can analysts agree? The problems of consensus and the psychoanalytic mannequin: I. A proposed solution. *Journal of the American Psychoanalytic Association* 41:493–511.

Caston, J., and Martin, E. (1993). Can analysts agree? The problems of consensus and the psychoanalytic mannequin: II. A proposed solution. *Journal of the American Psychoanalytic Association* 41:513–548.

Cicchetti, D., ed. (1989). *The Emergence of a Discipline. Rochester Symposium on Developmental Psychopathology*, vol. 1. Hillsdale, NJ: Lawrence Erlbaum.

Clyman, B. R. (1991). The procedural organization of emotions: a contribution from cognitive science to the psychoanalytic theory of therapeutic action. *Journal of the American Psychoanalytic Association* 39:349–382.

Connell, P. J. (1990). Context, self, and action: a motivational analysis of self-systems processes across the life span. In *The Self in Transition: Infancy to Childhood*, ed. D. Cicchetti, and M. Beeghly, pp. 61–98. Chicago: University of Chicago Press.

Cortina, M. (1992). Review essay of *The Legacy of Erich Fromm* by Daniel Burston. *Psychoanalytic Dialogues* 2:571–580.

——— (1995). Las Trampas de La Fe. Una resena critica del libro de Victor Saavedra, "La Promesa incumplida de Erich Fromm." *Subjetividad y Cultura*. 4:90–92.

Crews, F. (1993). The unknown Freud. *New York Review of Books*, November 19, pp. 55–65.

Crittenden, M. P. (1992). Treatment of anxious attachment in infancy and early childhood. *Development and Psychopathology* 4:575–602.

——— (1994). Peering into the black box. An exploratory treatise on the development of self in young children. In *Disorders and Disfunctions of Self. Rochester Symposium on Developmental Psychopathology*, vol. 5, ed. D. Cicchetti, and S. H. Toth, pp. 79–148. Rochester, NY: University of Rochester Press.

Damasio, R. A. (1994). *Descartes' Error. Emotion, Reason, and the Human Brain*. New York: Grosset/Putnam.

Dobzhansky, T. (1962). *Mankind Evolving: The Evolution of the*

Human Species. New Haven, CT: Yale University Press.

Eckardt, M. H. (1978). Organizational schisms in American psychoanalysis. In *American Psychoanalysis: Origins and Development*, ed. J. Queen, and E. Carlson, pp. 141–161. New York: Brunner/Mazel.

Elkman, P. (1971). Universals and cultural differences in the expressions of emotions. In *Nebraska Symposium on Motivation 1971*, ed. J. K. Cole, pp. 207–284. Lincoln, NE: University of Nebraska Press.

_____ (1977). Biological and cultural contributions in body and facial movement. In *Explaining Emotions*, ed. O. Rorty, pp. 73–101. Berkeley: University of California Press.

Emde, N. R. (1988). Development terminable and interminable: 1. Innate and motivational factors from infancy. *International Journal of Psycho-Analysis* 69:23–42.

_____ (1992). Positive emotions for psychoanalytic theory: surprises from infancy and new directions. *Journal of the American Psychoanalytic Association* 39:5–44.

_____ (1994). Individuality, context and the search for meaning. *Child Development* 65:719–737.

Erdelyi, M. H. (1985). *Psychoanalysis: Freud's Cognitive Psychology*. New York: W. H. Freeman.

Erickson, M. T. (1993). Rethinking Oedipus: an evolutionary perspective of incest avoidance. *American Journal of Psychiatry* 150:411–416.

Erikson, E. (1950). *Childhood and Society*, 2nd ed. New York: W. W. Norton, 1963.

Fairbairn, W. R. D. (1952). *An Object Relations Theory of the Personality*. New York: Basic Books.

Fonagy, P. (1993). Psychoanalytic and empirical approaches to developmental psychopathology: an object relations perspective. *Journal of the American Psychoanalytic Association* 41:245–260.

Freud, S. (1912). Totem and taboo. *Standard Edition* 13:1–162.

_____ (1916). Introductory lectures on psychoanalysis. Lectures 20 and 21. *Standard Edition* 16:303–338.

_____ (1938). Moses and monotheism: three essays. *Standard Edition* 23:1–54.

_____ (1940). An outline of psycho-analysis. *Standard Edition*

23:141–208.

Fromm, E. (1941). *Escape from Freedom*. New York: Farrar & Rinehart.

_____ (1947). *Man for Himself: An Inquiry into the Psychology of Ethics*. New York: Holt, Rinehart & Winston.

_____ (1950). *Psychoanalysis and Religion*. New Haven, CT: Yale University Press.

_____ (1951). *The Forgotten Language: An Introduction to the Understanding of Dreams, Fairy Tales, and Myths*. New York: Holt, Rinehart & Winston.

_____ (1955a). The human implications of instinctivistic radicalism. *Dissent* 4:342–349.

_____ (1955b). *The Sane Society*. New York: Holt, Rinehart & Winston.

_____ (1959). *Sigmund Freud's Mission: An Analysis of His Personality and Influence*. New York: Harper Colophon.

_____ (1961). *Marx's Concept of Man*. New York: Frederic Ungar.

_____ (1962). *Beyond the Chains of Illusion: My Encounter with Freud and Marx*. New York: Simon & Schuster.

_____ (1964). *The Heart of Man: Its Genius for Good and Evil*. New York: Harper & Row.

_____ (1966). *You Shall Be As Gods: A Radical Interpretation of the Old Testament and Its Tradition*. Greenwich, CT: Fawcett Premier.

_____ (1968a). *The Revolution of Hope*. New York: Harper & Row.

_____ (1968b). *Siete Lecciones sobre Técnica Psicoanalítica*. Unpublished text in Spanish. Library of the Instituto Mexicano de Psicoanálisis.

_____ (1970). *The Crisis of Psychoanalysis: Essays on Freud, Marx, and Social Psychology*. New York: Holt, Rinehart & Winston.

_____ (1973). *The Anatomy of Human Destructiveness*. Greenwich, CT: Fawcett Premier.

_____ (1976). *To Have or To Be*. New York: Harper & Row.

_____ (1980). *The Greatness and Limitations of Freud's Thought*. New York: Harper & Row.

_____ (1992). *The Revision of Psychoanalysis*, ed. R. Funk. Boulder, CO: Westview.

Fromm, E., and Maccoby, M. (1970). *Social Character in a Mexican Village: A Socio-psychoanalytic Study*. Englewood Cliffs, NJ:

Prentice-Hall.

Fromm, E., Suzuki, D. T., and DeMartino, R. (1960). *Zen Buddhism and Psychoanalysis*. New York: Harper Colophon, 1970.

Frosh, J. (1991). The New York psychoanalytic civil war. *Journal of the American Psychoanalytic Association* 39:1037–1064.

Gill, M. M. (1982). *The Analysis of Transference*, vol. 1. New York: International Universities Press.

_____ (1988). Converting psychoanalysis into psychotherapy. *Contemporary Psychoanalysis* 24:262–274.

_____ (1994). *Psychoanalysis in Transition: A Personal View*. Hillsdale, NJ: Analytic Press.

Gould, S. J. (1977). *Ontogeny and Phylogeny*. Cambridge, MA: Harvard University Press.

_____ (1980). *The Panda's Thumb: More Reflections in Natural History*. New York: W. W. Norton.

_____ (1982). Exaptation: A crucial tool for an evolutionary psychology. *Journal of Social Issues* 47:43–65.

Greenberg, J., and Mitchell, S. (1983). *Object Relations in Psychoanalytic Theory*. Cambridge, MA: Harvard University Press.

Grey, L. A. (1993). The dialectics of psychoanalysis. A new synthesis of Fromm's theory and practice. *Contemporary Psychoanalysis* 63:645–672.

Guntrip, H. (1969). *Schizoid Phenomena, Object-Relations and The Self*. New York: International Universities Press.

_____ (1971). *Psychoanalytic Theory, Therapy and The Self*. New York: Basic Books.

Hoffman, I. Z. (1983). The patient as interpreter of the analyst's experience. *Contemporary Psychoanalysis* 19:389–422.

Holt, R. R. (1972). Freud's mechanistic and humanistic images of man. In *Psychoanalysis and Contemporary Science*, vol. 1, ed. R. R. Holt, and E. Peterfreund. New York: Macmillan.

_____ (1973). On reading Freud. In *Abstracts of the Standard Edition of the Complete Works of Sigmund Freud*, ed. C. L. Rothgeb, pp. 3–79. Northvale, NJ: Jason Aronson.

Horowitz, M. J., ed. (1989). *Psychoanalysis and Cognition*. Chicago: University of Chicago Press.

Ingvar, D. (1985). Memories of the future. An essay on the temporal organization of conscious awareness. *Human Neu-*

robiology 4:127–136.

Kagan, R. (1982). *The Evolving Self: Problems and Process in Human Development.* Cambridge, MA: Harvard University Press.

Kirschner, S. R. (1988). The assenting echo: Anglo-American values in contemporary psychoanalytic development. *Social Research* 57:821–857.

Lasch, C. (1995). *The Revolt of the Elites and the Betrayal of Democracy.* New York: W. W. Norton.

Lazarus, S. R. (1991). *Emotion and Adaptation.* New York: Oxford University Press.

Lesser, M. R. (1992). Frommian therapeutic practice. *Contemporary Psychoanalysis* 28:483–494.

Lichtenberg, D. J. (1983). *Psychoanalysis and Infant Research.* Hillsdale, NJ: Analytic Press.

_____ (1989). *Psychoanalysis and Motivation.* Hillsdale, NJ: Analytic Press.

Lichtenberg, D. J., Lachmann, F. M., and Fosshage, J. L. (1992). *Self and Motivational Systems. Toward a Theory of Psychoanalytic Technique.* Hillsdale, NJ: Analytic Press.

Loewald, W. H. (1979). The waning of the Oedipus complex. *Journal of the American Psychoanalytic Association* 27:751–775.

Maccoby, M. (1976). *The Gamesman: The New Corporate Leaders.* New York: Simon & Schuster.

_____ (1981). *The Leader.* New York: Simon & Schuster.

_____ (1982). Social character vs. the productive ideal: the contradiction and contribution in Fromm's view of man. *Praxis International* 2:70–84.

_____ (1988). *Why Work: Leading the New Generation.* New York: Simon & Schuster.

Mahler, M. S., Pine, F., and Bergman, A. (1975). *The Psychological Birth of the Human Infant.* New York: Basic Books.

Main, M. (1993). Discourse, prediction, and recent studies in attachment: implications for psychoanalysis. *Journal of the American Psychoanalytic Association* 41:209–244.

Main, M., Kaplan, N., and Cassidy, J. (1985). Security in infancy, childhood and adulthood: a move to the level of representation. In *Growing Points in Attachment Theory and Research. Monographs of the Society for Research in Child Devel-*

opment, ed. I. Bretherton and E. Waters, 50:66–104.

McLaughlin, N. G. (1995). *Escape from Orthodoxy: The Rise and Fall of Erich Fromm*. Ph.D. Dissertation in progress, City University of New York.

Mitchell, S. (1988). *Relational Concepts in Psychoanalysis*. Cambridge, MA: Harvard University Press.

Palombo, R. S. (1978). *Dreaming and Memory. A New Information-Processing Model*. New York: Basic Books.

Parkes, M. C., Stevenson-Hinde, J., and Marris, P. (1991). *Attachment Across the Life Span*. New York: Routledge.

Peterfreund, E. (1980). On information and systems models in psychoanalysis. *International Review of Psycho-Analysis* 7:327–345.

―― (1983). *The Process of Psychoanalytic Therapy: Models and Strategies*. Hillsdale, NJ: Analytic Press.

Philipson, I. (1993). *On the Shoulders of Woman: The Feminization of Psychotherapy*. New York: Guilford.

Pine, F. (1990). *Drive, Ego, Object, and Self: A Synthesis for Clinical Work*. New York: Basic Books.

Rapaport, D. (1967). Paul Schilder's contribution to the theory of thought process. In *The Collected Papers of David Rapaport*, ed. M. M. Gill, pp. 368–384. New York: Basic Books.

Rickert, J. (1986). The Fromm-Marcuse debate revisited. *Theory and Society* 15:351–400.

Rosenblatt, A., and Thikstun, J. (1978). Modern psychoanalytic concepts in a general psychology. *Psychological Issues*, monographs 42/43. New York: International Universities Press.

Saavedra, V. (1994). *La Promesa Incumplida de Erich Fromm*. México: Siglo XXI.

Sandler, J. (1994). Fantasy, defense and the representational world. *Infant Mental Health Journal* 15:26–35.

Schafer, R. (1976). *A New Language for Psychoanalysis*. New Haven, CT: Yale University Press.

Schecter, D. (1971). Of human bonds and bondage. In *The Name of Life: Essays in the Honor of Erich Fromm*, ed. B. Landis and E. S. Tauber, pp. 84–99. New York: Holt, Rinehart & Winston.

Shapiro, D. (1989). *Psychotherapy of the Neurotic Character*. New York: Basic Books.

Simpson, G. G. (1949). *The Meaning of Evolution*. New Haven, CT: Yale University Press.

Sperling, M. B., and Berman, W. H., eds. (1994). *Attachment in Adults: Clinical and Developmental Perspectives*. New York: Guilford.

Sroufe, A. L. (1986). Attachment and the construction of relationships. In *Relationships and Development*, ed. W. W. Hartup and Z. Rubin, pp. 51–72. Hillsdale, NJ: Lawrence Erlbaum.

——— (1989). Pathways to adaptation and maladaptation: psychopathology as developmental deviation. In *The Emergence of a Discipline: Rochester Symposium on Developmental Psychopathology*, vol. 1, ed. D. Cicchetti, pp. 13–40. Hillsdale, NJ: Lawrence Erlbaum.

——— (1990). An organizational perspective on the self. In *The Self in Transition: Infancy to Childhood*, ed. D. Cicchetti and M. Beeghly, pp. 281–307. Chicago: University of Chicago Press.

Sroufe, A. L., and Rutter, M. (1984). The domain of developmental psychopathology. *Child Development* 54:173–189.

Sroufe, A. L., and Wards, J. M. (1980). Seductive behavior of mothers of toddlers: occurrence, correlation and family origins. *Child Development* 51:1223–1227.

Stern, D. (1985). *The Interpersonal World of the Infant*. New York: Basic Books.

——— (1994). One way to build a clinically relevant baby. *Infant Mental Health Journal* 15:9–25.

Stolorow, R., Brandchaft, B., and Atwood, G. (1987). *Psychoanalytic Treatment: An Intersubjective Approach*. Hillsdale, NJ: Analytic Press.

Sulloway, J. F. (1979). *Freud, Biologist of the Mind*. New York: Basic Books.

Tyson, P., and Tyson, R. (1992). *Psychoanalytic Theories of Development: An Integration*. New Haven, CT: Yale University Press.

Weiss, J. (1993). *How Psychotherapy Works*. New York: Guilford.

Weiss, J., Sampson, H., and Mt. Zion Psychotherapy Group. (1986). *The Psychoanalytic Process: Theory, Clinical Observations, and Empirical Research*. New York: Guilford.

Westermarck, E. (1891). *The History of Human Marriage*, Vols.

1-3. London: Macmillan, 1926.

Whyte, H. W., Jr. (1956). *The Organization Man*. New York: Simon & Schuster.

Williams, M. L., and Finkelhor, D. (1995). Parental caregiving and incest: test of a biosocial model. *American Journal of Orthopsychiatry* 65:101-113.

I

CONTRADICTIONS AND CONTRIBUTIONS OF FROMM'S THOUGHT

2

The Two Voices of Erich Fromm: The Prophetic and the Analytic

Michael Maccoby

Erich Fromm's contribution to our knowledge of individual and social behavior has been neither fully appreciated nor developed. Fromm's most popular books, which expand our understanding of both love and destructiveness, have, to a large extent, been assimilated into that body of knowledge that forms the foundation of intellectual thinking in Europe and the United States. Although he introduced many American intellectuals of the 1940s and 1950s to the relevance of psychoanalysis to understanding twentieth century social pathology, typical intellectuals of today think of Fromm, if at all, as a critic of the mass consumer society.[1] A smaller number recognize the contribution he made in *Escape from Freedom* (1941) to understanding the psychic appeal of Fascism, an understanding relevant to events in the 1990s in Russia and the Balkans. But relatively few appreciate his most valuable and original legacy: understanding human character in relation to society.

Fromm explored the influence of culture on character development but strongly differentiated himself from "culturalists" such as Sullivan, Horney, and Margaret Mead, who described culture in terms of behavior patterns and did not analyze socioeconomic factors. Although Fromm agreed with Marx's analysis of social change and shared his messianic view of history, he was also a deeply religious nontheist who drew his concept of human development from the Jewish Bible (1966), Zen Buddhism (Fromm et al. 1960), and Christian mysticism (1976). Although he shared, to a large extent, its critique of capitalism, Fromm was rejected by the psychoanalytic left. His former colleagues at the Frankfort School, particularly Herbert Marcuse, dismissed him as a conformist unwilling to support the radical action necessary to change society. Inevitably, experts in one or another social science or version of psychotherapy were put off by Fromm's unlikely mix of Freud, Marx, and religious mysticism.

My purpose is not to defend Fromm from his critics. Like any major thinker, Fromm's views changed over time and there are, as I shall describe, contradictions in his views and limitations in his approach, especially his psychoanalytic technique. Rather, I shall try to describe and clarify what I hear as the two dominant voices in Fromm's work, the analytic and the prophetic. William James wrote that theory, like music, expresses the composer's personality, and both of these voices came from deep inside of Fromm. I believe that by scoring them separately, so to speak, they can be better understood and, most important, usefully developed. When Fromm is most convincing, the two voices harmonize. When he is least convincing, the prophetic drowns out the analytic.

My analysis of these two voices is based on not only my reading of Fromm, but also my work with him in the 1960s.

MY EXPERIENCE WITH FROMM

In the summer of 1960, when I drove from Cambridge, Massachusetts to Cuernavaca, México with my wife, Sandylee, it was to enter into an eight-year apprenticeship with Fromm. That June, I had received a doctorate from Harvard in social relations, combining clinical and cognitive psychology with sociology and anthropology. I had decided that my next step should be psychoanalytic training, since psychoanalytic investigation seemed the best way to further my understanding of human motivation. In seeking psychoanalytic education, I considered the Boston Institute, where I had helped Ives Hendrick with his research, and I talked with Erik Erikson about working with him at Austen Riggs. Both were encouraging. However, David Riesman, who had been analyzed by Fromm and whom I had worked with as a teaching assistant, reported that Fromm was looking for a research assistant in México and suggested that we meet. I decided to study with Fromm because of the appeal of both voices, the analytic and the prophetic. Fromm defined the meaning of human development in a way that appealed to me emotionally as well as intellectually. It seemed to me that Fromm's call to create a sane society was urgently required in a world teetering on the edge of nuclear war. World War II and the Holocaust were a recent and searing memory. Fromm's analysis of human destructiveness provided some understanding of behavior that seemed incomprehensible and inhuman. I hoped that through my personal psychoanalysis, Fromm would help me to develop not only my capability as a researcher, but also my capacity for love and reason.

I should note here that when I told Grete Bibring of the Boston Psychoanalytic Institute that I was considering training with Fromm, she said, "You will probably get along very well together, but he will never analyze the transference." To a large extent, she was correct, for reasons I shall describe.

Before leaving for México, I joined Fromm, David Riesman, and others in founding the Committee of Correspondence and writing for its newsletter, arguing for arms control and improved relations with the Soviet Union.

Fromm accepted me as an apprentice. He needed someone with training in research design, statistics, and projective testing to work with him on the sociopsychoanalytic study of a Mexican village, and in return for my assistance, he agreed to admit me to the Mexican Psychoanalytic Institute and to be my training analyst. He also made it clear that my personal goals for analysis and my political engagement were important in his decision to work with me. During the next eight years, I was Fromm's research assistant, analysand, supervisee, and collaborator, culminating in 1970 with the publication of our book, *Social Character in a Mexican Village*.

I agreed to Fromm's condition of apprenticeship, that I first learn his theory and work with it before criticizing it, as he expected I would someday do. He said that he hoped I would be able to express this theory in my own words and expand it, and this has been my goal.

The Two Voices

During the time I was in analysis with him, Fromm's technique changed from one that was extremely influenced by his then recent exploration into Zen Buddhism with D. T.

Suzuki to one that emphasized a more systematic investigation into the patient's character and psyche. At times,
he experimented with technique using the active methods
pioneered by Sandor Ferenczi, including relaxation exer-
cises and suggestion about associating to a theme. He also
tried techniques used by Wilhelm Reich to attack character
armor. While his shifting of analytic approach complicated
his attempts to describe his practice, this does not fully
explain his dissatisfaction with the drafts he wrote on technique. I believe that what blocked his writing on technique
and also limited his effectiveness as an analyst was the
inability to always harmonize the analytic and prophetic
voices.[2] This disharmony resulted in a confusion concerning the goals and methods of psychoanalysis.

At its purest, Fromm's analytic voice was exploratory,
experimental, and skeptical. It asked for evidence and
questioned conclusions drawn too quickly. His prophetic
voice was urgent, impatient, and judgmental. It contrasted
reality with a demanding ideal of spiritual development. It
condemned rather than analyzed evil. At times, Fromm the
analyst was transformed into Fromm the rabbi or Zen master who responded to the student's inauthentic behavior
not by analysis, but with disgust or the verbal equivalent
of cracking him over the head with a stick.

At his most analytic, Fromm conceived of psychoanalysis as a method to help suffering people to liberate
themselves from crippling fear and to realize more of their
creative potential. In this mode, he emphasized the importance of psychoanalytic diagnosis at the start of treatment, and he was realistic about the patient's prognosis
and limitations.

At his most prophetic, Fromm's mission was to bring
about a messianic age of peace and human solidarity, and
he used psychoanalysis as a spiritual discipline for himself
and his disciples. He viewed neurotic symptoms as a
partial rejection of oppressive or alienating authority. The

psychoanalyst's role was to help give birth to the revolutionary within the neurotic.

Fromm's inconsistent approach to therapy expressed the contradiction between his theory of social character and his ideal of the productive character, which became increasingly mystical. I shall return to this point, that the disciplines of therapeutic psychoanalysis and spiritual development, while they share elements in common, are essentially different, and that Fromm sometimes confused the two.

Fromm believed that his most original ideas were the theory of social character, the interpretive questionnaire as a method of studying character, and the theory of destructiveness. He described each of these in his analytic voice. In two major studies, one of German workers and employees in 1930 (Fromm 1984) and the other of Mexican villagers in the 1960s (Fromm and Maccoby 1970), Fromm tested and developed the theory and methods of social character research.

He continually elaborated his theory of destructiveness. The sociopsychoanalytic analysis of sadomasochism and malignant destructiveness was well tested both clinically and in the social character research. The more controversial and less well studied theory of necrophilia, defined as the love of death, decay, and rigid order, which he first described in his sixties (1964), expressed the prophetic view of evil and was contrasted to his concept of biophilia, love of life, which at the extreme expressed being versus having and the driving force of mystical development.

The Two Voices in Fromm's Approach to Character and Society

To appreciate Fromm's approach to clinical diagnosis, his theory of character must first be understood. While

Freud's libido theory with its analogy of forces and cathexes corresponds to a late nineteenth century view of
physics, Fromm's theory of character development is fully
consistent with modern evolutionary biology (Bonner
1989). Humans are distinguished from other animals by a
larger neocortex with fewer instincts. Character is the
relatively permanent way in which human drives for
survival and self-expression are structured in the socialization process. Thus, character substitutes for or shapes
human instinct. But human survival is not merely a matter
of physical survival. Man does not live by bread alone. We
are social animals who must relate to others, and we are
spiritual animals who must infuse our lives with meaning
in order to function. Our brains need to operate in the
past, present, and future simultaneously. Without a sense
of hope, they turn off. To survive in the early years, we
require caring adults. To learn to master the environment,
control our fears and passions, and live in harmony with
others, we need teachers. To give meaning to our lives, we
must acquire a sense of identity and rootedness. Religions
both sacred and secular (including tribalism and nationalism), with objects of devotion, guiding myths, and rituals,
serve this function.

We not only must live our lives, but also solve the
contradictions stemming from our existence—the animal
and human needs, and physical survival and emotional
sanity. Fromm said that given our contradictory tendencies and awareness of our mortality, the question of why
people remain sane is perhaps more difficult to answer
than the question of why they become insane.

Character is a solution to those contradictions. It is like
a complex computer program that takes the place of what
is to a greater extent hard-wired in other animals. Biological research indicates we are closer to other animals than
we like to believe, and this, perhaps, is what keeps many

of us sane. We imitate and identify with those most like ourselves. We can use the culture, or more precisely the social character, as an off-the-shelf solution to the problems of existence. Although other animals also develop cultures to transmit patterns of behavior between the generations, human culture is more complex and varied. With our large neocortex, we are able to learn and change. Although we share almost 99 percent of our genetic material with chimpanzees (Diamond 1993), the other 1 percent allows us to choose between either becoming more uniquely and fully human or regressing to tribalism and/or psychopathology. Fromm termed the striving to become more fully human as "progressive," and he believed the great monotheistic humanistic religions and Buddhism, which is nontheist, shared the goal of directing people to a solution of achieving unity with nature through individuation, love of the stranger, and reverence for life. This solution increases our consciousness and strengthens community, while the regressive solutions result in either individual psychopathology (symbiosis, narcissism, and destructiveness) or group narcissism and hostility to people outside the tribe.

Speaking in his analytic voice, Fromm describes the social character as the cement that holds society together. It is what adapts humans to their environment in such a way that they *want* to do what they *need* to do to keep a particular society functioning. In this sense, some emotionally disturbed persons have failed to develop the social character; their emotions do not support adaptive behavior. Or the social character of some disturbed people might clash with the environment, because it is adapted to a disappearing world. In this situation, the social character is transformed from social cement to social dynamite. Thus, in *Escape from Freedom*, Fromm (1941) describes how the lower-middle-class German suffered a sense of powerlessness and meaninglessness in the 1920s. Hoarding, dutiful, conservative, and hard-working emotional attitudes no longer guaranteed prosperity. The harsh conditions imposed by the Treaty of Versailles after World War I caused runaway inflation that destroyed savings, while money was being made by wild speculation. The humiliation of the kaiser by the allies was felt as a personal indignity and loss of meaning. The flaunting of a sexual freedom and burlesque of authority in the Wiemar Republic aroused indignation and anger, which Hitler was able to manipulate in forging an ideology, a new religion, that blended the desire for revenge and the focusing of hatred on the Jews as scapegoats with inspiring hopes to create a great new civilization.[3]

Analytically speaking, normality and mental health require that the child develop a social character in order to gain the competencies required for survival in a society. Jung's (1971) view was that only through adaptation to a culture could a person begin to achieve individuation:

> Under no circumstances can individuation be the sole aim of psychological education. Before it can be taken as a goal, the educational aim of adaptation to the necessary minimum of collective norms must first be attained. If a plant is to unfold its specific nature to the full, it must first be able to grow in the soil in which it is planted. [p. 448]

However, speaking in the prophetic voice, Fromm questioned whether adaptation produced healthy people.

If the society is itself not healthy, then to be normal is to acquire a "culturally patterned defect," in effect to be sick. The neurotic who will not adapt may be healthier than one who is adapted. What does healthy mean for Fromm?

> Mental health, in the humanistic sense, is characterized by the ability to love and to create, by the emergence from the

incestuous ties to family and nature, by a sense of identity based on one's experience of self as the subject and agent of one's powers, by the grasp of reality inside and outside of ourselves—that is, by the development of objectivity and reason. The aim of life is to live it intensely, to be fully born, to be fully awake. To emerge from the ideas of infantile grandiosity into the conviction of one's real though limited strength: to be able to accept the paradox that everyone of us is the most important thing there is in the universe—and at the same time no more important than a fly or a blade of grass. [Fromm 1955, p. 68]

With this definition, has any society ever produced many healthy people? Can any society, other than the messianic vision of the prophet Isaiah, achieve sanity?

The model of a sane society Fromm proposes is communitarian socialism. He quotes a description of Boimondeau, a cooperative watch factory in France, as an ideal. According to this account, workers balanced work and education, collective and individual development. But when I tried to find out what happened to Boimondeau, I learned that the factory did not survive in the competitive marketplace. Like many other promising and short-lived cooperative enterprises, Boimondeau depended on an exceptional leader who left.[4] This communitarian ideal remains theoretical. It is not a convincing solution.

MARKETING MAN

Is Fromm correct that modern industrial society forms an alienated social character? Is the prototypic modern individual a person who adapts to the market economy by making oneself into a salable commodity, thus becoming detached from authentic emotions and convictions? Is the modern person's goal nothing more elevated than success in the career market and the pleasure of continual consumption: having versus being? Does health require us to transform society and transcend the social character?

I have used Fromm's method of social character investigation, the interpretive questionnaire, in rural and urban México, the United States, the United Kingdom, and Sweden. In all of these societies, there are significant variations in social character. Overall, the greater the extent to which people leave village life and adapt to industrial society, the more abstract their language becomes and the more detached they are from direct emotion, authentic relationships, and, to some degree, dreams and the inner life. I say "to some degree" because villagers are extremely conformist and fear even perceiving anything that is new and different. Just as the urban individual steeped in book learning loses the peasant's reliance on keen observation, so the industrial person's detachment and abstract thinking also allows greater flexibility and willingness to adapt to the new. Furthermore, rural people are more likely to fear the stranger and distrust those who do not share blood ties.

Within industrial society, the factory and construction workers and engineers I have interviewed market their skills, not their pleasing personalities. Recently, advances in production technology require both increased technical skill and greater cooperation with others at work, but the latter is a matter of listening to others and solving problems together, not selling oneself. Bureaucratic middle managers and professionals are the ones most forced to market themselves, and their overadaptation can cause symptoms of depression and self-disgust (LaBier 1987, Maccoby 1976). These are also the people who are most likely to be victims of corporate downsizing due to the drive for continual innovation and productivity caused by frantic global competition. While the most educated and technically competent are swept up in this vortex, people in rural villages and ghettoes of prosperous cities struggle on the margins of the economy, within a hopeless culture of escapism and violence.

The description by Fromm and other intellectuals of the 1950s, for example C. Wright Mills (1951) and William H. Whyte (1956), of a complacent, conformist marketing society seems benign in the light of the last 30 years. They were writing during a brief historical period when U.S. industry controlled international markets and companies could afford to be stable bureaucracies stocked with middle managers.

Fromm uses the marketing character as a basis for his prophetic denunciation of modern society, but the question remains of how healthy any society can be and which societies allow the greatest opportunity for healthy development. Children have no alternative but to adapt to the family, which is the major carrier of social character. Those with healthier families or exceptional genes may adapt with greater resiliency and independence as compared with those with less-healthy families.[5] What would it mean to transcend the social character?

THE PRODUCTIVE IDEAL

Fromm's model of the healthy individual who transcends and transforms society is the "productive character," the individuated person who loves and creates. Unlike his other character types—receptive, hoarding, exploitative, and marketing—the productive character lacks clinical or historical grounding. It is a questionable ideal.

In our study of Mexican villagers, Fromm and I

searched for the productive character, but did not find one. The closest we came were independent farmers who were more productive and loving than the average. In my studies of workers, engineers, and managers, I have also found people who are more active and creative than the average, but they do not fit Fromm's description of the productive character. Furthermore, most of the more productive professionals are not loving. (Einstein is an example of an extremely productive thinker who was not loving.) Productiveness in work does not necessarily imply productiveness in caring about other people.

In *Social Character in a Mexican Village* (1970), Fromm and I contrasted productive and unproductive aspects of the social character, which was in line with Fromm's theory in *Man for Himself* (1947). The productive peasant shares many of the adaptive independent, hoarding, family-oriented traits of the dominant social character, but is more individuated and more innovative and hard working, while less suspicious and fatalistic. The productive peasant is more likely to relate to children in terms of furthering their development rather than, as is the more common pattern, demanding strict obedience. However, this is far from Fromm's ideal of the productive person whose aim is to live life intensely, "to be fully born, to be fully awake." The more productive peasant must still adapt to a mode of work that requires hoarding traits common to peasants throughout the world.

In *Man for Himself,* inasmuch as Fromm describes a real life productive character, it is an unnamed creative artist. In later works (e.g. *To Have or To Be?* [1976]), examples of productiveness are Zen masters and Meister Eckhart, a medieval Christian mystic.

In his search for the productive ideal, Fromm's prophetic voice suppresses his analysis of social character. The artist has been a romantic model for bourgeois society — the individual who resists pressures to conform and succeeds in setting his or her own terms of self-expression, which are ultimately accepted and appreciated by society. The artist shows qualities of craftsmanship, creativity, independence, and determination. However, many productive artists are not loving people (e.g., Monet, Picasso), and Fromm does not describe a single creative artist who fits his ideal. Furthermore, the very few artists who make a living from their work today are caught up in a marketing web of art dealers, changing fashion, and intellectualized hype.

In terms of social character, the religious masters cited by Fromm should be viewed within the context of feudal society. Zen masters are unchallenged authorities who rule monasteries and dominate the emotional life of their disciples. Eckhart was head of German Dominicans, and his vow of celibacy freed him from the demands of family. Fromm himself was attracted to a semifeudal role as head of the Mexican Institute of Psychoanalysis during the 1950s and 1960s. There he personally analyzed the first generation of analysts, and was the unchallenged arbiter of disagreements among members of the society.

These feudal models will not inspire the children of the information age. To develop the modern social character in a productive direction, it is first essential to understand its positive potential (Maccoby 1976, 1981, 1988).

THE TWO VOICES IN FROMM'S APPROACH TO CLINICAL WORK

In his analytic voice, Fromm criticized Freud's patriarchal attitude as limiting the development of psychoanalysis as a science. He criticized Freud's use of the couch and the routine of analysis as bureaucratizing psychoanalysis. In contrast, Fromm attempted to create what he called a more "humanistic" face-to-face encounter. Here the analytic and prophetic voices sometimes harmonized and sometimes were discordant.

Fromm's psychoanalytic technique was essentially different from Freud's psychic archeology. Like Ferenczi, Fromm emphasized the importance of experience rather than interpretation, and he believed the analyst must understand the patient by empathy as well as intellect, with the heart as well as the head. But unlike Ferenczi, he was searching not for childhood traumas but rather for present-day passions. Memory might serve to illuminate a pattern of behavior from childhood such as betrayal of one's ideals to gain approval from authorities. Fromm believed that what blocked development was not our memories but our choices, our irrational attempts to solve the human condition through such mechanisms as sadism, regression to the womb, or narcissistic invulnerability. His goal was not to heal a psychic wound, but to liberate, so that the patient could become free to make better choices.

Fromm believed that the psychoanalyst should be active and penetrating, bringing the session to life by demonstrating his own urgency to understand and grasp life fully. Here the prophetic voice sometimes overwhelmed analysis. Fromm became like a religious master who unmasks illusion and thus expands the limits of the social filter, dissolving resistances. By experiencing and confessing to one's unconscious impulses, the patient would gain the energy and strength to change his or her life, and to develop human capabilities for love and reason to the fullest. This is an unproven theory, and in practice Fromm's technique sometimes resulted in a very different outcome.

Although Fromm's thesis shares Freud's conviction that the truth will set man free, it moves in a different direction from Freud's emphasis on psychoanalysis as a process that patiently uncovers and interprets resistance in order to regain lost memories. Both Freud and Fromm define psychoanalysis as the art of making the unconscious conscious; both recognize that we resist knowing the truth and that resistances must be overcome. But their views of resistance are somewhat different. For Fromm, repression is a constantly recurring process. One resists perceiving and knowing out of fear of seeing more than society allows or because the truth would force one to experience one's irrationality or powerlessness. The pattern of repression set in childhood is like the refusal to see that the emperor has no clothes. The analyst is the fearless master who has gone further and deeper beyond convention and into his own irrationality. His attitude models productiveness and mature spontaneity, free of illusion. In contrast, Freud defines resistance more narrowly. Repressed, unconscious wishes to maintain infantile sexual fantasies, and the childhood fear of being punished (castration) because of one's libidinal impulses, act as resistances to memory. These repressions bind energy into neurotic patterns.

For Freud, the key to analyzing and overcoming resistance is transference. The patient directs or transfers desire and fear onto the analyst, who becomes a substitute for figures of the past. Resistance will be overcome only if the acting out within analysis is interpreted and transformed into emotionally charged memory, which can be worked through and reintegrated into a more mature psyche. The working through frees the blocked energy of repressed wishes and defenses. It allows the patient to give up infantile objects and desires and discover better ways to satisfy needs. If the analyst dramatically unmasks truth in this framework, it may strengthen the transferential resistance, either because the patient denies unbearable feelings or adopts another defense, such as passive acceptance. Overcoming this resistance requires patiently analyzing the various forms it takes.

Fromm proposes a broader concept of transference. The analyst represents infantile authority—the mother who solves all of life's problems or the father who is never satisfied with his son's achievement. Instead of facing reality independently, the patient continues to transfer interpersonal struggles and wishes. While this aspect of transference is not contradictory to Freud's views (in *The Future of an Illusion* (1927), he describes religion in these terms), Fromm's approach in fact tended to strengthen this type of transference and with it the patient's resistance to remembering. He would focus on feelings about the analyst in the here and now and the function they served. His urgency of getting to the truth short-circuited the process of working through the transferential feelings and their origins.

Although Fromm criticized Freud as too much the bourgeois patriarch and showed how this limited his insights, Freud's approach to technique can be more participative than Fromm's, especially if the Freudian analyst does not force fit the patient into a formula. To be sure, Freud advocated rules in the doctor–patient relationship, in part to protect himself. These are followed bureaucratically by many analysts. An example is that the patient lies on a couch and cannot see the analyst. Freud did not like to be stared at all day. However, Fromm's piercing blue eyes could and sometimes did freeze the patient, and his intensity, which could make one feel more alive, could also provoke defensive reactions. Freud did not describe the analyst as guru or model, and his own self-analysis showed him as all too human. He saw the analyst as a professional with technical training who, in addition, should have a radical love of truth, a broad education in the arts and sciences, and knowledge of his own unconscious. The goal for analysis was not to become a productive person, but to be liberated from crippling neurosis.

Freud cautioned against expecting too much from a neurotic who has been cured. In his prophetic voice, Fromm suggested that neurotics are humanly healthier than those with the dominant social character or socially patterned defect who have adapted to a sick society and are alienated from themselves. The Frommian neurosis as described in *The Sane Society* (1955) results from incomplete rebellion against constricting authority and lack of confidence or courage to follow one's insights, to take one's dreams seriously.

A number of narcissistic patients with grandiose ideals for themselves and society were attracted to Fromm's therapy. But the Frommian approach increased both transference resistances and the patient's sense of guilt about unworthiness, unproductiveness, and dependency. Patients compared themselves to the "productive" analyst, and instead of remembering and experiencing childlike drives, humiliations, rages, and fears as a means to mastering them and losing the need for narcissistic solutions, they attempted to resolve conflicts by becoming ideal persons, like the master. In so doing, patients fearing disapproval by the master again submitted to authority and repressed sexual or angry impulses directed against the parent. Frommian disciples identified with the master and self-righteously directed anger and contempt at others who were not good Frommians. As Saavedra (1994) writes, this became a pattern among Fromm's disciples at the Mexican Psychoanalytic Institute.

Thus, Fromm's humanistic voice, which sought to correct the more impersonal, obsessional, and dogmatic approach of the early Freudians, was never fully heard. The analyst-religious master's prescription for productive development blocked patients from discovering their own avenues for development.

THE PRODUCTIVE IDEAL AND RELIGIOUS CONVERSION

In Fromm's later works, the models of productiveness became more and more religious, closer to Zen enlightenment or the ideal of non-deistic cosmic unity than to the psychoanalytic aim of lifting infantile repressions and expanding the realm of ego in place of id. William James's (1902) observations in *The Varieties of Religious Experience* can help us to view Fromm from the perspective of religious thinking. James writes that both Buddhism and Christianity are religions of deliverance that preach that "man must die to an unreal life before he can be born into the real life" (p. 165). He also proposes that the full significance of these religions appeals to a particular type of person, who may develop an approach to life similar to Fromm's productive ideal.

James described and contrasted three personality types. The healthy minded are those with a "harmonious" personality. They tend to be upbeat and adapted to society. James used the word *healthy* in a rather ironic way. The healthy minded avoid or repress unpleasant perceptions. They have little tolerance for the second type, the morbid minded, who always see the downside of life. Acutely sensitive to painful realities, the morbid minded must struggle with depression and despair. A third type, which is closer to the morbid minded, suffer from a "discordant" personality. They struggle with two selves, ideal and actual. Like Saint Augustine and other religious figures, they search restlessly for "the truth" until, through self-analysis and religious discipline, they are reborn with "a new zest which adds itself like a gift to life, and takes the form either of lyrical enchantment or of appeal to earnestness and heroism." (p. 485.) The result of being reborn is similar to Fromm's ideal.

Fromm had this type of discordant personality; he told me that he continually struggled with irrational impulses. Like Augustine's wrestling with his sins and temptations, Fromm used analysis of both himself and his disciples to increase awareness of the split between ideal and actual selves, to experience regressive drives, and to frustrate rather than repress them, while at the same time strengthening productive needs.

Like Saint Augustine, Fromm came to believe that health as defined by the productive character is not gained merely by insight or even experiencing what has been repressed. This definition of health requires spiritual development achieved through a courageous practice of life that frustrates greed and overcomes egoism through meditation and service.

Fromm was deeply religious but did not believe in God. Yet, one can argue that his concept of the cosmos, like that of Spinoza, is a nonanthropomorphic view of God, consistent with Jewish tradition. (When I said this to him, he did not object but said that the only absolutely essential commandment for a Jew was that which forbids all idolatry.) In *You Shall Be As Gods* (1966), he describes the Bible as evolving the concept of God from a tribal deity to the unknowable God of Moses and the prophets. This God who cannot be made into an idol of any kind first establishes the law and then demands that the people transform themselves according to a messianic vision of harmony and justice. Fromm was attracted to Buddhism because it did not require belief in God, but was based on a rational analysis of overcoming pain and suffering by living a good life. Yet, the appeal of the Jewish tradition, especially Hasidism with its animation and joyful music, continually called him back. (He often hummed Hasidic music, interspersed with Beethoven and other German classics.)

Perhaps the most important aspect of religion for Fromm personally was the *hope* it offered. He was not a Christian, and he did not find hope in a life to come. Hope was to be found in two ways. One was the coming of the messianic age, which according to Jewish tradition could happen anytime the world was ready. The other source of hope was a mystical unity with the cosmos, a transcendence of life that would overcome the fear of death.

If one does not believe in an afterlife or reincarnation, there are two main ways to grapple with the fear of death. One is regression to the "oceanic feeling" of infantile preconscious unity with the mother. This is the appeal of alcohol and drugs. The other is to overcome one's egoism and experience the mystical sense of fully awakened, life-loving unity with nature. In this regard, Fromm practiced Zen meditation, and in his seventies he showed me how he also "practiced" dying, by lying on the floor and pretending to give up the ghost while feeling this oneness.

The source of Fromm's prophetic voice was his search for hope, not only for himself but for humanity. In his fifties, when he wrote *The Sane Society* (1955), hope sprang mainly from his messianic drive to save the world, and this was also the reason why he so admired Karl Marx. In this context, the productive orientation is that of the messianic revolutionary.

In his late years, although Fromm did not lose his messianic hope, he became increasingly disappointed with the revolutionaries of the 1960s, the failure of Eugene McCarthy to lead a movement with him in the United States (*The Revolution of Hope* [1968]), and the decline of Marxist humanism in Eastern Europe. In his final work (*To Have or To Be?* [1976]), his hope shifted, and the model of the productive person became less the messianic revolutionary and more the biophilic mystic.

THE ANALYTIC VOICE

For Fromm to write a book on technique that truly harmonized the two voices, he would have had to describe a systematic approach to understanding a patient. He would have had to critique Freud's papers on technique in the careful way he analyzed Freud's theory of aggression in *The Anatomy of Human Destructiveness* (1970). If he had attempted this, he might have recognized what was valuable in Freud's strategy, and he might have developed a more differentiated approach to therapy and analysis. Even then, I believe, he would still have had difficulty in resolving the contradiction between his discussion of analysis as a more participative, humanistic encounter and his attitude of the omniscient master. In my experience, Fromm was penetrating and compassionate but not particularly empathic. Indeed, while his writings on humanistic analysis leave the impression that a loving, productive analyst will be able to know patients from the inside by empathizing or listening to them in a way a Zen master listens to all of nature, his practice was to use the interview and sometimes projective tests as x-rays of the psyche. Unlike Ferenczi, he did not focus on the countertransference as a way to explore the analyst's irrational reactions. Rather, his ideal was the productive, rational, loving analyst whose emotional reactions revealed the truth repressed by the patient.

When Fromm focused on concrete cases as a teacher, he was closer to Freud, minus libido theory, than to either Ferenczi or Zen Buddhism. He was at his most analytic when he interpreted social character from an interview or questionnaire and when he described psychoanalytic diagnosis. I refer to notes from a seminar on diagnosis he gave in 1963 to our class at the Mexican Psychoanalytic Institute.

First, the analyst should determine the symptoms, goals, and pathology of the patient. What is the type and the degree of pathology, for example, regressive symbiosis, narcissism, and/or destructiveness? Fromm advised that most conflicts presented by the patient are screens. The analyst cannot help the patient decide whether or not to get divorced or leave a job. These hide the deeper conflicts, which Fromm sometimes called the secret plot. An example is Ibsen's Peer Gynt: the modern alienated man who claims he wants to be free and express himself but really wants to satisfy all his greedy impulses and then complains that he has no self, that he is nothing and nobody.

The prognosis is better if the patient's goal is to achieve health in terms of increased capability for freedom and loving relationships, rather than getting help to solve a specific problem that may be merely a symptom of the failure to maintain the cover story.

Second, the analyst should determine the strength of the resistance. Fromm suggested a test of telling the patient something that appears repressed, indicated by a slip of the tongue, a contradiction, or a dream. If there is a positive reaction, the prognosis is better. If there is anger or the patient doesn't hear, the prognosis is very bad. Fromm considered a sense of humor the best indication of a positive prognosis. Lack of it was an indication of "grave narcissism." Humor is the emotional side of reason, the emotional sense of reality. Fromm himself had a keen sense of humor with a taste for the sardonic. He loved good jokes.

Third, the capacity for insight is another indication of good or bad prognosis. The analyst should make small tests, such as, "You complain about your wife. Perhaps you are afraid of her." It is a bad sign if the patient either denies an interpretation too quickly or submissively agrees to everything the analyst suggests.

Fourth, what is the degree of vital energy? Is the patient capable of waking up? A person can be quite crazy, yet have the vitality essential for transformation.

At this time, Fromm was no longer claiming that neurotics were healthier than normal people. However, he did maintain that some patients with a severe psychopathology had a better prognosis than those with milder pathology. The key diagnostic factor was the patient's creative potential or ability to struggle against the pathology.

Fifth, has the patient shown responsibility and activity during his or her life? Fromm contrasted obsessive responsibility with the ability to respond to challenges. If the patient always escapes with a magical, irresponsible flight, analysis is not impossible, but extremely difficult.

Sixth, is there a sense of integrity? This refers to the difference between a neurotic and psychopathic personality. Does the patient accept a truth once experienced? Or is there a quality of bad faith, wiggling away from inconvenient truths, a bad sign for prognosis.

Fromm advised using the first hour to ask why the patient had come and to ask for a history, noting what was said, what was left out, and the feelings associated with events. He suggested asking for two or three dreams, especially dreams that are repeated and three memories of infancy (a technique first suggested by Adler). In the second hour, he advised testing resistance and insight, then writing out a summary of the diagnosis and a prediction of how long treatment should take.[6]

In the mid-1960s, Fromm began to send me his own patients for Rorschach tests, which he believed helped significantly in providing a better diagnosis, including both psychopathology and the strength of biophilic tendencies. In the late 1960s, Fromm emphasized the need for the analyst to understand patients within their particular cultural context. Our intensive study of Mexican social character revealed the importance of culture, class, and mode of production on the formation of emotional attitudes (e.g., the role of the mother in Mexican culture). Fromm came to believe that 50 percent of an individual's behavior resulted from social character, 25 percent from constitutional or genetic factors, and only 25 percent from early experiences. This implied different expectations and approaches with different social character types. For example, middle class Mexican patients tended to be in awe of authority and needed encouragement to express critical views, while patients from the same class in the United States are skeptical about authority in general. In México, the analyst needs first to overcome the fear of authority, while in the United States it may be necessary to demonstrate that rational authority can exist.

Fromm was impressed by the evidence of psychological well-being from the orphanage "Our Little Brothers and Sisters" (*Nuestros Pequeños Hermanos*), founded by Father William Wasson in 1955. In a study I directed with a group of Mexican analysts, we found that orphans who had suffered extreme psychic trauma became productive, remarkably happy children after an average of two years in an environment that balanced security, taking responsibility, sharing, and educational opportunity. Father Wasson guaranteed that the children would never have to leave their new family. (He made a rule that he would take all siblings from a family, but would not accept a child if the mother was living, since the Mexican child would never fully join the new family. This was not the case for the father.) He preached that dwelling on one's misfortunes made one forever a self-pitying victim. Children were encouraged to take advantage of their opportunities for learning and to help each other. Everyone shared in the work, including farming. For Fromm, the positive results achieved at the orphanage reinforced his view that a good community can transform emotionally damaged people. He contrasted the orphanage to psychotherapies that by focusing on childhood hurts and traumas, strengthened narcissistic self-preoccupation and resulted in a chronic feeling of resentment and entitlement.

In our discussions together during the late 1960s as we wrote *Social Character in a Mexican Village* (1970) we agreed that severe emotional disorders were not cured solely by analysis. This is especially true if the patient comes from a culture of poverty and hopelessness. Without a sense of possibility, the patient lacks the self-confidence and hope to face crippling feelings and impulses. Even for some patients from more advantaged backgrounds, a strategy of psychoanalysis should focus on understanding and en-couraging the patient to strengthen creative potentials before probing for pathology.

FROMM'S CONTRIBUTION

Fromm's contribution to psychoanalysis and social science remains to be developed further. He provides us with theory and methods to understand health and illness as concepts that refer not only to the individual alone, but also to the relationships of the individual to others and to social institutions. "I am myself and my circumstances," Fromm would quote Ortega y Gasset. "And if I do not change my circumstances, I cannot save myself."

To take Fromm seriously, to enter into a dialogue with him, is to accept the challenge of taking responsibility of who I want to be as opposed to what I want to have. But it also means examining his assumptions about human nature, what it is possible for people to achieve, and what are the best ways to achieve our goals.

Both Fromm's sane society and psychoanalytic technique are founded on questionable assumptions about human nature. Isaiah Berlin has criticized utopian philosophers from Plato to Marx for believing that "virtue is knowledge," that to know what is truly good for oneself and others is enough to cause rational behavior. Berlin (1991) points out that good values such as equality and freedom, or Christian love and republican vigilance against oppression, may be incompatible. Furthermore, different groups have different ways of structuring human needs. He writes:

> Perhaps, the best that one can do is to try to promote some kind of equilibrium, necessarily unstable, between the different aspirations of differing groups of human beings—at the very least to prevent them from attempting to exterminate each other, and, so far as possible, to prevent them from hurting each other—and to promote the maximum practical degree of sympathy and understanding, never likely to be complete, between them . . . . Immanuel Kant, a man very remote from irrationalism, once observed that "Out of the crooked timber of humanity no straight thing was ever made." And for that reason no perfect solution is, not merely in practice, but in principle, possible in human affairs, and

any determined effort to produce it is likely to lead to suffering, disillusionment and failure. [pp. 47–48]

Speaking in his prophetic voice, Fromm underestimated the need for individuals to adapt to a society before attempting to transform it. The work of Jean Piaget describes the stages of moral development and the social interaction essential to achieve them. It is through institutions such as family, schools, and organizations (political, legal, and economic) that we create health, wealth, and good relationships. In an increasingly complex, technology-based society, improving these institutions and organizations requires expert knowledge combined with pragmatic idealism and supportive colleagues. It can be slow and arduous work. There will always be conflicts of different interests that must be negotiated. There is no dramatic cultural transformation that will dissolve psychopathology, create harmony, and make a society sane.

This is not a program to inspire the young who carry banners in parades. Nor will it sell many books. I was once interviewed by a French journalist who said, "Dr. Maccoby, if I understand you correctly, you are saying that with great dedication and courage, one can succeed in taking small steps to improve the world. That view will appeal to no one, neither those on the left nor the right." Yet, in practice, productive hope is generated when people work together to protect civilization and to push forward the envelope of their culture, even a little bit. They are the responsible parents, dedicated teachers, community volunteers, union organizers, idealistic researchers, and environmental activists. Perhaps there are no sane societies, but there are saner societies or sane-enough societies that allow individuals to join together to develop themselves and their culture.

To conclude these observations on Fromm's two voices, there are perhaps relatively few discordant personalities, in James's sense, who like Fromm are drawn to religious conversion and mystical unity. But there are many of the would-be healthy minded who feel confused about life, who are not sick but who seek happiness in the wrong places and yearn for deeper understanding of themselves. The liberation of women, economic and emotional, from male domination makes it essential that people learn to love, otherwise the family is likely to disintegrate. For the children of the postmodern world, especially those who have already achieved the material goals of the eighteenth century Enlightenment, Fromm can be a guide who integrates the humanistic lessons of religion, literature, and philosophy with the discoveries of psychoanalysis. Even when he speaks in his analytic voice, the prophetic demands are not silent. He directs us to learn the language of the unconscious and at the same time evaluate our actions and institutions in terms of whether or not they stimulate us to wake up and act according to reason, whether or not they move us and our culture toward community rather than tribalism. Even if one does not believe it is possible to create utopia, it is possible for many of us to develop our productive capabilities of love and reason. By engaging in a serious dialogue with Erich Fromm, we expand our awareness of the choices, sharpen our concepts, and deepen our sense of meaning.

As a student of Fromm, I believe the task remains of integrating the analytic and the prophetic voices, the understanding of what *is* and what *can* be with a compelling vision of what *ought* to be in order to create a better life and a more humane world.

ENDNOTES

1. For example, David Riesman (1950) credits Fromm for the concept of social character in *The Lonely Crowd*. Peter Gay (1985)

reports that he was first attracted to psychoanalysis by the writings of Erich Fromm.

2. In one of the last letters I received from him (December 10, 1979), in response to a question about the state of his book on technique, he wrote, "As to the book on technique. I thought about writing one but it is not more than a vague project at this moment." Recent publication of some of his drafts (Fromm 1992) by his literary executor, Rainer Funk, present the more prophetic approach.

3. The historian E. P. Thompson (1966) also used Fromm's social character theory to explain the anger and turmoil in *The Making of the English Working Class, 1790–1830* when the rise of the factory system destroyed both cottage industry, and the free, expressive life of the villagers, who were forced into a repressive, regimented working life.

4. An exception to the rather depressing history of cooperatives is Mondragon in the Basque country of northern Spain. Since its founding by a Spanish priest over 50 years ago, Mondragon has created many new companies, including a bank and a research and development center. Rather than communitarian socialism, it is more like humanistic capitalism.

5. I am indebted to Dr. Mauricio Cortina for making this point and for his useful comments on an earlier draft of this lecture.

6. For example he suggested the following formulas:

1. Psychological orientation, 3 months maximum.
2. Psychotherapy for mild neurosis, 1 year.
3. Psychoanalysis of neurosis where regression is not so malignant and there are positive prognostic indicators, 3 years.
4. Psychoanalytic therapy for very malignant cases, borderline disturbances, no time limit.

Influenced by Dr. Ramon de la Fuente, Fromm considered that medication could be helpful with some patients suffering from serious depressions or cyclical illness.

REFERENCES

Berlin, I. (1991). *The Crooked Timber of Humanity*. New York: Knopf.

Bonner, J. T. (1989). *The Evolution of Culture in Animals*. Princeton, NJ: Princeton University Press.

Diamond, J. (1993). *The Third Chimpanzee*. New York: Harper Perennial.

Freud, S. (1927). *The Future of an Illusion*. Standard Edition, 21:5–59.

Fromm, E. (1941). *Escape from Freedom*. New York: Rinehart.

_____ (1947). *Man for Himself*. New York: Rinehart.

_____ (1955). *The Sane Society*. New York: Rinehart.

_____ (1963, c. 1956). *The Art of Loving*. New York: Bantam.

_____ (1964). *The Heart of Man*. New York: Harper & Row.

_____ (1966). *You Shall Be As Gods*. New York: Holt, Rinehart & Winston.

_____ (1968). *The Revolution of Hope*. New York: Harper & Row.

_____ (1970). *The Anatomy of Human Destructiveness*. New York: Harper & Row.

_____ (1976). *To Have or To Be?* New York: Harper & Row.

_____ (1984). *The Working Class in Weimar Germany*. Cambridge, MA: Harvard University Press.

_____ (1992). *The Revision of Psychoanalysis*, ed. R. Funk. Boulder, CO: Westview.

Fromm, E., and Maccoby, M. (1970). *Social Character in a Mexican Village*. Englewood Cliffs, NJ: Prentice-Hall.

Fromm, E., Suzuki, D. T., and de Martino, R. (1960). *Psychoanalysis and Zen Buddhism*. New York: Harper.

Gay, P. (1985). *Freud for Historians*. New York: Oxford University Press.

James, W. (1902). *The Varieties of Religious Experience*. New York:

Longmans, 1928.

Jung, C. G. (1971). *Psychological Types*. Princeton, NJ: Princeton University Press.

LaBier, D. (1987). *Modern Madness*. Reading, MA: Addison-Wesley.

Maccoby, M. (1976). *The Gamesman*. New York: Simon & Schuster.

_____ (1981). *The Leader*. New York: Simon & Schuster.

_____ (1988). *Why Work*. New York: Simon & Schuster.

Mills, C. W. (1951). *White Collar*. New York: Oxford University Press.

Riesman, D. (1950). *The Lonely Crowd*. New Haven: Yale University Press.

Saavedra, V. (1994). *La Promesa Incumplida de Erich Fromm*. México: Siglo XXI.

Thompson, E. P. (1966). *The Making of the English Working Class, 1790–1830*. New York: Vintage.

Whyte, W. H. (1956). *The Organization Man*. New York: Simon & Schuster.

3

Beyond Freud's Instinctivism and Fromm's Existential Humanism*

Mauricio Cortina

INTRODUCTION

Fromm is generally credited with introducing one of the earliest revisions of libido theory, widening the narrow focus on oedipal conflicts to include a broad range of interpersonal, social and cultural factors that influence human development. This revision has now become adopted by the mainstream in psychoanalysis (Burston 1991, Cortina 1992, Greenberg and Mitchell 1983). The very significant differences between Freud's and Fromm's conceptions of human nature have attracted much less attention. Yet, an examination of these differences reveals

---

*I would like to thank Barbara Lenkerd, who has helped me clarify my ideas throughout the process of writing this chapter.

two distinct approaches to an understanding of the human condition.[1]

In the first section of this chapter I compare these two conceptions of human nature, examining some of the strengths and weaknesses of each. Building on John Bowlby, and the paleontologist Stephen Jay Gould's work, I propose an integration of these views that incorporates some of Fromm's strengths, namely his emphasis on what is new and distinctive in human nature—the discontinuities in our evolutionary descent—while affirming Freud's view that there are also significant evolutionary *continuities*, albeit of a very different nature than those proposed by Freud.

In the second section I examine how this revision of Fromm's concept of human nature challenges his views of (ontogenetic) development. Specifically, I argue that Fromm's overemphasis on evolutionary discontinuities—a relative absence of instinctive equipment in humans—parallels his views of ontogenetic development, that the route toward human individuation and growth is achieved by severing the symbiotic ties to primary caregivers (usually the mother). This view creates a false dichotomy by conceptualizing development as a choice between progressive and regressive solutions.

Attachment theory and developmental research published within the last two decades offers an alternative to the conceptual model of the mother–infant tie as symbiotic. The route toward autonomy and individuation is not based on the renunciation of this alleged symbiotic tie (a model of developmental discontinuity), but by a process involving the gradual construction of a relationship between the infant and his/her primary caregivers (Sroufe and Fleeson 1986). The internalization of this relationship is carried forward as a representational model of self and others, an internal organization that provides for a sense of continuity in development (Main et al. 1985, Sandler 1975, 1994, Sroufe 1990a, Sroufe and Fleeson 1986).

I conclude with a brief discussion of some clinical implications of this "secure base" model of development.

FREUD'S CONCEPT OF HUMAN NATURE

As is well known, Freud's view of human nature was enormously influenced by two major currents of nineteenth century science, namely Helmholtzian materialism, the basis for Freud's physicalistic conception of energy and drives (Bowlby 1969, Fairbairn 1941, Fromm 1973, Gill 1987, Holt 1968, 1989, Peterfreund 1971, Rosenblatt and Thikstun 1978, Schafer 1976), and evolutionary conceptions based on Lamarckism and Haekel's famous biogenetic law ontogeny recapitulates phylogeny (Gould 1977, Sulloway 1979). While all of these notions are now discredited, it must be said in Freud's defense that he made a valiant attempt to construct psychoanalysis within the framework of a natural science. I will briefly review some of the flaws of Freud's metapsychology.

Freud's conception of drives as having an inherent tendency to reduce tension to a minimum (the pleasure/ unpleasure principle) created many conceptual problems. It can be argued that Freud's model fit well with drives that are egoistic or antisocial. Given the pressure of socialization—civilizing tendencies, in Freud's terminology—there would be a need to either repress, discharge, or sublimate these drives together with the negative emotional components associated with these impulses. (The distinction between the aim of a drive and the emotional component that accompanies the drive is usually confused in theories of motivation [Lazarus

1991].) One of the most serious flaws of Freud's model is that it does not do justice to positive emotions such as joy, interest, or intimate affection, and the importance of relatedness that penetrate so many facets of development.

Pro-social motives do not fit the tension reduction model (Bowlby 1969, Emde 1992). Under normal conditions positive emotions are regulated at an optimal level of tension without the need for discharge or repression. The regulatory function of emotions is a major role of primary caregivers that is gradually taken over by the child. Contrary to what the tension model predicts, joy begets joy, interest begets interest, and love begets love. Organized complexity, which gives rise to new (emergent) properties, is now recognized as a fundamental concept in evolutionary theory (Gell-Mann 1994), developmental psychology (Cicchetti 1993, Cicchetti and Tucker 1994, Emde 1992, Sroufe 1990a), and at the cutting edge of scientific paradigms (Waldrop 1992). This is a far cry from Freud's energy models of cathexis and decathexis.

Due to his allegiance to Helmholtzian principles, Freud had to shoehorn his theory of motivation into a tension reduction (drive) model of development. He also limited his theory of motivation by postulating a dualistic drive theory—sexual and self-preservative drives, and in a later rendition of the drive model, life and death instincts. Major theorists in developmental psychology (Connell and Wellborn 1991), organizational psychology (Maccoby 1988), and psychoanalysis (Emde 1992, Lichtenberg 1989) have moved away from dualistic models toward a multi-motivational systems approach based on new scientific paradigms. I will return to this point when I discuss Fromm's multimotivational theory.

Freud's evolutionary assumptions are fundamental to his model of human nature. The phylogenetic assump-

tions also influenced his ontogenetic model of development (Sulloway 1979) and became central to an oedipal
interpretation of the origin of neurosis. As is well known,
Freud believed that parricidal and incestuous impulses
were a legacy of our human prehistory. These impulses
had originated in our phylogenetic past at a time when a
band of brothers rebelled against a tyrannical father,
murdering the father and appropriating the women for
themselves (Freud 1913). Following Freud's Lamarckian
belief that acquired characteristics are inherited and that
ontogeny (developmental history) recapitulates phylogeny (evolutionary history), it was just a step to enshrine
these evolutionary beliefs as part of the ubiquitous Oedipus complex. The Oedipus complex is by far the most
notorious example, but by no means the only instance, in
which Freud applied this evolutionary formula to support
ontogenetic theories of development (Sulloway 1979).

To summarize, Freud's concept of human nature postulated a developmental conflict between opposing drives,
and between socialization pressures of civilization and
atavistic impulses that had to be repressed or tamed. The
aim of development for Freud was to master irrational
passions in the service of the ego's rational control of these
drives. The prototype of Freud's concept of human nature
is embodied in the oedipal drama, where parricidal and
incestuous impulses, originating in phylogeny, are reca-
pitulated ontogenetically as the Oedipus complex.

These inherent conflicts have mental representations in
Freud's structural theory of the mind. The struggles are
transformed into conflicts between different mental agencies, the id and the superego, leaving an embattled ego to
find a compromise.[2]

While Freud's metapsychology and evolutionary assumptions have been abandoned by even the most die-
hard Freudians, his vision of the darker side of human

nature as a primitive legacy of phylogenetic impulses had the great merit of maintaining an evolutionary perspective of human nature at center stage. Perhaps because Freud's phylogenetic speculations were seen as extreme by even his most loyal adherents—Jones (1957) pleaded with Freud to abandon his Lamarckism, to no avail—an evolutionary framework was almost completely abandoned in psycho-analysis until Bowlby's seminal work began to appear in the 1960s. It is my intention to build on Bowlby's recasting of evolutionary theory.

Before picking up this thread of the argument, I will first describe briefly Fromm's vision of the human condition. Fromm's view of human nature also had an explicit evolutionary basis.

FROMM'S CONCEPT OF HUMAN NATURE

Fromm never accepted Freud's tension-reduction meta-psychology nor his phylogenetic beliefs (Fromm 1973). However, he did agree with Freud that there is a basic conflict in humans between life-affirming and life-strangling passions (eros versus death instinct). Fromm developed a radically different interpretation of the origin of this conflict. He first published his conception of human nature in *Man for Himself* (1947). This conception of human nature remained a unifying theme of his work, and it was elaborated in further publications (1955, 1956, 1964, 1973).

In stark contrast to Freud, Fromm believed it was the relative *absence* of instincts, not our atavistic retention of instincts, that defined, to a large measure, the human condition. In *The Anatomy of Human Destructiveness* (1973), Fromm speculated on the evolutionary process that led to this development:

Considering this data, man can be defined as the primate that emerged at the point of evolution where instinctive determination had reached a minimum and the development of the brain a maximum. This combination of minimal instinctive development had never before occurred in animal evolution and constitutes, biologically speaking, a completely new phenomena. [p. 224, Fromm's italics]

Fromm, in effect, saw homo sapiens as a species that was uprooted from the bonds of nature, a "freak of nature" as he put it:

Man's life cannot be lived by repeating the pattern of his species; *he* must live. Man is the only animal that does not feel at home in nature, who can feel evicted from paradise, the only animal for whom his existence is a problem that he has to solve and from which he cannot escape. He cannot go back into the prehuman state of harmony with nature, and he does not know where he will arrive if he goes forward. Man's existential contradiction results in a state of constant disequilibrium. This disequilibrium distinguishes him from the animal, which lives, as it were, in harmony with nature. This does not mean, of course, that the animal necessarily lives a peaceful and happy life, but that it has a specific ecological niche to which its physical and mental qualities have been adapted by the process of evolution. Man's existential and hence unavoidable disequilibrium can be relatively stable when he has found, with the support of his culture, a more or less adequate way of coping with his existential problems. But this relative stability does not imply that the dichotomy has disappeared: it is merely dormant and becomes manifest as soon as the conditions of this relative stability change. [Fromm 1973, p. 225]

Building on this dialectical model of human nature, in *The Sane Society* (1955) Fromm developed a theory of human motivation that went far beyond Freud's dual drive theory. In Fromm's work the source of motivation is not rooted in the clash between opposing biological drives, but originates in a new biological condition. This condition produced new (emergent) properties such as the capacity to provide meaning, foresight, and self-awareness, creating a set of new contradictions that characterizes human existence. According to Fromm (1955, p. 54), "the most powerful forces motivating man's behavior stem from the conditions of existence," the "human situation or condition" as he called it.

Fromm (1955) proposed five specifically human motives that were somewhat modified in his later work. In this first version these motives are considered as dialectical opposites:

Relatedness versus narcissism
Transcendence (creativeness versus destructiveness)
Rootedness (brotherliness versus incest)
Sense of identity (individuality versus herd conformity)
A frame of orientation and devotion (reason versus irrationality).

In *The Anatomy of Human Destructiveness* (1973) Fromm simplified this scheme and named five basic human needs:

A need for a frame of orientation and devotion (a cognitive and spiritual map)
A need for roots (relatedness)
A need for unity (coherence, sense of belonging)
A need to be effective (competence motivation, mastery)
A need for active stimulation.

These specifically human motives are constrained or enhanced by a complex mixture of individual, social, cultural, and historical factors that give rise to different manifestations of human nature. Each of these manifestations can be considered a solution to the riddle posed by the human condition. But for Fromm it is the "questions," not the historically conditioned "solutions," that are the essence of the human condition.

Freud's and Fromm's theories of human nature present interesting contrasts. Freud, the sobered enlightenment figure with a deep faith in the capacity of reason to unveil truth and destroy illusions, was a pessimist when he considered the possibilities for improving the human condition. Witnessing the First World War and the triumph of the Nazi movement only confirmed Freud's conviction of the power of our atavistic inclinations.

Fromm came from a long rabbinical tradition, with teachers who instilled an abiding faith in the humanistic tradition and an iconoclastic distrust of ideologies and political leaders (Burston 1991, Funk 1984). Fromm saw in Freud's theories a method to unmask deception and free humans from the bonds of illusion. This belief he shared with Freud. But Fromm also had a rigorous sociological and philosophical training. He saw as naive attempts to explain complex social phenomena, such as war, as being caused by innate aggressive drives. These views were also enormously blind to the realities of power. The capacity of leaders to manipulate people's fears and socially sanctioned narcissistic identifications were ignored by biological speculations (Fromm 1973). For Fromm, it was not our "bestial" phylogenetic heritage that was the main problem, but rather our specific *human* nature, emerging as a completely new evolutionary phenomenon, which cried out for understanding.[3]

FROM INSTINCT TO HUMAN MOTIVATION

Bowlby's evolutionary framework supports the view that pro-social and altruistic motives—not just aggressive and egoistic drives—are deeply rooted in evolution. While Bowlby's evolutionary view is radically different from Freud's, Bowlby's work also calls into question Fromm's model of human nature. Fromm thought that human evolution marks a fundamental break with nature. However, the continuity of pro-social motives in primate evolution suggests a different interpretation. I will try to show that the increase in behavioral flexibility evidenced in primate evolution is not due, as Fromm thought, to a reduction of our instinctual equipment. Most likely this outcome evolved through a different evolutionary process.

Before examining weaknesses in Fromm's model of human nature and proposing an alternative, it is important to summarize its strengths. Fromm's revision of Freud avoids questionable metapsychological constructs providing a more straightforward relational model. He moves away from Freud's atavistic reconstruction of human origins by calling attention to what is new in human evolution. He also provides a model of human motivation that is multimotivational rather than dualistic, the first attempt by a major psychoanalytic theorist to pioneer this approach. To my knowledge, Fromm has never received credit for this achievement.

Any conceptual bridge that helps identify continuities between our phylogenetic instinctive endowment and human motivation is indebted to the seminal work of Bowlby, who first looked at development from the point of view of separation-anxiety phenomena. His collaboration with the Robertsons in the late 1940s and early 1950s documented in film the classical observation of the three stages that follow brief separations: protest (anger), despair, and detachment. This universal reaction of young children to brief separations from their primary caregivers raises the question about the nature of the infant's tie to the mother. Bowlby felt that the extant models used to explain the tie were unsatisfactory.[4]

Looking for alternative theories, Bowlby turned his attention to the data from the field of ethology. Here he found that ethologists had been making careful observations that showed that in mammals and most species of birds, attachment behavior was ubiquitous. The data suggested that a motivational structure that was present across so many species must have been selected for very powerful reasons. Once having considered this tie from an evolutionary perspective, it became evident that the tie must perform a vital protective function, which Bowlby conceived (narrowly, I believe) as a protection from predators. I will return to this point later.

Bowlby's work can be seen historically as having provided a synthesis between Freud's outmoded drive theory based on frustration and control of instinctual urges and the relational model exemplified by Fairbairn's, Fromm's and Suttie's work (Burston 1991, Cortina 1992, Greenberg and Mitchell 1983). Bowlby redefines instinct in modern evolutionary terms using cybernetic models and control set theory, thus bridging the gap between these positions. He adds to the relational model an understanding of affiliative needs as instinctive in nature, yet powerfully influenced by experience.[5]

This ancient motivational system continues to have a vital function in humans. There is no break in evolutionary lineage even though there may be significant transformations. The similarities between attachment behavior in humans and other primate species is striking and uncanny to observe (Harlow 1961). Where we humans diverge is in the meaning these vital ties have for us, a meaning that becomes transformed by our symbolic capabilities that far exceed the cognitive capabilities of even our closest relatives (Zuckerman 1991).

Here we encounter a major problem. The issue that led Fromm to the minimal instinct hypothesis is compelling. Is not the enormous behavioral flexibility in humans a proof that we are no longer determined by "fixed action patterns" that characterize instinct? If, as I contend, instinctive endowment is not diminished but is transformed, how do we account for a transformation that led to flexibility and openness to experiential learning?

AN ALTERNATIVE TO FROMM'S EVOLUTIONARY HYPOTHESIS

Let us first consider some salient human characteristics that need to be accounted for in any evolutionary reconstruction of human origins: an enlarged brain (the basis for expanded symbolic capacities such as language, foresight, and imagination), erect posture, a very prolonged childhood, delayed sexual maturation, increased adaptive flexibility, and the development of intimate affectional bonds and extensive sociability. These characteristics produce in turn a new form of evolution that is not mediated by the genes, namely cultural evolution. While no single explanation is likely to account for all these attributes, in recent years Gould has advanced a comprehensive and coherent hypothesis that deserves our full attention.

In his book *Ontogeny and Phylogeny* (1977) Gould explains how flexibility can be selected directly by modifying developmental rates of growth (heterochrony). A relatively simple modification in the genetic regulation in the timing of development affecting the growth hormone can have profound effects on the adaptive capabilities of organisms. Accelerating development, a phenomenon known as progenesis, has the effect of producing precocious sexual maturity. Retarding development has the opposite effect, delaying sexual maturation. In a phenomenon known in biology as neoteny, this retardation of development affects not only sexual maturity but the organism as a whole. The hallmark of neoteny is retarded development with retention of juvenile forms. Retention of juvenile characteristics is associated with greater flexibility, playfulness, and malleability of organisms. Note that the mechanism that produces flexibility is mediated through selective forces that influence the genetic regulation of the timing of development (acceleration or retardation of development). There is not a direct effect on instinctive behavioral patterns per se.

However, instinctive patterns are profoundly affected by retarded development, particularly parenting behavior and attachment behavior in infants. If development is accelerated and sexual maturity is reached precociously, the need for parental care is minimal. If, however, sexual maturity is delayed, there will be a much greater need for parental care to protect and nurture offspring over a protracted juvenile stage of development. The selection for attachment bonds will cement the relationship between parents and their offspring. As it turns out, humans are the most neotenic of any known species (Gould 1977). That is to say, there is a pronounced retardation across all developmental processes requiring extensive parental care.

Why would there be a selective advantage to species that produce fewer offspring (the result of delayed sexual maturity) and require so much care? To provide an answer it is necessary to consider the environmental niche in which populations are reproducing.

In environments characterized by abundant resources, rapidly fluctuating conditions, and few competitors, a strategy that favors rapid colonization is clearly advantageous. In this environment species that can reach sexual maturity quickly (accelerated development) and produce large litters are rewarded. However, in environments that have reached a point of saturation (have reached their "carrying capacity") but are relatively stable, a strategy that favors the selection of fewer, but more competent offspring is clearly an advantage. Delaying sexual maturation can produce this effect (retarded development). The first strategy is known in biology as r selection and the second as K selection. Hominid evolution has been a typical example of a K selection within environments that are relatively stable but highly competitive (density dependent).

The selection of flexibility and the retention of juvenile forms; a very delayed sexual maturation; a protracted period of development; the development of attachment bonds, with fewer but more competent offspring—all have evolved as a common evolutionary matrix. A general retardation of development also produces a retention of embryonic rates of growth beyond birth. This effect is particularly relevant to human evolution. The human brain continues to grow at fetal rates until the second year of extrauterine life. This effect contributes to the enormous cerebralization observed in our species.

To summarize, the enormous growth of the neocortex together with a minimal instinctive equipment were invoked by Fromm as two converging evolutionary tendencies that explain the human's adaptive flexibility and plasticity. The alternative interpretation of human plasticity based on neoteny has the great advantage over Fromm's hypothesis of explaining both processes (growth of the neocortex and adaptive flexibility) by the single mechanism of retarded development (neoteny). It is also worth noting that it is out of this whole evolutionary matrix, and not just the protection from predators, as Bowlby believed, that attachment bonds emerged. Gould (1977) observes:

> By now, this associated complex of characters—neoteny, large brains, K selection, slow development, small litters, intense parental care, large body size—must have suggested a look at the mirror. A neotenic hypothesis of human origins has been available for some time but it has been widely ridiculed and ignored. Nonetheless, I believe it is fundamentally correct and the framework I have established may help vindicate it. [p. 351]

In the next section I will examine the effect this different interpretation of human origins has on Fromm's conceptions of ontogenic development.

THE DIALECTICS OF HUMAN DEVELOPMENT

As I indicated in the introduction, there is a parallel between Fromm's views of phylogeny and ontogeny. Just as Fromm saw the emergence of the human species as a break with our evolutionary ties to nature, so ontogenetic development required a break with the primary ties with mother. According to Fromm (1973), at the moment of birth the human infant is symbiotically attached to its mother and remains so longer than any other animal. The more complete the separation, the greater the need to replace the symbiotic tie with new ties. Fromm (1973) assumes that there remains a regressive craving to preserve primary ties or to find a substitute that can provide absolute protection and security, "a return to paradise":

> But the way to paradise is blocked by man's biological, and particularly by his neurophysiological constitution. He has only one alternative: either to persist in his craving to regress, and to pay for it by symbolic dependence on mother (and on symbolic substitutes, such as soil, nature, god, the nation, a bureaucracy), or to progress and to find new roots in the world by his own efforts, by experiencing the brotherhood of man, and by freeing himself from the power of the past. [pp. 232–233]

Fromm has set up a false dichotomy based on his own premises. Fromm assumes that the route toward independence in humans implies giving up the primary ties with caregivers and replacing them with new ties that are not based on symbiotic relatedness. Fromm never explains how this developmental transformation takes place. As a result we are left with a critical gap in our ability to understand normal development. This gap opens the door to view any manifestation of the need for attachment as potentially regressive.

THE LIMITATIONS OF THE SYMBIOTIC UNITY CONCEPT, AND AN ALTERNATIVE MODEL OF DEVELOPMENT

Fromm was not alone in the tendency to pathologize normal development. Most clinical theory derived from psychoanalysis follows this trend by postulating early stages of normal development in terms of later stages of psychopathology, a tendency Peterfreund (1978) has called the "adultomorphization of infancy." Perhaps this has been inevitable, as psychoanalysts began to build developmental theory from the basis of its practice with clinical populations. Insights about development gained from clinical work remain a treasure house of rich hypothesis. They remain to be developed and tested by other methodologies. Moreover, they need to be compared with what we know of normal development.[6]

Fromm, who coined the term *symbiosis*, and Mahler (1975) who developed an enormously influential stage theory of separation-individuation process, relied heavily on the assumption that the roots of human development could be traced to a primitive undifferentiated infant–mother bond. A corollary to this assumption was that development required breaking away from primary ties (Fromm), or "hatching" (Mahler) from this symbiotic unity.

There are now several excellent critiques of the concept of symbiosis applied to human development (Horner 1985, Stern 1985). I will not repeat their arguments here. Suffice it to say that conceptions of infancy have changed dramatically over the past twenty years. As infant research has focused on infant competencies, new data have forced us to rethink concepts such as infant omnipotence, fusion, and primary narcissism. Simultaneously with these developments another line of research influenced by Bowlby has been carefully documenting in longitudinal studies the vicissitudes of these "primary ties." Sroufe (Sroufe and Fleeson 1986) points out that the relationship between an infant and his or her primary caregiver is no different in principle from any other relationship. That is to say, both mother and infant have to become acquainted with each other as they develop an intimate relationship. While this relationship is highly motivated given our biological origins, the gradual construction of this relationship can take many routes—some healthy, others less than optimal, and some frankly pathological (see below). As the route to emotional security is constructed gradually, infants and toddlers begin to explore the world and to discover their individuality using their parents as a "secure base" of operation (Ainsworth et al. 1978).

It is here that Bowlby's work, and the research tradition it has spawned, has provided a much-needed corrective to models of growth and psychopathology based on concepts of regression, symbiosis, and fusion. Longitudinal research convincingly demonstrates that a major influence on socioemotional development is the quality of relatedness between a child and his/her primary caregivers, (Ainsworth et al. 1978, Arend et al. 1979, Bowlby 1980, Sroufe 1983, Sroufe et al. 1984, Urban et al. 1991) or to use Fairbairn's (1952) terminology, "the quality of the dependence." Fromm (1949) also believed that the quality of relatedness was a central issue in development:

> In a theory that is centered on the quality of interpersonal relatedness the most relevant datum would be the mother's attitude toward her child, i.e. her love, acceptance and so on. [p. 4]

Unfortunately, Fromm never developed this line of thought explicitly, even though in theory he considered modes of socialization (relatedness to others) together with assimilation of sociocultural factors as the two main determinants of character formation (Fromm 1947). Had Fromm followed this lead, it might have provided an alternative to the view that severing of primary ties was necessary in order to break the bonds of dependency. Attachment research has shown convincingly that a secure attachment relationship means less dependence later in life (Sroufe et al. 1984). Securely attached children are free to explore the world with confidence. In contrast, insecurely attached children by preschool age are seen by teachers as more clinging and dependent and take more passive or aggressive roles with their peers (Sroufe et al. 1984).

If the polarity between regressive and progressive developmental tendencies is misleading, how best can we conceptualize developmental tensions? No one single dialectic can capture the complexity of human development (Eagle 1995). Nonetheless, it is the case that attachment and exploration move in opposite directions, attachment toward and exploration away from mother as a secure base. While this dialectic is most obvious in early childhood, it continues to be played out, albeit transformed by new meanings and capabilities, in the course of development. Fromm's polarity between regressive and progressive tendencies or Mahler's separation-individuation process can be understood, in light of attachment theory, as an attachment-exploration or attachment-individuation process (Lyons-Ruth 1991). The move in either direction of this dialectical process can be healthy (progressive) or defensive (regressive) depending on the context and the overall quality of the relationship.

We are indebted to Mary Ainsworth for much of what we know about patterns of attachment and the development of the infant–mother bond. Her generative collaboration and expansion of Bowlby's work revolutionized the field of developmental psychology, providing an opening in academia for psychoanalytic concepts and ideas. The strange situation (SS) laboratory procedure is a landmark in this effort and was the culmination of a one-year naturalistic study of mothers and infants in an American middle class sample (Ainsworth et al. 1978). Based on the SS procedure Ainsworth described three patterns of attachment.[7]

Pattern B (secure attachment) is found in 55 to 60 percent of nonclinical middle-class samples in the United

States (Ainsworth et al. 1978). There are important cross-cultural differences in samples from other countries (Bacciagaluppi 1994). Secure infants explore the new environment freely in the presence of mother and express their delight about playing with toys. Upon their mother's first exit from the room, they protest mother's departure and do not settle down with the stranger. After being left alone during the first and particularly the second separation episode, secure infants immediately seek their mother when she returns and characteristically mold into her arms. They settle down after contact with the mother is reestablished and they regain their composure. The hallmark of a secure attachment is that the infants' reunion with their mother is effective in alleviating distress. At home, mothers of secure infants are observed to be responsive and sensitive to the infants' signals and communication. As histories of responsive and sensitive care (secure attachments) are internalized, young children show an inner sense of confidence and effectiveness and use their parents as a "secure base" from which to explore the world (Main et al. 1985, Sroufe, 1983, 1989a). Normal development is characterized by this back and forth confident movement, using mother as a secure base.

Pattern C (anxious-ambivalent or anxious-resistant pattern) is found in 7 to 15 percent of nonclinical population samples in the United States (Cassidy and Berlin 1994). Ambivalently attached infants' poverty of exploration is evident in the SS procedure even in the presence of mother. Upon reunion with the mother (after the separation episodes), the infants manifest their intense desire to be soothed by crawling toward mother and asking to be picked up, extending their hands toward their mother. Once in mother's arms, these infants settle down momentarily, but soon become distressed. Pattern C babies oscillate between wanting to be comforted and rejecting the comfort. The contact with mother is not effective in alleviating their distress. Lyons-Ruth (1991) observes that this ambivalence that Mahler considered to be universal during the rapprochement stage of development is only characteristic of children with anxious ambivalent patterns of attachment.[8]

Infants who exhibit this pattern in the SS procedure were observed at home as being cared for inconsistently and at times insensitively. Development of this pattern of attachment leads to children who are less competent and more dependent than securely attached children. Later in life these children maintain a hypervigilant attention and preoccupation toward attachment figures (Arend et al. 1979, Cassidy and Berlin 1994, Sroufe 1983).

Pattern A (anxious avoidant attachment) is present in 20 to 25 percent of population samples in the United States (Ainsworth et al. 1978). Avoidantly attached infants explore freely in the presence of mother or the stranger. After separation from their primary caregivers, pattern A infants may make an initial effort to reestablish contact with their mother, but they then either ignore their mother and/or get distracted with a toy or object. It may seem by their reunion behavior that these infants are more independent and less distressed than either their secure or anxious-ambivalent counterparts. However, when their heart rate (Sroufe and Waters 1977) or cortisol levels are measured (Spangler and Grossmann 1993), it becomes clear that these infants are very distressed. At this early stage of development, pattern A babies have learned to suppress their anger and desire to be soothed. As is evident from home observations, primary caregivers ignore or reject their children's bids for attention, particularly when caregivers are distressed. Very often the parents are uncomfortable with physical contact and are rejecting (Main and Stadtman 1981). As these infants

develop, they continue to defensively exclude from awareness attachment needs and embrace exploratory behavior
as a strategy to divert attention from attachment figures
and hide their anger (Crittenden and Ainsworth 1989).

Recently a fourth, disorganized/disoriented (D) pattern
of insecure attachment has been described by Main and
Solomon (1986). This pattern is found in 5 percent of
nonclinical U.S. populations, but much higher percent-
ages (50 to 60 percent) are found in children with a history
of maltreatment (Carlson et al. 1989, Lyons-Ruth et al.
1991) or a history of a parent that has suffered a significant
loss that remains unresolved (Main and Hesse 1990).
Unlike Ainsworth's ABC patterns of attachment, infants
exhibiting the D pattern do not exhibit a coherent behavioral strategy in the strange situation (SS). The lack of
behavioral coherence has been interpreted as being the
result of intense fear and confusion (Main and Hesse
1990).

It is important to note that only the anxious-ambivalent
pattern, characterized by clingy, enmeshed relationships
in later development, fits more closely with Fromm's
concept of a pathological symbiosis. However the symbiosis is better understood as a developmental line with its
own internal logic and not as a regression or as a "mother
fixation." On the other hand, a pattern of early independence from attachment figures can be a sign of serious
trouble. In extreme situations, these pseudoindependent
infants develop as toddlers an attachment disorder characterized by accident proneness and a reckless disregard
for signs of danger (Lieberman 1993).

There is a growing body of evidence based on longitudinal research that coherence of these patterns (defined as
broad-band-base measures of adaptation) persist into preadolescence (Urban et al. 1991). Mediating factors are both
intrapsychic (Main et al. 1985) and environmental (Ege-

land and Farber 1984). Children with histories character-ized by sensitive and respectful care develop an inner sense of confidence and belief in their capacity to master new experience. With histories characterized by intrusive, inconsistent, overstimulating, or rejecting care, this inner sense of confidence and effectiveness is shaken. Intrapsy-chically, representational models of self as unworthy and others as unavailable begin to crystallize.

Evidence suggesting continuity of relational patterns across generations is based on a sophisticated and inten-sive interview, known as the the adult attachment inter-view (AAI) (George et al. 1985), that examines memories of childhood and attachment-related experiences. The interviews are judged in terms of their coherence, defen-siveness, and cogency. Four prototypes have been de-scribed that roughly correlate with attachment patterns identified in childhood.

Interviews classified as autonomous are characterized by responses that are coherent, clear, and relevant. These individuals value attachments, but do not idealize or denigrate past experience. Memories that are painful are not repressed and genuine sadness and joy can be ex-pressed. This type of interview corresponds to the secure pattern.

Interviews classified as preoccupied are characterized by an ambivalent attitude toward attachment figures that is passive, angry, or both. Memories, positive or negative, are poorly integrated, and unconvincing evidence is pro-vided to sustain idealization of parents. While there is no rejection of the need for intimacy, there is a quality of anxious preoccupation in regard to attachment figures. Responses are often vague and nebulous. This pattern is similar to the hypervigilant strategy of anxious-resistant infants.

Interviews classified as dismissing are characterized by

individuals whose discomfort with the interview process is disguised as a superficially cooperative attitude. Responses are aimed unconsciously at minimizing the importance of attachment-related experiences. Few memories are recalled, and when they are, they have not been reflected upon. The interviewee usually prefers to talk about the present and tends to dismiss the importance of intimacy in the past and the present. Responses are constructed poorly. This category is similar to the avoidant strategy of minimizing attachment needs evident in the SS procedure with infants.

Interviews classified as unresolved/disorganized show evidence of brief mental disorganization and disorientation and magical thinking when traumatic memories are evoked (Main 1993). Not infrequently one finds highly functioning individuals in this adult category.

Based on studies from five different countries in low-risk samples, about 56 percent of the population are judged autonomous, 16 percent are dismissing, 10 percent are preoccupied, and 18 percent are judged in the unresolved/cannot classify category (Main 1993).

Perhaps one of the most striking research findings in the attachment literature is that adult categories based on the AAI predict attachment patterns of these adults to their infants. There are now several studies using the AAI before and after pregnancy (Benoit and Parker 1994, Fonagy et al. 1991, Grossmann et al. 1988) that find that a woman's AAI classification correlates in 80 to 85 percent of the cases with their infants' attachment status at one year. Benoit and Parker's (1994) study is the first to study attachment patterns in three generations (grandmother's AAI, mother's AAI, and her infant's attachment pattern in the SS procedure). Again, across the three generations there are strong correlations between the AAI in grandmothers, the categories of AAI in mothers, and the SS procedure in infants.

SOME CLINICAL IMPLICATIONS

At the most general level, the secure base phenomenon provides a model for thinking about psychotherapy and the therapeutic alliance. The role of the therapist is to provide a secure base from which the patient and therapist can explore together dysfunctional relational patterns in and out of the consulting room, as they are expressed in the present and as they originated in the past (Bowlby 1982).[9] The secure base model emphasizes not only the "holding" (Winnicott 1965) or "containing" (Bion 1967) function of psychotherapy, but also the exploratory function (Basch 1988, Peterfreund 1983) that leads toward competence and individuation. Another psychotherapy model that builds on the security-mastery polarity is Joseph Weiss (1993, 1994) and the Mt. Zion psychotherapy group. This model also has in common with attachment theory an emphasis on real experience. From infancy onward there is a need to understand and adapt to reality (Sampson 1992). Another distinctive feature of the Mt. Zion model is the importance given to the need to correct maladaptive relational patterns and beliefs. This emphasis on a self-righting tendency is consistent with attachment theory and has been expressed by other authors (Horney 1950, Lichtenberg 1989). Greenberg (1991) calls for a "safety-effectance" drive model to replace Freud's motivational theory. Given the strong similarities to the secure-base phenomenon it is surprising Greenberg barely mentions Bowlby's work.

Attachment theory powerfully calls attention to the importance the sensitivity of caregivers has on the development of secure relatedness. Needless to say, there are important differences between the responsiveness required by parents and psychotherapists. The psychotherapeutic relationship with adults is based on a greater degree of mutuality. Exploration is guided by mature cognitive capacities involving narrative structures, self-reflection, and insight. As psychotherapists, we must be more alert than the average parent to the impact of even our most well-intentioned efforts. A reassuring comment may be perceived as condescending and an interpretation as a threat. This requires a constant vigilance and monitoring of the relationship with patients (Casement 1991). Sandler's (1976) concept of free-floating responsiveness captures some of the complexity required by this attunement to patients' overt and covert messages that goes beyond the usual considerations given to transferential and countertransferential reactions. Other roles, such as encouraging patients to face up to debilitating fears, humiliations, and despair and seek out new and more hopeful alternatives, are also essential (Fromm 1968, Menninger 1959).

Finally, I would like to mention another area where longitudinal research based on attachment theory can be of great clinical importance. Developmental paths identified by longitudinal studies may serve as useful "story lines," model scenes (Lichtenberg 1989), or search strategies (Peterfreund 1983) that illuminate narrative structures as they unfold in clinical work. Some of these developmental paths follow histories of intrusive and overstimulating care (Jacobovitz et al. 1991, Sroufe 1989b), seductive care (Sroufe 1980), or paths that follow various forms of maltreatment (Cicchetti 1991).

Clinically I have found that listening with these story

lines in mind has helped me and my patients as we try to make sense of their histories and understand the origin of interpersonal patterns that are disruptive to their lives.

CONCLUSION

We humans have emerged from an evolutionary matrix that has put a very large premium on the protective and socializing function of affiliative ties, particularly on offspring who remain relatively helpless during a very protracted period of growth and development. This view differs from Freud's more atavistic evolutionary model that focused almost exclusively on egoistic and aggressive strivings. It also differs from Fromm, whose model was based on "an eviction from paradise" metaphor that emphasized the need to break from the ties to "nature, blood, and soil" (Fromm 1955, p. 48) as a condition for human development.

Fromm recognized the central importance of human relatedness; indeed, his whole approach is based on this premise. However, in the absence of a good model for normal development, he held a view of development based on human symbiosis rather than on the growth-promoting effects of human bonds. I attempt to summarize findings from attachment theory and research to fill this critical gap in Fromm's model of development with an alternative model. I explore some of the clinical implications of a secure-base model of psychotherapy derived from attachment theory and research.

ENDNOTES

1. Fromm did not identify his position as *existential humanism*, although he did use the term *humanistic psychoanalysis* to

characterize his approach, only to retract it later. I have used the term *existential humanism* as a shorthand term to characterize his thought, despite Fromm's attempt to distance himself from Sartre and Heidegger's brand of existentialism, which he thought was an expression of despair. Nonetheless, Fromm's thinking has a distinct existential flavor. Burston (1991) has compared it to Heidegger's concept of "thrownness," a sense of being cast in a world with no guarantees of safe havens. Fromm's belief that the fundamental contradictions in humans are rooted in biological and historical conditions of existence justify, in my opinion, the term *existential humanism*.

2. Fromm (1973) believed that Freud's second rendition of drive theory, eros versus the death instinct, allowed for a much richer view of human nature. Particularly eros, steeped as it was in a vitalistic conception of life, could have allowed Freud to move toward a more organic model of human nature. Freud never resolved the contradiction between vitalism and materialism (Fromm 1973, Holt 1968). Despite Freud's allegiance to his earlier materialistic mentors, who saw their mission as stripping science of the corrosive influence of vitalism, eros was a tribute to vitalism.

3. Whatever else may be said of this view of human nature, Fromm was more explicit than most psychoanalysts in working through a coherent vision of the human condition and applying this vision to psychoanalysis and a broad range of social, cultural, and religious phenomena. Any serious critique of Fromm has to take into consideration the premises of his model of human nature. In psychoanalytic circles, with few exceptions, Fromm's work was seriously distorted, either by seeing him as a student of Rousseau, with a rosy and naive picture of the human condition (Pruyser 1974), or by dismissing his work as a superficial "culturalist," who did not take into consideration unconscious motivation (Rapaport 1967). Neither of these critiques stands up to close scrutiny. Fromm did not see man as inherently good nor did he eschew the irrational. The charge that Fromm believed all pathology to be the product of cultural or interpersonal factors alone is a caricature of his position. His

views are better understood as dialectical, giving weight to the
influence of formative years, constitutional and socially patterned traits (social character) in the etiology of mental illness,
and personality development (Cortina 1992).

4. One set of theories saw the nature of the tie as secondary
to the infant's physiological needs (Freud). Another set of
theories based on behavioral principles believed the tie was
learned. A third set of theories postulated a craving to return to
the womb (Rank 1929). A variation of this theory sees Rank's
birth trauma as a symbolic representation of a process of
psychological birth from the embeddedness of the primary tie
with the mother (Fromm 1941, Mahler 1967, Schachtel 1959,
Schecter 1973). Fromm was first in developing the idea of
symbiosis (Fromm 1941) and the concept of psychological birth
(Fromm 1955). Mahler never acknowledges Fromm, a case that
borders on plagiarism. Finally, Suttie (1935) and Fairbairn (1941)
anticipated Bowlby's work by seeing the tie as primary but not
necessarily symbiotic.

5. Bowlby's concept of attachment has been criticized as too
behavioral and ignoring intrapsychic phenomena (Greenberg
and Mitchell 1983, Sutherland 1989). I think this is a fundamental misunderstanding of Bowlby's work. Motivation can be
seen from two complementary perspectives. Seen from the
outside, an infant's needs to maintain proximity to mother can
be described in behavioral terms as attachment behaviors (clinging, protesting, crying, crawling after mother, etc.). However
seen from the inside, this urge is experienced subjectively as a
felt experience, that, depending on the context, may trigger
different emotions such as anger, affectional intimacy, shame,
sadness, or despair. Bowlby maintains that attachment is monitored by a whole gamut of feelings (Bowlby 1969). As the child
develops more sophisticated cognitive abilities, the environmental context is internalized in models of self and others
("internal working models") that are associated with patterned
emotional responses and behavioral strategies (Bowlby 1980).
The difference between Bowlby's model of intrapsychic development and most object-relational perspectives is a matter of

emphasis, with a greater role given to the actual quality of experience in Bowlby's work than to the role of fantasy as in object relations theory.

6. The study of normal and abnormal together is the goal of the new field of developmental psychopathology (Cicchetti 1989, Sroufe 1990b).

7. The SS situation consists of seven episodes, 3 minutes or less each, and lasts 18 to 21 minutes. The idea behind the procedure is to see how an infant responds to an increasingly stressful challenge in which the balance between attachment behavior and exploratory behavior are examined. There is a sequence of episodes that gradually tips the balance away from exploration and toward attachment: entrance into a new environment, arrival of a stranger, two brief separations from mother, and two subsequent reunions with her. Infants are usually 12 and/or 18 months old when the procedure is used.

8. When I mentioned this issue to Anni Bergman, Mahler's close collaborator and coauthor, she agreed. At the time they were doing the research there was no good model of normal development available that would have helped them recognize that even mild ambivalence during brief separations could be a sign of potential trouble (personal communication, 1992).

9. Compare with Sullivan's (1953) "security needs" or "need for tenderness" and Leston Havens's (1989) discussion of a "safe place" in psychotherapy.

POSTSCRIPT

After writing this chapter, I came upon McKinney and McNamara's (1991) *Heterochrony: The Evolution of Ontogeny*. Their book is the first attempt to summarize the literature since Steven Jay Gould's masterful *Ontogeny and Phylogeny* (1977). McKinney and McNamara build on this body of work and fine-tune it. Heterochrony in general (the study of rate and timing of development) and the neotenic hypothesis in particular call attention to the enormous importance for evolution of changes in the rate and timing of development. However, according to McKinney and McNamara, the neotenic hypothesis—outlined in the chapter—conflates two distinct processes. The *rate* of ontogenetic development can be slowed down (retarded) or can be accelerated in comparison to the rate of development of phylogenetic ancestors. Neoteny is *retarded* development. The *timing* of development refers to *when* ontogenetic development begins or ends in comparison to phylogenetic ancestors. The onset (starting point) or offset (end point) of development in a descendent species can begin earlier or later in comparison to its ancestors' phylogeny. A late offset of development is called hypermorphosis. What is characteristic of the human species is that this *offset* of ontogenetic development (not its rate) is very delayed in comparison with other primates. This is evident in brain development that continues to grow at *rapid* fetal rates until the end of the second year of extra-uterine life. In fact, humans have the most prolonged development of any primate. Most likely this late offset of development was strongly selected during hominid evolution.

In short, the neotenic hypothesis of human evolution confuses retarded development (neoteny) with prolonged development (hypermorphosis). It remains to be seen whether McKinney and McNamara are correct in their critique. If they are, everything I said regarding neoteny should be described as hypermorphosis. Although this is an important distinction, it does not change the main thesis of the first part of the chapter, namely that humans did not evolve by "losing" their instinctual equipment but by its transformation. This transformation has probably taken place by selection for a late offset of ontogenetic development. As I have noted, many human characteristics, including an enlarged brain, prolonged development, late sexual maturation, long life, large size, intense need for parental care, and flexible behavioral repertoire can be explained by means of this unifying hypothesis. In turn, this evolutionary matrix produces emergent properties described by Fromm as existential needs for purpose and meaning.

REFERENCES

Ainsworth, M. (1985). Patterns of mother–infant attachment: antecedents of development. *Bulletin of the New York Academy of Medicine* 61:771–790.

Ainsworth, M. D. S., Blehar, M., Waters, E., and Wall, S. (1978). *Patterns of Attachment*. Hillsdale, NJ: Lawrence Erlbaum.

Arend, R., Gove, F. L., and Sroufe, L. A. (1979). Continuity of individual adaptation from infancy to kindergarten: a predictive study of ego resiliency and curiosity in preschoolers. *Child Development* 50:950–959.

Bacciagaluppi, M. (1994). The relevance of attachment research to psychoanalysis and analytic social psychology. *American Academy of Psychoanalysis* 22:465–479.

Basch, M. (1988). *Understanding Psychotherapy: The Science Behind the Art*. New York: Basic Books.

Benoit, D., and Parker, C. H. K. (1994). Stability and transmission of attachment across three generations. *Child Development* 65:1429–1443.

Bion, W. R. (1967). *Second Thoughts*. London: Heinemann.

Bowlby, J. (1969). *Attachment*, vol. 1. New York: Basic Books.

———— (1980). *Attachment and Loss*, vol. 3. New York: Basic Books.

———— (1982). *A Secure Base*. New York: Basic Books.

Burston, D. (1991). *The Legacy of Erich Fromm*. Cambridge, MA: Harvard University Press.

Carlson, V., Cicchetti, D., Barnett, D., and Braunwald, R. (1989). Disorganized/disoriented attachment relationships in maltreated infants. *Development and Psychopathology* 25:525–531.

Casement, J. P. (1991). *Learning from the Patient*. New York: Guilford.

Cassidy, J., and Berlin, J. L. (1994). The insecure/ambivalent pattern of attachment: theory and research. *Child Development* 65:971–991.

Cicchetti, D. (1989). Developmental psychopathology: past, present and future. In *The Emergence of a Discipline: Rochester Symposium on Developmental Psychopathology*, vol 1, ed. C. Cicchetti, pp. 1–12. Hillsdale, NJ.: Lawrence Erlbaum.

_____ (1991). Attachment organization in maltreated preschoolers. *Development and Psychopathology* 3:397–411.

_____ (1993). Developmental psychopathology: reactions, reflections, projections. *Developmental Review* 13:471–502.

Cicchetti, D., and Tucker, D. (1994). Development and self-regulatory structures of the mind. *Development and Psychopathology* 6:533–549.

Connell, J. P., and Wellborn, J. G. (1991). Competence, autonomy and relatedness: a motivational analysis of self-system processes. In *Self Processes and Development*, ed. G. R. Megan and L. A. Sroufe. Hillsdale NJ: Lawrence Erlbaum.

Cortina, M. (1992). Review essay. *The Legacy of Erich Fromm*, by D. Burston. *Psychoanalytic Dialogues*. 4:530–538.

Crittenden, P. M., and Ainsworth, M. D. S. (1989). Child maltreatment and attachment theory. In *Child Maltreatment: Theory and Research on the Causes and Consequences of Child Abuse and Neglect*, ed. D. Cicchetti and V. Carlson, pp. 432–463. Cambridge, MA: Harvard University Press.

Eagle, M. N. (1985). Review Essay. Oedipus and beyond: a clinical theory by J. Greenberg. *Psychoanalytic Dialogues* 5:83–92.

Egeland, B., and Farber, A. E. (1984). Infant-mother attachment: factors related to its development and changes over time. *Child Development* 55:753–771.

Emde, R. N. (1992). Positive emotions for psychoanalytic theory: surprises from infancy research and new directions.

Journal of the American Psychoanalytic Association 39:5–44.

Fairbairn, W. R. D. (1941). A revised psychopathology of the psychosis and the neurosis. *International Journal of Psycho-Analysis* 22:250–279.

_____ (1952). *Psychoanalytic Studies of the Personality*. New York: Routledge.

Fonagy, P., Steele, H., and Steele, M. (1991). Maternal representations of attachment during pregnancy predict the organization of infant–mother attachment at year one. *Child Development* 62:891–905.

Freud, S. (1913). Totem and taboo. *Standard Edition* 13:1–100.

Fromm, E. (1941). *Escape from Freedom*. New York: Farrar & Rinehart.

_____ (1947). *Man for Himself: An Inquiry into the Psychology of Ethics*. Greenwich, CT: Fawcett.

_____ (1949). Psychoanalytic characterology and its application to the understanding of culture. In *Culture and Personality*, ed. S. S. Stanford and W. M. Smith. New York: Viking Fund.

_____ (1951). *The Forgotten Language*. New York: Grove.

_____ (1955). *The Sane Society*. New York: Holt, Rinehart & Winston.

_____ (1956). *The Art of Loving*. New York: Bantam, 1970.

_____ (1964). *The Heart of Man: Its Genius for Good and Evil*. New York: Harper & Row.

_____ (1968). *The Revolution of Hope*. New York. Harper & Row.

_____ (1973). *The Anatomy of Human Destructiveness*. Greenwich, CT: Fawcett Premier.

Fromm, E., and Maccoby, M. (1970). *Social Character in a Mexican Village: A Socio-psychoanalytic Study*. Englewood Cliffs, NJ: Prentice-Hall.

Funk, R. (1984). *Erich Fromm*. Hamburg: Rowohlt Taschenbuch Verlag.

Gell-Mann, M. (1994). *The Quark and the Jaguar: Adventures in the Simple and the Complex*. New York: W. H. Freeman.

George, C., Kaplan, N., and Main, M. (1985). *The Berkeley Adult Attachment Interview*. Unpublished protocol. Berkeley, CA: Department of Psychology, University of California.

Gill, M. M. (1987). Point of view of psychoanalysis: energy discharge or person. In *Attachment and The Therapeutic Process*, ed. F. Sacksteder, D. Schwartz, and Y. Akabane, pp. 17–41. Madison, CT: International Universities Press.

Gould, S. J. (1977). *Ontogeny and Phylogeny*. Cambridge, MA: Belknap and Harvard University Press.

Greenberg, R. J. (1991). *Oedipus and Beyond: A Clinical Theory*. Cambridge, MA: Harvard University Press.

Greenberg, R. J., and Mitchell, S. (1983). *Object Relations in Psychoanalytic Theory*. Cambridge, MA: Harvard University Press.

Grossmann, K., Fremmer-Bombik, J., Rudolph, J., and Grossmann, E. K. (1988). Mother attachment representations as related to patterns of infant–mother and maternal care during the first year. In *Relationships within Families: Mutual Influences*, ed. R. A. Hinde and J. Stevenson-Hinde, pp. 241–260. Oxford: Clarendon.

Harlow, H. F. (1961). The development of affectional patterns in infant monkeys. In *Determinants of Infant Behavior*, vol. 1, ed. B. M. Boss. New York: Wiley.

Havens, L. (1989). *A Safe Place: Laying the Groundwork of Psychotherapy*. Cambridge, MA: Harvard University Press.

Holt, R. (1968). Beyond vitalism and mechanism: Freud's concept of psychic energy. In *Psychoanalysis and Contemporary Psychoanalysis*, ed. R. Holt and E. Peterfreund. New York: Macmillan.

––––––– (1989). *Freud Reappraised*. New York: McGraw-Hill.

Horner, M. T. (1985). The psychic life of the young infant: review and critique of the psychoanalytic concepts of symbiosis and omnipotence. *American Journal of Orthopsychiatry* 55:324–344.

Horney, K. (1950). *Neurosis and Human Growth*. New York: W. W. Norton.

Jacobovitz, B. J., Morgan, E., Kretchmar, D. M., and Morgan, Y. (1991). The transmission of mother–child boundary disturbances across three generations. *Development and Psychopathology* 3:513–527.

Jones, E. (1957). *The Life and Work of Sigmund Freud*, vol. 3. New York: Basic Books.

Lazarus, R. (1991). *Emotion and Adaptation*. New York: Oxford University Press.

Lichtenberg, D. J. (1989). *Psychoanalysis and Motivation*. Hillsdale, NJ: Analytic Press.

Lieberman, A. F. (1993). *The Emotional Life of the Toddler*. New York: Macmillan.

Lyons-Ruth, K. (1991). Rapprochement or approchement: Mahler's theory reconsidered from the vantage point of recent research on early attachment relationships. *Psychoanalytic Psychology* 8:1–23.

Lyons-Ruth, K., Rapacholi, B., McLeod, S., and Silva, E. (1991). Disorganized attachment behavior in infancy: short term stability, maternal and infant correlates, and risk related subtypes. *Development and Psychopathology* 3:397–412.

Maccoby, M. (1988). *Why Work: Leading the New Generation*. New York: Simon & Schuster.

Mahler, M. (1975). *The Psychological Birth of the Human Infant*. New York: Basic Books.

Main, M. (1993). Discourse, prediction and recent studies in attachment: implications for psychoanalysis. *Journal of the American Psychoanalytic Association* 41:209–244.

Main, M., and Hesse, E. (1990). Parents' unresolved traumatic experiences are related to infant disorganized attachment status: Is frightened and/or frightening parental behavior the linking mechanism? In *Attachment in the Preschool Years: Theory, Research and Intervention*, ed. M. T. Greenberg, D. Cicchetti, and E. M. Commings, pp. 161–182. Chicago: University of Chicago Press.

Main, M., Kaplan, N., and Cassidy, J. (1985). Security in infancy, childhood and adulthood. A move to the level of representation. In *Growing Points in Attachment Theory and Research. Monographs in the Society for Research in Child Development*, ed. I. Bretherton and E. Waters, pp. 50:66–104.

Main, M., and Solomon, J. (1986). Discovery of a new, insecure disorganized/disoriented attachment pattern. In *Affective Development in Infancy*, ed. T. B. Brazelton, and M. Yugman, pp. 95–124. Norwood, NJ: Ablex.

Main, M., and Stadtman, J. (1981). Infants' response to physical rejection by the mother: aggression, avoidance and conflict. *Journal of the American Academy of Child Psychiatry* 20:292–307.

McKinney L. M., and McNamara, J. K. (1991). *Heterochrony: The*

Evolution of Ontogeny. New York: Plenum.

Menninger, K. (1959). Hope. *American Journal of Psychiatry* 116:481–491.

Peterfreund, E. (1971). Information, systems and psychoanalysis. *Psychological Issues*, monographs 25/26. New York: International Universities Press.

_____ (1978). Some critical comments on psychoanalytic conceptualizations of infancy. *International Journal of Psycho-Analysis* 59:427–441.

_____ (1983). *The Process of Psychoanalytic Therapy: Models and Strategies.* Hillsdale, NJ: Analytic Press.

Pruyser, P. (1974). The anatomy of human destructiveness. *Theology Today* 31:256–260.

Rank, O. (1929). *The Trauma of Birth.* London: Kegan Paul.

Rapaport, D. (1967). Clinical implications of ego psychology. In *The Collected Papers of David Rapaport*, ed. M. M. Gill, pp. 17–39. New York: Basic Books.

Rosenblatt, A., and Thikstun, J. (1978). Modern psychoanalytic concepts in a general psychology. *Psychological Issues*, monographs 42/43. New York: International Universities Press.

Sampson, H. (1992). The role of "real" experience in psychopathology and treatment. *Psychoanalytic Dialogues* 2:509–528.

Sandler, J. (1975). Infant and caretaking environments. In *Explorations in Child Psychiatry*, ed. J. Anthony. New York: Plenum.

_____ (1976). Countertransference and role-responsiveness. *International Journal of Psycho-Analysis* 3:43–47.

_____ (1994). Fantasy, defense and the representational world. *Infant Mental Health Journal* 15:26–35.

Schachtel, E. (1959). *Metamorphosis.* New York: Basic Books.

Schafer, R. (1976). *A New Language for Psychoanalysis.* New Haven: Yale University Press.

Schecter, D. (1973). On the emergence of human relatedness. In *Interpersonal Explorations in Psychoanalysis*, ed. E. Wittenberg, pp. 17–39. New York: Basic Books.

Spangler, G., and Grossmann, K. E. (1993). Biobehavioral organization in securely and insecurely attached infants. *Child Development* 64:1439–1450.

Sroufe, L. A. (1980). Seductive behavior of mothers of toddlers:

occurrence, correlates and family origins. *Child Development* 51:1222-1229.

_____ (1983). Infant-caregiver attachment and the patterns of attachment in the preschool: the roots of competence and maladaptation. In *Minnesota Symposia in Child Psychology*, vol. 16, ed. M. Perlmutter, pp. 41-83. Hillsdale, NJ: Lawrence Erlbaum.

_____ (1989a). Relationships, self and individual adaptation. In *Relational Disturbances in Early Childhood*, ed. A. J. Samerof and R. Emde, pp. 70-94. New York: Basic Books.

_____ (1989b). Pathways to adaptation and maladaptation: psychopathlogy as developmental deviation. In *The Emergence of a Discipline: Rochester Symposium on Developmental Psychopathology*, ed. D. Cicchetti, pp. 13-40. Hillsdale, NJ: Lawrence Erlbaum.

_____ (1990a). An organizational perspective of the self. In *The Self in Transition: Infancy to Childhood*, ed. D. Cicchetti and M. Beeghly. pp. 281-308. Chicago: University of Chicago Press.

_____ (1990b). Considering normal and abnormal together: the essence of developmental psychopathology. *Development and Psychopathology* 2:335-347.

Sroufe, L. A., and Fleeson, J. (1986). Attachment and the construction of relationships. In *Relationships and Development*, ed. W. W. Hartup and Z. Rubin. pp. 1-26. Hillsdale, NJ: Lawrence Erlbaum.

Sroufe, L. A., Fox, N., and Pancake, V. (1984). Attachment and dependency in developmental perspective. *Child Development* 54:1615-1627.

Sroufe, L. A., and Rutter, M. (1984). The domain of developmental psychopathology. *Child Development* 55:17-29.

Sroufe, L. A., and Waters, E. (1977). Heart rate as a convergent measure in clinical and developmental research. *Merrill Palmer Quarterly* 23:3-27.

Stern, D. N. (1985). *The Interpersonal World of the Infant*. New York: Basic Books.

Sullivan, H. S. (1953). *The Interpersonal Theory of Psychiatry*. New York: W. W. Norton.

Sulloway, J. F. (1979). *Freud: Biologist of the Mind*. New York: Basic Books.

Sutherland, D. J. (1989). *Fairbairn's Journey into the Interior*. London: Free Association.

Suttie, I. D. (1935). *The Origins of Love and Hate*. London: Kegan Paul.

Troy, M., and Sroufe, A. (1987). Victimization among preschoolers: role of the attachment history. *Journal of the American Academy of Child and Adolescent Psychiatry* 26:166–172.

Urban, J., Carlson, E., Egeland, B., and Sroufe, L. A. (1991). Patterns of individual adaptation across childhood. *Development and Psychopathology* 3:445–459.

Waldrop, M. M. (1992). *Complexity: The Emerging Science at the Edge of Order and Chaos*. New York: Simon & Schuster.

Weiss, J. (1993). *How Psychotherapy Works: Process and Technique*. New York: Guilford.

_____ (1994). The analyst's task: to help the patient carry out his plan. *Contemporary Psychoanalysis* 30:236–254.

Winnicott, D. W. (1965). *The Maturational Processes and the Facilitating Environment*. New York: International Universities Press.

Zuckerman, L. (1991). Apes R not us. *New York Times Book Review*, May 30, pp. 43–47.

4

The Greatness and Limitations of Fromm's Thought: On Dreams[1]

Paul Lippmann

Dreams and Fromm together have been deeply inter-twined in my personal and professional life. From the outset of my graduate training in psychology in New York almost forty years ago, Fromm's spirit permeated the intellectual atmosphere. Imagine—one could think about psychology, psychoanalysis, socialism, Zen Buddhism, and Hasidism all at once. I attended his lectures at the 92nd Street Y, and my analyst and clinical teachers were all deeply influenced by him. My teacher and closest friend, David Schechter, had come to New York from Montreal to study with Fromm, eventually to become his devoted student and friend. He introduced me to Fromm at his home in Switzerland. With warm generosity, upon

[1]This title is taken from Erich Fromm's (1980) *The Greatness and Limitations of Freud's Thought*.

learning that it was my birthday, Fromm arranged an impromptu party, one of the highlights of which was Fromm's urging us to join him in Hasidic song and dance to celebrate the occasion—a strange scene on the streets of Locarno.

For many years now, following Edward Tauber and Maurice Green, I have had the opportunity to teach the advanced seminar in dreams at the William Alanson White Institute, a course originally taught by Fromm. To engage with Fromm is to wrestle with him, and through the years, I have attempted to wrestle with his ideas and with his powerful and often dominating nature and influence.

It is an extraordinary time in the relationship between psychoanalysis and the surrounding social and political climate to think about dreams and about Erich Fromm's contribution to their understanding. The victory on the world stage of American materialism and the accompanying mindless destruction of nature in the pursuit of profit have found their way into the inner recesses of the consulting room. For those who have learned from Fromm, the impact of social, economic, and political reality on the lives and dreams of our patients and ourselves comes as no surprise. Yet modern psychoanalysis with its increasing relational emphasis seems to ignore the larger world beyond the confines of the nursery, of the mother–infant bond, and of the narrow relationship between patient and analyst. Psychoanalysis in this narrow perspective is ill-prepared to explore the impact on our work and thought of the fateful relationship between social forces and psyche. But now we have no choice. Political and economic reality has forced its way into our work.

The recent and growing large-scale effort to manipulate, control, and dominate the mental health field by American corporate interests through managed care insurance and its unethical bottom-line profit mentality has been aided and abetted by our own willingness, even eagerness, to maintain our own economic interests by rushing to join the managed care game. In this ruthless takeover, there is no room for psychoanalysis, for depth of psychology, for an interest in the innermost aspects of human life. There will be no insurance reimbursement for working with dreams. Try talking to a managed care clerk on the telephone about the significance of dreams, try writing on a form that dreams lead the analysis, try referring to yourself as a psychoanalyst on a managed care insurance application, try saying that it takes time to know the mysteries of the human heart, and you will soon learn that this new world has no place for you and your thinking. Thus, it is an interesting time to be talking about dreams and Fromm. Both are afforded little room in this new world; both represent freedom and rebellion; both together deserve our attention.

From the beginning, the dream occupied a place of special and central importance in the theory and practice of psychoanalysis. Freud's monumental opus, *The Interpretation of Dreams* (1900), threw open the gates of the twentieth century to the dream and brought the world of the spiritual and mystical to the world of the scientific, brought the imagery of the soul to the soullessness of modern times. And in turn, the dream opened to psychoanalysis no less than the mysteries of the unconscious. An intimate relationship—dream and psychoanalysis. No wonder psychoanalysis reveled in the dream, at first. The "royal road" was a broad, happy, bustling, crowded thoroughfare.

But too soon, the adventurous and creative spirit of early psychoanalytic work with dreams lost its originality and fresh vitality. Under the domination of Freud's ge-

nius, his gift became a noose. Dreams were subjected to a
rigid method with the outcome of inquiry never in doubt.
All dreams were reduced to a handful of doctrinaire
interpretations reflecting psychoanalytic preconceptions.
When orthodox psychoanalytic theory peered into the
mysteries of the dream, it saw reflected only its own
familiar face. In countless papers, books, and scientific
meetings, the quirky freedom and specifically individual
nature of dreams were increasingly subjected to a rote and
sterile treatment. The adventure down the royal road had
become a lockstep for the faithful on a narrow and rigid
path.

Against this background came Erich Fromm's contribution to the psychoanalytic discussion of dreams, *The
Forgotten Language* (1951). Its central view of the richness
and deep insightfulness of dreams stood in sharp contrast
to the increasing airlessness of orthodoxy. Emerging from
Fromm's characteristic respect for Freud's genius, it boldly
challenged the assumptions and methods that had led to a
dead end in the psychoanalytic engagement with dreams.
Further, it anticipated many of the developments in contemporary thinking, while providing a significant counterpoint within interpersonal psychoanalysis to Harry Stack
Sullivan's dismissive attitude toward dreams.

It should come as no surprise that Fromm would
wrestle with dreams. His deep and prolonged wrestling
match with Freud would of necessity bring him to Freud's
central and most favored contribution. In addition, it is of
interest that Fromm, so deeply engaged with the impact of
social and political reality on human life, would turn his
attention to that most internal and private realm of nighttime phantom experience. The relationship between social
conditions and the dream world is compelling, puzzling,
challenging. While, as Schorske (1980), Bettelheim (1990),
and others have pointed out, interest in the inner world of

night visions can represent a turn away from disagreeable daily life on both a personal and social level, it is Fromm who brought these realms into a single discourse. And so, Fromm took his turn to peer into the dream.

It should first be pointed out that almost every orientation, every theorist, every individual looking into the dream, like Narcissus looking into the pool, sees the reflection of one's own secret nature, one's own mind. It may well be that the puzzling ambiguity of dream content calls forth the innermost concerns and private preoccupations of the interpreter—for Freud, repressed infantile sexual wishes; for Jung, shadows and archetypes; for cognitive theorists, styles of mentation; for relational analysts, modes of interaction; for contemporary psychoanalysts, aspects of transference, and so on. In teaching analytic candidates, as Tauber (1963) has pointed out, it becomes evident that each student in the group discussion of patients' dreams sees a reflection of his or her own conflicts and concerns.

This is an interesting phenomenon in its own right—the Rorschach-like experience of looking into the dreams of others and finding one's own face. It is as though, despite our professed intention, the dream's own nature remains elusive as we rush past ambiguity and puzzlement to our own more familiar territory, to our own needs. "Staying with the dream's own imagery," as Hillman (1979) and others have advised, is more difficult that we imagine, for doing so opens one to the mind of the other in its most personal, private, and creative dimensions, areas often surprising and unfamiliar, outside our own needs and concerns. And yet, at times, it seems therapeutically useful, in the short run, for the analyst to project his or her own interests and theories into the dream. The analyst, for example, who sees every figure in the patient's dream as representing the analyst or as disguise for theoretically popular aspects of the patient's own nature may well be advancing a narrow view of the therapeutic task, but it may have little or no relationship to the dream itself and its own concerns. (I am reminded of the self-serving analyst who emphatically interpreted the number 8 mentioned in passing in a dream as referring to the $800 the patient owed on the last unpaid bill. The point was driven home until the patient got the message.) Fromm stressed the unwilled freedom of dreams to go their own way often against social and conscious personal expectations. Free association to dream elements for Freud, amplification of portions of the dream for Jung (1974)—both can lead away from the dream's own nature and into other, albeit interesting, matters. The intimate relationship between the associations of dreamer and interpreter is an area of study in its own right. But for now, it should not surprise us that when Fromm takes *his* turn to look into the dream, he sees . . . Fromm!

I have always found it difficult to evaluate Fromm's discussion of dreams. On the one hand, in shaking Freud's dogmatic reductionism, he freed the discussion of dreams, over forty years ago, opening powerful new dimensions in a typically direct and understandable language. On the other hand, he brings with him all his own dogmatism, his polemical style, his capacity for oversimplification and sweeping generalization, his either-or reductionism, his straw-men battling, and so on. The best and the worst are intimately intertwined through the pages of *The Forgotten Language* (1951). However, the fact that mainstream psychoanalytic discussion of dreams more or less completely ignored this work has little to do with the kind of ambivalent assessment I am suggesting. It has more to do with the way in which traditional psychoanalysis turned a deaf ear to dissent, particularly from an outsider. Fromm's respect for Freud, notwithstanding, he could not pay lip service to the entire psychoanalytic edifice, while suggesting modifications, in the manner, for example, of Erikson or Kohut. As to dreams, his critique of Freud's fundamental dictum—all dreams are disguised fulfillments of repressed infantile sexual wishes—and its replacement with Fromm's view that "dreams can be the expression of both of the lowest and most irrational *and* of the highest and most valuable functions of our minds" (p. 47) had no place at that time in mainstream psychoanalytic discussion. The dream as creative and symbolic expression of mind in all its complex capacities comes closer to a contemporary view.

Let us bear in mind that at the time of publication of *The Forgotten Language*, Aserinsky, Kleitman, and Dement's pioneering work resulting in the vast domain of rapid eye movement (REM) sleep studies (Ellman 1992) had not yet burst upon the scientific stage. Nor had the neuroscientists yet discovered the dream (Hobson 1988). Nor had we entered the revolution in thinking about mind characterized by cognitive psychology (Foulkes 1985). Nor had the literary imagination entered the debate with Freud (States 1988). Nor had the intimate relationship between Freud's view of dreams and the Talmud's extensive discussion been uncovered (Frieden 1990). Nor had we yet entered the current era of the widespread discussion and use of dreams in healing, far removed from the psychoanalytic arena (Castaneda 1993). And yet Fromm's contribution anticipated many of these developments that have enriched our understanding of and appreciation for extraordinary capacity of mind in its nightly adventures.

Fromm begins *The Forgotten Language* with the following:

If it is true that the ability to be puzzled is the beginning of wisdom, then this truth is a sad commentary on the wisdom of modern man. . . . This attitude is perhaps one reason why one of the most puzzling phenomena in our lives, our dreams, gives so little cause for wonder and raising questions. [p. 1]

Since he believes, with Freud, that all dreams are meaningful, he calls for us to open our minds to these puzzling nightly events. Unfortunately, he does not go on to develop this particular theme in relation to the use of dreams in psychoanalysis, but its appearance at the very outset of the work gives it a special place that merits commentary.

While there has been outstanding work on dreams in the past ten or twenty years, dreams remain a mystery. Despite thousands of years of probing exploration, despite the efforts of philosopher and scientist, of imagination and machine, the dream remains elusive, puzzling, evocative. Like the oft-dreamt dream itself, it moves silently just barely beyond our outstretched reach. Pursued by our daytime deliberations, it slips into its own realm: "Catch me if you can." Given this state of affairs, it seems both prudent and respectful for clinical psychoanalysis to allow itself a response of appreciation, of puzzlement, of wonder, of question, when meeting up with a dream. Yet we find too often the expectation both of patient and analyst that the analyst is the knower, the interpreter, of the dream. The patient does the job of dreaming, the analyst of uncovering and translating its meaning. No wonder many analysts, particularly early in their professional lives, dread their patients' dreams, and show evidence of constricted rather than more relaxed and playful thinking when dreams are reported. Thus, the unrealistic expectations that come with the role of "dream expert," particularly "paid dream expert," make it difficult to allow that necessary attitude of unknowingness at the outset of working with a dream. Despite Fromm's beginning his book with the virtues of puzzlement, despite Jung's (1933) emphatic insistence on an attitude of ignorance at the outset of dream interpretation and on the desirability of living with a dream over time, turning it over and over to see its different facets, despite Bonime's (1962) excellent emphasis on the merits of genuine collaboration in working on dreams, and especially despite the fact that we have not yet come near to a full understanding of the nature and function of dreams, the erroneous conviction persists that the psychoanalyst should be the knower of the dream (Lippmann 1990).

While Fromm expands our view of dreams in *The Forgotten Language*, he discusses dream after dream in a fashion that can lead away from an attitude of puzzlement and uncertainty. In this he is no different from Freud or Jung. While Fromm emphasizes context, character, the necessity of personal associations, stage of development, and so on, his dream analyses tend more to foster an attitude of knowingness, of certainty, of clarity about central motivations and central problems. This is Fromm's way—direct to the heart. But when it comes to dreams in their creative, evanescent, complex, multilayered nature, Fromm's strength and certainty often leaves the dream itself pinned to the mat.

I believe the above represents a central underlying contradiction in Fromm's approach. In the following, Fromm (1951) shows his deep appreciation for complexity in regard to the nature of dreams in contrast to Freud's apparently reductionist conclusions:

> In view of the fact that there is no expression of mental activity which does not appear in the dream, I believe that the only description of the nature of dreams that does not distort or narrow down the phenomenon is the broad one

that *dreaming is a meaningful and significant expression of any
kind of mental activity under the condition of sleep*. [p.
25] . . . Not only do insight into our relations to others or
theirs to us, value judgments and predictions occur in our
dreams, but also intellectual operations superior to those
in the waking state. . . . Sometimes one finds exceedingly
complicated intellectual considerations occurring in
dreams. [p. 45] . . . Dreams express any kind of mental
activity and are expressive of our irrational strivings as well
as of our reason and morality, that they express both the
worst *and* the best in ourselves. [p. 109] . . . What is
important is to understand the texture of the dream in
which past and present, character and realistic event, are
woven together into a design which tells us a great deal
about the motivation of the dreamer, the dangers he must
be aware of, and the aims he must set himself in his effort
to achieve happiness. [p. 157]

This is Fromm at his best, expansive, generous, open-
minded, a worthy and respectful partner for the task of
beginning to enter the mysteries of the dream. In addition,
he broadens the discussion by introducing us not only to
the related areas of symbolic language, myth, and fairy
tale, but also to the contributions of a wide array of
intellectual companions: Socrates, Plato, Aristotle, Lucre-
tius, Artemidorus, Cicero, Talmudic sources, Synesius of
Cyrene, Thomas Aquinas, Hobbes, Voltaire, Kant, Goethe, Emerson, Nietzsche, Bergson. And further, he mentions in passing views of dreams of the Ashanti, of Kiwai
Papuans of New Guinea, and of Mohave, Yuma, and
Navaho Indians. His scholarship also brings to our attention a consideration of dreams in the Old Testament.

And yet, in his extensive reporting of dreams and their
analyses, including Freud's dreams in which he chides
Freud for never going far enough in self-analysis, he

narrows the field considerably and his own preoccupations take over.

> In this as in every other dream, we can decide whether the dream is expressive of irrational passion or of reason. [p. 38] . . . From our theoretical considerations about the meaning and function of the dream, it follows that one of the most significant and often most difficult problems in the interpretation of dreams is that of recognizing whether a dream is expressive of an irrational wish and its fulfillment, of a plain fear or anxiety, or of an insight into inner or outer forces and occurrences. Is the dream to be understood as the voice of our lower or our higher self? [p. 148]

Clearly, a decision to be made, one way or the other, rather than complex combinations and interweavings.

One of Freud's greatest contributions was his consideration of the way in which thoughts, impulses, and conflicts combine and are expressed in compromise. Ideas and their associated feelings bred in the unconscious join with conscious impressions, memories, and concerns to produce the images and ideas found in the dream. The former cloaks itself, or better, interweaves itself in the latter. The richness of dream imagination lies in part in the way in which experience from different psychic layers can be combined into images with multiple meanings. Thus, for example, a dream of an unbalanced checkbook can reflect concerns with feeling unbalanced, as well as with finances, with the dreamer's struggle with mixed idealization and hatred of Kafka (the unbalanced Czech book writer), and with a finite host of other possibilities expressed in a single image. A patient dreams of an aunt with cerebral palsy and bursts into laughter when she realizes she is also commenting on my first name (Paul) and my overideational approach to her problems. The extraordinary economy of dream thought is one way to put it—many ideas, memories, and experiences from many layers, from many eras in one's life, associated along many dimensions, carried in a single expression. Complex metaphor, intricate poetry.

We are familiar, for example, with the related experience in analysis of listening to a statement about a particular current concern that may have considerable applicability to the therapeutic relationship. "The landlord has keys to my studio. He feels he has the right to enter and go through my things, my paintings, my materials, it's my whole life, without permission. I can't stand it! I hate him, the creep! And I have to pay him for the right to be violated!" The more the patient goes on, the more the analyst tries to remain open to hearing about unacknowledged feelings toward himself, as well as about the father, the mother, an older brother, art critics, teachers, aspects of the patient's own self, God, and much else, all at once, all intertwined. Thus, ideas about dream formation, symptom formation, transference, creative expression, as well as views about thinking proceed from a consideration of Freud's hypothesis about the way in which unconscious mentation links with conscious thought in complex compromise formation. Fromm's going to the heart, either-or, bottom-line way of thinking rushes past such considerations in his respectful denigration of Freud's hypothesis. But in addition to a lack of patience with the subtle architecture of the mind suggested by Freud, Fromm takes particular pains to do battle with the doctrinaire supposed contents of the contribution from the unconscious, not so much with its forms. Again and again, he derides Freud for supposing that the irrational, repressed infantile sexual wishes of children are central participants in the creation of dreams, thus seeming to leave little possibility for a view of multilayered meanings.

In the analysis of dream after dream, we find Fromm's concerns with moral courage, with rebellion, with struggles against irrational authority, with the higher power of rational thought, with the limiting nature of modern culture, with the superior nature of the freedom of dream thought, with the socialist and humanist idealization of the possibilities of nonexploitation of human beings. In short, we find Fromm. While affording us the opportunity to view dreams in wide perspective, the limitation touches upon the way in which people seem reduced to caricatures, their situations two-dimensional, their struggles oversimplified, the solutions to their problems too clear-cut.

To his credit, he introduces a critique of Jung's contribution to thinking about dreams. It should be noted how few psychoanalysts of any orientation have anything at all to say about Jung; his participation in the Nazi era, his ambivalent view of Jewish culture, his erotic engagement with patients, his mysticism, his bitter split from Freud— whatever the complex reasons for the wholesale dismissal of his work, he has become the unwelcome one at the psychoanalytic table. Yet his ideas about dreams are significant and useful. His students have produced an extensive literature that offers countless insights into the nature of dreams and their use in psychotherapy. His influence on the burgeoning, current nonpsychoanalytic use of dreams is profound. And yet, most psychoanalytic writing keeps an enormous and safe distance from Jung's work. Fromm (1951) displays an admirable quality of scholarship in his willingness to take on some of Jung's ideas. He wrestles with Jung and while he finds his work flawed, one-sided, dogmatic, Fromm is in full agreement with Jung that "the unconscious mind is capable at times of assuming an intelligence and purposiveness which are superior to actual conscious insight" (p. 96).

While Fromm clearly expanded the traditional psychoanalytic view of dreams, and while his contribution was largely ignored within mainstream psychoanalysis, his greatest value, from my point of view, lies less in the impact of his work on the general discussion of dreams than in his influence within interpersonal psychoanalysis. Sullivan and Fromm were the two major architects of early interpersonal thinking. Whereas Fromm engaged with dreams directly and found their deep usefulness in psychoanalytic therapy, Sullivan (1953) had little use for dreams. Neither pretending to love nor to be particularly interested in dreams, Sullivan (1953) went beyond mocking Freud's mythologizing and stultifying misuse of dreams in clinical work and demonstrated that he had very little use for dreams at all. In his effort to shape psychiatry into a scientific enterprise, he turned sharply away from what he believed to be the unverifiable and often clinically useless, even harmful, theories of mind of the Europeans, and particularly from what was not manifest in social interchange. Dreams, representing that most private of human thought process, inaccessible in their construction and experience, distorted in their remembered and reported versions, were a perfect target for Sullivan's contempt expressed as operational scientific zeal. While acknowledging that dreams (and myths) represent "a relatively valid parataxic operation for the relief of insoluble problems of living" (p. 342), he asserted that attempts to convert such operations into the syntaxic mode, that is, into consensually valid statements, were both foolish and a waste of time. This wholesale dismissal of dreams is also seen in his description of his own way of working with dreams. After listening to a dream, he first "clears up as much as he can of what is irrelevant and obscuring in the reported dreams" (p. 338). That is, he first strips and removes "all the little personal details, confusions and obscurities" that may hide what Sullivan believed to be significant. He then presents back what he thinks is a summary of what he thinks the patient has been dreaming about and asks for response. Clearly, he had neither the temperament nor the inclination to spend time with a dream as dreamt.

There are undoubtedly many reasons, both personal and professional, for Sullivan's turn away from dreams (see, for example, Levenson's [1983] discussion of Sullivan's spider dream). Certainly his critique of the classical theory and method and his overriding concern with the treatment of schizophrenia turned him away from a free-associational approach to nightly dream phantoms and toward real talk about real problems in living. His genius and his enormous contribution notwithstanding, the subtleties of the dreaming mind were not for him. What I believe matters in all this is that his dismissive attitude toward dreams took root and spread in the clinical work of his students. The private world of inner experience as expressed in dreams was just not particularly important subject matter for the work of many early interpersonalists. Just as Freud had his Freudians, cigars and all, so did Sullivan his Sullivanians, with their scientistic derision of dream analysis along with other manifestations of the more private realms of human experience.

Fromm came to the psychoanalytic engagement with a fully developed and articulated appreciation for the deep intertwining of the social and the private. For him, an understanding of psyche without the social dimension in all its meanings would be unthinkable. It was not a turn away from awareness of the impact of culture on personality that led him to an understanding and appreciation of the value of dreams and their use in psychoanalysis. He

came to dreams with his awareness of the social fully
intact. The critique of an insular instinct theory leveled at
the Freudians could not be made of Fromm. Yet he
explored the dream, the private realms of experience, the
soul. His point of view prevented the interpersonal tradition from dismissing dreams, both in theory and in
practice. It made it possible, in my own experience in
training at the William Alanson White Institute, to develop a complex and plural view of mental life, in general,
and of dream life, in particular. That is, in the political
world that is an analytic institute, Fromm gave weight to
an appreciation of dreams. Tauber and Green's (1959)
work follows in this path. It seems to me extremely
important to have within a social view room for the private
dimension. Otherwise the interpersonalists, by necessity
in contrast with the Freudians, would have been in danger
of as one sided a view of human life (the purely interpersonal) as were the Freudians (the purely instinctual).
There is no one without the other. All is emphasis. All is
complex, deeply layered, richly enmeshed. Like the
dream itself. Despite evident limitations, one aspect of the
greatness of Fromm's thought was his appreciation of the
very complexity that we now sense is at the heart of all
life. His work on dreams is an openhearted expression of
the richness of that complexity and of the potential for
insight and wisdom that can emerge from the innermost
mental recesses at the center of human complexity.

As Fromm teaches, sleep frees the mind from the
immediate concerns of adaptive functioning, the creative
result in dreams affords an unparalleled opportunity to
study the way in which ideas, feelings, memories—psychic experience in all its astonishing variety intermingles
and expresses itself in highly specific imagination. If we
take the time, if we approach the dream not so much with
preconception but with an open, questioning and playful
mind and heart, if we are willing to be taken by surprise,

then we have a chance to learn about the way the mind in its specificity gathers, integrates, and expresses all levels of experience during its nightly creative weaving. Further, a broadly interpersonal perspective brings us to interesting questions not only about the functioning of mind (e.g., the ways in which dreams integrate social and private meanings, the ways in which conscious and unconscious aspects of self and others and their interactions are represented), but also about the ways in which minds interact and affect one another in the most extraordinary ways (e.g., highly specific images created in the mind of one by the other's descriptions, the conscious and unconscious ways in which dream images can lead to potentially integrative and insightful images in the mind of the listener). Whether from the point of view of mind alone or minds in communication, analyst and patient together, as they learn of the intricate way the sleeping mind approaches life, can come to a growing and trustworthy confidence in one's natural capacities to engage in, struggle with, enjoy, and survive life's challenge. Fromm's vision embraces the dream and enlarges our capacity to understand its vast potential for human life. We are deeply in his debt.

REFERENCES

Bettelheim, B. (1990). *Freud's Vienna and Other Essays*. New York: Knopf.

Bonime, W. (1962). *The Clinical Use of Dreams*. New York: Basic Books.

Castaneda, C. (1993). *The Art of Dreaming*. New York: Harper-Collins.

Ellman, S. J. (1992). Psychoanalytic theory, dream formation, and REM sleep. In *Interface of Psychoanalysis and Psychology*, ed. J. W. Barron, M. N. Eagle, and D. L. Wolitzky, pp. 357–374. Washington, DC: American Psychological Association.

Foulkes, D. (1985). *Dreaming: A Cognitive-Psychological Analysis.* Hillsdale, NJ: Lawrence Erlbaum.

Freud, S. (1900). The Interpretation of dreams. *Standard Edition,* 4,5.

Frieden, K. (1990). *Freud's Dream of Interpretation.* Albany: State University of New York Press.

Fromm, E. (1951). *The Forgotten Language.* New York: Grove.

———— (1980). *The Greatness and Limitations of Freud's Thought.* New York: Meridian.

Hillman, J. (1979). *The Dream and the Underworld.* New York: Harper & Row.

Hobson, J. A. (1988). *The Dreaming Brain.* New York: Basic Books.

Jung, C. S. (1933). *Modern Man in Search of a Soul,* translated by W. S. Dell, and C. F. Baynes. New York: Harcourt Brace Jovanovich.

———— (1974). *Dreams,* translated by R. F. C. Hull. Princeton, NJ: Princeton University Press.

Levenson, E. (1983). *The Ambiguity of Change.* New York: Basic Books.

Lippmann, P. (1990). *Dreams and interpersonal psychoanalysis: a love-hate story.* Paper presented at the William Alanson White Institute Clinical Conference, New York, October 16.

Schorske, C. E. (1980). *Fin-de-Siecle Vienna: Politics and Culture.* New York: Knopf.

States, B. O. (1988). *The Rhetoric of Dreams.* Ithaca, NY: Cornell University Press.

Sullivan, H. S. (1953). *The Interpersonal Theory of Psychiatry.* New York: W. W. Norton.

Tauber, E. S. (1963). The dream in the therapeutic process from the therapist's standpoint. In *Dreams in Contemporary Psychoanalysis,* ed. E. T. Adelson, pp. 228–235. New York: Society of Medical Psychoanalysts.

Tauber, E. S., and Green, M. R. (1959). *Prelogical Experience—An Inquiry into Dreams and Other Creative Processes.* New York: Basic Books.

5

Fromm's Humanistic Ethics and the Role of the Prophet

Marianne Horney Eckardt

Fromm rarely wrote in the conventional style of psycho-analysis, and he seldom spelled out the relevance of his writing to psychoanalysts. But as I will show, relevance is everywhere. It is important to appreciate the explicitness of Fromm's style. It is as explicit as that of Picasso or any painter of recent deconstructionism. He paints in stark black and white; there are no grays. He paints a message. The message is to stir people out of any illusion that life can be lived well with any degree of passive submission; rather, it has to be lived actively with the knowledge that life constantly offers alternatives and that choice is important.

Fromm (1962) believed that no one can save a fellow being by making a choice for him or her. "All that one man can do," he writes, "is to show him the alternatives truthfully and lovingly, yet without any sentimentality or illusion. Confrontation with the true alternatives may awaken all the hidden energies in a person, and enable him to choose life, no one else can breathe life into him" (p. 176).

The phrase "all that one man can do" is deceptively simple, but it is full of significance. It points to Fromm's chosen style. This style, like so much of his basic belief, has roots in rabbinical traditions, in biblical themes reinterpreted by him. The style is that of the prophets. Fromm describes the prophet's role. Prophets do not predict the future. They present reality free from the blindfolds of public opinion and authority. They feel compelled to express the voice of their conscience to say what possibilities they see, to show the alternatives, and to warn the people. It is up to the people to take the warning and change or to remain deaf and blind. Prophetic language is always the language of alternatives, of choice, and of freedom; it is never that of determinism. The prophets dissent and protest when man takes the wrong road, but they do not abandon the people. They do not think in terms of individual salvation, but believe that individual salvation is bound up with the salvation of society.

Fromm's foremost reaffirmation is the biblical fight against idolatry. We cannot understand God; we can try to understand what God is not. It is a negative theology. The same is true of our understanding of human beings. We can describe their personae, the masks they wear, their egos, but living human beings cannot be described like things. They cannot be described at all. One's total individuality, one's suchness, which is unique, can never be fully understood not even by empathy, for no two human beings are entirely alike.[1] That is the fundamental message. Separate from it, although not less important, are the specific messages of the wrong and right roads as Fromm sees them, based on his humanitarian ethics.

TOWARD A HUMANITARIAN ETHICS

I will place Fromm's concerns with humanitarian ethics in the context of the history of psychoanalytic interest in moral values in order to highlight his beliefs. The relationship of moral values and neuroses has been an uncomfortable issue in the history of psychoanalysis. Freud's superego is related to the biological force of the id and specifies taboos on murder and incest, but there is little else that one can construe as a broader ethic.

Heinz Hartmann (1960) first confronted the issues in *Psychoanalysis and Moral Values*, a thoughtful book in which he affirms the separate realms of psychoanalysis and moral issues, and writes that neurosis is not a "moral problem." He writes:

> You know how carefully we avoid, in analysis, imposing ethical demands on our patients. [p. 92] . . . Analysis is as little a never-failing key to morality as it is, as Freud was the first to remind us, a reliable key to happiness. [p. 87] . . . The recognition of one's authentic values and their distinction from those which are not authentic, is not infrequently sharpened in the course of analysis. This will not change a "bad" person into a "good" person, or only rarely. What it means is that the codes can become less distorted, often less one-sided expressions of the moral aspects of the personality. [p. 92]

The neo-Freudians took this problem much more seriously. For them neurosis was indeed a moral problem. This was a radical shift—a shift as important as their abandonment of the libido theory. Neurotic forces cause self-alienation and thus interfere with productivity, creativity, and relationships to others. Karen Horney's first chapter in her last book, *Neurosis and Human Growth* (1950) is called, "A Morality of Evolution." Neurotic forces, according to her, interfere with man's nature-given strivings for self-realization:

> You need not, and in fact cannot, teach an acorn to grow into an oak tree, but when given a chance, its intrinsic potentialities will develop. Similarly, the human individual, given a chance, tends to develop his particular human potentialities. He will develop then the unique alive forces of his real self: the clarity and depth of his own feelings, thoughts, wishes, and interests; the ability to tap his own resources, the strength of his will power; the special capacities or gifts he may have; the faculty to express himself and to relate himself to others with his spontaneous feelings. [p. 17]

Horney, with her usual clarity, here describes the mental health norm that became widely accepted – a norm that not only measured what could be, but also what "was not given a chance," meaning the interplay between environment, anxiety, and neurotic defensive strategies that interfere with natural growth. These ideal norms helped to create the widely accepted notion that being neurotic was being bad or less of a human being, and not being neurotic was equated with health and human integrity. The 1940s and 1950s were the years of the greatest idealism about the role of psychoanalysis as the savior of mankind. Money-Kyrle (1961), an associate of Melanie Klein, in his book *Man's Picture of His World* speaks of the hope that, if carried out on a scale wide and deep enough, psychoanalysis could affect the world as a whole and point toward a happier future for mankind.

In spite of differences, Freudians and neo-Freudians share the idea that moral issues are not directly their concern or responsibility. Freudians feel their therapeutic realm is distinct from such issues; neo-Freudians rely on nature's inherent positive forces. Fromm, although a co-builder of the neo-Freudian position, arrived at a different philosophy. Man has the potentiality for good and evil. Evil is not just a by-product of psychopathology. Our notions of mental health are not just a measure of disease, but a mixture of neurotic psychopathology and beliefs in our Western ethics. Fromm accepted the challenge, which is most succinctly expressed by Stephen Jay Gould (1987) when he writes of our biased view of evolution as inherently progressive; that is, to believe that good design or harmony of the system is entailed in the laws of nature. Gould writes:

> We are left with two choices in reinterpreting our oldest hope that moral messages might be extracted from nature: either the messages are there and they are terrible . . . or moral messages cannot be derived from nature's facts. The ethical standards of human life are not written upon the heavens or etched into a blade of grass. These are human concepts, fit only for human definitions and human struggles. Thus we need humanists of all stripes, for science does not touch these deepest questions. [p. 146]

Fromm is such a humanist. He called his philosophy radical humanism, its character dialectic, its spirit critical and challenging. The word *radical* is used in the sense of going to the roots of a matter. The words *critical* and *challenging* are important to indicate that "being" is an ever-changing activity with no final answers. *Dialectic* connotes a similar emphasis on processes involving tension, challenge, and attempts at solutions. Tension is inherent in the essence of man, as Fromm sees it. This essence of man evolves out of a dichotomy in his biological nature—"being in nature" and thus subject to its laws, and yet simultaneously transcending nature, being aware of himself and his existence, an awareness that demands solutions. "The energies of man," Fromm (1992) writes, "have as their aim the transformation of the unbearable dichotomy into a bearable one and the creation of ever new and, as far as it is possible, better solutions of this opposition" (p. 25). We are forced to react as long as we live, seeking relief from this unbearable tension, which is experienced as helplessness.

No absolute answers exist. Human beings find many ways, of course, of meeting this existential dilemma. Fromm points to regressive and progressive solutions, to wrong and right turns at the fork of the road. The sense of helplessness causes the average person to look for all-wise, powerful, all-caring figures. Strong affective bonds develop to such magic helpers, be they religious forces, people, or institutions. Fromm refers to these figures as idols. It is this yearning for and relying upon idols that leads to regressive solutions, rather than to constructive solutions that aim at man's unfolding of his own resources. Fromm's books were written with the hope of making people aware of existing alternatives and their consequences.

FROMM'S REVISION OF PSYCHOANALYSIS

Fromm's main body of writings, as mentioned, is not about psychoanalysis. However, in 1992 his *The Revision of Psychoanalysis*—written as part of a larger project, never completed, on a systematic work on humanistic psycho-analysis—was published by Dr. Rainer Funk, the editor of Fromm's literary estate. This little book illustrates Fromm's philosophy of radical humanism as applied to the particulars of psychoanalysis. He challenges psychoanalysis to make efforts toward a creative revision if it intends to live up to its promises of helping people develop greater authenticity and find their right way of being. Fromm writes:

> A creative renewal of psychoanalysis is possible only if it overcomes its positivistic conformism and becomes again a critical and challenging theory in the spirit of radical humanism. This revised psychoanalysis will be critical of all social arrangements that warp and deform men; and it will be concerned with the process that could lead to the adaptation of society to the needs of man, rather than with man's adaptation to society. [p. 19]

Fromm lists six areas that need revision: the theory of drives, the theory of the unconscious, the theory of society, the theory of sexuality, the theory of the body, and psychoanalytic therapy. The common elements in the philosophy of these revisions are (1) a shift to process thinking away from static concepts, (2) a concept of knowledge that emphasizes experience rather than scientific knowledge, (3) the full realization that man is primarily a social being who functions in the context of his particular environment, (4) a clear humanistic orientation, and (5) the socially critical insight into the ever-present conflicts between the interests of most societies in the continuity of their system and the interests of man in the optimal unfolding of his potentialities. "This insight," Fromm writes, "implies refusal to accept ideologies at their face value: rather it urges consideration of the search for the truth as a process of liberating oneself from illusions, false consciousness, and ideologies" (p. 21). Fromm challenges societies, institutions, and the individual.

FORKS IN THE ROAD

While Fromm and Horney agree on what a human being could be at best, they differ in that Horney believes in innate forces that strive toward self-realization. Fromm does not believe that people necessarily know their way, even if not diverted by neurotic forces. Most people fail in the art of living, not because they are inherently bad or so without will that they cannot live a better life, but rather because they do not wake up and see when they stand at a fork in the road. They need to be alerted to their fate that they have to struggle to find the directions for living, that they have to work out their lives by active participation.

Gould and Fromm differ only in their hopes. Gould has no illusion that nature provides the answer, while Fromm continued to flirt with nature. In his book, *The Revolution of Hope*, Fromm (1968) asks, almost with nostalgia, whether there is objective evidence at least suggestive that our norms should be guiding principles for all. He falls back on the premise of harmony and the maximum of vitality and well-being, and, given that premise, the biophilic norms would be more conducive to the optimum of growth and well-being.

In spite of Fromm's belief in a negative theology, he describes the art of being alive in many ways. As his notion of a fully alive being is not different from our own implicit or explicit conception, I will give only a few of his descriptions.

> The person who fully loves life is attracted by the process of life and growth in all spheres. He prefers to construct rather than to retain. He is capable of wondering, and prefers to see something new rather than looking for the security of finding confirmation of the old. He loves the adventure of living. He sees the whole rather than the

part. He wants to mold by love, reason and persuasion, not by force. He enjoys life rather than just craving excitement. [1964, p. 45]

What then is his identity in a human sense? Identity is the experience which permits a person to say legitimately "I" as an organizing active center of the structure of all his actual or potential activities. This experience of "I" exists only in the state of spontaneous activity, but it does not exist in the state of passiveness and half-awakeness, a state in which people are sufficiently awake to go about their business but not awake enough to sense an "I" as the active center within themselves. This concept of the "I" is different from the concept of the ego. [1968, p. 87]

Fromm (1976) describes being in conversation:

They come fully alive in the conversation, because they do not stifle themselves by anxious concern with what they have. Their own aliveness is infectious and often helps the other person to transcend his egocentricity. . . . The conversation becomes a dialogue in which it does not matter any more who is right. The duelists begin to dance together, and they part not with triumph or sorrow—but with joy. [p. 34]

Fromm here makes his few references to psychoanalytic treatment. "The essential factor in psychoanalytic therapy," he writes, "is this enlivening quality of the therapist. No amount of psychoanalytic interpretation will have an effect if the therapeutic atmosphere is heavy, unalive, and boring" (p. 34).

Even this short description would be incomplete without mentioning the quality of hope. Hope to Fromm is ever important. It is an intrinsic element of the structure of life, of the dynamic of the human spirit. Hope is a psychic concomitant of life and growth. It is ever implied by the nature of life. Hope is looking forward to, is faith, is intention, is active wishing, is the excitement of ideas or of an encounter. Hope is inherent in caring and in any creative endeavor. It is the emotion that energizes our search, our ideas, our activities, and enhances the intensity of meaning. Hope is, however, a constantly endangered phenomenon. Its vulnerability is extreme. Resignation, the no-hope counterpart, is destructive of life by omission.

Fromm aimed at addressing a spiritual dimension in us that potentially can inform our modes and acts of living, no matter what we may be doing. He described an ideal to strive for, even though our complex nature and world continuously demand or lead us into compromises. Fromm did not present prescriptions, just food for thought and consideration. These spiritual values also have relevance, of course, to the art of being a therapist and doing therapy.

QUALITIES OF BEING "FULLY ALIVE"

I will group my own considerations of this relevance around the topics of the meaning of "being fully alive," "idolatry," "dualistic thinking," "caring," and "hope." It is easy to embrace the mentioned values. I will point to some of the inevitable conflicting stresses that give an ever-present poignancy to our quest for being what we want to be.

How many of us maintain or even strive after a schedule that is compatible with full aliveness? We overschedule, in a hectic existence we place one foot in front of the other, which permits little thought or contemplation to what may have transpired. How many of us have time for walks we greatly need to feel refreshed and to let our brain do what it does best when least attended to by conscious thought, namely, to arrive at a sense and a perspective of what is going on. I once came across a study that showed that patients who are scheduled during the first part of the day statistically do better than the ones who are attended to in the more fatigue-laden latter part of the day. I was amused, but it could be true.

Idolatry

The admonition against idol worship is never to be forgotten. Our perspective is blurred over and over again by our wish for knowledge to be certain and for an understanding that is right. We can appreciate the quality of our perception and yet be open to other possibilities of meaning. Often one sentence of a patient shifts our understanding of some particular, reminding us that we see what we construct, not necessarily what is there. We need schools of thought (idols) to learn potential patterns of being and different ways of conceiving them, but then we also need to be able to cut the umbilical cord. Ideologies and umbilical cords are perpetuated by institutions and our involvements with them, but living requires organization. We evolve our preferred manner of approach and procedures. They are essential. But we easily think of these as not just preferred, but as being right—with a banner attached.

Our chosen procedures are starting points and then take on a life of their own and undergo modification in our mutual therapeutic dance. While it is hard to guard against our yearning for certainty, it is equally hard, if not harder, for our patients. They like to see us as bearers of wisdom, not recognizing the wisdom in themselves. One patient's frequent expression, "You are right," filled me with discomfort, as I aim at dialogue. Another patient's responses, "While you were talking I thought . . . " or "That may be so, but . . . " filled me with delight. My emphasis here is on paradox and conflict. How can we spread Fromm's knowledge without running the danger of idolizing or ideologizing Fromm and negating his message? It can be done, but it is difficult.

Dualism

Freud was a dualist. I refer to his life and death instincts, the ego and the id, and others. In religion we meet good and evil. In our field, the duality turns around normal versus pathology. Most of our so-called defenses (pathology) are also modes of adaptation or coping with a difficult world. The less we think or speak in terms of pathology, the closer we are to natural human struggles and the spirit of such struggles. Yet our professional training is steeped in the language of dualism and pathology.

Caring

We care about our patients. Yet many aspects of our procedures touch on self-interest and are not necessarily the best for the patient. We aim at the patient's growth. Growth takes place largely outside the therapeutic office. Many patients would do well with occasional breaks from treatment to stretch their own muscles. Yet regularity of attendance is easiest on our schedule and sense of security about not having too many vacancies. The same goes for frequency of sessions a week. Frequent sessions may encourage dependency. Again, I am just emphasizing conflicts, for financial pressures will intrude and sway us. Awareness at least allows us not to rationalize such influence and to encourage consideration of alternatives.

One aspect of caring may be curtailed by time. Patients enjoy our interest and participation in their activities outside the office. We gain much from reading poetry or books that have had special meaning for them. If they are artists or writers, our appreciation of their work shows that we care. But we are often too busy to extend our interest in them beyond the paid-for hour.

Hope

Hope touches on the core of what it means to be alive. Thus an essential aspect of therapy is to actively encourage our patients to attend to planning ahead, planning for joy, for venturing out, for vacations, for what they would like to do. This aspect far too often suffers from neglect as the fascination with the past or even the present takes precedence over possible hopes for the future. Any bubble of past enthusiasm, shrunk by inattention, should be given a chance to reexpand. Disappointed hope leads to resignation. Our capacity for resignation is great; it restricts and locks the doors to new unfolding. Again our desire for regularity of treatment may interfere with our encouraging this more spontaneous venturing of the patient.

CONCLUSION

I have attempted to portray Fromm's vision of the spirit that would inform true aliveness. It is a vision to guide us in our inevitable human struggles to live a good life. I have also tried to emphasize the challenges. Psychoanalysis evolved in a period of determinism, a determinism that became woven into the fabric of its theory and its therapeutic approaches. As students we learn to follow blueprints. But only experience will teach us to use our knowledge, our intuition, and teach us the basic truth that there is no answer written on the blackboard out there on how to conduct life or how to conduct therapy. There is a moral dimension to life, whether it is our own or our patient's life. This moral dimension can be actively nurtured and is not consequent to the absence of pathology. We are children of our Western cultural tradition. Our cultural values as well as our personal values are active ingredients in our way of conducting therapy, in what we respond to with pleasure or with concern. We do want to make our patients into beings who are more capable of loving, of being creative and less destructive. Let us affirm the fact that those are our own precious values that guide our enterprises.

Fromm's vision emphasized finding solutions, wrong and right forks in the road, and an admonition that it is up to us to choose. But he also radiated an embracing vitality, joy, and caring which in turn sparked and still spark our vitality and our courage to embrace life.

ENDNOTE

1. Fromm's major work on aggression (1973), malignant aggression in particular, which he calls necrophilia, is written in part to tell us what is not biophilic.

REFERENCES

Fromm, E. (1962). *Beyond the Chains of Illusion*. New York: Simon & Schuster.

_____ (1964). *The Heart of Man*. New York: Harper & Row.

_____ (1968). *The Revolution of Hope*. New York: Bantam.

_____ (1973). *The Anatomy of Human Destructiveness*. New York: Holt, Rinehart & Winston.

_____ (1976). *To Have or To Be*. New York: Harper & Row.

_____ (1992). *The Revision of Psychoanalysis*, ed. R. Funk. Boulder, CO: Westview.

Gould, S. J. (1987). A poet's Darwin. *Parnassus Poetry Review* 14:146.

Hartmann, H. (1960). *Psychoanalysis and Moral Values*. New York: New York University Press.

Horney, K. (1950). *Neurosis and Human Growth*. New York: W. W. Norton.

Money-Kyrle, R. (1961). *Man's Picture of His World*. New York: International Universities Press.

6

Erich Fromm's Contribution to a Theory of the Development of the Malevolent Personality

Carl Goldberg

There are thousands hacking at the branches of evil to one who is striking at its roots.

Henry Thoreau

THE PROBLEM OF EVIL

Evil is not merely a pejorative metaphysical concept that has historical fascination and can easily be explained away. It is a presence and destructive force that has decisively shaped our lives. Senseless acts of cruelty and destructiveness have become an ubiquitous component of daily life and involve us all. The rampage of crimes of violence perpetrated against people in all segments of American society has become a dominant force in contemporary life. Few people feel safe from menace even in their own homes.

Not only are evil deeds an extremely destructive component of the human condition, but no less importantly, the sense of imposing evil in our everyday world demoralizes us, leaving us feeling depressed, pessimistic, and alienated from what is good, hopeful, and worthy in our lives. It leaves us with a chronic sense of overwhelming oppression and an unwillingness to strive for what we believe in and cherish.

A NEGLECT OF THE PROBLEM OF EVIL BY THE BEHAVIORAL SCIENCES

Whereas each of us as private citizens can attest to the calamitous presence of malevolence in our own lives, we as behavioral scientists for the most part have assumed either one or both of two overriding distancing beliefs about the problem: One, evil can be safely ignored, because it is a moral problem and, as such, the province of the theologian and the philosopher, rather than a legitimate concern of the mental health professional. Two, there is no such person as an evil human, because the character structure of the perpetrators of heinous actions can be reduced to known and well-understood clinical concepts.

In my book *Speaking with the Devil* (Goldberg, in press), I sought to demonstrate that the above assumptions about evil are fallacious denial and reductionism, and as such have not well served behavioral scientists' mandate to provide meaningful explanations and understanding of social problems to the public. Without a deep insight into the crucial influences and dynamics of evil, we cannot fashion viable strategies for efficaciously responding to the malevolent perpetrator or modify societal institutions to curb future atrocities. An ancient saying tells us: "Those who avert their eyes from evil commit the worst sins."

Before I examine the ideas of Erich Fromm for his insights into the causes of evil and then propose my explanation based on Fromm's views, I need to define what I mean by evil.[1]

A DEFINITION OF EVIL

The notion of evil involves treating another person without respect for that person's humanity. Operative in malevolent behavior is one or both of two crucial beliefs. The first is a situation in which one creates or accepts the assumption that another person is weak, stupid, incompetent, and so forth, and on that basis treats him or her as an object rather than someone who deserves decency. The second is a situation in which the perpetrator assumes that because the victim is regarded as dangerous to the physical or psychological safety of the perpetrator that any destructive action taken against the victim is justified. My definition presupposes that the agent of malevolence has the capacity to understand the consequences of his or her actions. Therefore, *evil*—as I will be using the term—is the deliberate infliction of cruel and painful suffering on another living being.

A comprehensive definition of evil also must include its powerful effects on nonparticipants as well as those directly involved. Acts of atrocity, such as torture, cruelty,

and serial and mass murder, defy not only our understanding of what might have caused these events, but
even our capacity to imagine what might have actually
taken place. Committed acts of serious malevolence are
singular among human experiences in their commanding
effect on people who are not directly involved or may not
even be present when they occur. Acts of evil invoke
discomfort in those who try to understand the causes of
these heinous acts. This tension results from the curious
fascination we have about mysterious power in uneasy
amalgamation with the feared dangers of its unsanctioned
exercise. Such events engender a simultaneous paradoxical response, from those who witness, read, or are simply
told about the events, of both captivating excitement and
total bodily fear.

Finally, the context of possibility in which evil takes
place must be included in its definition if its dynamics are
to be meaningfully described. Evil is an act that lacks
justification because it can be feasibly replaced by more
rational, decent, and humane behaviors. For instance, it is
reasonable to protect oneself against an armed attacker,
even if one's efforts cause serious harm to the other. On
the other hand, one would be acting malevolently if he or
she unnecessarily remained in a situation just so one could
assault an attacker even after that person had been ren-
dered helpless. Our system of justice is constituted on the
premise that it is one's right (perhaps even one's duty) to
protect one's self and others from arbitrary and destructive
actions by whatever force is necessary. However, our
forceful actions are regarded as unjustified if they are
based on premeditated revenge, retaliation, or other
harmful actions taken against past or supposed future
behavior of another person. In short, our system of justice
legitimizes protective action only in the immediate situation in which one is endangered.

THE THESIS OF THIS CHAPTER

Modern psychological theories have not provided a cogent understanding of the senseless acts of cruelty and destructiveness that have become commonplace in our society. The general approach in the modern era for understanding malevolence is contained in the assumption that the childhood influences in the formation of the character of the people involved are the sole crucial sources of all tragic events. Psychoanalysts, in particular, have reduced character to the resultant of childhood experiences, with an emphasis on the attribution of early trauma. In so doing, they have largely ignored the ongoing formation of character forged by the choices and decisions each person makes. In this way, modern psychological explanation for malevolence parts company with classical theory about human events, which provides an abundance of clear examples of the arbitrary nature of our destiny and the crucial role one's moral choices have for tempering one's fate, as exemplified in the story of Job. His catastrophes were not due to any flaw in his pious and kind character. They were caused by Satan slyly and maliciously convincing God to make a wager with him about Job's future behavior. In this parable, the resolution of Job's unfair suffering was directly related to the way in which he responded to his dilemma.

In this chapter I will show that character is gradually molded by prior actions. My thesis, simply put, is that we learn by doing. Impulses to do good or evil occur continually in our daily lives. Usually they come in small matters; and yet, how we respond to earlier decisions shape our moral choices in the future. Extreme behavior, such as heinous cruelty, usually is the last of many steps along a continuum of unkind and indecent acts, made possible and facilitated by earlier acts of insensitivity and disregard for others that were rationalized and thereby justified.

My clinical experience with patients I have treated in psychiatric hospitals, forensic facilities, and private practice suggests that there are five distinct stages that a person passes through in forging a personal identity as a malevolent person. (I will describe these stages shortly.) I will demonstrate with a case vignette the specific conditions that gradually prepare a person for acts of cruelty and malevolence, and the social and political factors that increasingly forge malevolent behavior as a committed way of life. My account of malevolence at once strives to do justice with the discoveries of science and psychoanalysis, while at the same time, in the spirit of Fromm (1964), retains the traditional significance of choice, freedom, and responsibility in human affairs.

FROMM'S THEORETICAL DISCUSSION OF MORAL CHOICE

Fromm provided one of the few comprehensive psychological theories of evil. In this chapter, however, I will confine my discussion to his insightful ideas about moral choice and its implications for the expression of aggression.

Fromm was a highly regarded, best-selling author in the 1940s and 1950s, but in recent decades behavioral scientists have largely ignored his work. In two very accessible books, Fromm proposed a number of important ideas to explain how malevolence develops in personality. He began with an examination of the following contradictions in human nature:

1. Although we are animals, our instinctual equipment in comparison with other mammals is incomplete. Unlike

them, we are not born with essential survival skills—in our species, speech and manual dexterity—but have to develop them.

2. We share with other animals the capacity to attain practical, immediate aims, but we alone have an awareness of ourselves and our past and a sense of our influence on the future. While this existential sense offers us opportunities to plan ahead and create, it also casts the disturbing shadows of diminution, powerlessness, and termination across our path. As Fromm (1964) wrote in *The Heart of Man*, "Human self-awareness has made man a stranger in the world, separate, lonely and frightened" (p. 117).

3. We are subject to nature. But because of our awareness of history and our understanding of how we influence others' actions toward us, we have the intellectual capacity to override our instinctual natures. To do so, however, we must recognize that the contradictions in our nature demand continual choices and decisions, many of which cause *angst*.

Based upon these three basic contradictions, Fromm maintains that human character prior to experience is neither good nor bad, caring nor antagonistic, compassionate nor indifferent. Rather, our character is shaped by the choices we make throughout our lives:

> There is no such thing as the choice between "good" and "evil"—there are concrete and specific actions that are means toward what is good, and others that are means towards what is evil, provided good and evil are properly defined. Our moral conflict on the question of choice arises when we have to make a concrete decision rather than when we choose good or evil in general. [Fromm 1964, p. 128]

But rather than regard human choices in absolute terms, Fromm conceptualized them as either more progressive or more regressive in the development and realization of our humanity. These choices continually forge our character. He also believed that some people lack the freedom to choose the more virtuous options:

> Their character structure has lost the capacity to act in accordance with the good. Some people have lost the capacity of choosing evil, precisely because their character structure has lost the craving for evil. In these two extreme cases we may say that both are determined to act as they do because the balance of forces in their character leaves them no choice. In the majority of people, however, we deal with contradictory inclinations within the person's character. [Fromm 1964, p. 135]

If in most cases people actually do have freedom of choice, why have so many philosophers argued that it does not exist?

> The argument for the view that man has no freedom to choose the better as against the worse is to some considerable degree based on the fact that one usually looks at the *last* decision in a chain of events, and not at the first or second ones. Indeed, at the point of final decision the freedom to choose has usually vanished. [Fromm 1964, p. 155]

Fromm's ideas are based on his reading about malevolent people he never met, rather than on examinations of patients he treated.[2] Consequently, his intuitive theory is not supported by a discussion of the specific psychological forces that influence the choices and decisions he recognized as leading to evil.

As I sought to demonstrate elsewhere (Goldberg, in press), the key concepts that account for malevolent personality development are available to us. In the following account I describe the interplay of these conceptualized forces and events in a journey toward malevolence that typically progresses through five stages. My terms for these stages are intended to underscore the profound emotional stakes at issue here:

Stage I—Child of scorn: the shaming of the vulnerable child;

Stage II—Child of the devil: the inculcation of the "bad" self;

Stage III—Transition from victim to perpetrator of malevolence;

Stage IV—Experimental malevolence: the proliferation of contempt;

Stage V—Forging the malevolent personality: the devil's representative in atrocity.

Before I discuss more closely each of these phases, let me make clear that they are not rigorously separate from one another. On the contrary, there is usually an overlap from one stage to the next.

The concept of separate stages is nonetheless valuable, however, because each can be seen as a distinctive crucible for a specific type of healing approach. The therapist working with a child experiencing stage I, for example, can work most effectively in transforming her supposedly "wicked" or "immoral" behavior by dealing with the issue of negative personal identity.

Stage I: Child of Scorn

Shame and pride are the monitors of our personal identity (Goldberg 1991). When a child can feel pride in his competence and knows that he has won the esteem of others, he forms a sense of positive personal identity. But if he is instead disregarded and mistreated, and indeed subjected to a pattern of humiliation and shame, he will acquire a negative personal identity. This depleted sense of self-worth is not passive. It will continually inform him in painful, destructive ways that he is incompetent, inadequate, unwanted. In thus diminishing one's sense of self-regard, chronic shame prevents the individual from positively defining himself to others and also leaves him vulnerable to their further abuse and neglect. In sum, shame undermines both the child's sense of well-being and his interpersonal relationships.

If she is unable to express clearly her feelings of hurt and anguish, she develops a disparaging inner "narrative voice" that constantly warns her away from situations in which she might again be hurt or painfully exposed. Her dilemma is especially cruel, because the situations that test or reveal vulnerability are likely also to be the most opportune occasions for receiving attention and affection. In other words, the child afflicted with a negative personal identity is always at risk when she asks for what she craves most.

Stage II: Child of the Devil

Children begin to imagine the ideal intimate encounter during the "age of belief," that is to say, between the ages of 4 and 8. This ideal person, embellished with details borrowed from actual people the child encounters, is sought over the years, until the age when objects of desire actually become accessible.

If a child's early experiences of lust and desire are treated in healthy ways by his caregivers, he will have good feelings about these yearnings. But if his caregivers react with shame and betrayal to his first awakenings of strong desire, they will impose a sense of badness upon his personal identity; that is, they will inculcate a "bad" self in the child. This conviction that he is somehow bad will be strengthened when others continually inform him, either verbally or through their actions, that he is flawed and unwanted.

To try to hide from his painful badness, a child in this second stage of malevolence will lie and practice deceit, with himself as well as with others. Such deceit makes effective self-examination very difficult.

In other words, since the sense of badness cannot readily be recognized and understood, it cannot easily be uprooted and replaced with reasonable expectations for oneself. On the contrary, the inculcated, hidden feelings of self-contempt gradually stabilize the child's negative personal identity. He becomes convinced that he is helpless and all alone in the world.

Stage III: Transition from Victim to Perpetrator of Malevolence

Unrelieved, unremitting self-contempt is virtually unbearable. To survive both psychologically and physically, the sufferer must somehow cast off the terrible feelings of self-hate. Some sufferers try *bravado*, performing risky or heroic deeds in order to restore self-esteem. If this course fails, *shamelessness* is likely to follow, demonstrating indifference toward society's approval or disapproval of one's behavior.

In the two previous stages, the sufferer passively tolerated shame and humiliation inflicted by others; now, she will lash out, becoming the perpetrator of malevolence.

Using rationalizations and other forms of justification for insensitive behavior, she convinces herself that any indecencies she is about to commit have already been, or will soon be, directed at her. Indeed, the perpetrator comes to believe that everyone in the world should become held responsible for committing or permitting mistreatment of her.

Deprived of the benefit of self-examination, the self-hating individual is prone to *magical thinking*, a suspension of any critical assessment of her personality or behavior. She does not need to improve her character when magically convinced that she is already special; obviously, only the flawed perceptions of others prevent her superiority from being recognized. As perpetrator now, she will use whatever means are available to convince others of her special status.

Stage IV: Experimental Malevolence

To continue behaving contemptuously toward others over the years, the self-hating individual must rationalize ever more desperately, thereby ever more inaccurately perceiving himself and other people. Each rationalized choice to behave insensitively chips away at his freedom of choice until inevitably, cruel behavior is always and unarguably justified. At one extreme, the malevolent criminal may rationalize that he is providing a social benefit; that is, he explains that he does what others would like to do if they were not too "gutless" or dishonest to admit it. He is a role model for the fearful, inspiring them to stand up for their authentic aspirations.

At this fourth stage, other people can be seriously harmed as a result of the perpetrator's indifference to their well-being. He has not yet, however, begun to inflict cruelty or cause destruction intentionally.

Stage V: Forging the Malevolent Personality

At this stage, the perpetrator is accustomed to using magical thinking instead of self-knowledge to deal with his disquieting doubts about the possible absence of meaning in his life. When reality threatens his magical notions, he is likely to erupt in the cruel, destructive behaviors of atrocity.

Basically, three types of people practice atrocity—foot soldiers, leaders, and lone wolves.

Under normal circumstances, such heinous criminals as Adolph Eichmann, the paramilitary killers in Serbia, and the terrorist followers of fanatical religious leaders will appear as innocuous and absurd as Uriah Heep[3]—perhaps annoying because of petty displays of self-importance but easily dismissed and forgotten. Fearful and unreflective, they are emotionally trapped in barren lives. But during stressful periods of great social unrest, these people find themselves magnetically drawn to malevolent leaders and become the *foot soldiers* of atrocity. They make a terrible bargain: in exchange for their services, the forces of evil grant them a role in a powerful movement that gives to their lives at last some semblance of meaning, however vicious.

The *leaders* of such movements have, like their foot soldiers, progressed into the fifth stage of malevolence. People are drawn to them because of some outstanding physical, social, or psychological attribute and because they are skillful in articulately justifying their advocacy of brutality. To accept their message is to participate in a magical triumph over one's own weakness by joining in attacking others; the malevolent leader is seen to be living an enviably higher "good" than are the weak and cowardly upon whom he imposes his will.

Lone wolf perpetrators are most often involved in serial or mass murder and are more likely than the other two types to be diagnosed as mentally ill. Their psychological disabilities prevent them from interacting easily with other people; even other perpetrators regard them as "odd." Typically, they commit their crimes either alone or with only one other similarly disturbed lone wolf.

The frightening consequences of stage V may seem far removed from stage I, but the progression can be like a boulder rolling down a hill, gradually and terribly accelerating. It all begins simply enough with shame, the crucial concept in stage I.

JASON'S STORY

No one becomes bonded to malevolence except to inure himself to some great suffering. The problem the behavioral sciences have had in dealing with malevolence is in recognizing the precise ways in which such suffering is psychologically transformed in malevolence.

Jason, a writer in his early thirties, explained in our first session that he had come to me because of his problems with intimacy. For as long as he could remember, the important people in his life scolded him for living solely for the moment, neither building bridges to others nor showing them sufficient compassion and concern.

Still, he was doubtful that psychoanalysis could really help him. Having already been in analysis for many years, he knew that the process depends upon words, and he had come to believe that words cannot accurately convey immediate personal intent. Like Pirandello, Jason felt that each of us has within himself a special world of meaning, and even though we believe that we understand what another person means in his words, in fact we never do.

On the contrary, Jason went on, words are used in the vacuous pursuit of a reality that is treacherous. That is to say, we all use words to make definite-sounding commitments, such as pledges of eternal love, for a future that is uncertain. Without words, we cannot make these false promises. Words are inherently ambiguous or ambivalent; actions are not. Jason reasoned that his own inability to love resulted from his having to use words to declare and commit himself in a relationship.

His specific reason for contacting me was a series of deceptions he had committed in collusion with Sonia, a beautiful married publisher with whom he was sexually involved. Sonia demanded that during sex he declare his love, whether he meant it or not, but didn't expect him to pretend any love for her afterward. Yet the mutual deception troubled Jason:

"I thought at the moment: what does it matter what I say to her in the heat of passion? After all, the affair won't last forever. But something kept telling me that we should scrutinize our every word to each other, as if we will live together forever and have to bear each other's suffering. Nevertheless, to my surprise—because it's contrary to my usual personal proclivities—I was compelled by my sympathy for her dependence on my words to tell her each time we were passionate that I would love her forever. It disgusts me that I told her what she wanted to hear."

An unfortunate lifelong legacy for many patients born to wealth and privilege is that their parents gave them therapists in childhood instead of nurturing emotional responses. Jason was introduced to the world of psychoanalysis and the power of language at the age of 5; when he came to me he was a veteran of twenty-five years in analysis.

I learned that the second of his many therapists felt the need to write for advice about the boy's problematic behavior

to a world-renowned British child psychiatrist. The letter
cited Jason's lack of compassion for others, his violent tem-
per, and reveries in which he spent hours imagining himself
to be one of the heroes in the classical novels given to him by
his parents. Unfortunately, the analyst failed to mention that
Jason's lack of empathy resulted from his parents' making
impossible demands upon him to save them from their
suffering.

According to behavioral science studies, destructive behavior is linked with difficulty in forming empathic bonds
with others. If one is unable or unwilling to take into
consideration how someone else feels—in effect, psychologically take the place of the other person—one tends to treat
others as objects of no importance rather than as beings like
oneself, with feelings and concerns and the right to be treated
with decency.

Perhaps using this reasoning in response to a letter that
provided an incomplete patient history, the British expert
wrote back that Jason was evidently a child schizophrenic in
need of extensive psychoanalysis. Jason, of course, was told
about this assessment.

His actual story suggests an alternative diagnosis. His
European parents, understanding the implications of Nazism
early on, had scrambled frantically to smuggle out their
jewels and gold certificates, taking little thought of their
equally threatened relatives. In the United States, Jason's
father combined this stake with his astute technological sense
and business acumen to make a fortune in industry. Such
success, of course, could not assuage the parents' gnawing
sense of guilt and shame for abandoning their relatives to
horrible fates in the Holocaust. They desperately sought for
evidence that their flight to safety had produced some socially
redemptive consequence.

To Jason's mind, they had criticized him virtually from
birth for any perceived faults, as if their anxious, demanding
attentions implied that only if their precious child became an
exceptional, flawless person could they be forgiven. In Jason's daydreams, he tried to imagine ways of escaping from
their desperate emotional concentration on him.

The adult Jason was tall and powerfully built, with dark wavy hair and chiseled features. With a very high I.Q. and verbal fluency, he became a successful writer, well regarded in literary circles. Yet, not surprisingly, he felt alone in the world, having no close male friends. Probably, one of his strongest motives for continuing analysis in adulthood was that the therapeutic session was the only place where he could achieve even a modicum of intimacy with another man.

To satisfy his inner emptiness, Jason became a sexual athlete. A new woman was like a drug; he experienced the same "rush" he got with cocaine. Unfortunately, this heightened excitement waned immediately after a successful seduction, and he became depressed. Although he felt trapped by this addiction, the sexual "highs," short-lived as they were, energized his will to live. When there was no new candidate in sight, he was not interested in returning to previous conquests; instead, he felt intensely agitated and self-punitive.

In short, Jason was a "stimulus addict," the kind of person who does not feel alive unless involved in encounters that are risky and uncertain. He was incapable of securing pleasure or harmony from close, intimate relationships. For Jason, such relationships with women were always marred by his fear that any woman who really came to know him would find out that he was a schizophrenic. Throughout his childhood and into the present, he harbored a deep resentment toward all women, convinced that they considered him physically attractive but emotionally impaired.

Rationalizations for Jason's increasing indifference, insensitivity, and cruelty toward women were easy to find, given his sharp intelligence and practiced imagination. When he tired of a partner, or tried to initiate a relationship with a highly unstable woman, he could easily precipitate some sort of crisis in a relationship in order to deal with his feelings of "deadness." He coolly rationalized such contemptuous behavior as putting a pillowcase over his lover's head during sex because he had convinced himself that he was superior to conventional morality. By boasting about his cleverness in manipulating others, he was actually trying to reverse the humiliated status he suffered. As we have learned, each rationalized choice of insensitivity toward others eroded his freedom of choice, and thus his cruel behavior inevitably became unassailably justified.

Pivotal in Jason's unstable life was his unwillingness to take responsibility for his difficulties. For example, he could not bear to consider the possibility that his inability to reach out and form close relationships was a sign of incompetence. Rather, he portrayed it as a virtue; that is, his dedication to a relentless pursuit of knowledge precluded becoming involved with other people's sensibilities. This quest for knowledge, of course, was directed almost entirely outward and only rarely included examination of his own hurt psyche.

Jason's torment fueled a serious addiction to cocaine. At his publisher's Christmas party, he insulted Elyse, an editor who was a longtime friend, by proposing that they make love in the office washroom with the door ajar. She was not entirely surprised, having heard many rumors about Jason seducing women then subjecting them to degrading experiences. In one tale, he had allegedly spent the night with some new woman in a hotel, pushed her nude out into the hall the next morning and bolted the door, evidently enjoying her frantic efforts to get back in. It was said that she later committed suicide. Elyse, who was a patient of mine, decided that her friend needed immediate help. It was she who recommended me to Jason.

Soon after our sessions began, I became aware that Jason would sometimes take on another persona, a personification he referred to as "Stud." Jason explained that this second self was the part of him that did not age and lived in accord with Nietzschean philosophy; that is, Stud regarded his behavior as beyond the strictures of conventional morality. He justified his belief on the basis that he was sufficient unto himself, needing no one else.

"I don't give a shit," Stud said. "I enjoy myself and indulge any whim or desire I have. Anything else in life is too dull and uninteresting, or it requires too much effort."

Stud took over or was heard from when Jason felt inadequate or apprehensive about making the correct life decisions. He argued that society's highest possible morality would be to allow people like him to exercise their superior capacities to the full. If lesser people suffered thereby, that would be regrettable but unimportant.

Throughout his growing years, Jason had experimented with the "technicalities" of morality. As a young child, he purposely strode across lawns with signs saying, "Keep Off the Grass." In adolescence, he parked his car in spots reserved for the handicapped or people with special permits. He cheated on college tests even though he was always well prepared and usually the brightest in class; the thrill of outwitting the teacher "turned me on." In adult life, he intentionally lit up cigarettes in "No Smoking" sections or carried on distractingly loud conversations during concerts or lectures. In all of these situations, his facile, glib charm usually spared him the wrath of the people he annoyed.

Eventually, when his grandiosity convinced him that he could talk his way out of virtually any kind of trouble, he graduated to more serious offenses against conventional morality.

The degrading acts against women were rationalized as uncompromising scientific curiosity about human behavior. According to Stud, Jason had pushed the naked woman into the hotel corridor in order to enact authentically the disturbing legacy of schizophrenia bestowed upon him by the psychiatric profession.

"I have been told all my life that I'm incompetent to do the right things," Jason was in effect saying to this second self. "Maybe they were right! Someone else will have to make decisions for me. I'll let that other part of me, the confident part, take charge."

Not surprisingly, given this analysis, Stud first appeared to Jason during a cocaine "trip." During the subsequent months of continuing drug usage, however, Stud made himself known quite apart from any chemical inhalation. Soon, it was Stud who bought the drugs, and Stud who planned Jason's escapades with women.

In their extensive study of criminals, Yochelson and Samenow (1993) pinned down the drug factor:

More than the nonusing criminals, the users [of drugs] lacked the courage to take responsibility initiatives and make the required efforts. Drugs always offered a rapid and effective way of achieving the desired mental state of being "ten feet tall" and simultaneously dispelling the tedium of responsible living. [p. 40]

Colin Wilson, based upon his own study of criminals, believes that each of us has a "shut-off" mechanism that allows our other self to make decisions about the choices we face. Suppose, for example, that we are feeling some strong biological craving, but suddenly hear a voice cry out, "Help me, I'm hurt!" Most of us will push aside our own need and focus on the crisis facing the other person. This is not an automatic process; we deliberately choose to control our own needs until a more appropriate moment.

But the criminal, Wilson (1984) found, makes a *decision* not to abandon his own needs and concerns:

He can see no sound reason why he should waste his time establishing a higher level of self-control [than what seems to him to be in his best interests]. Let other people worry about that. [p. 59]

This description fits Jason. When he had decisions to make that involved the welfare of others, he pushed those concerns out of his consciousness.

Jason's parents always told him that he need not worry about the practical aspects of life. Others could tend to such mundane matters while he concentrated on developing his superior intellectual and creative talents. In truth, Jason now feels incompetent to handle practical matters. When a difficult decision has to be made, his mind wanders off and Stud takes over, carrying out the necessary actions.

Jason's rationalizations in regard to the woman who committed suicide are particularly revealing about choice and responsibility in the malevolent personality. The night of the incident in the hotel, he had taken a large dose of Ecstasy before leaving home. From articles in medical journals and his own experiences, he was very familiar with the often violent side effects of this drug, once thought to be a "wonder drug" for heightening erotic arousal and prolonging sexual endurance. He had taken Ecstasy several times and gone "out of control," endangering himself and others around him.

On this occasion, as on many others, he justified taking the drug on the basis that women did not offer themselves for his private delectation because they expected straitlaced, conservative behavior. They wanted excitement. Also, he was looking forward to the best possible sexual encounter, rationalizing that his previous loss of control was a result of his inexperience with this particular drug. Since he had learned how to handle cocaine and other psychoactive drugs by not allowing himself to become too fearful of their harmful effects, he believed that he could also control his experience with Ecstasy and luxuriate in its aphrodisiac qualities.

In fact, as Jason later realized, he was deluding himself. Almost immediately upon reaching the hotel, he felt irritated and annoyed in some unfathomable way. He set those feelings aside for later examination. In a manner of speaking, he gave Stud tacit permission to act upon him, without knowing what Stud might do.

Because pushing the woman nude into the hallway was not the action of the person he was raised to be, Jason provided himself with a highly convoluted set of rationalizations.

In the first place, he claimed, he became angry because his partner accused him of needing to sleep with a great many women, then relented and said it was all right with her, for the present. Once he got his head straight, she went on, he would realize that he cared more for her than for anyone else. What enraged Jason was that he had never professed love for this woman or discussed his addiction to serial sex, and yet, ironically, many of his lovers had excused or explained his womanizing in much the same terms that she had.

In his emotional and chemical-induced agitation, Jason told himself that women who claimed to find his womanizing unacceptable but also condoned it had no integrity. They didn't merit his consideration. Therefore, he could—and would—do as he pleased with these shallow women. His many experiments with breaking the rules, beginning with walking on the grass, proved that rules were only for others. What conventional morality regards as wicked he rationalized into a "philosophy of good"; his experiments, then, had a socially redemptive value.

As this set of rationalizations might suggest, Jason's course of treatment with me was difficult and demanding. Intensely competitive, he could not easily accept the role of patient, which he defined as having to pay me money because he was weak and inferior and needed to be cared for by someone superior. Virtually snarling, he said that his twenty-five years of shameful indoctrination at the hands of analysts were enough.

I realized that Jason would continue to battle me and there would be no therapeutic progress if I continued to play the role of "knowledgeable analyst." Besides, I had been shouldering all of the therapeutic risks in our sessions by trying to deal with the contemptuous, irrational Stud. By contrast, Jason had assigned himself the easier role of "intellectual observer," standing aside and criticizing me for failing to outwit Stud in my office or to curb his malevolent behavior outside.

I threw the ball into Jason's court.

"You seem to know it all!" I said, again and again. "If you have the answers, than *you* have to tell me how to deal with Stud."

At first, Jason was stunned that I refused to grapple with him and his second self intellectually. Then he became infuriated, taking moral offense. He pointed out that if he had the answers, he wouldn't be paying me. I countered that he seemed to take a morbid pride in acting as if he knew how to deal with Stud but refused to let me use this insight in a practical way.

As Jason kept repeating that I did not understand him, I recognized him as an *antihero*, that is, the sibling rival of the hero (Goldberg 1989). As I had seen often enough by now, Jason felt jealousy, envy, and resentment toward the ideal image of himself that others held up to him, the self they wanted him to be. If the hero stands for hope, courage, and risk, Jason was a depressed version of the hero, so irritated by those values that he not only rejected them but also took a morbid pride in acting against them.

Being misunderstood is a central theme in the life of the antihero. Jason preferred to be misunderstood because being fully understood by his parents, previous therapists, or me would be dangerous. He had an urgent need to differentiate and hold himself apart from others. Because malevolent irritants are hard to endure, Stud served as a defense against his being consumed and incorporated by others.

I shared this observation with Jason, explaining exactly how he, along with Stud, had effectively taken control of all of our therapeutic sessions.

From then on, Jason focused on his apparent command of situations, not only in my office but outside. As he did so, he slowly but steadily became emotionally in touch with his deep hurt and despair. Often, he would plead with me to understand him.

"Why don't you understand me?" he'd complain. "You're making me feel the way I always did with my family . . . helpless, and incompetent. They expected me to do something no one realistically could."

I urged him to elaborate, but he refused.

A few sessions later, he tried to explain, perhaps in reaction to the disappointment that he read in my face at being unable to reach him.

"I remember the look my mother would get on her face whenever I said or did something she didn't like," he said. "Her face froze. And I felt all alone in the world. I feel that way right now."

At this point, we were able to begin working on the force that generated his self-contempt.

Those who feel inordinately flawed or shamed are constantly escorted in the background of consciousness by a vigilant, rarely silent "judge" who examines and comments upon their every thought, feeling, and action. This critical voice has been scripted and incorporated into the self from among the myriad of interactions with parents and significant figures in the past. Leaping upon a bare minimum of information and experience in any given situation, this judge decisively forms a condemning opinion, thus intruding, impeding, and aborting behavior. In this way, the critical voice obstructs any effort made toward self-discovery, exploration of possibility, or any other deepening of experience. Rather, its moral judgments advise the ashamed individual that his behavior and actions are contemptible, then insist that he defend and justify himself.

In short, the behavior of shame-prone people demands continual justification.

I have found in my own work that people addicted to rationalization can take a critically important first step toward healing, once they are willing to spend the time and effort taking note of how often and in what ways their critical voice demands justification. Most begin by taking daily notes in a journal.

Then, they become able through their observations to take the second step: confronting and disarming the critical voice just as they would an actual person who might try to abuse or humiliate them.

Third, they define themselves both to the critical voice and to themselves in terms of their ideal self.

Fourth, they learn to dissuade the critical voice from making disparaging remarks about their thoughts, feelings, and actions.

Fifth, the first four steps result in an increasingly fewer number of rationalizations, since the gradual cessation of critical inner judgments presents fewer obstacles to new, exploratory behavior. Now, patients learn to make more penetrating discoveries about themselves, for example, the revelation of one's deeply buried despair about human limitations. The bracing new opportunity of dealing with such discoveries helps patients learn to live more legitimately as purposive people and to develop a courageous, creative consciousness of human possibility.

To sum up, Jason's inability to empathize with others was forged in childhood, when his parents made impossible demands upon him to alleviate their guilt. As we have seen, the predilection to malevolence comes from a variety of sources in addition to abuse or neglect. It is very high among people like Jason, who have been subjected to unreasonable expectations they are not equipped to meet.

In traditional analysis, Jason would undoubtedly be diagnosed as a psychopath. Like many other so-called psychopaths, however, his emotional difficulties did not arise from an absence of feeling for others, but from too much (Goldberg 1991). His childhood identification and empathy with his parents was too painful to sustain. Therefore, he felt forced to cut his bonds with them, and subsequently with everyone else. Eventually, his impotence to help others in combination with his image of himself as a psychiatric patient imbued him with shame and self-contempt.

Self-hatred, one of the most virulently destructive forces visited upon humankind, leads to all of the malevolence that plagues our world.

The shame Jason felt, so subtly inflicted, is more common in children than most people realize. His parents did not physically or psychologically abuse him, they were clearly decent people by any standards, but they were anxiously overconcerned about appearances and firmly discouraged his natural curiosity and sense of wonder. Consequently, Jason learned that he could not reach out toward people simply for the intrinsic pleasure of intimacy; rather, people were there to be used in his unending search for knowledge. And since his parents had suppressed his curiosity because it was too suggestive of personal limitations they found abhorrent, he sought knowledge primarily from the outside, rarely turning inward to examine his damaged psyche.

Jason was shamed into compliance with parental expectations by the conviction that being less than perfect is equivalent to being evil, and undeserving of human company. People like him, when they reach adulthood, convince themselves that there is a mitigating greater good behind their malevolent acts that renders such behavior not only justified but necessary. Jason believed that he and his family could save themselves from the pettiness of ordinary human weakness by being brutally honest about their desires. And so he justified his cruelty with the assumption that his frank submission to his desires, even when they led to violent acts, was a greater good than the willful intellectual dishonesty of the women he met.

However, it should also be pointed out that Jason's parents' overindulging him, together with making unreasonable demands of him, cannot totally account for his cruelty. Here is where Fromm's valuable distinction between benign forms of aggression that are in the service of human survival and malignant aggression that serves no constructive purpose, as it is a cumulative reaction to hurt and disappointment (Fromm 1973), provides an insightful, possible account of the deeper influences of his cruelty.

Jason may have been considerably humiliated by his parents' cowardly and indifferent behavior in turning their backs on their family in Europe during the Holocaust and instead investing their concerns in becoming affluent. Despite their large contributions and active participation in charities, their preaching about the need to care for others and their attention to Jason's self-centeredness must have struck Jason as hollow. Understandably, words came to have no real meaning for him. Despite their show of concern, the only moral code his parents lived by were dictated by selfishness and material comforts. A highly cynical attitude and an identification with aggressors who cruelly humiliate others may have been Jason's response to his parents' disavowed guilt and shame. By his aggression and cruelty, Jason was trying to show that he was not a weak victim; nor was he, he liked to believe, forced to lie to himself and others about his actual motives (Mauricio Cortina, personal correspondence).

Over the course of treatment, as Jason learned to deal with his shame and irrational counteractions to his lifelong inner pain, he was able to share his vulnerabilities with others. In this way, he came to recognize that his personal growth would require continual sacrifice of his false securities. Previously, he preferred to "look good" to others rather than to be actually competent as a human being. To find healing, however, he had to relinquish this image; he couldn't pretend to have all the "right" answers.

As we continued to work together, Jason grew more curious about the undiscovered parts within himself and the sensibilities of others. Eventually, he established a fulfilling and intimate relationship with a woman.

Jason's case shows that seriously malevolent personality patterns can be transformed. But the corrective process depends upon a cogent understanding of the conditions that produce these patterns, along with a capacity and willingness to work with intersubjective shame (Goldberg 1991).

ENDNOTES

1. In this chapter evil and malevolence are used interchangeably. Nevertheless, in examining the philosophical and theological obstacles to understanding the problem of cruelty and destructiveness in the world, it is important to separate the question of evil from the problem of malevolence. Evil, historically, is concerned with metaphysical questions, such as, Is there a superordinate being who tolerates the evil committed in the world, or who itself is the cause of evil? and phylogenetic questions, such as, Is there a universal inherent human tendency toward cruelty and destructiveness? The sheer volume of

controversy and printed material on the question of evil throughout the millennia shows the problem to be as yet insoluble. The problem of malevolence, that is, the social and psychological issues, factors, and conditions that influence cruelty and destructiveness, I seek to demonstrate in a five-stage theory of the forging of the malevolent personality, outlined in this chapter. It is within our current understanding of human behavior.

2. According to Michael Maccoby, who worked with Fromm when he was writing his book on human aggression, clinical cases were discussed. However, Fromm thought he could not use this material without risking disclosure of patients' identities (personal correspondence, M. Cortina).

3. Uriah Heep, a character in Charles Dickens's *David Copperfield*, is a famous example of the passive–aggressive personality. He pretends to be humble, meek, and benevolent, but is actually scheming, hateful, and resentful. His strategy is based on the assumption that most people find it convenient to believe the best of others and therefore are easily deceived. He gains the advantage of others by telling them what they want to hear.

REFERENCES

Fromm, E. (1964). *The Heart of Man*. New York: Harper & Row.
_____ (1973). *The Anatomy of Human Destructiveness*. New York: Holt, Rinehart & Winston.
Goldberg, C. (1989). The role of passion in the transformation of anti-heroes. *Journal of Evolutionary Psychology* 9:2–16.
_____ (1991). *Understanding Shame*. Northvale, NJ: Jason Aronson.
_____ (In press). *Speaking with the Devil: The Culture and Psychology of Evil and Malevolence*. New York: Viking/Penguin.
Wilson, C. (1984). *A Criminal History of Mankind*. New York: Carroll & Graf.
Yochelson, S., and Samenow, S. S. (1993). *The Criminal Personality*. Vol. I. Northvale, NJ: Jason Aronson.

7

The Relational Perspective in Fromm and in the Stone Center's Work

Douglas LaBier

In this time of reassessing Fromm's contributions to psychoanalysis, I would like to discuss Fromm's contribution to current relational theories in psychoanalysis, a contribution that has been insufficiently recognized. His thinking and perspectives concerning, for example, the significance of mutuality and emotional connection for health, the meaning of pathology, and the goals of psychoanalysis are all underpinnings of the relational perspective.

Relational theory in general emphasizes that the human being is fundamentally a part of a network of relationships. In contrast to drive or developmental arrest theories, the relational perspective sees the person as continually motivated by the need for relationship and an active participant in shaping the internal consequence of external experience (Mitchell 1988).

But relational theory is not monolithic. Nor, ironically, is it always "relational" in its concepts. In this chapter I focus on the linkage between Fromm's work and a particular relational theory of development and clinical treatment that has emerged in recent years. It diverges, in certain important respects, from the main body of relational thinking. It is known as the Stone Center model because of its origin within a group of researchers and clinicians, led by Jean Baker Miller, who are associated with the Stone Center for Developmental Studies at Wellesley College (Jordan, et al. 1991, Miller 1976, 1988).

The Stone Center model has developed independently from and without explicit reference to Fromm's work. In addition, it originated from within a specific context: revised thinking about women's development within patriarchal culture. Nevertheless, it has clear similarities with some of Fromm's major contributions. These include his emphasis on the overriding human need for mutual affirmation and authentic relational connection, and his original thinking about the impact of patriarchy and gender socialization upon the individual's potential for health or sickness (Fromm 1947, 1955, 1956, 1970, 1976, 1980, 1992a,b).

The Stone Center model has developed original perspectives about pathology and human development that resolve some conflicting aspects of Fromm's work, particularly his dual tendency to embrace a relatively conventional view of separation and individuation while simultaneously arguing that positive human development is a process of evolving and maturing forms of connection (see Cortina, Chapter 3 in this volume, for a critique of this contradiction).

The Stone Center model also stands alone among relational theories in incorporating an explicit analysis of the role of gender, culture, and values upon human development and pathology. This makes it, in my view, the most promising and relevant relational model—and the one most compatible with Fromm—for understanding and treating men and women in today's career-oriented, technologically advanced consumer culture.

FEATURES OF RELATIONAL THEORY

The relational perspective addresses and corrects some of the limitations and inadequacies of both the drive theory and self psychology or arrested development models. For example, Benjamin (1988) has argued that conventional psychoanalytic formulations that equate maturity with separation and individuation portray, essentially, an un-related self—tightly bounded, internally structured, and without empathic recognition of others as subjects.

The relational perspective limits our understanding, however, to the degree that it ignores or discounts forces within the larger culture that distort or damage the nature and quality of relational connection from birth through old age. These include gender socialization, patriarchy, and careerist values.

Fromm stressed the role of such forces in determining the avenues open to healthy or unhealthy development, and thereby brought a political dimension into a theory of human development. This acounts, no doubt, for much of the opposition to and dismissal of his work by other analysts. But this dimension is also what continues to make his work ever-relevant, even critical, to under-standing and treating troubled men and women in today's culture. And it is also the point of intersection between his work and the Stone Center model, which emphasizes the roles of mutuality, empathy, and strengthening of the "relational self" as elements of healthy development. These elements are affected by the system of power relations operating in the family and larger culture.

CONNECTION, DISCONNECTION, AND MUTUALITY

Fromm maintained that a continuum of relational connection always exists between self and other, as well as between self and the larger natural world. It is rooted in the human need to restore lost connection with the world that is part of the human condition, and that generates isolation, powerlessness, and helplessness.

The relational continuum extends from deeply regressive, to dominant-subordinate forms of social and intimate relations, to relationships based on the practice of mutuality, authenticity, and reciprocal affirmation. All forms of relationship are attempts to establish and maintain some form of connection, although some are at the expense of one's emotional reality and health. All forms of distortion in human relationship originate in a striving for authentic, affirming, mutual connection.

To the extent that family and cultural life within contemporary culture is founded on disconnection and patriarchy, it is inherently pathogenic. This distortion potential is further reinforced through adulthood, particularly through adaptation and rewards within the workplace. Cultural values that define various forms of disconnection, inauthenticity, and "power-over" (i.e., domination, in contrast to "power-with," or shared power) also have distorting roles toward mature adult development. The damage this produces for men is less overtly visible than that for women, because men move into the power positions, identify with them, and are rewarded by them.

THE STONE CENTER PERSPECTIVE

These perspectives of Fromm's provide a backdrop to much of the relational theory developed by Miller and her colleagues. This model originated in the recognition that equating successful male adaptation with health for both sexes is a faulty assumption. Miller and her colleagues (Jordan et al. 1991, Miller 1976, 1986, 1988) argue that a sense of connection to others is a central organizing feature of women's development, and that disconnection, or violation of mutuality, produces pathology in some form.

Miller found that most women develop a heightened sense of value and effectiveness from a context of relationships, which leads to a greater sense of connection, rather than a sense of separation, which has been defined as healthy individuation—essentially a quality of isolated, disconnected autonomy. This point of view links with Fromm's perspectives about the distorted forms of social and individual relations that occur within patriarchal, authoritarian cultures.

The work of Gilligan (Brown and Gilligan 1992, Gilligan 1982, Gilligan et al. 1990, 1991) has added to this perspective through research that shows that the traditional psychoanalytic model of development and individuation was rooted in male development, which was accepted as the norm of human development. Yet male development is, itself, distorted and deformed within a culture of patriarchy, the very conditions that create, in Fromm's terms, the "normal" social character oriented to domination-submission—or further along the pathological spectrum, to sadism and masochism—as solutions to the need for relatedness.

Gilligan argued that in contrast to boys, girls develop a relational ethical structure privileging affiliation between and among people, and that a devaluing of sense of self occurs among girls as they pass through adolescence.

Similarly, Miller and her colleagues observed that women typically occupy a subordinate power position within a social system that is organized around domination-subordination as the dominant mode of relationship. Interpersonal relationships then take shape in response to the structure of hierarchy and "power-over others." Women's development becomes increasingly marked by more fluid and permeable intrapsychic boundaries, in contrast to men's.

As boys learn to separate from the mother and the world of emotional connection, they identify with what becomes a false, inauthentic self, a culturally defined voice of the dominant male role. Fromm's description of the contemporary, well-adapted person, largely cut off from one's own emotional reality, and whose mask conceals such feelings as helplessness, powerlessness, and an unclear identity, is a clinical picture of the outcome of this process, particularly for men.

More broadly, Fromm pointed out that patriarchy produces inherently distorting and damaging consequences for relationships and overall health for both men and women. For example, Fromm (1980) explained that a patriarchal bias makes it impossible to think in terms of equality. A view of development that sees sexuality as essentially an inner chemical process within the male, with the female as the proper object of the drive, precludes recognizing the female as an equal *subject*, as an actor with her own desire, voice, and intention.

Gilligan's work extended such thinking by demonstrating the disconnections that typically occur during girls' adolescence. By adulthood, women become largely selfless and voiceless in relationships. They use empathy and their capacity for relationship to cover over their own feelings and thoughts. A paradox then occurs in the form of the tendency to give up authentic relationships for the sake of preserving "relationships." This is at the heart of women's emotional disturbances. Learning to "not know" protects them from the consequences of relationships they cannot have. For example, in relationships of disconnection they fear that getting angry will make things worse.

One can see much of this as an extension of Fromm's marketing character orientation, including the silencing of one's sense of self, alienation from one's own desires, the lack of interest in nature, and seeing oneself as a commodity. All produce detachment and disconnection, both from inner truth and from relationships in which mutual affirmation as separate subjects is possible.

In short, conventional socialization crystallizes in the silencing of women's sense of self and autonomous desire, and adaptation to the role of the controller, the dominator, for men. This process underlies what Gilligan, Miller, and others have described as the damage of disconnection.

MUTUALITY AND THE RELATIONAL SELF

The Stone Center model holds that mutuality, or mutual intersubjectivity plays the central role in healthy development. Jordan (1991) defines mutuality in terms of interest in and cognitive-emotional awareness of the subjectivity of the other, through empathy, a willingness and ability to reveal one's own inner states, needs, and experiences, and a valuing of the process of knowing and learning about the other. Central to Fromm's thinking is a similar recognition that there can be no authentic contact between two people that does not affect both of them, that no interaction leaves either one of them unchanged.

This view of mutuality, however, contrasts with the views of relationship shared by most object relations theorists. Miller (Miller and Stiver 1993) argues that much current relational theory ignores the key role of mutual empathy and mutually empowered relationships. For example Kohut's (1984) selfobject relationship is one that essentially serves the narcissistic needs of the individual. In addition, much of relational theory does not take into account distortions to relationships that accrue within a culture of having, possessing, and objectification of the other. One sees this absence, for example, in much of the work associated with the New York University model of relational psychoanalysis. As Miller has pointed out, this model uses the language of objectification and does not take into account the distorting impact of cultural values and socialization.

In contrast, one can describe the Stone Center relational model as more a model of "subject relations." That is, it views healthy human interaction as occurring between two or more fully realized subjects, people who recognize and affirm each other as subjects who have mutual impact on and recognition of the other. Interaction serves to extend and enhance mutual affirmation, an essential part of the biophilic orientation that Fromm described.

The Stone Center model attributes pathology to the consequences of the breakdown of mutuality. This links with Fromm's view of the outcome of the "having" orientation, which can include narcissism, greed, and sadism. Fromm argued that the more malignant passions are oriented toward transforming everything in the world, including people, into objects one possesses.

The person who is well adapted to the power position, then, also tends to experience diminished pleasure in giving, sharing, and community. He or she is fundamentally unrelated and isolated, but may have little conscious awareness of this. The male who experiences this is often externally well adapted, particularly to the culture of work (LaBier 1986). In this sense, successful oedipal resolution for the male produces new, hidden pathology through a reinforcement of disconnection and the absence of critical emotional awareness.

Predating relational theory by several decades, Fromm argued that the most powerful drives derive from seeking solutions to the disconnection, sense of separation, and isolation that is part of the human condition. The human is attempting to create meaning through a connected, affirming relationship with the world beyond oneself. The need to establish connection, and the need for meaning and purpose, therefore underlie the fundamental conflicts.

Central, here, is the Stone Center model's concept of the "relational self." In this view, the self is experienced in the context of relationship. It is not a bounded, fixed, self-contained entity, relating to external objects. The relational self develops to the degree that the person is able to experience mutual connection and validation with a larger community.

Seeing the self as relational shifts how one interprets symptoms and the process of change. One example would be interpreting anger as a symptom of a disconnection within a relationship. Clinical treatment would be based on illuminating the source of disconnection within the relationship, and working to shift or change one's participation in that relationship. This focus on emotional experience as a product of the relational system and how it affects one's sense of self is different from traditional formulations trying to "fix" the "anger problem" within the person.

This perspective is consistent with Fromm's view that awareness of emotional truth about family and other relationships is a precondition for change. It is also consistent with his view of understanding symptoms as part of an entire relational system, the outcome of a way of life that became established in family relations and continues to be reenacted or practiced in adulthood.

EMOTIONAL CONNECTION AND HEALTH

Miller argues that qualities of the relational self, such as interpersonal sensitivity, capacity for vulnerability, and empathy, are strengths rather than weaknesses. But they are defined as weaknesses because they are associated with a form of self relegated to women in a hierarchical power structure. And as participants in a culture that rewards "power-over" others, women could only achieve power through indirect means, such as manipulation, undercutting, or hidden exploitation.

The crucial point, here, is that healthy self-definition can only occur in the context of connection. Relational theory argues that because the self is always in relationship, healthy growth is dependent on mutually affirming relationships. A healthy self involves constant, continuous oscillation between the experience of separation and connection. Growth, then, means the practice of authenticity and relational capacity, through which one becomes simultaneously more self-defined and connected.

These views are closely related to Fromm's argument that striving for healthy connection, including the experience of unity and oneness with life, rests upon practicing and acting upon such capacities as reason, caring, and mutual affirmation.

In healthy relationships, the person becomes one with his or her "objects." That is, objects cease to be objects. Fromm's concept of the being mode describes, essentially, the model of healthy interpersonal relations stressed by the Stone Center model. Active, engaged, mutual relatedness to the world reflects the being mode, in contrast to feeding one's self as an isolated entity, one's status, image, and so on.

In this respect, the concept of the relational self has much in common with the perspective of Eastern traditions such as Zen, and the Christian mystics. The Stone Center has developed some of these implications more fully by demonstrating that healthy growth of the individual does not mean severing connections, but rather the growth of the capacity to engage in interactions which foster the development of all people involved. Both self-delineation and connections are enhanced through affirming relationships.

In this sense, the Stone Center model corrects a contradiction within Fromm's work. He used language that suggests independence and individuation require "severing" of incestuous, regressive ties. Yet his overall theories and clinical perspectives regarding treatment suggest the opposite, that healthy development means transforming rather than severing connection. That maturation of cognitive and emotional capacities is an evolution in the direction of greater practice of mutuality and connectedness.

For Fromm, becoming aware of truth and struggling to remove illusions is part of the practice of simultaneous independence and connection. By recognizing that certain kinds of relationships support and enhance mutual subjectivity, one experiences what Fromm described as the "awakening" process that can occur in treatment. Similarly, the Stone Center model holds that a person who feels and thinks as a fully realized subject—similar to what Fromm described as the "being" mode—will not be threatened, emotionally or psychologically, by confronting and recognizing another's subjectivity. This underscores the significance of the quality of the relational connection as a determinant of health or pathology.

PATHOLOGY AND DISCONNECTION

The Stone Center model argues that emotional disconnection and the breakdown of empathy produce pathology. The forces of disconnection are broad-based and pervasive within our culture. They include all forms of relational violation, from an abusing family to a traumatizing society, including its institutions and values, which support a false self.

This is consistent with Fromm's analysis of the damaging consequences of "normal" forms of adaptation upon character and the solutions people create in response to human relational needs. He argues that most illness, whether more malignant or more benign, represents failed or distorted attempts to establish positive solutions to the striving for meaning, purpose, and connection. That is, the fundamental human strivings, under favorable developmental and social conditions, lead to enhanced relatedness and positive connection. More severe disturbance represents the dominance of irrational passions, which, by definition, are nonrelational.

The irony is that the greater amount of disconnection within relationships, the more individuated one feels. Yet, beneath this adaptive facade, one may be alienated and disconnected from oneself.

Fromm's description of the disconnection women and men experience within contemporary culture predated current views of the impact of gender socialization in pathology. For example, he described the alienation and fear of losing what one has and possesses that lurks beneath the facade of many men who are well adapted to their roles of socially sanctioned power and position, which carry with them a sense of isolated autonomy.

One often sees the consequence of this erupt during midlife, when failed solutions to needs for human relatedness and sense of purpose generate new conflicts and questions about one's choices in life, one's way of being. That is, the maintenance of rationalizations and other defenses is extremely draining, and often tends to unravel during midlife when the needs for authenticity, mutuality, and meaning come to the fore. Jordan (1991) states, with reference to this period, that the man may feel great anxiety about what he defines as a passive or exposed position regarding his own feelings and the other person.

Miller (1986) describes, in particular, an overall sense of isolation, different from the experience of being alone, that results from disconnection. She states that the feeling of desperate loneliness is "usually accompanied by the feeling that you, yourself, are the reason for the exclusion. It is because of who you are. And you feel helpless, powerless, unable to act to change the situation" (p. 94).

Both sexes seek to escape what Miller described as a combination of condemned isolation and powerlessness. Relationships of disconnection, then, can lead to either overt disturbance or arrested development. Each party participates in a process of making the other an object to possess or control, rather than a mutually recognized subject.

THE ROLE OF PASSIONS

Fromm's concept of passions was also a precursor of the relational perspective, in that Fromm described passions as relational by definition (Fromm 1976, 1992a,b). His description of passions like love, justice, and freedom as oriented toward development, while hate, suspicion, sadism, and so on are destructive, is foreign to conventional psychoanalytic thinking, yet congruent with the Stone Center's clinical perspectives regarding values and prac- tices that enhance mutual empowerment and health.

For example, the Stone Center model emphasizes such principles and values as love, truthfulness, and mutual respect as particularly suited to the fulfillment of human needs, and that violating them produces pathology. Fromm's argument that it is necessary to evaluate per- ceived needs in terms of whether they are conducive to growth and well-being or damaging to them is similar to Miller's discussion regarding the qualities of relationships that further healthy growth versus pathology.

Fromm argues that it is more difficult to recognize such passions as the desire for fame, power, possessions, revenge, or control as damaging because they are often adaptive and rewarded. In relational theory, such pas- sions require disconnection with others and with the world because they are rooted in possession and control, which are attempted solutions to helplessness and pow- erlessness.

The Stone Center model's portrayal of the clinical consequences of disconnection elaborates in new ways some earlier emphases of Fromm. For example, his por- trayal of the "having mode" is one of pervasive discon- nection and disengagement, which may take the form of narcissistic isolation or sadistic control. Such manifesta- tions originate from seeing the other as the object of one's own needs and desires, rather than as an equal subject, an actor within his or her own life.

THE AIMS AND METHODS OF TREATMENT

The methods and goals of psychoanalytic treatment con- stitute additional areas in which the Stone Center model is rooted in and extends many of Fromm's seminal contributions.

For example, the Stone Center model gives a key role to mutual empathy and mutual empowerment in the therapeutic process. Miller and Stiver (1993) stress the clinical importance of being empathic with strategies patients use to stay out of connection in the therapy relationship. She argues that because the process of development so often involves moving away from knowledge about the self, away from authenticity, the therapeutic process must be seen in terms of alternating connection/disconnection, and the cultivation of mutual empathy. Through repeated cycles of connection–disconnection–connection between therapist and patient, the patient brings more and more of oneself into the relationship, including aspects of thinking, feeling, and awareness that one has learned to exclude.

The paradox here is that the person has learned to practice disconnection as a means of remaining in connection—at the expense of one's sense of truth, inner reality, or self-affirmation. The process of relinquishing such strategies feels frightening, but gradually unfolds as the desire for authentic relationships awakens.

The necessity to support everything that enhances the patient's capacity for heightened awareness of truth and for critical thinking was central to Fromm. From the Stone Center perspective, this would be seen as a necessary part of recognizing the distorting, damaging effects of disconnected relationships.

Such awareness, in turn, helps generates a struggle for greater freedom by enlisting the patient's desire to confront the truth and restore the lost "voice." This is what Fromm described as the struggle between one's irrational passions and the healthy, adult passions. For Fromm, the origin of cure is in the conflict created by the two forces.

What makes the Stone Center model particularly relevant to contemporary conflicts, and further linked with
Fromm's work, is its explicit focus on the distorting effects
of gender and cultural values, and on the liberating effects
of restored connection, which can be aided through the
analytic process. This extends and deepens the implications of Fromm's work in original and unique ways.

Fromm emphasizes the importance of conveying an
absence of sham and deception to the patient, and establishing an atmosphere of truth and nonjudgmental compassion. This is congruent with the Stone Center's emphasis on the role of openness, mutuality, and respect for
the patient's connection–disconnection strategies that the
Stone Center describes. Fromm's focus here is on the
analyst's striving to experience in himself or herself what
the patient is talking about, to see the patient as a hero of
a drama, not as a collection of symptoms, a person
fighting to live and deal with the world that one experiences.

This represents one of the streams of Fromm's work
that flow directly into the perspectives of the Stone
Center, particularly the latter's emphasis on bringing into
relationship aspects of awareness that have been sub-
merged or distorted through adaptation to cultural norms.
The consequence is less concern with strengthening the
ego against the force of internal drives, or of the self-
cohesion and stability concerns of self psychology theory,
and more concern with enlisting a person's struggle between, in Fromm's language, irrational and malignant
passions, and life-affirming passions.

Both Fromm and the Stone Center model advocate the
analyst taking an explicitly value-based stance on the side
of life, affirming the patient's active struggle toward
seeing and acting upon truth, a biophilic aim oriented
toward mutuality in relations, love, and creativity.

The more radical, political aspect of both Fromm's work and the Stone Center model is present in their shared rejection of the goal of analysis being for the patient to suffer no more than the average member of one's social class. In contrast, both support the goal of becoming more human, more free, independent, and mutually related.

This necessarily involves exposing false consciousness and self-deception, within oneself and the larger society. Grey (1992) has written that by challenging the implicit values within the "pathology of normalcy" of the patient, the analyst elicits increased participation and more active sense of responsibility from the patient. The analyst attempts to achieve a connection with the patient while not becoming caught up in the patient's cover story.

This expresses much of what Miller and others have described as the process of connecting through mutual empathy with the patient, a process essentially the same as what Fromm referred to as "center-to-center" relatedness with the patient. Fromm argued that it is necessary for the analyst to enter inside the patient, while at the same time remaining himself or herself. In this sense the analytic work is a process of engagement between two subjects, who experience a center-to-center relatedness. This key concept, which generates a sense of vitality, stimulation, and aliveness within the session, illustrates, in Fromm's terms, the "being" mode, and, in the Stone Center model, the experience of mutual empathy.

THE ROLE OF THE ANALYST

A central feature of the analyst's role within the Stone Center model is dealing with one's own fear of vulnerability and desire to stay out of relationships oneself.

Practitioners may mask this by emphasizing the need to remain "objective," or seeing "overinvolvement" as leading to regression. Consistent with Fromm's emphasis on immediacy, presence, and authenticity in the analytic hour, the Stone Center model calls for recognizing the tendency of the analyst to rationalize self-protective strategies, and shift to a fuller resonating with the patient.

Miller (Miller and Stiver 1993) argues that strategies of disconnection in the patient can arouse similar strategies in the analyst. This happens particularly when the patient is moving from connection to disconnection, in which the analyst is prone to mobilize his or her own defensive strategies. The key, in Miller's view, is the therapist's being empathic with the patient's need to oscillate, without which the patient would feel out of control and alone.

Similarly, Jordan (1993) maintains that the difficulty of many analysts are rooted in their own limitations or defensiveness, which interferes with empathy and mutuality. This, in turn, reflects that the dominant culture is highly invested in isolation and in denying vulnerability. Here she underscores the political dimension of therapy, through supporting the patient's becoming aware that adaptation to the dominant culture contains a problem, to the degree one accepts dominance and "power-over" as solutions.

The Stone Center's analysis of therapeutic strategy is both congruent with and further extends Fromm's portrayal of empathic connection within the analytic hour. Though using somewhat different language, he spoke of the need to transform the analytic process from the detached observer model, in which one studies and treats an object, to interpersonal communication, grounded in the full, emotional experience of the patient.

Fromm argued that if the experience of a patient fails to strike a chord of experience within the analyst, the latter does not understand the patient. Anticipating what the Stone Center model has since elaborated upon regarding the analyst–patient relationship, Fromm emphasized that the analyst must permit him/herself to be vulnerable, and not hide behind the role of the professional who knows all the answers. At the same time the analyst must not collude with the patient's pathology through fear of confronting the truth, or through avoidance of painful material to "protect" the patient.

In this view, both analyst and patient are engaged in a common task: creating a shared understanding of the patient's experience. This must be linked with the analyst's full response to that experience. Fromm contrasts this, as does Miller and her colleagues, with the traditional model of seeing conflict as essentially a repetition of the past, and the aim of treatment as bringing infantile awareness into conflict in order to strengthen the ego to better cope with instinctual material.

The Stone Center model maintains that in order to move away from participation in violating and disconnecting relationships, one needs to experience validating and encouraging relationships, based on genuine connection. Therefore, healing can occur only when authenticity is present during treatment.

In showing the linkage between past, present, and cultural forces, Fromm argued that such experiences as powerlessness are not limited to the experience of the child. The adult is powerless also, both because of fundamental conditions of human existence and because of historical realities, such as the exploitation of the majority by an elite. For both sets of reasons, people will seek magic helpers and new idols to submit to, in order to create an illusion of security.

All of these forces contribute to the ways in which conflicts from early family relationships will present themselves in adults. Fromm's continuing emphasis on the damage to one's sense of authenticity and spontaneity that can result from struggling with irrational authority systems is similar to the Stone Center's view about the pathological consequences of learning to ignore or deny one's voice, one's recognition of truth, while growing up within a patriarchal culture.

This latter dimension, concerning the impact of power relationships upon one's potential for health or sickness, was a central pillar of Fromm's thinking. It is also an underpinning of the Stone Center model. One sees this, clinically, through the form of participation in power relationships, either through the dominant or subordinate position. Miller and her colleagues have pointed out, for example, that women are faced with undertaking a political act when attempting to heal the damage of disconnection, particularly at midlife, when the desire to restore the "lost voice" often resurfaces.

In terms of the outcome of conventional socialization that the analyst must work with, Fromm maintained that a person may achieve a range of awareness or awakeness, from a partial—based on what is necessary to win, destroy, or survive—to a more optimal awareness, which expands beyond immediate self-oriented needs to include full awareness of oneself and others. In such a relationship, one experiences heightened awareness of the moment, of the mutual stimulation that occurs. It also means experiencing feelings, not thinking about feelings.

This description is essentially what Miller and her colleagues describe regarding the growth that occurs in therapeutic work with women whose voice has been silenced and distorted by socialized unawareness. One develops heightened capacity to face life and mobilize one's inner strengths to struggle with fears. For both Fromm and the Stone Center, truth is liberating. It is nourished by mutually empathic relationships, through which one becomes freer to embrace the truth and deal with it courageously.

THE CRITERIA OF HEALTH

The Stone Center model's understanding of health shares much of the same perspective and values orientation of Fromm's. For example, Surrey (1991) describes some of the features that one finds in relationships that grow in healthy ways. Her research indicates three processes that underlie relationships of healthy connection: mutual engagement, mutual empathy, and mutual empowerment. When all three are present in relationships, specific capacities are strengthened. Miller and her colleagues have described these as a heightened sense of vitality; increased experience of empowerment, based on each individual's active presence within the moment; increased clarity of truth, derived from increased knowledge about the self and other; and increased capacity for activeness.

These qualities are quite similar to Fromm's description of the capacities of the healthy individual, qualities of the "being" mode, and with what he called the "transtherapeutic" aims of psychoanalysis, those beyond symptom relief. These goals include heightened capacity for concentration, capacity for deepening relationships, and mindfulness and clarity in interactions and in other spheres of activity.

Additionally, Fromm's emphasis on recognizing that a person's conflicts are part of an entire system, a "practice" of life, also links with the Stone Center model's emphasis on bringing into one's awareness and relationships more of one's emotional reality. The aim is developing an increasingly more authentic, integrated, aware self—a concept similar to Fromm's.

One may question how this perspective differs from any good psychoanalytic or psychotherapeutic treatment. There are three critical differences: first, it brings into therapeutic focus the dimension of the culture and gender forces that link with the patient's childhood conflicts; second, it explicitly affirms and supports human values embodied in the broader aim of the treatment to build and enhance relational connection; and third, it emphasizes integrating awareness with shift of "life practice," that is, the totality of one's attitudes, relational orientation, values, and behavior. Awareness is meaningless if it is not incorporated into one's way of being.

When Fromm argues that the sanity of normal adaptation is paid for by emotional numbness and false consciousness, he is describing the kinds of experiences that Miller and her colleagues have worked with in troubled women, whose symptoms of anger and depression are part of the price of their socialized adaptation.

Again, the political component is apparent in both. Fromm points out that family and developmentally based conflicts may exist parallel to, or even serve as a mask for, conflicts regarding integrity, authenticity, or self-interest, which derive from adaptation to adult roles and culture. Miller and her colleagues describe the latter with respect to typical expressions of women patients about their conflicts, in which they are more likely to attribute their anger in an unequal relationship to an internal defect.

The analyst can help the patient face alternatives, both those turned away from in the past and new ones in the present, that are aroused by new awareness and grounded in the experience of mutual empathy. The task of the analyst is to help the patient envision new alternatives that can awaken energies.

Fromm (1992a) gives the example of a person struggling with submission. The person must not only become aware of the developmental roots of it, and of all its qualities, forms, and experience in the present, but also work to make actual shifts in what he does, how he relates in practice, in order to become more free. As one becomes aware of the experience of nonsubmission, then one begins to practice courage in the face of it. Through the process of mutual empathy between patient and analyst, one begins to find new questions about one's condition and symptoms and seek healthier solutions with greater courage.

Helping the patient to experience the strategies of distortion and rationalization he or she adopted as a child enables the patient to envision shifts in his or her belief systems and values, away from the old, and to free up capacity for productive relationships with people and life in general. Fromm describes this in terms of confronting the sick part of the patient with the healthy part, the infantile with the adult.

In discussing Fromm's perspectives on treatment, Biancoli (1992) points out that certain forms of sickness in relation to the social structure may indicate the disobedience of the healthy and hidden part of the person, which has not found any other way of affirmation. This also describes how the relational model interprets pathology in terms of failed or thwarted forms of connection within early relationships, which can be repeated throughout adulthood. The healthy capacity for relationship is expressed in damaged form through the symptom, and this can be understood more fully by looking at the relational systems of the patient.

In his many respectful critiques of Freud's work, Fromm often reminded his readers that "from the shoulders of a giant, one can see farther than the giant." This is a good description of Fromm's own legacy with respect to the relational theory I have discussed in this chapter.

The major pillars of the Stone Center relational model rest, in my view, on many of the original psychoanalytic and sociobiological contributions of Fromm. From this foundation, the relational perspective in general and the Stone Center model in particular are extending and deepening a new vision of healing emotional damage and broadening the possibilities for human growth in contemporary culture.

REFERENCES

Benjamin, J. (1988). *The Bonds of Love*. New York: Pantheon.

Biancoli, R. (1992). Radical humanism in psychoanalysis. *Contemporary Psychoanalysis* 28:695–730.

Brown, L., and Gilligan, C. (1992). *Meeting at the Crossroads*. Cambridge, MA: Harvard University Press.

Fromm, E. (1947). *Man for Himself*. New York: Rinehart.

_____ (1955). *The Sane Society*. New York: Rinehart.

_____ (1956). *The Art of Loving*. New York: Harper & Row.

_____ (1970). Freud's model of man and its social determinants. In *The Crisis of Psychoanalysis*. New York: Holt, Rinehart & Winston.

_____ (1976). *To Have or To Be?* New York: Harper & Row.

_____ (1980). *Greatness and Limitations of Freud's Thought*. New York: Harper & Row.

_____ (1992a). *The Art of Being*. New York: Continuum.

_____ (1992b). *The Revision of Psychoanalysis*. Boulder, CO: Westview.

Gilligan, C. (1982). *In a Different Voice*. Cambridge, MA: Harvard University Press.

Gilligan, C., Lyons, N., and Hanmer, T., eds. (1990). *Making Connections*. Cambridge, MA: Harvard University Press.

Gilligan, C., Rogers, A., and Tolman, D., eds. (1991). *Women, Girls, and Psychotherapy*. Cambridge, MA: Harvard University Press.

Grey, A. (1992). Society as Destiny. *Contemporary Psychoanalysis* 28:344–363.

Jordan, J. V. (1991). The meaning of mutuality. In *Women's Growth in Connection*, ed. J. V. Jordan, A. G. Kaplan, J. B. Miller, et al., pp. 81–96. New York: Guilford.

_____ (1993). *Challenges to connection: the traumatizing society.* Lecture presentation, Harvard Medical School Conference, "Learning from Women," Boston, April 30.

Jordan, J. V., Kaplan, A. G., Miller, J. B., et al., eds. (1991). *Women's Growth in Connection.* New York: Guilford.

Kohut, H. (1984). *How Does Analysis Cure?* Chicago: University of Chicago Press.

LaBier, D. (1986). *Modern Madness.* Reading, MA: Addison-Wesley.

Miller, J. B. (1976). *Toward a New Psychology of Women*, 2nd ed. Boston: Beacon, 1986.

_____ (1988). *Connections, Disconnections, and Violations.* Work in progress, no. 33. Wellesley, MA: Stone Center Working Paper Series.

Miller, J. B., and Stiver, I. (1993). *The therapy connection.* Lecture presentation, Harvard Medical School Conference, "Learning from Women," Boston, May 1.

Mitchell, S. A. (1988). *Relational Concepts in Psychoanalysis.* Cambridge, MA: Harvard University Press.

Surrey, J. L. (1991). The self-in-relation: a theory of women's development. In *Women's Growth in Connection*, ed. J. V. Jordan, A. G. Kaplan, J. B. Miller, et al., pp. 51–66. New York: Guilford.

II

THE CLINICAL ENCOUNTER

8

Fromm's Clinical Practice: Insight or New Experience?

Marco Bacciagaluppi

Hirsch (1987) lists two essential therapeutic factors: insight and the experience of a new relationship. In my paper on Fromm's technique (Bacciagaluppi 1989) I remarked that "there is something paradoxical in Fromm's discussion of this subject" (p. 241). Fromm differs sharply from Freud on the role of the analyst, and advocates an attitude of active and empathic participation on the part of the analyst. Yet, following the classical tradition, he stresses insight as an essential therapeutic factor, although, to be sure, his view of insight is much wider than the classical one (Bacciagaluppi 1989). "His insistence on direct, 'core-to-core' relatedness implies that the patient's experience of a new relationship with the analyst would inevitably become the second major factor in a Frommian analysis. Yet, Fromm never discussed this factor in theoretical terms" (pp. 241–242).

Following Hoffman (1983) and Hirsch (1987), I suggested three groupings of analysts according to the degree of their participation (Bacciagaluppi 1989): (1) orthodox Freudians, characterized only by observation aimed at insight, with two qualifications—the therapeutic alliance and countertransference; (2) analysts characterized by observation and by what Greenberg (1981) calls "participation with," namely an empathic participation; and (3) analysts characterized by the recognition and use of what Greenberg calls "participation in," which implies an inevitable confirmation of the patient's negative expectations. Thus, there is a discrepancy between Fromm's traditional theoretical view according to which insight is the most important therapeutic aim, which would place him in the first category of analysts, and his clinical practice, which shows a high degree of empathic participation, thus providing the patient with the experience of a new relationship and placing Fromm in the second category of analysts.

In other respects, there is an opposite discrepancy between Fromm's theory and practice (Burston 1991), that between his advanced theoretical formulations and his alleged classical practice, at least prior to 1955. I recently discussed a third discrepancy, in terms of a contrast between certain very advanced theoretical formulations of Fromm's, which actually place him in the third category of analysts, and his clinical practice, which places him in the second (Bacciagaluppi 1993). I shall limit myself to discussing the first discrepancy, that between the theoretical stress on insight and the practical emphasis on a new relationship. I shall stress the importance of the new experience provided by the analyst. I shall also show that the new experience is seldom entirely new. Often, we find in the patient's past a "weak precursor" (Hoffman 1983) of the therapeutic experience.

CASE MATERIAL

One example of the first discrepancy is provided by a 1964 lecture of Fromm's, which I edited and which was recently published both in *Contemporary Psychoanalysis* (Fromm 1991a) and in the German edition of Fromm's posthumous works (Fromm 1991b), and which contains one of Fromm's very rare clinical accounts (see postscript).

The case is that of a Mexican woman of 25, whose presenting symptom is homosexuality. She has an affair with another woman who, according to Fromm, "treats her abominably," but the patient is afraid of being abandoned and submits to the relationship. She is the illegitimate daughter of a rich man and his mistress. The father was never present. The mother, says Fromm, "was an utterly scheming mother who only used this little girl to get money out of the father." The mother's sister was the owner of a brothel who tried to induce the little girl into prostitution. Then, when the patient was 15, the father, "in one of his whims," sent her to college in the United States. There she met a girl who was affectionate to her, and they started a homosexual affair. Fromm finds that "a girl so frightened, with a past like that, would start a sexual affair with anyone . . . who shows real affection; it's the first time that she gets out of a hell." The patient eventually moved to a heterosexual position and got married.

Fromm, in Ferenczi's tradition, quotes this case as an example of the importance of trauma as a real-life experience. "The trauma is something which happens in the environment, which is a life experience, a real-life experience" (Fromm 1991a, p. 589). I would like to remark that this Ferenczian emphasis on real-life events is matched in Great Britain by John Bowlby, "Psychoanalytic Champion of 'Real-Life Experience,' " as Christopher Fortune (1991) titles an interview with Bowlby.

In his presentation, Fromm shows great warmth and sympathy for his patient, as he presumably showed to the patient herself during therapy. He thus seems to have followed in the footsteps of Ferenczi, who, according to Fromm's (1980–1981, originally published in Suzuki et al. 1960) account in his book on Zen, held that the analyst "had to be able to love a patient with the very love which the patient had needed as a child" (p. 111).

However, as an example of the discrepancy between Fromm's empathic participation in practice and his theoretical emphasis on insight, in this lecture Fromm (1991a) repeats his theoretical emphasis on insight: "For me the essence of analytic cure lies in the very conflict engendered by the meeting of the irrational and the rational part of the personality" (p. 591). Instead, the personality of the analyst is listed as the last of seven other factors. To be sure, in this connection Fromm calls for a capacity for empathy: "If one doesn't experience this as one's own, then I don't think one understands it." On the other hand, he seems to downplay the role of the analyst when he compares him/her merely to "a good mountain guide" (p. 598).

In the debate "over whether insight or a new experience with the psychoanalyst is the primary mutative agent in psychoanalysis" (Hirsch 1987, p. 205), a range of views is held. In this connection the most balanced view is probably that of Merton Gill (1983), who holds that "every interpretation is also an intervention," and that "both insight and new experience play a role in bringing about change in psychoanalysis" (p. 233). Fromm seems to uphold the first factor in theory and the second in practice.

THE "WEAK PRECURSOR"

I suggest that Fromm's case also allows a step forward to be taken in this debate. In the literature, the mutative

factor alternative to insight is always called a "new experience," but, in my view, it is seldom entirely new.
Hoffman (1983) recognizes this possibility when he speaks
of "weak precursors in the patient's history that were not
pathogenic but rather growth promoting" (p. 419). In
Fromm's case, I suggest that the patient's father may be
viewed as such a weak precursor when he sent his
daughter to college. In his fatherly role he was weak
because he was personally distant, but he did provide the
patient with an important alternative experience—a necessary, if not sufficient, condition for her further development. The effect of the weak precursor had to be confirmed and extended by Fromm's therapeutic intervention
in a warm parental role, although he does not make this
explicit.

Fromm does not recognize any merit to the patient's
father, and actually downplays the father's contribution
by saying that he sent his daughter to college "in one of his
whims." There may be a special reason for this neglect.
Although Fromm does not make his own parental role
explicit, there may be a retrospective jealousy at work
here, and the wish to be the only one to take the credit for
the patient's well-being. We are all prone to these narcissistic temptations, and have to be aware of them and
overcome them, but it may be especially useful to do so in
order to be on the lookout for weak precursors and give
them their due recognition, thus strengthening their influence.

Following Hoffman (1983), I suggest that the existence
of an alternative good relationship in the patient's past
may be an important therapeutic factor. In my experience,
there is a range of possibilities in this connection. At one
extreme, the patient may be conscious of this alternative
relationship and mention it from the start. At the other,
the patient may not be aware of it, and it may remain

hidden for a long time. I shall give an example of each of these extremes.

ORIGINAL CASE MATERIAL

Case 1

This is an example of the first extreme, in which the patient is aware of the weak precursor from the start. This patient was a 40-year-old married woman at the beginning of treatment. When the patient was a child her father used to beat her severely, and she hated him. When she was 15 years old the father committed suicide, as his own mother had done before him. The patient's mother never did anything to prevent the father's beatings. On her side, the mother was ashamed of the patient when she was born because she was hairy. The only supportive figure in the patient's childhood was the maternal grandmother, who was sympathetic but ineffective in preventing the father's beatings. After the father's death the patient had a psychotic breakdown and for some years was in analytic treatment, in which she greatly improved. She graduated from school and became very creative in her field. She married early. The husband was a sadistic man who had affairs with other women and was resentful of his wife's creativity.

At the start of therapy, the image of the grandmother, who had been dead some years, was present to an almost hallucinatory degree. She often appeared in the patient's dreams, and, when in distress, the patient would imagine talking to the grandmother and being comforted by her. As therapy proceeded, the presence of the grandmother gradually subsided.

A basic interaction took place between the patient and me at the very start. At the end of our first meeting I made a slip and marked the next appointment on my calendar one week in advance of the actual date. I obviously liked her and wanted to see her sooner. I told her of my slip a few months later. I viewed it as belonging to an alternative line of development in her life history—a minority set of good relationships, which, before me, comprised her grandmother and her first analyst.

In her fourth year of therapy, after separating from her husband, the patient reported the following dream: "My father was relaxed. From behind the wallpaper, which was peeling off, appeared two old photographs of my grand-mother. My father (who was a keen photographer) says he will make new prints of the photos for me." I told her that she sees me performing a fatherly role in an alternative way, and that this reactivates the good parental image of the grand-mother. This dream marks a change in what Bowlby (1969) calls internal working models.

Case 2

This is an example of the second extreme, in which the weak precursor lies hidden and only emerges after a long time. Again, this case shows a history of physical abuse. In contrast to the first case, the memory of the abuse, like that of the weak helper, emerged only after a long time.

After some years of treatment, this patient, a 35-year-old unmarried woman at the beginning of therapy, told me that when as a child she was alone with her mother, her restless-ness used to irritate the mother. "Once she nearly killed me," she said smiling, "by beating me with a slipper." I remarked that although she now smiled, she must have been very frightened at the time. In the next session she had what she called a "horrid vision" of a woman being killed by being beaten with a wooden clog—an incident she had read about in the newspaper. In the next session I revealed a situation from my own life: I told her that as a child also I had been confronted by my mother's outbursts of rage. This proved to be what Arnold Rachman (1993) calls "judicious self-disclosure," because the patient was stimulated to recall a typical example of a weak precursor. She said that there was a neighbor who used to try to restrain her mother, but to no avail, since she was small and suffered from a weak heart. In my self-disclosure I presented myself as a fellow victim, a sympathetic but ineffective helper; but this reactivated the memory of the original weak helper.

In the ensuing months her working model of a mother gradually changed. Maybe recalling the weak helper had a positive effect in leading the patient to search for a strong helper in the present. She at first recalled an ambivalent mother figure, namely her pediatrician, who on the one hand protected her from an unnecessary tonsillectomy, but on the other used to threaten to cut off her hands if she insisted on biting her nails. Finally, she dreamed of a sturdy colleague who had an invalid husband and used to envy the patient her freedom, but since her husband's death had been on entirely friendly terms with her. I remarked that this at last was an alternative female figure who was neither weak nor ambivalent.

DISCUSSION

The weak precursor gives rise to positive expectations, which are initially in the minority as compared to the prevailing negative expectations. A continuity between a positive experience with the therapist and the alternative experience in the past may emerge only after much testing of the therapist on the patient's part, and, maybe, only after the therapist has failed the test and made mistakes, following Gill's (1983) third principle of the transference, according to which, sooner or later, we inevitably confirm the patient's negative expectations.

This may actually be the most effective therapeutic experience of all. Maybe, the alternative experience only emerges fully after the analyst has fallen into the trap, has then acknowledged it, and has worked his/her way out, as Levenson (1972) says, or "participated in," as Greenberg (1981) says.

On the strength of these two cases, I find that this therapeutic pattern, however, is not inevitable. My response in the first case I reported above was to a positive expectation that the patient brought into therapy. This was based on an alternative set of positive experiences, in particular that with the first analyst, which was specifically reactivated when the patient started on a second analytical experience. In Fromm's case report, he confirmed and strengthened a positive expectation that came from the patient's experience with her father. In Fromm's case and in my first case, the analyst identified with a positive parental figure. There was thus a direct strengthening of the weak precursor. In my second case, I primarily identified with the patient herself, which seems to have indirectly led to the same result.

The response of the analysts in all these cases was an example of what Greenberg (1981) calls "participation with." However, Gill's (1983) third principle of the transference, and Sandler's (1976) concept of role-responsiveness, can still be applied in a more general form. Provided weak precursors were included in the patient's experience, the patient's expectations will be both positive and negative. If we confirm the negative expectations, we shall provide an experience of "participation in." If we confirm the positive expectations, we shall provide an experience of "participation with." In both cases we change the past. In one case, we reproduce the original mistakes, acknowledge them, and remedy them. In the other case, we strengthen the original weak helper.

CONCLUSION

The concept of "participation in" had already been anticipated by Ferenczi (1933) when he stated that to admit our
mistakes creates in the patient a confidence in the analyst.
He went on to say that "it is this confidence that establishes the contrast between the present and the unbearable traumatogenic past" (p. 160). I suggest that in the
recognition of "participation in" and in the provision of
"participation with" there is not only a contrast with the
prevailing past negative experience, but also a strengthening of the weak precursor—not only a new experience,
but also the strengthening of a minority positive experience in the past. In Fromm's case, in particular, the
mutative factor seems to have been not primarily insight,
but a new experience strengthening an earlier positive,
although incomplete, experience.

I believe, however, that these detached formulations
miss the essence of the therapeutic interaction. I suggest
that what happened in these cases corresponds to
Fromm's (1947) definition of motherly love, which "is
unconditional, based only upon the child's request and
the mother's response" (p. 106). This description may be
regarded as the essence of an ethological definition of
love, based on parental caregiving behavior. This is the
love that as Ferenczi said and Fromm restated, the patient
had needed as a child.

POSTSCRIPT

After having presented this work, I was informed by Dr.
Sonia Gojman, of the Mexican Psychoanalytic Institute,
that the patient discussed in Fromm's lecture was not

treated by Fromm himself, but by Dr. Eduardo Zajur, who published the case in 1974. I am grateful to Dr. Gojman for the information, and must apologize for my faulty reading of Fromm's lecture. I find, however, that the correction does not belie my remarks on Fromm's warm attitude toward the patient and his downplaying of the father's role. It does confirm that Fromm left practically no record of his own clinical practice. It is possible that my faulty reading was unconsciously directed by the hope that I had discovered one such record.

REFERENCES

Bacciagaluppi, M. (1989). Erich Fromm's views on psychoanalytic "technique." *Contemporary Psychoanalysis* 25:226–243.

_____ (1993). Ferenczi's influence on Fromm. In *The Legacy of Sandor Ferenczi*, ed. L. Aron and A. Harris. Hillsdale, NJ and London: Analytic Press.

Bowlby, J. (1969). *Attachment and Loss, vol. 1, Attachment.* New York: Basic Books and London: Hogarth.

Burston, D. (1991). *The Legacy of Erich Fromm.* Cambridge, MA and London: Harvard University Press.

Ferenczi, S. (1933). Confusion of tongues between adults and the child. In *Final Contributions to the Problems and Methods of Psycho-Analysis*, ed. M. Balint. London: Karnac, 1980.

Fortune, C. (1991). Psychoanalytic champion of "real-life experience": an interview with John Bowlby. *Melanie Klein and Object Relations* 9:70–86.

Fromm, E. (1947). *Man for Himself.* New York: Fawcett, 1975.

_____ (1980–81). *Gesamtausgabe*, ed. R. Funk. Stuttgart: Deutsche Verlags-Anstalt.

_____ (1991a). Causes for the patient's change in analytic treatment. *Contemporary Psychoanalysis* 27:581–602.

_____ (1991b). Wirkfaktoren der psychoanalytischen Behandlung. In *Von der Kunst des Zuhörens. Therapeutische Aspekte der*

Psychoanalyse, ed. R. Funk. Weinheim/Basel: Beltz.

Gill, M. M. (1983). The interpersonal paradigm and the degree of the therapist's involvement. *Contemporary Psychoanalysis* 19:200–237.

Greenberg, J. R. (1981). Prescription or description: therapeutic action of psychoanalysis. *Contemporary Psychoanalysis* 17:239–257.

Hirsch, I. (1987). Varying modes of analytic participation. *Journal of the American Academy of Psychoanalysis* 15:205–222.

Hoffman, I. Z. (1983). The patient as interpreter of the analyst's experience. *Contemporary Psychoanalysis* 19:389–422.

Levenson, E. (1972). *The Fallacy of Understanding*. New York: Basic Books.

Rachman, A. W. (1993). *Judicious self-disclosure by the psychoanalyst*. Presented at The Fourth International Conference of the Sandor Ferenczi Society, "The Talking Therapy: Ferenczi and the Psychoanalytic Vocation," Budapest, July 18–21.

Sandler, J. (1976). Countertransference and role-responsiveness. *International Review of Psycho-Analysis* 3:43–47.

Suzuki, D. T., Fromm, E., and De Martino, R. (1960). *Zen Buddhism and Psychoanalysis*. New York: Grove, 1963.

Zajur, E. (1974). Un caso de seudo-homosexualidad femenina. *Revista de Psicoanálisis Psiquiatria y Psicologia* 4:14–36.

9

The Analyst as a Person: Fromm's Approach to Psychoanalytic Training and Practice

Sonia Gojman

Each situation is different, each child is a world, and each teacher should learn something new every day.

Martin Buber

From the relational perspective of psychoanalysis (Greenberg and Mitchell 1983, 1993) our role as analysts is no longer seen as one of a neutral expert who applies technical methods to discover the unconscious striving of our patients. Rather, the analyst is recognized as an active participant in the treatment process, as an important factor in its affective development and in the attainment of its goals. The analyst's values and personal attitudes color the mutual relationship as much as the patient's.

Our role as therapists in the analytic process has been increasingly emphasized (Casement 1985, Gill 1982) by referring to our own feelings as useful tools.[1] These feelings are no longer seen exclusively as countertransferential distortions, but also as an affective resource. Becoming aware of our own feelings can help us understand the patient (Balint and Balint 1961, Peterfreund 1971). Some authors explain this emotional resonance of the analyst as an "intersubjective phenomenon" (Natterson 1991, Stolorow and Atwood 1992) that is accessible only through each person's own inner experiences and sensitivity.

Many of Fromm's criticisms of orthodox technical methods (Evans 1966, Fromm 1935, 1968, 1974, 1979) show him to be well ahead of his time, an important forerunner, of these relational views. As early as 1935 Fromm discussed the relationship between analyst and patient as essential in understanding the deeper meaning of the communication developed between them. The actual, "here and now" relationship is always interwoven with the patient's past.

The subtle interpersonal events occurring between the analyst and the patient, mutually observing each other, must be taken into account to understand how and to what extent they can be utilized by the patient in the phenomenon of transference. Our attention to our own feelings helps us understand the patient. This means, in Fromm's terms, recognizing our "participant-observer" role (Fromm et al. 1960) in the treatment process. But Fromm's recognition of such an active, intimately related role needed extensive clinical examples such as those provided by Casement (1985), Gill (1982), and Mitchell (1993), in order to have a thorough understanding of the mutual process involved.

As I will try to show, in Fromm's earliest articles and later in his clinical seminars in México and New York, he rejected many technical prescriptions on the grounds that they were not focused on the actual content of the analytical relationship. Because of Fromm's having more fully understood the unique interactional context and complexity for each treatment, these considerations have become important in current discussions of psychoanalytic technique (Bollas 1992, Gill 1994, Lippmann, Chapter 4 in this volume). The open recognition of this complexity saves clinicians from having to conceive of ourselves as "infallible experts" and frees us from the burden of our longings for certainty.

Some critics of Fromm's clinical approach (Burston 1991, Maccoby 1982) do not fully appreciate this complex perspective that supports Fromm's approach. Maccoby, for example, criticizes Fromm's technical approach for not having built on Freud's detailed technical recommendations. Maccoby argues that Fromm's failure to analyze the transference originates in a model of "productivity" that describes not a real character but rather an "ideal" to be pursued. According to Maccoby, Fromm's value system interferes with his ability to analyze an idealizing transference, a fact that inevitably limits the patient's autonomy.

I agree that Fromm contradicts himself by supporting a modest and self-critical attitude by the analyst and at the same time adopting the role of an "expert" (see Margolies's discussion in Chapter 15). But not analyzing resistance and transference carefully and imposing the analyst's values are analytic failures that are not just the result of a theoretical contradiction. These failures are also experiential realities that become enacted with the patient whenever we are not aware of our own participation in the analytic process. Moreover, failures in analyzing a patient's idealization are a common difficulty with practitioners from all orientations and are not exclusive to Fromm's clinical approach.

Idealization by our patients and difficulties in analyzing transference can today be more easily recognized and understood by focusing in our countertransferential reactions. This countertransference involves our own feelings and reactions to our patients. We also need to explore with the patient the impact of our personality and how our analytical position is experienced by the patient. Difficulties in analyzing transference and patients' idealizations interfere with treatment when (and while) we are unable to understand the patients' own perspective and until we become aware of their nonverbal messages. These complex messages can also be understood as "projective identifications" (Casement 1985).

Fromm's approach to psychoanalytic practice and training was not aimed at an intellectual transmission of external knowledge, but rather at the awakening within the analyst of a meaningful, honest, and profound interest in the patient (Aramoni 1970, Millán and Gojman 1981). For Fromm this meant that as clinicians we must develop the capacity to be aware of ourselves, to realize and recognize how we participate in the treatment process. We must not be deceived by the desire to eliminate personal characteristics from the relationship with the patient by use of technical means.

Ferenczi, tragically and prematurely, tried to develop an "active" technique that would acknowledge our essential role in the analytical process, and Fromm tried to build on this legacy (Forest 1954). This tradition has continued to grow with the contributions of Casement (1985), Gill (1994), Hirsch (1994), and Mitchell (1993), among others. Supported by extensive clinical material, these authors point out the importance of becoming aware of ourselves and how we relate to the patient during the psychoanalytic process. This awareness expands our capacity to analyze the transference.

Fromm's self-critical and sociopsychoanalytic approach offers an alternative model of clinical work that has been

taken to its logical conclusion by contemporary intersubjective (Natterson 1991, Stolorow et al. 1987) and relational
approaches (Gill 1994, Hirsch 1994, Mitchell 1993).[2] Indeed, a nonprescriptive approach to technique is precisely
the view that is most consistent with the core of Fromm's
theoretical, clinical and educational contributions.

Fromm went beyond current relational perspectives
with his view that demystifying awareness must also
recognize the full impact of the social systems to which we
and our patients are compelled to adapt.[3] The social,
self-critical, and nonprescriptive approach to technique
also emphasizes sensitive, careful attention to the patient,
including the patient's legitimate *observer* role, which may
be of immense help in demystifying the technical illusion
of the "neutral" knower.[4]

REPRESSION AND RESISTANCE

In 1935, Fromm developed his earliest critique of orthodox
psychoanalytic technique (the article was published only
in German and Italian). Fromm thinks that the main origin
of repression is not intrapsychic; rather, it is driven by
anxiety produced by external forces, namely the fear of
losing the love of important figures and the fear of
isolation from social supports, leading to ostracism.

A repressed impulse, Fromm explains, does not cease to
exist as such, but rather its access to consciousness is
thwarted. The mechanism by which this is accomplished
is called "resistance." Every time the repressed material is
touched upon, resistance appears, and its power depends
on the strength with which it is repressed. If resistance
appears in the analysis of a person, the analyst has,
according to Freud, a proof that unconscious material is

being touched upon. The intensity of the resistance, however, does not always indicate that important thera- peutic results will be achieved. There are occasions when resistance is so strong as to be impossible for the patient to overcome.

Being an unconscious process, says Fromm, resistance is not a question of the patient having difficulty "saying" the things that occur to him—a difficulty gradually over- come as the patient's willingness to change increases—but rather a process of which the patient is not aware. Through the psychoanalytic process the patient revives the original childhood relationship with the authority that caused the repression. The patient "transfers" to the analyst the anxiety that led to the repression of the impulse. Here Fromm follows the classical psychoanalytic model closely. A friendly, objective, and nonjudgmental attitude on the part of the analyst will support the gradual development of the patient's confidence. This confidence is necessary to overcome the resistance and become con- scious of the repressed impulse during the treatment process.

From a purely Freudian, intrapsychic point of view, it is assumed that the result of the treatment depends essen- tially on the strength of the resistance presented by the patient. It is here that the emphasis of Fromm, and the whole relational perspective, differs so greatly from Freud. Fromm criticizes Freud's scheme for not taking into account more centrally the actual relationship between patient and analyst. Fromm believed this actual relation- ship is enormously important in determining the outcome of treatment. The anxiety, anchored in the past, can become greater or lesser, largely depending on the specific personal characteristics of the analyst and the nature of the relationship between analyst and patient.[5] The freer the analyst is of condemnatory attitudes concerning the

patient's unconventional acts or tendencies, and the more
he establishes himself as wholeheartedly interested in the
search for the patient's happiness, the sooner the patient's
resistance will yield. This was for Fromm the basic factor
in psychoanalytic treatment, in the training of psychoanalysts, and in the supervision of cases handled by students
in training.[6]

The adherence to technical guidelines or conscious
beliefs about what would be helpful, was, according to
Fromm, much less important than the attributes the
analyst brought into treatment as well as the socially
determined character traits of the analyst. The character
required for an effective clinical practice is one that includes a certain independence from the conventionalism
and taboos of the time. There exists, according to Fromm,
the possibility of accepting things as they are, yet transcending them and establishing a critical distance from
common attitudes. Social restrictions can then appear for
what they are—only means to maintain a certain social
order and its contradictory class relations that deprive
men and women of their own authority (Gojman 1983).[7]
Recognizing the power of compelling social tendencies
may allow the discovery that social norms are not absolute.

Acknowledging the historical justifications for certain
moral standards through critical study of social systems
(and understanding the power structures involved in
them) can produce a change in our own attitude toward
human beings. Our reactions and affects can cease to be
automatic and abstract. Indeed, critically understanding
these power structures can lead, according to Fromm, to
recognizing the obstacles that keep us from developing
the solidarity and support that a successful treatment
requires.

An analyst who is not so free and open mentally,

however intelligent or well trained, will repeat the experience that the patient originally went through with his parents when he was a child, and later on with teachers and other oppressive figures. In other words, the analyst will permit the repetition of authoritarian constellations that inhibit development.

THE PERSON OF THE ANALYST AS THE CENTRAL AXIS IN CLINICAL PRACTICE

More than thirty years after Fromm's 1935 article, in his clinical seminars with students in México (1968), he attempted to clarify the technical questions of clinical practice. He emphasized anew that the person of the analyst is the central axis in clinical practice. What is really important is the analyst's vitality, his capacity for enjoyment, and ability to be unconventional and to promote without restriction the patient's striving for happiness.

To "jump inside the patient" as Fromm puts it (Aramoni 1983, Fromm 1968, Narvaez 1981), is only possible if one knows oneself; only then can we establish intimate contact with another person and understand what is happening to the patient from his or her own vantage point. The analyst may thus discover within the patient aspects that the patient is ignorant of or unable to articulate.[8] Treatment is thus posed as a dialogue between two unconsciouses. In this process analysts must become aware of their active participation in the treatment in order to help develop the patient's own resources and overcome resistances. This is only achievable with a genuinely egalitarian attitude. We take the responsibility for this search, according to Fromm, together with the patient. Analysts must be alert to their own resistance to helping the process along as a first step toward a successful outcome.

This self-questioning role should be nurtured during psychoanalytic training, avoiding the temptation to fall back on an illusory scientific technique. According to Fromm, we must abandon longings for certainty in doing the right thing or of thinking we are better informed than the patient on what they should believe about themselves or about the analyst. This also includes giving up any certainty concerning what patients should or shouldn't do with their lives, and when they should terminate treatment.[9]

Fromm (1968) spelled out some of the problems involved in applying technical rules. *Free association* Fromm observes, was originally proposed as a means to penetrate the unconscious by sidestepping the frame of reference of logical, rational, and conventional thought. However, says Fromm, it can also do the opposite by permitting the patient to talk ad infinitum about trivia that lead to nothing, thus reinforcing resistance. The analyst may also misuse technique to rationalize passivity, laziness, or avoidance of difficult problems.

The use of the couch can also, according to Fromm (1968, 1974), present problems. Keeping the patient from seeing the analyst was used by Freud as a means to prevent the patient from observing the analyst's reactions, assuring the analyst's neutrality. As Fromm sees it, this technique may in fact only increase the patient's curiosity about the analyst and, as in pornography, stimulate the patient's desire to know more about the analyst than otherwise would have been the case. At the same time the couch does not prevent the patient (unless he or she is extremely disturbed) from getting to know who the analyst really is and how he or she reacts. A significant communication can only be established by being intimately in contact with another person (Evans 1966).

The common practice of interpreting the patient's hos-

tility toward the analyst as being motivated by "transferential distortions," may also, says Fromm (1968), be a
veiled threat from the analyst to the patient, a subtle
warning (to the patient) that she or he must stop. These
defensive interpretations curtail the full manifestation of
the hostility and the possibility of being able to analyze
it.[10] Fromm (1968) also believed that to invoke resistance
every time the patient appears to be uncooperative can be
a subtle way of coercing the patient into compliance.

Schafer (1992) reaches a similar conclusion, noting that
Freud's clinical interventions, couched in a martial language, reflected a countertransferential problem. What is
really expected from the patient-enemy's "cooperation" is
unconditional surrender. The patient must submit to what
the analyst says is wrong with him, for ostensibly patients
are incapable of developing their own criteria for what is
best for them. By means of this countertransferential
communication, the patient is led to believe that only the
analyst can recognize what the patient does not know and
what is going on in his unconscious. Yet consciously,
analyst and patient may hold an opposite belief. Moreover, if a patient does not give in and accept the interpretations, the analyst concludes that resistance has made its
appearance. In this warlike countertransference vision of
Freud, the analyst cannot count on the patient as an ally in
the process of gaining insight and overcoming resistance.

According to Fromm, amiability and tact are required
elements for a good analyst. A prolonged silence may be
experienced by the patient as an unnecessary torment. A
detached and objective attitude may come across as cold
and uncaring. Fromm also noted that genetic interpretations and continual references to the past might also be a
resistance on the part of the analyst to seeing how and
why the symptoms are sustained in the present.

Fromm's approach reflects an attitude of respect for the

ability and rights of patients to express their own inner worlds in their own language, to make sense out of them through the analytic process, and make decisions about their own lives based on a deep comprehension and relief of symptoms. This respect has to be granted to the patient, according to Fromm, without concealing it beneath rules and technical jargon. Furthermore, the meaning of any given technique depends ultimately on who uses it, how it is used, and whether we like it or not (Fromm 1968). Depending on our own attitude, we may use techniques as a resource to carry out a significant investigation or as a self-deceiving tool that favors resistance.

Techniques in conventional analysis can in fact be used to defend power relations and class interests rather than to question them. Our profound interest in the patient, says Fromm, implies a building, synthesizing, and searching dialogue to discover different paths leading to therapeutic solutions (Aramoni 1988). This is a far cry from the neutral and detached stance of the classical analyst.

PSYCHOANALYTIC TRAINING

Fromm never finished writing his own technical advice for psychoanalytic practice, but in his clinical seminars Fromm (1964, 1968) frequently examined the many different ways in which the analyst can make inappropriate use of technique. He criticized technical prescriptions because they distracted from what he considered to be the real psychoanalytic task—understanding the patient's unconscious motivation from within and discovering new possibilities of bringing about change.

The most important element in psychoanalytic training is to get first-hand personal experience by practicing and

monitoring the process involved. This process has been
described by Casement (1985) as "internal supervision and
trail identification" and can be a valuable tool that leads
the way to greater understanding during difficult moments in the treatment process. In fact, power struggles
and other serious difficulties between analysts and patients often precede a profound insight. These difficulties
are frequently a manifestation of the well-established
transference and represent the patient's ways of effectively reviving original traumatic experiences. Sandler's
(1976) concept of "role responsiveness" identifies the
emotional atunement required by analysts during a therapeutic impasse.

Fromm did not develop an explicit "technique" that
would help analysts use their emotional responsiveness to
further treatment goals. But his rejection of a prescriptive
technique and his discussion of an analytic attitude appropriate to the task of understanding the patient are clearly
consistent with Casement's and Sandler's concepts. Some
of the criticisms of Fromm's clinical practice (Burston 1991,
Maccoby 1982) can now be addressed from a more fully
developed conception of a nonprescriptive technique that
was implicit earlier in Fromm's (1968) Cuernavaca seminars.

From this perspective of psychoanalytic treatment, it
becomes essential to be able to relate to another person in
a close, intimate way, to be affectively in contact and
recognize each other's feelings (Crowley 1952) (the analyst's as well as the patient's). It follows that a good
psychoanalytic training would seek to develop, to a considerable extent, precisely this capacity. This relational
capacity, to be effective, must engage both participants in
a mutual and profound dialogue. Instead of offering a
prescriptive technique, Fromm's most important aim was
to sensitize analytic candidates and practitioners to the

actual processes, through their own treatment, the supervision of clinical cases, and in seminars oriented to achieving a descriptive account of the psychoanalytic process.

A basic premise of most programs in psychoanalytic education is that the psychoanalysis of the trainee (the so-called didactic analysis) will bring about the competence and capacities mentioned above through the self-knowledge obtained in treatment. Most training institutions do not take into account, however, how much the two participants in the therapeutic relationship are involved in the educational life of the institution and how this affects the real psychoanalytic setting. Furthermore, there is a tendency for students to see their didactic analysis as a part of the curriculum requirements, altering the whole motivational scheme of analysis. This is particularly the case when the analysis is undertaken as one of the conditions for enrollment (Bernfeld 1962).

Most of the technical prescriptions that facilitate the process of transference in psychoanalytic treatment insist on the neutrality of the training analyst. This neutrality is supposed to facilitate the analyst's role as a blank screen on which the patient can project his transferred relations with the authority figures of his childhood. As Fromm saw it, this ideal is never met in any regular analyses and is even more evidently absent during didactic analyses because of the frequent encounters between analysts and candidates outside of treatment. I believe these encounters and the reactions they engender—on both participants—can and should be acknowledged and examined more openly. Didactic analysts must begin to take these encounters seriously as they unfold in the educational setting. Awareness of the participative nature of the analytic process is essential for establishing a solid therapeutic alliance. By acknowledging these extraanalytical encounters the patient-student and the didactic analyst will be able to distinguish more clearly the degree and extent to which these encounters are influenced by transference–countertransference reactions.

Unfortunately, in most psychoanalytic institutes these encounters are either ignored or at best acknowledged as inevitable interferences with the treatment process. Didactic analysts ambivalently struggle, trying to perform their difficult and at times irreconcilable roles of teacher, supervisor, and analyst. This remains true whether in reporting or nonreporting programs.[11] In fact, as didactic analysts we become colleagues with our trainees, working in the same professional circles. We are pressured not to become aware of these encounters or discuss them obliquely. This mutually collusive role prohibits the discussion of these forbidden encounters. The personal knowledge gained in this interaction is suppressed and leads these encounters to become hidden burdens. This reality is very seldom described in the psychoanalytic literature.

In the real everyday environment of psychoanalytic institutes, trainees gain a good deal of information about their analysts-teachers in one way or another even if they do not seek it out purposely. This information consists of knowledge of analysts' teaching and professional activities, their status as members of the institution, and their relationship with colleagues. Instead of seeing this information as nonexistent and as a useless source of knowledge, examining this interaction as a common experience and as an educational opportunity would free the student analyst and the training analyst from the burden of disowned knowledge.[12] This examination would also help distinguish transferential distorting elements that belong to either participant. This can be done only if the roles of both participants are conceived with modesty and within a spirit of mutuality, without granting certainty to either of the participants.

The institutional relations among colleagues could be taken more seriously and honestly if the power and prestige structure of the common group were examined through their respective perspectives as participant-observers, each with different hierarchical positions.

Being aware of the way in which social reality intrudes on the didactic psychoanalytic process implies a demanding commitment from both participants, but it also represents the relief of acknowledging our real participation and not struggling to conceal it. It forces us and our trainees to be attentive to oneself and to one another, as two people. This task is perfectly in tune with Fromm's approach to psychoanalysis—an honest examining of each one's participation.

It must be recognized that taking part in the teaching functions of psychoanalytic training programs and at the same time analyzing trainees demands an enormous effort from the analyst. It exposes us to a great deal of anxiety. It can lead analysts into an extremely difficult situation wherein, after a long and well-recognized practice, training analysts find themselves surrounded by analysands or former analysands as junior colleagues in very high-risk professional communications in groups ridden by all sorts of secrets and nonusable information.[13] Not taking into account the relevance of these facts of everyday life cannot lighten, but on the contrary only worsen, the incommensurable psychoanalytic task of the training analyst.

Assuming openly the role of colleague with the didactic analyst does in fact demand from the patient-student a more responsible commitment. This commits our junior colleagues to exposing themselves fully and sharing the experience of one's internal life, not protected by the mythical "neutrality" of the analyst. The student-patients understand that they are also exercising, legitimately, their role as observers, thus coming to know the analyst as a person instead of idealizing him or her. The student-patients will gradually recognize their analysts' strengths and limitations. That the student-patients become aware of their analysts' weaknesses need not impede the fundamental psychoanalytic goal for both participants—being able to open oneself, to recognize and understand the unconscious through mutual nonauthoritarian participant-observation.

The analyst must thus be aware of and accept a limit to the exercise of power and authority. Analysts must also be objective and critical toward the social realities in which the patient and the analyst live. By practicing openly and attentively, the analyst comes to know how much one can learn from the learner (Fromm 1994).

TEACHING METHODS CONGRUENT WITH A NONPRESCRIPTIVE APPROACH TO TECHNIQUE

For the analyst not to repeat the schemes of childhood that led to repression means acceptance of the other's nonrepressed person, in this case the patient-student, with his or her notions, desires, and values. This means understanding the person and respecting his or her right and competence to exercise personal authority. This attitude can only come from the analyst's knowledge of the hidden power structures that stand behind repression, and not from thinking that the consulting room, the teaching seminars, and training institution can really be neutral or hidden from trainees.

In conclusion, an intellectual conception of psychoanalysis as an exercise of established technical rules may be intended to lighten the complex psychoanalytic task of the analyst. Paradoxically it may have an opposite effect by mystifying the analytic process in the guise of useful technical devices that put a rationalized distance between analyst and analysand-colleague. This rationalization serves the purpose of hiding the analyst's own insecurity when confronted by not being able to have the last word with analysands. Such an approach cannot help but obstruct the necessary intimacy, equality, and shared search for truth required in the psychoanalytic process.[14]

ACKNOWLEDGMENTS

I am most grateful to Drs. Barbara Lenkerd and Mauricio Cortina who helped me clarify my ideas in English.

ENDNOTES

1. Previous approaches are worth reviewing: Clara Thompson's article "Counter-transference" (1952), Ralph M. Crowley's "Human Reactions of Analysts to Patients" (1952), and Eduard S. Tauber's "Observations on Counter-Transference Phenomena" (1952).

2. This same approach has been developed in the social sciences (Bertaux 1989, Bryman 1984, Bulmer 1979, Geertz 1973, 1984, Saltalamacchia 1992).

3. The transcription of the lectures offered to the William Alanson White Institute's students in 1974 in Locarno (Fromm 1974) fully support this view. See also Rainer Funk's (1993) development of the social aspect of Fromm's clinical practice.

4. Miriam Greenspan (1993) calls for a similar approach to psychotherapy and labels it "feminist," emphasizing its egalitarian (or nonauthoritarian) aspects. I agree with her perspective. However, I think it is misleading and divisive to call it feminist.

5. For a lively description on how cultural differences affect the underlying analytic process, see Taketomo (1989) and the many cases described by Devereux (1967).

6. See the educational plan of the Mexican Psychoanalytic Institute developed with Fromm's participation (Universidad Nacional Autonoma de México, Facultad de Medicina 1972). It is worth also reviewing the bylaws of the Instituto Mexicano de Psicoanálisis (1963) and those of the Sociedad Psicoanalitica Mexicana (1956). These educational blue prints are very similar to those developed by the International Federation of Psychoanalytic Societies in which Fromm actively participated as a founding member. See also Aramoni and Derbez (both in Millan and Gojman 1981) for an account of Fromm's role in psychoanalytic training in México. For a description of Fromm as a supervisor see Feiner (1975), Norell (1975), Moulton (1975), and Lesser (1992).

7. See Siirala's (1993) article on transference for a different way of expressing the idea of the analyst as one who contains shared social burdens imposed on the patient.

8. Casement (1985) calls this procedure trial identification.

9. See Menaker (1989) for a critical view of how an analyst's interpretations and attitudes may interfere with the treatment process, based on recollections of her analysis with Anna Freud and her husband's analysis with Helene Deutsch. See also Deutsch (1983) on supervised analysis and Roazen (1985) on Deutsch.

10. See Strean (1993) for a contemporary approach that is consistent with these guidelines.

11. Some very interesting efforts are under way to address these difficulties by eliminating most of the supervising and analyzing requirements for trainees within the training institution. Some recent experiments involve offering only clinical and theoretical seminars to students. The training institution takes the position that it does not officially sanction or offer any guarantees as to the clinical competence of the trainees (Kemper 1994).

12. Bowlby's (1988) article, "On Knowing What You are not Supposed to Know and Feeling What You are not Supposed to Feel," shows clearly how one hides from oneself what one knows, particularly if this knowledge is a threat to a relation with an authority figure. This hiding in turn affects further relationships and undermines credibility in oneself and in others.

13. See the sensitive description of these difficulties by Rawn (1991) and by Freudenberger and Robbins (1979).

14. Contemporary participatory social research methods imply a similar approach (Sanchez and Almeida 1991, Lenkerd 1980) as does Gilligan's (1982) analysis of women's "different voice." Women's "ways of knowing" (Belenky et al. 1986) describe a more relational view of education that is beginning to be put into practice in a few places. Jordan et al. (1991) describe a method of education based on conversations that help articulate each person's hidden knowledge and promote a "growth in connection."

REFERENCES

Aramoni, A. (1970). *En busca de la Verdad, Arte y Técnica del Psicoanálisis*. México: IMPAC.

_____ ed. (1983). *Cuatro Neurosis en Busca de Argumento. La Praxis Psicoanalítica*. México: Siglo XXI Editores and Instituto Mexicano de Psicoanálisis.

_____ (1988). *Hombre Sueño Razón. Ensayos sobre Psicoanálisis Evolucionista*. México: EOSA, Serie Alterna.

Belenky, M. F., Clinchy, B. M., Goldberger, N. R., and Torule, J. M. (1986). *Women's Ways of Knowing: The Development of Self, Voice and Mind*. New York: Basic Books.

Balint, M., and Balint, E. (1961). *Psychotherapeutic Techniques in Medicine*. London: Tavistock.

Bernfeld, S. (1962). On psychoanalytic training. *Psychoanalytic Quarterly* 4:3–14.

Bertaux, D. (1989). Los Relatos de Vida en el Análisis Social. In *Historia Oral*, ed. J. Aceves, pp. 87–96. México: Instituto Mora UNAM.

Bollas, C. (1992). *Being a Character: Psychoanalysis and Self Experience*. New York: Hill and Wang.

Bowlby, J. (1988). On knowing what you are not supposed to know and feeling what you are not supposed to feel. In *A Secure Base*, pp. 99–118. New York: Basic Books.

Bryman, A. (1984). The debate about quantitative and qualitative research: a question of method or epistemology? *British Journal of Sociology* 35:75–92.

Bulmer, M. (1979). Concepts in the analysis of qualitative data. *Sociological Review* 27:651–677.

Burston, D. (1991). *The Legacy of Erich Fromm*. Cambridge, MA: Harvard University Press.

Casement, P. J. (1985). *Learning from the Patient*. New York: Guilford.

Crowley, R. M. (1952). Human reactions of analysts to patients. *Samiksa* (Published by the Indian Psychoanalytical Society) 6:212–219.

Derbez, J. (1981). Fromm en México: Una Reseña Histórica. In *Erich Fromm y el Psicoanálisis Humanista*, ed. S. Millán, and S. Gojman, pp. 27–53. México: Siglo XXI.

Deutsch, H. (1983). On supervised analysis. Introduction by Paul Roazen. *Contemporary Psychoanalysis* 19:53–70.

Devereux, G. (1967). *From Anxiety to Method in the Behavioral Sciences*. Paris: Mouton, and Ecole Practique de Hautes Etudes.

Evans, R. I. (1966). *Dialogue with Erich Fromm*. New York: Harper & Row.

Feiner, A. H. (1975). Reminiscences of supervision with Erich

Fromm. *Contemporary Psychoanalysis* 11:463–473.

Forest, I. (1954). *The Leaven of Love. A Development of the Psychoanalytic Theory and Technique of Sandor Ferenzci.* New York: Harper.

Freudenberger, H. J., and Robbins, A. (1979). The hazards of being a psychoanalyst. *Psychoanalytic Review* 66:275–296.

Fromm, E. (1935). Die Gesseschaftliche Bedingtheit der Psychoanalytischen Therapie. In *Gesamtausgabe Band I, Analytische Sozialpsychologie,* ed. R. Funk, pp. 115–138. Stuttgart: Deutscher Taschenbuch Verlag, 1989.

_____ (1968). Typewritten transcription of Fromm's seminars on clinical and technical aspects. México: Instituto Mexicano de Psicoanálisis.

_____ (1974). Typewritten transcription of the lectures offered in Locarno to the students of the William Alanson White Institute. Erich Fromm Archives.

_____ (1979). Erich Fromm: Du Talmud à Freud. Interview avec Gerard Khoury. *Le Monde* October 21.

_____ (1994). *The Art of Listening,* ed. R. Funk. New York: Continuum.

Fromm, E., Suzuki, D. T., and de Martino, R. (1960). *Zen Buddhism and Psychoanalysis.* New York: Harper.

Funk, R. (1993). Fromm's approach to psychoanalytic theory and its relevance to therapeutic work. In *Cuadernos IV,* ed. S. Millán, S. Gojman, Seminario de Sociopsicoanalisis, pp. 17–42. México: Instituto Mexicano de Psicoanálisis.

Geertz, C. (1973). Thick description. In *The Interpretation of Cultures.* New York: Basic Books.

_____ (1984). From the native's point of view: on the nature of anthropological understanding. In *Culture Theory: Essays on Mind, Self and Emotion,* ed. R. A. Shweder and R. A. Levine, pp. 123–136. Cambridge: Cambridge University Press.

Gill, M. (1982). *Analysis of Transference, vol. 1: Theory and Technique.* Psychological Issues, Monograph 53. Madison, CT: International Universities Press.

_____ (1994). *Psychoanalysis in Transition: A Personal View.* Hillsdale, NJ: Analytic Press.

Gilligan, C. (1982). *In a Different Voice: Psychological Theory and*

Women's Development. Cambridge, MA: Harvard University Press.

Gojman, S. (1983). Vampirismo y Poder. In *Cuatro Neurosis en Busca de Argumento,* ed. A. Aramoni, pp. 78–108. México: Siglo XXI.

Greenberg, J. R., and Mitchell, S. A. (1983). *Object Relations in Psychoanalytic Theory.* Cambridge, MA: Harvard University Press.

Greenspan, M. (1993). *A New Approach to Women and Therapy.* Blue Ridge Summit, PA: Tab Books.

Hirsch, I. (1993). Countertransference enactments and some issues related to external factors in the analyst's life. *Psychoanalytic Dialogues* 3:343–366.

_____ (1994). Dissociation and the interpersonal self. *Contemporary Psychoanalysis* 30:777–792.

Instituto Mexicano de Psicoanálisis. (1963). *Statutes.* México: IMPAC.

Jordan, J. V., Kaplan, A. G., Miller, J. B., et al. (1991). *Women's Growth in Connection.* Writings from the Stone Center. New York, London: Guilford.

Kemper, J. (1994) Personal communication. Brazil: Circulo Psicoanalitico do Rio de Janeiro.

Lenkerd, B. (1980). Participant Research at ACTION: Understanding the Limits to Change. Paper presented at the American Anthropological Association, Washington, DC.

Lesser, R. M. (1992). Frommian therapeutic practice: a few rich hours. *Contemporary Psychoanalysis* 28:483–494.

Maccoby, M. (1982). Social character vs the productive ideal: the contribution and the contradiction in Fromm's view of man. *Praxis International* 2:70–84.

Menaker, E. (1989). *Appointment in Vienna.* New York: St. Martin's Press.

Millán, S., and Gojman, S. (1981). *Erich Fromm y el Psicoanálisis Humanista.* México: Siglo XXI.

Mitchell, S. (1993). *Hope and Dread in Psychoanalysis.* New York: Basic Books.

Moulton, R. (1975). Memorias de mis recuerdos de cuando fui supervisada. *Revista de Psicoanálisis Psiquiatria y Psicologia*

9:93-99.

Narvaez, F. (1981). La Terapéutica Humanista. In *Erich Fromm y el Psicoanálisis Humanista*, ed. A. Aramoni. México: Siglo XXI.

Natterson, J. (1991). *Beyond Countertransference: The Therapist's Subjectivity in the Therapeutic Process*. Northvale, NJ: Jason Aronson.

Norell, M. (1975). Reminiscences of supervision with Erich Fromm. *Contemporary Psychoanalysis* 11:456–462.

Peterfreund, E. (1971). Information, systems, and psychoanalysis. *Psychological Issues*, vol. 7. Monographs 25/26. New York: International Universities Press.

Rawn, M. L. (1991). Training analysis and training psychotherapy. *Psychoanalytic Psychology* 8:43–57.

Roazen, P. (1985) *Helene Deutsch. A Psychoanalyst's Life*. New York: Doubleday Encore.

Saltalamacchia, H. (1992). *Historia de Vida*. Puerto Rico: Cijup.

Sanchez, M. E., and Almeida, E. (1991). La relación humana simétrica: Fuente de acción y conocimiento. In *Cuadernos* vol. 2, Ed. Seminario de Sociopsicoanalisis, pp. 30–43. México: Instituto Mexicano de Psicoanálisis.

Sandler, J. (1976). Countertransference and role responsiveness. *International Journal of Psycho-Analysis* 3:43–47.

Schafer, R. (1992). *Retelling a Life: Narration and Dialogue in Psychoanalysis*. New York: Basic Books.

Siirala, M. (1993). From transfer to transference, or let us not forget Laios when we recognize Oedipus. *International Forum for Psychoanalysis* 2:90–101.

Sociedad Mexicana de Psicoanálisis. (1956). *Statutes*. México.

Stolorow, R. D. and Atwood, G. E. (1992). *Contexts of Being. The Intersubjective Foundations of Psychological Life*. Hillsdale, NJ: Analytic Press.

Stolorow, R. D., Brandchaft, J. B., and Atwood, G. E. (1987). *Psychoanalytic Treatment*. Hillsdale, NJ: Analytic Press.

Strean, H. D. (1993). *Resolving Counter-resistances in Psychotherapy*. New York: Brunner/Mazel.

Taketomo, Y. (1989). An American–Japanese transcultural psychoanalysis and the issue of teacher transference. *Journal of The American Academy of Psychoanalysis* 17:427–450.

Tauber, E. S. (1952). Observations on counter-transference phenomena. *Samiksa* 6:220–228.

Thompson, C. (1952). Counter-Transference. *Samiksa* 6:205–211.

Universidad Nacional Autonoma de México Facultad de Medicina, División de Estudios Superiores. (1972). *Curso de Especialización en Psicoanálisis*. México: IMPAC.

10

Opening of Alternatives and Modification of Character Traits in Psychoanalysis

Romano Biancoli

CLINICAL APPLICATIONS OF ALTERNATIVISM

The opening of alternatives in the life of a patient is one of the tasks of psychoanalysis (Fromm 1968). The art of psychoanalysis, as opposed to the technique (Fromm 1991), is the practice of creativity and vitality, which is also expressed through seeing the concrete and real alternatives that a patient has. Indicating alternatives that had not been considered or conceptualized before can reawaken new energies.

Alternativism is a theory of human freedom with origins in the rejection of both "hard determinism" and "free will" (Fromm 1964). "The possibility of freedom lies precisely in recognizing which are the real possibilities between which we can choose, and which are the 'unreal possibilities" (p. 261). In order to choose, it is necessary to be aware of the alternatives and ensure that they are realistic and not illusory. We must also recognize the force of our conscious and unconscious inclinations toward these alternatives and be aware of the consequences of choosing one alternative over another. This choice cannot only be intellectual, but must also be emotional. When the chosen alternative is difficult, and therefore liberating, conflictual and prevailing interior inclinations must be opposed. Thus, it is necessary to be strong willed, to mobilize emotions, to pay the price and face the material disadvantages that such a choice brings (Fromm 1964). A choice is real only if it is a responsible one. Responsibility means answering for one's choices and paying for the consequences. The possible loss of a material advantage is compensated by an increase in personal freedom.

These working concepts were later reformulated by Fromm (1992 and Bacciagaluppi and Biancoli 1993). In the context of the autobiographical approach to self-analysis, Fromm introduces two concepts: the "forks of the road," and the "secret plots." Of the former, Fromm (1992) writes: "What were the forks of the road, where I took the wrong direction and went the wrong way?" (p. 72). In writing about the latter he maintains: "In many persons there are two such plots: a conscious, 'official' one, as it were, which is the cover story for the secret plot which dominates our behavior" (pp. 73–77).

The existence of secret plots can make freedom of choice an illusion and can hide the real alternatives. It often happens during analysis that unconscious forks of the road are discovered, situations in which the individual is faced with real alternatives but does not realize it. The exploration of these alternatives must become an act of total discovery, both intellectual and emotional. It is an inner transformation that must then be translated into external action in order to produce real change in character traits. In fact, for an alternative to be put into practice, its depression must find expression in the external world in which we live.

THE BEGINNING OF A CLINICAL CASE

During her third session of analysis, a 20-year-old woman reports her first dream:

I'm walking down the street. I see a small group of people. I go nearer to see what's happening. There's a big brown bear on the ground, it's dead and all its bones are broken. The people are standing around looking at it.

A patient's first dream helps us to identify his/her main problem (Silva-Garcia 1982). It is the first, unconscious visiting card that is presented after the analyst has entered the life of the dreamer. A dream, as a "global symbol," is an "instantaneous portrait" of the dreamer. (Silva-Garcia 1982).

Through the symbol of the bear the patient tells her analyst that there is a big, strong being in her life that was savagely and viciously killed by having all its bones broken. In the manifest content of the dream the physical pain that the animal had to endure before dying is implicit. Implicit also is a feeling of sorrow, without tears, that the scene provokes.

The main questions that must be asked about this dream are: Who does the bear represent? Why was this awesome symbol of life killed so cruelly? Who killed it? Is the dreamer capable of crying? Why does she not cry? Why does she not even protest against this savage, sadistic cruelty? Is she so afraid of life? Is she a berserker (Eliade 1978), one so full of rage?

This symbol will be our guide in understanding who the dreamer is and why she is like she is, how she relates to others, and what aggressive transference she will have toward the analyst. Also the transference will show her to be distant from others, an observer who hides her feelings.

The patient is the youngest of five children, of which the first three, all boys, died in infancy and the last two, both girls, survived. Her mother is a well-off housewife who does not love her husband. Seemingly, she only married in order to get away from her parents, with whom she had a conflictual relationship. Soon after her wedding she apparently told her two sisters that she did not want children. Once pregnant, she told them she was unhappy and that she hoped at least the baby would be a girl. With each successive pregnancy she expressed the same preference. The first baby was born premature and died soon afterward; the second died of meningitis when he was 10 months old; the third was born two years later and died at 4 or 5 months of an illness the patient cannot name. The patient discovered that her maternal grandparents felt that their daughter was neither mature nor responsible enough to have children. They offered to help when the third child was born but were turned down and they maintained that this baby too (like the second) was neglected. The patient's mother's feelings of guilt were inevitable as was the involvement of her father, who must have felt particularly impotent, as the patient's dream suggests. It could be thought that the psychopathology and conflicts of the couple did not allow a healthy elaboration of their grieving (Bowlby 1980). Moreover, as there was no dialogue or solidarity between them, the patient's parents could have unconsciously carried over to the two daughters their painful experiences with their first three children (Bowlby 1980).

Three years after the death of the third child, a fourth pregnancy resulted in the birth of a girl. According to what the patient heard from her aunts, her mother was happy and caring toward the baby. Toward her youngest daughter, too, the mother seemed to be attentive and considerate, but she showed a preference for her other daughter. Thus our analysand grew up with the feeling of not being loved but merely looked after by her mother. The patient's father was an engineer who worked for a large company and was competent at his job. However, his ethics did not allow him to make the compromises necessary to advance his career in the company. His wife could not understand his scruples and she exasperated him to the point where he resigned. He found another job that he did not like and he started to suffer from depression. He was an upright man, capable of facing both professional and political challenges, but he was afraid of his wife and of women in general, which only increased his wife's hatred and contempt for him. His depression was the expression of his failure as a husband and father. He died of a heart attack at 52, when the patient was 17.

The apparent divisions in the house were that the elder sister, who was more diplomatic, seemed to defend her father, whereas the younger sister allowed herself to be bought by a show of affection from her mother and attacked her father. The father preferred the younger daughter, the analysand, but he did not know how to show his affection for her. Thus the child, in love with her father, became more and more disappointed, angry, and desperate.

Everyone thought that the patient loved her mother and hated her father and she thought so, too. The only person who saw the truth was a friend, who was unable, however, to make the patient aware of the situation, no matter how hard she tried. This shows us that the patient had the positive experience of an intimate friendship in preadolescence with a girl of the same age, even if this isophilic relationship (Sullivan 1953) was not entirely successful. The problem was how to bring out the truth, that the patient loved her father, that she admired him for his upright spirit and idealistic beliefs. What language could be used? (Ferenczi 1933). What language can a bear understand? After about one month of analysis, of her own accord the patient said that her father was a bear, thus explicitly clarifying one aspect of the symbol of her dream. How could she rouse this big bear? By making him angry? By doing badly at school? By running away from home? She had tried all of these but to no avail. Is she not also a bear, who breaks her own bones? She was now 15 years old. Having dismissed the idea of suicide she was left with not eating. For two months she struggled against hunger and refused any food. Force-feeding in the hospital convinced her to start eating again and she rejected anorexia as a strategy for life. She decided to leave home and drop out of school, going to live with a maternal aunt who lived in the same city and finding a job in a bar.

Because of her touchiness and verbal aggression she lost one job after another, caused difficulties for her aunt, and upset her father who expressed his concern. She argued with him but experienced his depression as a gloomy reproach, as if it were her fault.

The patient became engaged. Her boyfriend was accepted by everybody and this led to a few happy weeks, but she treated him badly and finally left him without any explanation. This introduced a period of short and stormy affairs, intended to provoke her parents, especially her father, whose sudden death ended this phase.

The patient's life is now divided between her aunt's home and her mother's, to which she returns periodically. She has fairly intimate but rather conflictual relationships with some female friends. She is full of anger and blames herself for her father's death. She currently works in a big electrical goods shop but the arguments are inevitable, and her relationships with men are virtually impossible. She asks for help.

In analysis, as we have already seen, the bear appears immediately and it is soon apparent that it was not the patient who broke his bones. Unconsciously, the patient already knew that other women, her mother and grandmother, had broken those bones. Blaming herself for her father's death was a way of keeping her really damaging outbursts of aggression at bay. As the bear is examined, especially with the understanding that he was afraid of women and thus of her too, even of his little girl, this little girl softens, finds herself again, and cries. These tears mark the start of a new course, an alternative presents itself in the patient's life.

CHARACTER TRAITS

Fromm's characterology (Biancoli 1992, Burston 1991, Fromm 1947, 1973, 1976, Fromm and Maccoby 1970, Funk 1978) distinguishes productive from nonproductive character orientation. The latter can be divided into receptive, exploitative, hoarding, marketing, or necrophilous. There is no such thing as pure character orientations, but rather they blend and mix, both among nonproductive orientations and/or as a combination of productive and nonproductive orientations (Fromm 1947). Productiveness gives the nonproductive aspects of character positive and constructive qualities.

In *Man for Himself* (1947), Fromm first introduces the various character types as "ideal types," and then for each of them gives a list of corresponding positive and negative aspects. For example, in the case of the receptive orientation, the negative aspect "passive" is transformed by productiveness into the positive aspect "accepting," "parasitical" becomes "charming," "sentimental" becomes "tender," and so on. In the same way, in the exploitative orientation, "exploitative" becomes "active," "aggressive" becomes "able to take initiative," and so on. Thus, for every type of nonproductive orientation there are various negative aspects that the productiveness in a character can transform into their positive counterparts.

If we examine the patient's character, we can see a blend of orientations in her case, too. The productive component is clearly important. This can be seen both from the fact that the patient has managed to survive without becoming psychotic in an extremely unfavorable family atmosphere, and that she managed to register a strong protest and look for economic independence as soon as she left home. She is courageous as well as "impulsive," this latter being a positive aspect of the exploitative traits. Some negative aspects of receptive orientation (accepting) are evident, especially "sentimental" and "unrealistic." The latter does, however, tend toward its positive side, "idealistic," partly due to her father's influence. Other negative exploitative traits are "aggressive," "egocentric," and "arrogant."

Each character orientation corresponds to certain modes of relating to other people (Fromm 1947). According to the table put forward by Rainer Funk (1982), the receptive orientation relates to others masochistically, while the exploitative orientation does so in an oral-sadistic way. In fact, sadomasochism is the recurring mode of relating in this patient.

A FRAME OF ORIENTATION AND DEVOTION IN ANALYSIS

The patient had hardened in her anger and in her dissent, and she had not cried for years. She used to cry a lot when she was little, but soon stopped, becoming aggressive as she started to believe in force (the bear?) as the best way of getting what she needed. Following the model of her cold mother, she tried to remain detached from people but was unable to do so, either with her parents or her friends. When she was not on the losing side she dominated. Her frame of orientation and devotion (Fromm 1950, 1955) was predominantly authoritarian, with some humanistic elements that seem to have come from her father.

During analysis, the confrontation with the humanistic frame offered by the analyst leads to tears. The patient cries as she used to when she was little, before she acted out her protests. These child's tears open up the corridor of her life history and allow her heart to soften, to feel liquid pain. These are therapeutic tears, but they are insidious if they last. They risk becoming the permanent wail of a person who does not want to grow up and they leave the way open for the masochistic mode of relating to others. The analyst tells her all this and the patient reacts by continuing to cry, but now her tears have a different quality. She cries for the shy bear who was killed and had all his bones broken. She cries for his clumsy, touchy, impotent kindness. She cries because she realizes that, even though he was a coward with his wife, he gave the best part of himself to his daughter.

This is the alternative: either the masochistic tears of self-pity, or the mature tears of pain for the other. When humanistic values penetrate the spirit, something happens to the character. The receptive trait "sentimental" becomes "tender."

The negative aspects of character change into their positive counterparts as the frame of orientation and devotion changes in a humanistic sense (Silva-Garcia 1990). A character does not change directly as its structure tends to be permanent, but the change in a person begins with his/her frame of orientation and devotion, which is closely linked to character. When analysis transforms an authoritarian frame by introducing a humanistic component into it, it works on the patient's whole personality, both on his/her character traits by pushing them toward their positive counterparts and on his/her mode of relating to others.

CHANGE IN "MODES OF SOCIALIZATION"

Fromm (1964) shows in schematic form the passions that lead to the "syndrome of decay" – narcissism, necrophilia, and incestuous symbiosis; and those that lead to the "syndrome of growth" – love, biophilia, and independence-freedom. All these passions express modes of relatedness and socialization and correspond to character orientations.

The patient's sadomasochism is a result of her incestuous-symbiotic passion, but is, however, countered by yearnings for freedom. Her narcissism is not too strong and should decrease enough to enable her to love. Necrophilia is not in evidence and it is to be suspected that life-loving tendencies have been repressed. These modes of relating are consistent with her character orientation.

The patient is more fixated on the father figure than on the mother figure. Her father fixation intensified with his death and it will probably require a lot of work in analysis to unravel it. After her father's death the patient tried to get nearer to her mother but she was disappointed. Her mother's coldness becomes the subject of analysis. After one year of treatment the patient starts to ask her mother if she loves her. Her mother avoids the question but the patient insists so much that her mother finally tells her own truth: she did what she could, her marriage was unhappy, her childhood was unhappy, do not ask her to give what she is unable to give. The truth is very bitter. The analyst comments to the patient that her suffering over this is quite understandable and, in another session, adds that there is a positive side to the mother's confession: she was honest and told the truth. The appreciation of the fact that her mother did not try to disorient her is accepted by the patient.

The patient again distances herself from her mother and stops visiting the house even occasionally. She phones but more and more rarely. Her mother also rarely phones. Her hostility toward her mother gradually decreases. She shows an increase in autonomy.

TRANSFERENCE AND "CENTER-TO-CENTER" RELATEDNESS

In certain important moments of the analysis, communication between the analyst and the patient is intuitive and empathic.

This happens, for example, when the tenderness and tears for her father appear and later when the pain and bitterness emerge for her mother's inability to love. The analyst feels what the patient feels and both participate in a nonverbal and verbal atmosphere. A "center-to-center" relatedness is created (Fromm 1960, 1968), which makes the analysis spontaneous and effective.

At other times the patient seems to be hostile and polemical with the analyst and tries to get him into difficulty. The analyst no longer feels he has the patient's trust and the analytic dialogue becomes difficult. The patient behaves toward the analyst in the same way she behaved toward her father and still behaves toward her employers. This is the same oral-sadism that tries to humiliate and make the interlocutor suffer. The patient's authoritarian frame of orientation and devotion does not distinguish rational from irrational authority (Fromm 1947) and does not allow her to trust the analyst's competence. The patient's transference is an expression of how this authoritarian frame must be transformed in a humanistic sense (Silva-Garcia 1991), by favoring the productiveness in the patient's character orientation. After a year and a half the transference becomes a defense that impedes the analysis. During a difficult and intense session, the analyst shows the patient an alternative: either she continues to see him through the angry and resentful distortions of past experiences or she manages to see him as a real person, distinct from her father. The second alternative is the one that allows the analysis and the patient's evolution to continue. The patient replies with the following dream:

I'm standing on a rock and looking out to sea. A beautiful ship is approaching. Not far from me are a boy and a girl who keep diving into the sea from different rocks to show the ship's captain how deep the water is and how close the ship can come. The captain is on the deck, watching them. When the ship comes near, it comes up against the rocks and cannot find an opening, an inlet. The captain is afraid of hitting a rock, but the boy and girl help him with their diving to get as near as possible to the coast.

In the dream we find both the impossibility of docking and the offer of cooperation. Why does the patient dream of rocks? Why does she send a boy and a girl to help the captain? Who are these people?

The rocks imply that the patient still needs to defend herself and thus keep her aggressive character traits. The analyst-captain is not only rejected, but also helped to get as near as possible as long as he follows the precise instructions of the divers, otherwise he will run aground. In fact, he watches the divers very closely. The dreamer watches the whole scene without taking part directly, but she sends a boy and a girl. We still do not know who these two people are or who they symbolize, with their image of a close and cooperative couple. So far no answer has appeared in her associations.

This dream expresses the patient's inner struggle to trust a rational authority. The sadomasochistic components in her frame show the analyst a barrier of rocks, while the humanistic elements cooperate. Even if the rocks could make us think of isolation, they would seem, rather, to represent the barrier of cutting words that the patient turns on the analyst in her need to feel that she is hurting him, that he feels pain. Thus, the rocks too are a mode of relating. The dream contains both alternatives—on the one hand, the distrustful, resentful transference, represented by the barrier of rocks, and on the other, the willingness to be open for dialogue and cooperation. Also the dream seems a variation of her first dream of the bear, all of whose bones were broken; only now a boy and a girl protect the "beautiful ship" from breaking her ribs, "bones," on the rocks.

This patient is still in analysis today. The negative aspects of her character, which have not yet changed, especially the aggressive and arrogant aspects of the transference, correspond to her oral sadism. They can only be overcome by her own productiveness, the boy and girl divers who encourage and foster the intellectual, emotional, and affective values of radical humanism, in an open analytical dialogue, in a "center-to-center" relatedness.

REFERENCES

Bacciagaluppi, M., and Biancoli, R. (1993). Frommian themes in a case of narcissistic personality disorder. *Contemporary Psychoanalysis* 29:441–452.

Biancoli, R. (1992). Radical humanism in psychoanalysis or psychoanalysis as art. *Contemporary Psychoanalysis* 28:695–731.

Bowlby, J. (1980). *Attachment and Loss. vol. 3: Loss: Sadness and Depression.* London: Hogarth.

Burston, D. (1991). *The Legacy of Erich Fromm.* Cambridge, MA: Harvard University Press.

Eliade, M. (1978). *Histoire des croyances et des idées religieuses.* Paris: Payot.

Ferenczi, S. (1933). Confusion of tongues between adults and the child. In *Final Contributions to the Problems and Methods of Psycho-Analysis.* New York: Brunner/Mazel, 1955.

Fromm, E. (1947). *Man for Himself. An Inquiry into the Psychology of Ethics,* vol. 2. London: Routledge, 1990.

_____ (1950). *Psychoanalysis and Religion.* New Haven and London: Yale University Press, 1978.

_____ (1955). *The Sane Society.* New York: Holt, Rinehart & Winston.

_____ (1960). *Psychoanalysis and Zen Buddhism.* London: Unwin, 1986.

_____ (1964). *The Heart of Man.* New York: Harper Torchbooks, 1987.

_____ (1968). *Transcripcion de seis conferencias.* Ciudad de México, Febrero 4–Marzo 18 de 1968. Tubingen: Erich Fromm Archives.

_____ (1973). *The Anatomy of Human Destructiveness.* London: Penguin, 1977.

_____ (1976). *To Have or to Be?* London: Abacus, 1979.

_____ (1991). *Von der Kunst des Zuhorens.* Weinheim und Basel: Beltz.

_____ (1992). *The Art of Being.* New York: Continuum.

Fromm, E., and Maccoby, M. (1970). *Social Character in a Mexican Village: A Sociopsychoanalytic Study.* Englewood Cliffs, NJ: Prentice-Hall.

Funk, R. (1978). *Erich Fromm: The Courage to be Human.* New

York: Continuum, 1982.
Silva-Garcia, J. (1982). Fromm y la comprension de los suenos. In *Simposio International sobre la obra de Erich Fromm*, ed. A. Gallego Mere, pp. 107–124. Madrid: Universitad Internacional Menendez Pelayo.

_____ (1990). *Some of Erich Fromm's contributions to Freud's psychoanalytic method*. Paper presented at the 34th Winter Meeting of the Academy of Psychoanalysis, San Antonio, December.

_____ (1991). *La transferencia en la perspective humanista*. Paper presented at the psychoanalytic seminar of the Istituto Erich Fromm di Psicoanálisi Neofreudiana, Bologna, September.
Sullivan, H. S. (1953). *The Interpersonal Theory of Psychiatry*. New York: W. W. Norton.

A Commentary

Ana Maria Barroso

Dr. Biancoli shows us possible clinical applications of some of Fromm's theoretical concepts. He focuses on Fromm's concept of alternativism and explores the opening of alternatives in a person's life in therapy that can lead to changes in character traits.

Dr. Biancoli presents us with a very stimulating and difficult clinical case. In a fresh and intuitive style, he discusses decisive moments in the course of the treatment. He conveys his clear interest in understanding and helping the patient.

I have directed my comments in the same direction, attempting to open up alternatives that may offer a different interpretation of the case. I will take up some aspects in the clinical material that seem to me fundamental.

The case is about a young 20-year-old woman from a conventionally stable marriage characterized by a long struggle between the parents that engenders a climate of coldness and violence (exemplified by the mother's emotional outbursts and her contempt and scorn toward her husband). The husband responds passively and feels defeated. It is important to understand the causes of this struggle.

Dr. Biancoli suggests that there is a war between the sexes (Fromm 1987) that among other consequences, leads to the neglect of the male siblings during their early childhood. What I think is fundamental is that in this environment the daughters, and particularly the patient, are used as weapons by the parents. According to Dr. Biancoli the patient experiences this situation as the "feeling of not being loved, but merely looked after by her mother, who is kind to her only when she uses the daughter in her outburst against the husband." I believe this is the basis for the patient's statement that she does not love her mother, yet she belongs to her as her tool and appendage. She only seems to exist in her mother's eyes when she is attacking her father. This situation seems to repeat itself with other men in her life and might be connected with a longing to be near her mother and be accepted by her.

Another piece of information that might be indicative of her relationship with her mother is the episode of anorexia at age 15 from which she nearly died. Anorexia can be understood as a violent rejection of the changes produced in the body by puberty and a profound fear of passing from girlhood to womanhood and therefore a rejection of sexuality. This fear of growing up could have been aggravated by guilt of becoming like her mother.

The anorexia could be also understood as an unconscious "communication" (Casement 1985), that is, an attempt to send a message by means of her body. Starving herself could be a way to reject (albeit destructively) the failure of mother's nurturing care. Perhaps once she had made her statement and faced the possibility of death, she was then able to make a decision to live.

Insofar as the male figure is concerned, her experience teaches her that, in contrast to the omnipotent mother, men are weak, vulnerable, and passive, and hence untrustworthy.

From all this we can infer that for a little girl immersed in this world, the only way to survive is to maintain a submissive bond to her mother, with a consequent identification with her. In other words, given the symbiotic tie to her mother, she has no option but to "decide" in favor of coldness and distrust. This allows her to survive at the price of leading a sterile life devoted to resentment and isolation. As is well known, the recognition of the importance of the bond with the mother was one of Fromm's most novel concepts and occupied a preponderant place in his thinking.

I believe the patient made an "identification with the aggressor" (A. Freud 1936). Based on this identification she has learned to treat those around her as she was treated by her mother. The fact that her short and stormy amorous adventures ended with her father's death may have been the result of the intense guilt of her having become an ally of her mother against her father. A deeper irrational belief in the omnipotent power of her "badness" having caused her father's death may also have played a role. At this point she makes a hasty decision to marry, perhaps a desperate attempt to escape this predicament.

Her first dream shows us a picture of violence and cruelty in which she is only an onlooker. The patient seems emotionally "frozen" (Winnicott 1958). From the very first moment she transmits to the therapist the feeling of pain and sadness that she ought to experience, a mechanism that Klein (1946) called projective identification and has been reelaborated by Casement (1985) in his work on countertransference responses.

With her tears the thaw begins. This is what I believe marks the first step in establishing a working alliance with the analyst, a situation that in Fromm's terms opens up the possibility of "joining forces" in order to face the transference together. As Bettelheim (1967) has put it, it is only possible to cry when there is someone there to listen to the weeping.

After one year in therapy and feeling more supported, the patient reorients her analysis and confronts her mother insistently, wanting to know what her mother's feelings toward her are. She gets an answer. The suffering emerges, and in an attempt perhaps to alleviate the pain, the analyst points out "the positive side of her mother's confession."

A different strategy might have been to contend with the suffering and encourage the expression of the contained resentment and anger that are at the basis of her sadomasochistic relationships (Maccoby 1969), in other words to allow the development of the transference in order to make this force useful for growth. In Fromm's (1964, 1987) terms, this force is a "compensatory violence," a force as intense as the wish to live, the rebellion of life against impotence.

Six months later a very important interaction takes place. The patient becomes "hostile and polemical, attempting to get the analyst into difficulty, so transference becomes a defense that impedes the analysis." The pressure seems to have been such that it leads the analyst to present the patient with an alternative, "either of continuing to see him through the distortion of the past or that she manage to see him as a real and different person." I consider this to be a decisive moment in the therapy because the patient could have been trying to communicate to the analyst the suffering she had been subjected to, a form of transference that Casement calls "communication by impact" and Weiss (1993) describes as "turning passive to active." The patient may have also wanted to test the therapist's ability to handle her hostile feelings, which she may fear are ungovernable.

I would suggest that the analyst may have identified countertransferentially with the analysand's fear of being annihilated, a fear that becomes manifest if the patient differs from her mother. Dr. Biancoli's ultimatum may have been a response to this anguish. Perhaps it is the same anguish that leads Dr. Biancoli to accentuate the positive aspects of the father and press upon the patient his belief that "the patient is in love with the father."

The patient responds with a dream that demonstrates her creative capacity for symbolism and her playfulness. I believe the dream is an attempt to vindicate the father, to keep him alive by letting the masculine figure take over the helm at the expense of her lingering in childhood. Perhaps if she were to become a woman *she* would steer the ship. Another possible interpretation is that she remains a child in order to keep the father and the dead siblings alive.

The dream can also be seen as a transferential gift. She flatters the analyst by placing him in her beautiful ship and making him a captain. The dreamer also makes a very subtle, perhaps controversial point. In the dream it is not the captain who is really navigating the ship, since he does not have the necessary instruments or resources to do so.

Therefore, she sends her emissaries to show the way. She thus transforms what had been a matter of life or death into a children's game. The responsibility for the ship's fate now rests on the emissaries.

I believe that the patient's unconscious hope (Bion 1967, Casement 1985) is to be able to entrust her experience— which until now has been unmanageable—to the therapist. As the therapist understands and contains the patient's experience, the patient is able to affirm her right to life, becoming different from her mother, with an identity based on the discovery and expansion of her own abilities. In other words, what she needs is to be seen not only for who she is, but for who she is capable of becoming.

REFERENCES

Bettelheim, B. (1967). *The Empty Fortress. Infantile Autism and the Birth of the Self*. New York: Kollier Macmillan.

Bion, W. R. (1967). *Second Thoughts*. London: Heinemann.

Casement, P. (1985). *On Learning from the Patient*. London: Mark Paterson.

Fromm, E. (1964). *The Heart of Man*. New York: Harper & Row.

_____ (1987). *La Condicion Humana Actual*. México: Editorial Paidos Mexicana.

Freud, A. (1936). The ego and the mechanisms of defence. In *The Writings of Anna Freud*, vol. 2., New York: International Universities Press, 1966.

Klein, M. (1946). Notes on some schizoid mechanisms. In *Developments in Psycho-Analysis*, ed. J. Riviere. London: Hogarth.

Maccoby, M. (1969). La estrategia de la interpretacion en el analisis de la destructividad. *Revista de Psicoanálisis, Psiquitria y Psicologia.* Sept–Dec 1969, pp. 15–21.

Weiss, J. (1993). *How Psychotherapy Works.* New York: Guilford.

Winnicott, D. W. (1958). *Through Paediatrics to Psycho-Analysis.* London: Tavistock.

11

Countertransference Redefined: Some Clinical Contributions of Fromm

Alan Grey

In its original usage, the word *trivia* referred to any intersection where three roads meet. At such gathering places, people tended to pause for the exchange of small talk, so trivia became associated in the popular mind with gossip and trivialities. Then, eventually, the word acquired that denotation. For vernacular meanings to change over the span of centuries is in the very nature of language. Little confusion results because the glacial pace of such transformations seldom requires relearning one's vocabulary in a single lifetime. Unfortunately alterations in the technical jargon of psychoanalysis have emerged at a far more rapid tempo, with consequences far from trivial. Analysts of different persuasions use the same words to convey widely different meanings. This lexical looseness not only confuses efforts at communication, but sometimes obscures important new ideas. This state of affairs certainly applies to several of the contributions of Erich Fromm.

Partly his retention of orthodox terminology, even for radically altered concepts, grew out of Fromm's sense of allegiance with Freud. Perhaps another factor was his impatience with words as faulty vehicles and, therefore, with terminological niceties. As Tauber (1959) said about Fromm's views in this matter, "It is not so much that he believes there is no science to the therapeutic enterprise but rather that much of what transpires is extremely difficult to formulate . . . somewhat similar to our artistic experience" (p. 1814). Thus it was that despite the abundance of Fromm's treatises on psychosocial matters, seldom did he write directly about treatment. To glean more about his clinical innovations than what appears in those few pages, we must rely largely on secondary sources.

Among those sources are the recollections of colleagues, analysands, and supervisees. Also quite informative is a book-length verbatim interview with Richard Evans (1966), published with Fromm's approval during his own lifetime. These sources help to document the extent to which Fromm brought a fresh approach into the psychoanalytic treatment repertoire, despite his retention of old labels. The three specific examples to be considered here of how he redefined the orthodox terminology are the unconscious, character, and countertransference.

THE UNCONSCIOUS

Although contemporary analytic thought is marked by numerous challenges to orthodoxy, if there is a single concept that is generally accepted it would seem to be that of unconscious processes and the part they play in subjective experience. None insisted on this cornerstone more staunchly than Fromm, who stated that Freud's greatness lay in his having been "the first to have made this discovery the center of his psychological system" (Fromm 1980, p. 21). The fact is, however, that the unconscious as understood by Fromm was significantly different from Freud's version.

For one thing, certain aspects of Fromm's portrait of the unconscious drew upon mystical teachings that considerably antedate the version offered by the founder of psychoanalysis. This is not to imply that Fromm entertained one of those popular views of mysticism that confuse it with magic or the occult, nor that he resembled those early Christian martyrs who sought revelations by withdrawing from the world and abasing the flesh. Rather, the province of the unconscious for him referred to phenomena described by serious scholars of mysticism like Underhill (1955). She sees it as a particular kind of experience motivated by love and drawing upon supernormal powers of the self for an understanding that she insists is "practical, not theoretical" (p. 82). Put another way, Fromm's unconscious continues to include irrational passions but it also encompasses attributes excluded from the Freudian unconscious, qualities like brotherly love, understanding, and sensitivity to the surrounding world.

No longer is the unconscious categorically dangerous, untrustworthy, and the enemy of civilization. In Tauber's (1959) words, it also can provide an avenue to

> experiencing the "here and now" in its immediacy where rational objective, discursive elements are subordinated to intuitive, nondiscursive, nonanalytic elements. . . . As Inge indicated in his Bampton Lectures at Oxford in 1899, mysticism need not even be theologically oriented; it is a philosophical position that historically

appears on the scene as an expression of man's deep
opposition to dogma and ritualization. Fromm feels that
one of the most serious dangers to the very life of psychoanalysis is the growing dogma and ritual. [p. 1812]

In the sense that it evades verbal awareness, such
valuable intuitive experience of the here and now is,
literally, unconscious. To recognize such processes as
integral to the psyche evokes a far different image of
humankind than does the conception of the unconscious
system, which "consists of wishful impulses" with their
"exemptions from mutual contradiction, primary process
(mobility of cathexes), timelessness and replacement of
external by psychic reality" (Freud 1915, pp. 186–187).
While Fromm's regard for the unconscious as a source of
wisdom may sound like Jung, unlike Jung's notion of
genetically transmitted universal truths, the Frommian
picture is of impressions attuned to immediate experience. Were this sketch of the matter to stop here, it might
invite the idea of an infallible fount of inspiration and
guidance.
    It would be far more accurate to say that for Fromm the
unconscious is not a homogeneous entity, either entirely
insightful or always infantile. Nor does he see any inherent antagonism between what is conscious and what is
not. The term is employed generically to refer to psychic
activity of any sort, so long as it is outside of awareness.
Today's unconscious impression may lead to tomorrow's
conscious ideation, and vice versa. It includes thoughts
not yet linguistically formulated and those inaccessible to
formulation because of the quality of their organization
and logic. They may be expressive movements, sensory
images evoked by everyday encounters, or dreams difficult to verbalize but captured in a work of art. If all of this
seems reminiscent of Sullivan's prototaxic and parataxic

modalities, or of Laing's vignettes of schizophrenic communication, the resemblance is more than coincidental.
The contributions of both these men are cited by Fromm
(1992) as in harmony with his own thoughts about unconscious processes.

Yet another variety of unconsciousness is repressed
ideation, somewhat as Freud defined it, albeit seen from a
very different perspective. The censor that drives
thoughts underground is not primarily a psychic force but
is imposed by what Fromm (1992) calls a "social filter."
Much of this filtering is accomplished via such cultural
tools as "language, logic and the mores" (p. 56). Our
definitions of words like *unconsciousness*, *character*, and
countertransference provide nice illustrations of how the
process works. Thus, because Fromm's understanding of
countertransference rests upon—is filtered through—the
other two concepts, an adequate understanding of this
meaning requires reconsideration of all three.

Definitions are shaped by the needs of the power
structure within which they operate. Typically it is the
socioeconomic power structure that captures Fromm's
attention. In his characteristically optimistic fashion, he
held that where the power structure is humanistic, in a
"sane society" that does not impose coercive meanings, all
unconscious mental processes are potentially available to
awareness, with appropriate effort. Under those circumstances, too, experiences may be unconscious without
being deemed evil. Unconsciousness now can be seen as
only a collective term for psychic activities molded by a
complex array of societal circumstances, the "social filter."
It follows, then, that unconscious experience can be creative as well as destructive, no longer the hereditary
opponent of civilization but a resourceful contributor to it.
Had he compared the Freudian and Frommian meanings,
Lewis Carroll (1896) surely would have concluded that the

term *unconscious* is "like a portmanteau, there are two meanings packed up in one word" (p. 198).

It is Fromm's meaning that would be especially favored by recent systematic research. Many studies indicate that these "intuitive orientations" (Grey 1993a) are essential for maintaining ourselves in the world. Some intuitive functions are as automatic and unvarying as word articulation, walking, or tying a shoe. Others can range in complexity through a series of graduations from the routine to inspired creative insights that spring to awareness from the blue. The processes themselves are mysterious, in the sense of inaccessibility to direct observation, but the competencies they produce often are readily apparent. A product particularly germane to what we do as analysts is what researchers call "appraisal." It refers to "the ways in which the individual defines and evaluates relationships in the environment" (Lazarus 1991, p. 10). In more familiar language, appraisal is involved in assessing the patient's character, and in the part played by the analyst's counter-transference reactions in that assessment, as well as in a wide range of everyday transactions.

As Lazarus (1991) put it, although much appraisal is unconscious, "we should resist equating the automatic with the premature, because automatic processing can involve complex, abstract and symbolic significances that through experience can be condensed into an instant meaning" (Lazarus 1991, p. 155). It flowed from Fromm's recognition of the positive capacities of the unconscious that he was among the first to accord a central place to his own intuitive reactions to the patient. Reliance on the analyst's own unconsciously derived impressions became a hallmark of his treatment approach. In his own words:

> Only insofar as I can muster within myself those experiences about which the patient is telling me either explic-

itly or implicitly, only if they arouse an echo within myself, can I know what the patient is talking about and give back to him what he's really saying. Then something very strange happens: the patient does not have the feeling that I'm talking about something alien to him—instead he feels that I'm talking about something we both share. [Fromm, quoted in Evans 1966, p. 46]

Ultimately, then, the "echo within myself," a confirmation from the unconscious, is essential for guiding and validating conscious appraisals. This clearly implies that, for Fromm, unconscious processes are substantially more than obstacles to mental health. Rather "awareness of the unconscious becomes an essential element of truth-seeking" (Fromm 1992, p. 59). Now an interpersonally sensitive unconscious is vital to locating the treatment focus. This treatment focus is on how patients contribute to their own repetitive difficulties, on what analysts call "character."

CHARACTER

Understanding character calls for more than sensitive observations. It also requires a conceptual frame within which to organize those observations. For such an orientation, Fromm stated that he found "the Freudian concepts of character are of immeasurable value" (Evans 1966, p. 2). And, in fact, as three of his character types, he continued to use the oral-passive, oral-aggressive, and anal syndromes developed by Freud and Abraham, now relabeled as the receptive, exploitative and hoarding orientations. But along with this relabeling went a rather basic reconceptualization, quite like the redefinition of unconsciousness and, again, with significant clinical implications.

Specifically, the Frommian idea of character draws upon Freud in at least four respects. The first and most obvious is the already-mentioned preservation of the Freud-Abraham syndromes. Second, he cautioned that no one or two behavioral characteristics of these syndromes but the entire gestalt is what identifies a character orientation, because, third, an orientation is determined not by actions alone but by the motivational theme underlying them, and this is best revealed by the overall patternings. Fourth, characterological strivings are substantially unconscious, so that one's character tends to be hidden from oneself.

It is precisely in this most crucial matter, that is, what motivates human beings, that Fromm broke with the past. As he described it: "The fundamental basis of character is not seen in various types of libido organization but in specific kinds of relatedness to the world" (1947, p. 58). This is the reason for relabeling character orientations. No longer are they bodily functions but rather modes of interactions, whether receptively, exploitatively, or by hoarding. Character is shaped through the interplay between individual and society, not in a preordained "epigenetic" unfolding but, potentially, along widely varying paths.

Endowed with flexible biological resources, each of us learns to exercise them as best we can in coping with the particular societal opportunities into which we are born. Thus, the receptive orientation is elicited in response to particular socioeconomic arrangements perhaps best exemplified in feudal culture. Similarly the exploitative type emerges under circumstances reminiscent of the world of venture capitalism that succeeded feudalism, and hoarding personalities are suited to the bourgeois lifestyle first shaped during the eighteenth and nineteenth centuries. These syndromes were known to Freud inasmuch as they all were observable in his day, reasoned Fromm. Subsequent societal changes, however, require recognition of a fourth patterning, particularly salient in America. "The character orientation which is rooted in the experience of oneself as a commodity and of one's value as exchange value I call the marketing personality" (Fromm 1947, p. 68). All of these are "social character types" have developed so that people are inclined to behave as their socioeconomic circumstances require.

Viewed within the complex context of their actual cultural settings, it becomes apparent that people are motivated by a wider range of drives than merely sex and aggression. Now we are required to pay attention to the full scope of relationships. To see all motivations in terms of one's infantile self and early transactions with parents can provide startling insights. Yet it becomes a reductionist game to perceive no more than that in the adult family, the workings of extended kinship groups, neighborhoods, relations with peers, friends, and colleagues, or in the influences of more encompassing societal entities, such as the culture heritage. Ingestion, defecation, procreation and aggression do not quite cover even the world of the patient on the couch.

In place of the instinct theory, what Fromm proposed as essential for clinical as well as theoretical understanding were five "most powerful forces motivating man's behavior [which] stem from the condition of his existence" (1955, p. 28). Each of these five needs was stated as a pair of opposites calling the analyst's attention not only to regressive tendencies but also to positive potentials. These needs are

1. relatedness versus narcissism

2. transcendence-creativeness versus despair
3. rootedness-brotherliness versus incest
4. sense of identity-individuality versus herd conformity
5. the need for a frame of orientation and devotion-reason versus irrationality.

To his credit, Fromm recognized that this list contained an implicit value system, one to which he adhered throughout the remainder of his career. This dispensed with the fiction of scientific neutrality heretofore claimed by psychoanalysts. At the same time, Fromm restored a claim to objectivity on the alleged basis that these values represent universal human psychological needs. The legitimacy of this formulation would have been enhanced had Fromm achieved greater specificity for the terms and further documentation for his assertions of cross-cultural validity.

In any case, it is a good list and the evidence would have tended to support at least some of the claims, as I have noted elsewhere (Grey 1993b). It provides a motivational perspective much needed for broadening our understanding of personality. It calls attention not only to the narcissism of patients but also to their capacity for loving, not only to incestuous impulses but also to capacities for caring and helpfulness beyond dyadic boundaries. It suggests that meaningful commitments to the larger community are not identical with dyadic intimacy.

To put this point more sharply, Fromm's reconceptualization of the unconscious and of motivation, combine to open the way for consideration of a fifth orientation, the productive character. The four types identified thus far, including the three inherited from Freud and the fourth added by Fromm, all describe unproductive or problematic types. This seems to imply, counter to the colloquial meaning of character, that analysts find all unconsciously rooted repetitive personality patterns to be pathological. But once the unconscious has been reassessed to include constructive motivations, then it becomes necessary to contemplate the possibility of an unconsciously motivated productive character.

In summing up the attributes of this productive type, Fromm hearkens back to Aristotle, "The good man for Aristotle is the man who by his activity, under the guidance of his reason, brings to life the potentialities specific of man" (Fromm 1947, p. 92). Somewhat simplistically, then, Fromm attributes a formidable list of virtues to such people. As actual studies of productive personalities have shown, however, the very circumstances that favor one particular productive attribute tend to discourage another one (Grey 1993b). At the same time Fromm cautions elsewhere that even the best of us is likely to be a mix of two or more types. With this qualification in mind, it still is likely that there are people with predominantly productive characters. Without being infallible, their intuitive responses to others will be essentially trustworthy as interpersonal guides. In short, their spontaneous reactions will tend to be appropriate and, in that sense, quite the opposite of countertransference as first understood.

COUNTERTRANSFERENCE

When asked whether "you mean by countertransference the same thing that Freud meant, namely that the attitude toward the patient is part of the therapeutic relation," Fromm's prompt and firm answer was "certainly" (Evans 1966, p. 33). Unfortunately the question itself is quite equivocal, since it fails to specify whether the reference is to Freud's (1913) usual insistence on eliminating counter-transference from the analytic work. The interviewer could possibly be alluding to those rare instances when Freud spoke of the analyst's unconscious reactions as a valuable "instrument with which he can interpret the utterances of the unconscious in other people" (p. 320).

This ambiguity reflects a persisting state of affairs within mainstream analysis itself. Some warn that these subjective messages are to be avoided as a liability, while others insist that they are therapeutically useful. Given that these debates are yet to be resolved, it seems more fruitful to examine what tends to be done in actual practice. For this purpose, a useful source is LaPlanche and Pontalis (1973), whose standard reference work describes the term itself as a kind of crossroad, offering three alternative routes to the analyst. One is the classical strategy of striving for neutrality so that treatment may be "structured exclusively by the patient's transference." A second path is for analysts privately to scrutinize their own countertransference reactions for their personal information from which to "interpret utterances of the unconscious in other people." The third road is for the analyst to disclose to the patient "the actual emotions [personally] felt." They add, "This approach is on the tenet that, resonance from the unconscious to the unconscious constitutes the only authentically psychoanalytic form of communication" (p. 93).

Despite its rhetorical appeal, any implication that historically most analysts actually have favored communication "from the unconscious to the unconscious" would fly in the face of the facts. At a clinical level the prevailing uses of countertransference have been limited to "a simple uncovering of the analyst's residual pathology," as Epstein and Feiner (1986, p. 16) put it. This persisting mistrust of the intuitive has been supported by a metapsychology that regards overt expressions of unconscious needs as likely to be defensive distortions of unrealistic infantile impulses.

It requires radical revision of metapsychological premises to foster adequate recognition of the unconscious as sensitive to current interpersonal realities. Yet intuitive perceptiveness is abundantly documented by clinical and research evidence, certainly enough to urge such revision. It clears the way for systematic use of intuitive resources for the improvement of treatment methods. While it brings hazards of its own, this emancipation of the analyst's intuition for therapeutic purposes is precisely what is accomplished by Fromm's altered conceptions of the unconscious, of character, and of countertransference.

How these redefinitions bring the deliberate use of the analyst's own unconscious into the actual treatment process is best conveyed in Fromm's own words (quoted in Evans 1966):

> Now I listen to you, and while I'm listening, I have responses which are the responses of a trained instrument. . . . I'll tell you what I hear. This will often be quite different from what you are telling me or intended to tell me. Then you tell me how you feel about my interpretation. . . . We move along this way freely. I am not claiming that what I hear is necessarily correct, but it deserves attention because of the fact that your words produce this reaction in me. [p. 35]

According to this approach, the analyst seeks to penetrate behind the patient's "official goals" for the "secret plot" motivating self-defeating behavior (Fromm 1992, p. 73). The intention is to activate a dialectic between these two facets of the patient's personality, as they bear upon an issue of crucial immediate significance in the patient's life. And it is true that treatment outcome studies find such therapeutic interventions contributing significantly to improvement (Thorne and Klohnen 1993).

Nor does Fromm stay outside the dialectic once the process has begun. For instance, he persists in calling attention to denied aspects of the patient's personality. In his opinion it might waste years to sit by and wait for patients to arrive at such discoveries for themselves. Yet another way to participate is to challenge values implicit in what he calls the patient's "pathology of normalcy." These confrontations and cornerings may prove discouraging to patients, but he found that more often they evoked increased participation and a more active sense of responsibility.

While Fromm did not encourage analysts to engage in autobiographical self-disclosure, these techniques do demand another sort of self-revelation. They require analysts to expose their own strengths and limitations of understanding and their own value systems far more directly than occurs with the earlier, enigmatic model of therapeutic neutrality. He relied upon

> what you might call a humanistic premise: that there is nothing human which is alien to us. . . . And only insofar as I can muster within myself those experiences about which the patient is telling me either explicitly or implicitly, only if they arouse an echo within myself, can I know what the patient is talking about and give back to him what he's really saying. [Fromm, quoted in Evans 1966, p. 46]

Clearly, Fromm chose the road less traveled, what LaPlanche and Pontalis had identified as the third path, based on the tenet that resonance "from the unconscious to the unconscious constitutes the only authentically psychoanalytic form of communication." Fromm took it one step further, however, in that this form of communication was intended to convey not only a message but a model. It was a vehicle for the patient to experience what he called "authenticity" in human relationship, a treatment approach quite different in conception from that heretofore prevailing. In more recent years, other therapists have embraced this goal of authenticity, often not realizing its theoretical source nor how radically it diverges from mainstream metapsychology.

As a cornerstone of treatment, the guideline of authenticity necessarily implies an unconscious encompassing more than infantile impulses and characterological tendencies beyond the purely defensive. It also dispels any notion that psychoanalysis is a uniform procedure, following the same course with any well-trained analyst. The practice of speaking one's mind spontaneously and directly to a patient, even when monitored by critical self-observation, can be justified only on the assumption that analysts have essentially productive character orientations, however else they may vary. Here lies the most debatable and hazardous premise of this method. And yet it can be argued that the very same dangers lurk equally, if less obviously, along other analytic paths.

Whatever one's opinions on this issue, still it is quite apparent that Fromm approached psychoanalytic treatment from a radically altered understanding of what constitutes countertransference. In his view, while it is inappropriate for the analyst to claim infallibility, it is equally unfitting to avoid disclosing one's sincere assessment on pertinent issues. In that sense, neutrality is a countertransference problem. As he put it: "The primary consideration is that the analyst not be afraid of his *own* unconscious for then he will not be afraid or embarrassed by opening up the patient's unconscious" (Evans 1966, p.

55). It is not the patient's right to free choice that Fromm rejects here. It is the myth of neutrality as an abdication of the analyst's responsibility.

REFERENCES

Carroll, L. (1896). Through the Looking Glass. In *The Complete Works of Lewis Carroll*. New York: Barnes & Noble, 1994.

Epstein, L., and Feiner, A. (1986). Introduction. In *Countertransference: The Therapist's Contribution to the Therapeutic Situation*. Northvale, NJ: Jason Aronson.

Evans, R. I. (1966). *Dialogue with Erich Fromm*. New York: Harper & Row.

Freud, S. (1913). The disposition to obsessional neurosis: a contribution to the problem of choice of neurosis. *Standard Edition* 12:317–326.

_____ (1915). The unconscious. *Standard Edition* 14:159–215.

Fromm, E. (1947). *Man for Himself*. New York: Rinehart.

_____ (1955). *The Sane Society*. New York: Rinehart

_____ (1980). *Greatness and Limitations of Freud's Thought*. New York: New American Library.

_____ (1992). *The Revision of Psychoanalysis*, ed. by R. Funk. Oxford: Westview.

Grey, A. (1993a). The interpersonal self updated. In *Narcissism and the Interpersonal Self*, ed. J. Fiscalini and A. Grey. New York: Columbia University Press.

_____ (1993b). The dialectics of psychoanalysis: a new synthesis of Fromm's theory and practice. *Contemporary Psychoanalysis* 29(4):645–672.

LaPlanche, J., and Pontalis, J.-B. (1973). *The Language of Psychoanalysis*. New York: W. W. Norton.

Lazarus, R. S. (1991). *Emotion and Adaptation*. New York: Oxford University Press.

Tauber, E. S. (1959). The sense of immediacy in Fromm's conceptions. In *American Handbook of Psychiatry*, ed. S. Arieti, pp. 1811–1815. New York: Basic Books.

Thorne, A., and Klohnen, E. (1993). Interpersonal memories as maps for personality consistency. In *Studying Lives Through Time: Personality and Development*, ed. D. C. Funder, R. D. Parke, C. Tomlinson-Keasy, and K. Widaman, pp. 223–253. Washington, DC: American Psychological Association.

Underhill, E. (1955). *Mysticism: A Study in the Nature and Development of Man's Spiritual Consciousness*. New York: Noonday.

III

THE INTERSECTION BETWEEN SOCIAL CHARACTER AND CLINICAL WORK

12

Freud, Fromm, and the Pathology of Normalcy

Daniel Burston
Sharna Olfman

Although Fromm is usually labeled a neo-Freudian, this is misleading if it blinds us to the differences between him, Karen Horney, Clara Thompson, and Harry Stack Sullivan. In some ways, the neo-Freudian Fromm resembled least was Sullivan, who had made consensual validation the chief or defining criterion of mental health. In fairness to Sullivan, most clinicians endorse his approach, and not Fromm's. After all, laymen and specialists alike gauge the sanity of someone's thought processes by the degree of consensual validation that attaches to their content, and the adequacy or intelligibility of their underlying process, so far as we can apprehend it. This is simply standard procedure, and many of the diagnostic instruments and protocols of the mental health professions are merely refined and systematic extensions of these commonsense assumptions.

Nevertheless, Fromm objected to this approach to mental health, and did not hesitate to say so. In *The Sane Society*, Fromm (1955) declared:

> It is naively assumed that the fact that the majority of people share certain ideas or feelings proves the validity of these ideas or feelings. Nothing is further from the truth. Consensual validation as such has no bearing whatsoever on mental health. . . . The fact that millions of people share the same vices does not make these vices virtues, and the fact that they share so many errors does not make the errors to be truths. [p. 23]

Having said that, however, Fromm hastened to add that consensually validated "errors" and "vices" do confer certain rewards, namely, that those who share in them are subject to less inner conflict and misery than their overtly neurotic counterparts. To distinguish this phenomenon from the more visible and disconcerting varieties of neurotic disturbance, Fromm gave it a special name, calling it a *socially patterned defect*. This term was first introduced in *Escape from Freedom* (Fromm 1941), in connection with the worship of irrational authority that characterizes the psychology of fascism. Here Fromm proposed the controversial idea that many neurotics are maladjusted because they do not share the socially patterned defects that are characteristic of the majority of "normal" people who compose their society. This claim in turn implies that in any society, a certain percentage of highly conflicted overtly maladjusted people are more healthy in some sense than the average person, even if they suffer much more. Fromm then went on to deduce that neurotic suffering of this kind should be attributed not to an ostensible lack of "normalcy," but to a failure of individuation, an ability to live soundly against the prevailing mentality of the age.

In his next book, *Man for Himself,* published in 1947, Fromm developed his ideas about socially patterned defects further, albeit this time in connection with the way market forces erode the sense of identity and personal agency in capitalist democracies. In *The Sane Society,* cited a moment ago, Fromm took this line of reasoning further still, although he now replaced the term *socially patterned defect* with a more colorful and arresting phrase, "the pathology of normalcy." I will not repeat his arguments in detail. I will simply note that, as the phrase implies, Fromm did not find the notions of pathology and normality to be mutually exclusive, as common usage (and Sullivanian psychiatry) suggests they are. In Fromm's estimation, those who share in the "pathology of normalcy" characteristic of their milieu are generally rewarded for doing so, partly by the absence of painful inner conflicts they might otherwise encounter, and partly by the degree of practical success and recognition they are likely to achieve if they play by prevailing rules of the game. Neurotics, by contrast, are often *penalized* for their personal idiosyncrasies, partly because they don't fit in, and partly because—for that very reason—they are subject to an inordinate degree of anxiety, insecurity, and self-doubt, in addition to whatever unresolved baggage they carry along with them as a result of genuine developmental arrest (Fromm 1944).

There is one trait or feature, however, that neurotics and normals share that is worth reflecting on. For lack of a better term we may call it an aversion or *hostility to truth.* There are notable differences in the forms in which this attitude emerges, however. A neurotic's rationalizations and defenses may be totally transparent to an outsider, because they reflect a relatively rare intrapsychic constellation, sociologically speaking. And because the patient must explore and understand the meaning of his symptoms in order to get well, eventually, these avoidance mechanisms can be confronted clinically, once the therapeutic alliance has been joined, and therapy is under way.

By contrast, the indifference or hostility to truth bred by conformist psychology has a much lower degree of social visibility because it is socially shared and reinforced (Fromm 1973). Here resistance to insight and change are not the product of individual or purely intrapsychic defenses, but of shared perspectives and definitions of reality that are anchored firmly in one's sense of corporate identity, constructed by what Fromm called *social filters*. The result of this process—a constriction or distortion of consciousness—resembles repression as we encounter it clinically, but for obvious reasons it cannot be addressed in the same way.

Moreover, and more to the point, the absence of consciously experienced suffering vouchsafed to the more conformist majority deprives them of any tangible incentive to change, and to see through those features of collective ideology that mask or distort existential actualities. This situation is pithily summed up in Fromm's oft repeated aphorism that, for the majority of people in society, "most of what is real is not conscious, and most of what is conscious is not real" (Fromm 1975, p. 403).

Fromm's claim that for the average person, most of what is real is not conscious, and most of what is conscious, unreal, is bound to strike the majority of people in any society—including most of its clinicians—as extravagant, if not slightly deranged. For if the majority of people thought that the majority of their counterparts were defective or impaired in some vital capacity, such as a desire or willingness to apprehend the truth, all trust in consensual systems of belief and the rituals of daily interaction would break down, with disastrous results.

Clinical experience indicates that even relatively normal individuals who experience a precipitous breakdown of "basic trust" in their environment are subject to anxious, depressive, or frankly paranoid reactions.

That being so, what prompted Fromm to espouse this stark and disturbing viewpoint, and what are its implications for therapy, if any? Before addressing these questions, it may be useful to point out that any perplexity or alarm we might feel in response to Fromm's arguments about everyday false-consciousness diminishes somewhat when we realize the basic idea is not original to Fromm. In fact, it is indelibly inscribed in both the prophetic and Platonic traditions, and forms an integral part of our Western cultural heritage. In *The Legacy of Erich Fromm*, Burston (1991) has argued this point at length, and noted the many vivid antecedents to Fromm's arguments in the history of Western thought.

We will not repeat those arguments now. Suffice it to say that many elements of the Platonic tradition are also present in the sociological reflections of Sigmund Freud, and accordingly, that there are noteworthy points of convergence between Freud and Fromm on this score. We lay particular emphasis on this point because our primary objective is to elucidate the differences between them if their essential similarities are borne in mind.

To begin with, like Fromm, Freud did not confuse consensus with truth, or even with mental health, for that matter. Though some of us may find it strange, Freud often remarked that many people who are healthy (i.e., happy and symptom free) are completely worthless, from a human or cultural point of view, while many neurotics, despite their intense suffering and psychological disabilities, have ennobling qualities and insights into reality that are rare or exceptional in the common run of humanity.

Another closely related point was Freud's firm belief

that the average human being is as allergic to truth as his neurotic counterpart. Freud was particularly emphatic on this point in *The Future of an Illusion* (1927) and again in *Moses and Monotheism* (1939). Even before these books were published, Freud gave a very clear indication of his leanings on this point in *Group Psychology and the Analysis of the Ego* (1921). Here Freud stated that the average individual's loyalties to social and political institutions like the state, the Church, and the military are based on idealizing transference toward their leadership, which presumably have a homoerotic basis. According to Freud, then, in society as we know it normal men create the institutions that regulate their lives by sublimating homosexual libido in ways that call forth altruism and obedience from those in the ranks, but at the expense of their capacity to apprehend the truth about their leaders, who are generally out for their own advantage, despite their noble rhetoric. Significantly, women do not even enter into Freud's analysis at the sociological level, although we gather elsewhere that they have a supposedly feebler disposition to truth than the average man for supposedly constitutional reasons.

Fromm did not share Freud's astonishing phallocentrism. Nor did he lend much credence to the role that sublimated homoerotic tendencies play in Freud's cultural *weltanschauung*. But deep as these differences are, the fundamental difference between Freud and Fromm stems from another source. Like Plato long before, Freud attributed the indifference or hostility to truth that characterizes the vast majority to a basic fault of human nature, which only rare and resolute natures can overcome. Fromm, by contrast, attributed this phenomenon to social and cultural processes that prevent the full and spontaneous development of our critical faculties. On reflection, Freud's attitudes bear a strong resemblance to the ideas of

Schopenhauer, Nietzsche, and Gustav Le Bon, whose aristocratic elitism and pessimism about politics hearken back to sentiments expressed in Plato's *Republic* and *Laws*. Thanks to Henri Ellenberger (1970), Paul Roazen (1986), and others, we now know that Freud read and appreciated these earlier authors. Fromm, by contrast, was rooted in the tradition of socialist humanism, and was more optimistic about human nature. Though his remarks about contemporary capitalism could be scathing, in the final analysis he had more faith in politics to effect change through rational planning and discussion than Freud did.

We should hasten to add that the point of these comparisons is not to establish that Fromm's line of theorizing is superior to Freud's. Whether that (or the reverse) is true depends entirely on your point of view. What we *are* trying to establish, however, and what is more frequently forgotten, particularly by Freud zealots, is that as disturbing or critical as Fromm's ideas may appear at first, there is ample precedent for this kind of reasoning in classical Freudianism. Indeed, if we take Freud at face value, Fromm's formulations regarding the shortcomings of the normal person sometimes seem quite tame by comparison.

Clinicians who have forgotten or minimized this dimension of Freud, including many ego psychologists, self psychologists, and object relations theorists, have lost something central to his whole intellectual orientation. But they are not entirely to blame for interpreting him this way, as critics like Russell Jacoby (1975, 1983) insist. In fact, Freud himself must shoulder much of the blame for this sad state of affairs, because his various formulations on the relationship between normality and mental health are riddled with ambiguity, and often lend themselves to being interpreted in terms that make adjustment to prevailing conditions of life the main criterion for mental well being. A good example of this is Freud's dictum that the aim of analytic therapy is to replace neurotic misery with everyday unhappiness. The presumption here appears to be that human beings are fated to be chronically unhappy, but that the quality and intensity of everyday unhappiness is bearable, if only just.

In response to this assessment, Fromm would have countered that the aim of analytic therapy is to restore the individual's capacity to live fully and authentically, from the core of their being, and to tolerate the suffering and emotional isolation that comes from experiencing and relating to the world in ways that are different from those of the majority. Meanwhile, for most of us, presumably, the range and limits that society imposes on the experience of affect, and of insight into our social surroundings, create the tepid boredom, the chronic frustration and the puzzling sense of aimlessness that constitute everyday unhappiness for so many people.

Another important difference between Freud and Fromm transcends the scope of clinical concerns. It has to do with the sources of conflict in society that engender conflict in individuals. It also has to do with the impact of economic factors on collective psychology, and the sharp and seldom remarked upon contrast between Freud's predominantly *quantitative* approach to the problem of repression historically, and Fromm's predominantly *qualitative* approach to the same issues.

According to Freud in *Civilization and Its Discontents* (1930), all societies are torn by an intractable conflict between the explosive libidinous and aggressive impulses that exist within its individual members, and countervailing collective requirements for the creation of solidary social bonds, through the secondary transformation of the libido by sublimation and reaction formations. Unfortunately, thought Freud, as our sexual energies become more constrained and desexualized in the service of solidarity—as we become, in effect, more civilized—we rebel at our loss of primitive self-expression. The resulting hostility to culture necessitates the emergence of powerful elites to curb, contain and coerce the mob, and to furnish them with "ego ideals" that inspire identification, idealization, and call forth acts of service and long suffering. It also requires that collective resentment be displaced onto external scapegoats, so that the ruling elite will not become the target of the larger collective's burgeoning aggression.

The upshot of this line of reasoning is that as things get better, they also, inevitably, get worse, because with the ever-increasing domestication of the libido required by the advance of culture, which favors the proliferation of science and technology, the resulting tensions between social groups that follow as a consequence act to widen and deepen the scope of human destructiveness, increasing the likelihood of genocide and ultimate self-extinction. The whole process is a vicious circle. And in keeping with this grim historicism, Freud's claim that the majority of people inhabit a quasi-hypnoid state in relation to their political, military and religious leadership—whether true or not—is an act of devastating and commendable frankness. It suggests that our sense of belonging to specific groups, and our identifications with their claims to truth, are fueled by the same infantile fixations that give rise to lively disturbances of reality testing in our interpersonal worlds and in the clinical situation.

Despite its deeply pessimistic coloration, Freud's analysis of our civilized malaise occupies an important place in the history of ideas. Leaving its clinical ramifications to one side, it represents a critical response to the philosophy of the Enlightenment, and to the progressivist optimism of the nineteenth century. Granted, Freud believed in progress. But it is progress with a price tag; progress at the expense of physical and emotional fulfillment, at the expense of equality and peace. Furthermore, in Freud's estimation, appreciable gains in solidarity *within* a given group are inevitably compensated for by increasing hostility to outsiders, who bear the brunt of the group's displaced hostility to "culture," that is, the ruling elite. This is a blow to Enlightenment optimism. The most advanced representatives of the Enlightenment believed that the dissemination of reason through science, technology, and universal education would eventually liberate humanity from want and superstition, and thereby create the climate necessary for a universal world order based on peace, justice, and human equality—a secularized version of the messianic age.

Freud had no patience for this kind of nonsense. In contrast to the belief in progress that the nineteenth century embraced and espoused, for the most part, Freud, following Schopenhauer, Nietzsche, and Le Bon, declared that the limits of human rationality are reached the moment we enter the political arena, where instinct and irrationality are destined to prevail, despite our best intentions and most elaborate plans and safeguards.

Finally, Freud regarded our basic inner conflicts, or the conflicts between groups of instincts and between the individual and society, as givens or universals that vary only in intensity, not in kind. The repression and sublimation of eros—and the corresponding resentment among the masses—increase cumulatively in quantitative terms as history unfolds, but are not subject to any qualitative change or variation, as the cultural/interpersonal school of analysis later insisted.

As Fromm noted in the early 1930s, the belief in a timeless, unchanging unconscious mind, whose core constructs are inscribed deep in phylogenetic memory enabled Freud to project the psychological structure of his own milieu backward to prehistoric times, showing a naive indifference to the vast changes that social, technological, and economic changes have wrought on human nature since then. The most striking example of this tendency of Freud's was his attempt to universalize—indeed, ontologize—the Oedipus complex and render it culture constitutive, by tracing the basic coordinates of contemporary kinship and political systems, and the roots of religious belief, back to hypothetical events in the "primal horde" (Fromm 1932).

Unfortunately, it is not possible now to review all of Fromm's early rejoinders to Freud or explain how they foreshadow his later work. Suffice it to say that between 1929 and 1934 Fromm wrote several germinal papers on psychoanalytic social psychology within a more or less orthodox framework. But having studied Marx and Weber, he was already keenly aware that trying to explain a state of affairs that is prevalent in one's own society by reference to imagined events in remote prehistory, as Freud did with the Oedipus complex, is a dubious and ethnocentric undertaking, no matter how eloquently or persuasively you appear to carry it off (Fromm 1932).

Fromm's landmark paper, "The Social Limitations of Psychoanalytic Therapy" (1935), like all of his early papers, was characterized by a densely woven counterpoint between clinical and sociological concerns. However, this paper had a new urgency that reflected Fromm's deepening disenchantment with the constraints and limitations of classical Freudianism. Fromm focused specifically on Freud's clinical posture and directives, and argued that analytic neutrality, as Freud evidently conceived it, is frequently a cover-up for the analyst's unconscious sadism or indifference to the patient.

Furthermore, Fromm charged that patients invariably discern the analyst's real feelings and attitudes beneath their surface neutrality—whether consciously, or otherwise—and that this frequently results in the reactivation or intensification of old traumas, not their careful and methodical resolution, as Freud had hoped. The clinical orientations of Groddeck and Ferenczi, Fromm added, point the way beyond the austere strictures of classical theory toward a radical and humanistic therapeutic practice.

This paper is interesting for a number of reasons. From a historical perspective, Fromm's critique of Freud and his glowing remarks on Ferenczi are remarkably similar to the contemporaneous work of Glaswegian psychiatrist Ian Suttie, an early figure at the Tavistock and author of *The Origins of Love and Hate* (1935). Both Fromm and Suttie reproached Freud for being excessively imbued with a patriarchal spirit and allowing his healing discoveries to be shackled by them.

Moreover, although Fromm had not yet coined the phrase "the pathology of normalcy," the obvious and direct implication of his whole line of analysis is that Freud's bourgeois, patriarchal attitudes were the product of a socially patterned defect that Freud shared with the majority of his middle-class contemporaries, whose pejorative assessment of neurotic suffering he only partially transcended. (Ferenczi's influence is patent here.) To be sure, this was not the only time Fromm said so. Later, in *Sigmund Freud's Mission* (1959) he voiced a very similar objection in connection with Freud's psychology of women.

From 1935 onward, we see a dramatic shift in Fromm's manner of theorizing. Having dropped the libido theory, Fromm now focused increasingly on what he called "existential needs" that are rooted in the conditions of human existence and not in specific tissue needs or somatic drives. Fromm now insisted that the core conflict between the individual and society was not the repression or sublimation of the instincts per se, but how a given society meets or disappoints the individual's need for self-actualization and core to core relatedness to other people. From this point of view, a society could be substantially lacking in sexual repression—like Aldous Huxley's *Brave New World*—and still be profoundly deranged. By redefining the source and the nature of the needs that safeguard and threaten our sanity and well-being, Fromm transposed Freud's notion of "the pathology of civilized communities" into an entirely different key.

Moreover, observing developments around him, Fromm saw no real reason to posit a strong or significant correlation between the repression or sublimation of eros and the advance of technology per se. This marks another significant break with Freud, who imagined that all cultural and technological achievement—and he scorned to differentiate between the two—is based on the repression or transformation of the libido, and therefore that progress is contingent on the dampening of sexual appetites and self-expression.

This kind of theorizing used by Freud may sound quaint or even a little bizarre to contemporary ears, but it was perfectly intelligible in Victorian times. After all, the industrial and scientific revolutions that began in the late seventeenth century, which brought the bourgeoisie to power, seemed to climax in an atmosphere of unprecedented prudishness and sexual privation—particularly for the middle class, whose strength was steadily increasing, relative to the aristocracy. Meanwhile, Victorian adventurers and ethnographers were journeying to exotic archipelagos and remote African highlands, where they encountered tribal societies whose sexual life was comparatively free and unrestrained. At the time, the inference seemed obvious—progress, prudishness, and continence go hand in hand.

Unfortunately, Freud and his contemporaries were mistaken on this point. A general relaxation of sexual mores set in soon after the First World War, and continued during the pre- and post–Second World War era, barring a brief interlude in the 1950s. With the advent of AIDS and the religious right, this progressive relaxation of sexual behavior may change or reverse itself, in time. But no one can deny that during this period of history, the development of technology accelerated at an unprecedented rate. Moreover, the progressive movement toward the relaxation of sexual constraints did not result in a more peaceful world, as Freudian theory would have predicted. On the contrary, it was a time of unprecedented slaughter and brutality on a global scale despite more enlightened sexual mores. Whatever developments may await us in the future, these facts speak strongly against Freud's historicism, and the argument that history represents some inexorable and unified progression that necessitates the repression or domestication of eros, and a corollary intensification of aggression as a result.

In retrospect, Fromm's reflections on clinical constructs and historical trends leave us with some intriguing questions. One objection raised by clinically minded critics is that his tendency to regard neurosis as being symptomatic of health, so to speak, gives many neurotics an ersatz sense of identity as misunderstood heroes or geniuses, an illusion they use to rationalize their insistent anger and their persistent neediness. There is merit to these objections, and so Fromm (1964) redressed the initial one-sidedness of his earlier pronouncements by emphasizing that a neurotic may also be in conflict with society because he or she is *less* healthy than the average person.

The problem with this important caveat is that it leaves us, theoretically, with two classes of neurotic individuals—one group that is insufficiently individuated to throw off the shackles of convention and express its opposition constructively, and another, even more damaged variety that is more alienated than the average person and incapable of joining the mainstream as a consequence. For the latter group, achieving a "normal" level of functioning would presumably be a big step forward, and a valid therapeutic objective.

Intuitively, and at first sight, these distinctions seem to make a lot of sense, but by and large, Fromm said very little about how to discriminate between these different types of neurotic disturbance, and many clinicians would no doubt object that some people appear to combine aspects of both types simultaneously.[1] Moreover, to the best of my knowledge, Fromm said nothing about how to distinguish genuine, existential suffering from neurotic misery, either in qualitative or quantitative terms. In the absence of clear-cut theoretical guidelines, some clinicians may still feel that they can make reliable discriminations of this kind on a clinical-experiential basis. But sometimes the two are very, very hard to disentangle, even on a purely experiential level.

Another serious problem is raised by Fromm's critique of Freud. Fromm argued that Freud was deeply affected by the socially patterned defects that prevailed in his sociocultural milieu. And in retrospect, no doubt, many of us agree that Fromm's criticisms were on target. Still, if this was true of Freud, it stands to reason that this same criticism applies with equal justice to the majority of less visionary people who make up the majority of practicing analysts—and indeed, potentially all mental health practitioners. For if we really take the idea of socially patterned defects seriously, we cannot exclude their effects on the majority of "normal" psychotherapists *a priori*, unless we wish to maintain, against all the evidence of experience and against common sense, that the training or selection of psychotherapists somehow makes them privileged or exempt, a society apart from society, or that our own society is somehow unblemished or unaffected by these deformations of consciousness.

Obviously, this is a sobering prospect. Nowadays, many analytically oriented psychotherapists feel quite comfortable condemning Freud's incorrigible sexism, or his cold, pedagogical posture as a clinician, although when Fromm began writing about these topics, doing so was considered an act of betrayal, if not slightly bizarre. Still, even now, few psychotherapists relish the idea that they are somehow implicated in perpetuating a status quo that precludes the full emergence of their client's critical faculties or the unfolding of their humanistic conscience. We tend to think of the present naively, as a definitive transcendence of the past, and often forget that those who seek therapy nowadays, like those who provide it, still live in a global context of poverty, oppression, exploitation and genocide, to which all must adapt willy nilly, often at the expense of objectivity and compassion. And whether we are aware of it or not, many of us simply prefer to think *that* sort of thing only happened before, in the bad old days, that we have outgrown all that now.

In short, inasmuch as they assimilate it at all, most psychotherapists tend to appropriate Fromm's ideas on the pathology of normalcy as a way of dwelling on the defects of previous generations of therapists, by way of illustrating to themselves what wonderful, unbiased, progressive people they are. The idea that our own society, though quite different from Freud's, and from Fromm's, needless to say, has an equally pervasive tendency to shape and distort awareness, and to blunt the deep and differentiated experience of feelings and ideas that the majority would deem inappropriate, infantile, or paranoid is not an idea that appeals to the vast majority of psychotherapists. Yet this *is* the upshot of Fromm's theorizing. It is also the reason why Fromm repeatedly emphasized that unless psychoanalysts face the socially patterned defects characteristic of their own society, psychoanalysis would succumb to bureaucratic routinization, and eventually dwindle or perish due to irrelevance and/or widespread lack of credibility (Fromm 1970).

Meanwhile, as Paul Roazen reminds us, psychoanalysis is alive and growing in Paris and Buenos Aires, and throughout much of Latin America. Perhaps its status there is due to the fact that many of its Parisian and Latin American practitioners refused to treat psychoanalysis as a mere clinical specialty divorced from culture and politics. Indeed, many analysts there were recruited from the ranks of people who were actively involved in the struggle for social justice, as were many of their socialist counterparts in Vienna and Berlin in the movement's early days (Jacoby 1983).

Whether or not the current decline of psychoanalysis in the United States is attributable to the causes Fromm adduced is debatable, however. After all, other causes may be at work, including the rise of competing therapies, the revival of biological psychiatry, and the decline of a stable, leisured middle class. But this last possibility, which looms large in my mind, prompts further reflection. Fromm addressed the "pathology of normalcy" in Fascist Europe and the postwar United States. While he noted the differences between these societies—the former being excessively patriarchal, the latter inimical to old-fashioned patriarchalism—the common feature they shared was the way in which the average person's capacity to reason and respond compassionately to life was eroded by consensus and convention, and by the desire to promote personal security or success at the expense of recognizing and acting on the truth.

In fairness to Fromm's critics, some positive developments have occurred since he wrote about these issues. The civil rights, feminist, and environmental movements, which address socially patterned defects like racism, sexism, and environmental degradation, have made their way into the mainstream, albeit against considerable resistance and with debatable effectiveness in many instances. Moreover, the Cold War is over, diminishing the likelihood of nuclear holocaust, at least in the short term.

Even so, in the broad sweep of history, these apparent gains may be comparatively short lived. If we take Fromm seriously, we must do for our time what he did for his, recognizing that Fromm wrote in a period when the middle class, which furnishes the majority of analytic clients, enjoyed greater stability and prosperity than it does at present or is likely to any time in the foreseeable future. Indeed, with the increasing proletarianization of younger professionals and academics, and increasing alienation and insecurity due to new technology, downsizing, and competition, it is possible that we are witnessing the end of middle-class affluence as Fromm, for example, knew it.

The causes and consequences of this process are too numerous and complex to enumerate here. But one is that, like their working-class counterparts of days gone by, both spouses in middle-class marriages must now work in order to pay the bills. It is not a question of having a choice. And characteristically, their careers require more time and energy than they did in days gone by. Indeed, by and large, people have to train and work longer to achieve less and less than they did twenty or thirty years ago. The combination of stress, insecurity, and erratic parenting that results from these new economic trends and pressures is inimical to the development of intimacy and injures parents and children alike, even when the damage is offset somewhat by relative affluence for more fortunate people, or rationalized by such off-putting euphemisms as "quality time" (see, e.g., LaBier 1986).

There is a grim irony in all of this. Technology was originally conceived of as a labor saving device, and in theory, perhaps, it still is. In practice, however, the proliferation of new technologies tends to result in joblessness for many, and in *too much* work for those who have it. Another consequence of rapid technological development is the progressive decline of historical mindedness, of genuine literacy, and of what Erik Erikson termed "transgenerational identification." In traditional societies, the pace of technological change was slow, enabling younger people to identify with the attitudes and experiences of their elders.

Now, however, each emergent revolution in society's infrastructure renders it increasingly difficult for the young to empathize in a meaningful way with the experience of their predecessors, as the parameters and proverbial rules of the game shift rapidly to respond to new social and technical realities. Apart from fostering the disintegration of intergenerational ties, this results in an increasingly anxious eye to the future, and an impoverished sense of the past, which stands in marked contrast to the attitudes and sensibilities of previous ages and contributes appreciably to what Fromm termed the "marketing character," which lacks a strong sense of rootedness (Burston 1991). It also contributes to an overall decline in literacy, which is increasingly becoming the domain of academic specialists. And as literacy and historical mindedness evaporate, entertainment, with its standardized and homogenized perspectives on reality, jumps in to fill the gap. The decline in real literacy—as opposed to "computer literacy" or mere escapist reading— is fostered, in turn, by the time and effort it takes to continually recalibrate one's skills and attitudes to adapt to shifting market forces. Who has time to read, *really* read, a book, to meditate on it, allowing the author's ideas and experiences to penetrate into the deeper recesses of one's soul?

Leaving vexing economic issues like third-party payment and managed care to one side, can psychoanalysis survive in a society bereft of leisure, literacy, and a sense of connectedness with the past? Not very likely. And because Europe and Latin America lag behind the United States in the decline of leisure and literacy, they will probably be a more hospitable environment for psychoanalysis in the future.

As unfortunate and uncompromising as these developments are for the future of psychanalysis, there are other, more serious possibilities to ponder. The galloping resurgence of fascism around the world is an ominous backdrop to these domestic developments in the United States. If past history is any guide, the current dislocation and downward mobility of the middle class will probably lead to increasing political polarization, with an increasingly angry and militant right-wing eventually leaping into the vacuum created by the disintegrating center. Who says that it can't happen here?[2] Or that if it does not, that we can surmount or even survive the damage to the biosphere that would inevitably result from a confrontation with nuclear fascism abroad. Even if we avert planetary death, life as we know it will change forever, and an increasingly totalitarian political culture would almost inevitably emerge, albeit one that may pay lip service to the liberal and emancipatory ideals of days gone by as a rhetorical justification for its repressive practices.

One need not subscribe to Freud's philosophy of history to appreciate the element of truth it contains. If Marx tended to celebrate the liberating potentialities unleashed by new technologies, Freud drew our attention to the price we pay for progress. While there are always grounds for hope, optimism, in the conventional sense, may actually be detrimental to our collective interests, if it prevents us from seeing the writing on the wall. This attitude of sober realism, which is not despair, but an unflinching assessment of global actualities, is especially apparent in the later Fromm, whose message reached fewer people because of his decline in popularity after 1968.

Unfortunately, despite (or because of) Fromm's many best-sellers, Fromm bashing was a popular pastime among the liberal and left-wing intelligentsia during the late 1960s and 1970s—so much so, in fact, that nowadays his ideas are hardly remembered or discussed. Despite his prescient critiques of Freud's sexism and authoritarianism, Fromm has acquired the reputation of being a pedant, a popularizer, and a fashioner of trite, homiletic platitudes who was secretly impervious (if not actually hostile) to the deeper implications of Freudian theory. Fromm's work is not beyond criticism or reproach, but most of the fashionable indictments that have shaped the current public perception of him, such as it is, suffer from an excess of polemical zeal, and a lack of genuine historical understanding. In truth, the real reason he is ignored nowadays is that Fromm at his best was too provocative and disturbing to be readily assimilated into the analytic mainstream.

ENDNOTES

1. Michael Maccoby informs me that Fromm did in fact provide clear clinical criteria for distinguishing between healthier-

than-normal and less-healthy-than-normal neurotics in a work-shop for students of the Mexican Psychoanalytic Institute in México (Cuernavaca, México, 1963). However, the fact that those remarks were never published, and that Fromm apparently saw no need to publicize them, remains something of a mystery, as does the hypothetical distinction between neurotic and existential suffering.

2. Editor's note: This statment was particularly prescient. Burston made this observation in May 1994, before the Oklahoma City bombing and the increased public awareness of the existence of home-grown fanatic militia groups and antiabortion terrorist tactics.

REFERENCES

Burston, D. (1991). *The Legacy of Erich Fromm*. Cambridge, MA: Harvard University Press.
Ellenberger, H. (1970). *The Discovery of the Unconscious*. New York: Basic Books.
Freud, S. (1921). Group psychology and the analysis of the ego. *Standard Edition* 18:69–143.
_____ (1927). The future of an illusion. *Standard Edition* 21:5–56.
_____ (1930). Civilization and its discontents. *Standard Edition* 21:64–145.
_____ (1939). Moses and monotheism. *Standard Edition*. 23:7–137.
Fromm, E. (1932). On the method and function of an analytical social psychology. In *The Crisis of Psychoanalysis*, pp. 110–134. Greenwich, CT: Fawcett Premier 1970.
_____ (1935). Die Gesseschaftliche Bedingtheit der Psychoanalytischen Therapie. (The social limitations of psychoanalytic therapy.) In *Gesamtausgabe Band I: Analytische Sozialpsychologie*, ed. R. Funk, pp. 115–138. Stuttgart: Deutscher Taschenbuch Verlag, 1989.
_____ (1941). *Escape from Freedom*. New York: Avon, 1965.
_____ (1944). Individual and social origins of neurosis. *American Sociological Review* 9(4). Reprinted in *Science of Man: Yearbook of the International Erich Fromm Society*. 4:231–237, 1993.

_____ (1947). *Man for Himself*. Greenwich, CT: Fawcett Premier.

_____ (1955). *The Sane Society*. Greenwich, CT: Fawcett Premier.

_____ (1959). *Sigmund Freud's Mission: An Analysis of His Personality and Influence*. New York: Harper & Row, 1970.

_____ (1964). *The Heart of Man: Its Genius for Good and Evil*. New York: Harper & Row.

_____ (1970). *The Crisis of Psychoanalysis*. Greenwich, CT: Fawcett Premier.

_____ (1973). *The Anatomy of Human Destructiveness*. Greenwich, CT: Fawcett Premier.

_____ (1975). Humanism and psychoanalysis. *Contemporary Psychoanalysis* 11(4):396–406.

Jacoby, R. (1975). *Social Amnesia*. Boston: Beacon.

_____ (1983). *The Repression of Psychoanalysis*. New York: Basic Books.

LaBier, D. (1986). *Modern Madness: The Emotional Fallout of Success*. Reading, MA: Addison-Wesley.

Roazen, P. (1986). *Freud: Political and Social Thought*. New York: Da Capo.

Suttie, I. (1935). *The Origins of Love and Hate*. Harmondsworth: Penguin, 1960.

13

The Social Dimensions of Transference

Salvador Millán

TRANSFERENCE: A KEY FOR THERAPEUTIC SUCCESS

Freud's earliest views of psychoanalytic treatment were premised on developing a positive transference in the form of an almost complete faith on the part of the patient in the authority of the psychoanalyst. This transference was seen as the basis for a successful treatment outcome. Patients who revealed doubts about the treatment or the competence of the analyst were deemed poor candidates for treatment.

It is true this strategy had a historical function and facilitated the early practice of psychoanalysis among Freud's closest followers. Nonetheless, the treatment had strong authoritarian and paternalistic overtones. In his writing on technique Freud recommended great care in the selection of cases. He believed that only neuroses in which the patient was able to transfer the conflict and deposit it into the figure of the therapist (Freud 1912) were appropriate for psychoanalytic treatment. The therapist would then become a "father image" (Freud 1912, p. 100). The concept of transference became a fundamental key to therapeutic success. The patient's confidence in the therapist contributed to a positive transference that would become crucial to weather the storms of the negative transference (Freud 1913).

This technical strategy originated the division of the neuroses into two categories: the transference neuroses (hysterias and obsessions), and the narcissistic neuroses. The latter neuroses were thought of as incapable of transferring the conflict. Hence the leverage obtained by transferring this hope of a cure onto the figure of the therapist was lost. Freud reaffirmed this principle many times and warned therapists that trying to treat neuroses in which there was a failure to deposit this conflict into the figure of the therapist was doomed to fail. Without this transference the therapist would lose the most powerful lever of success.

This lack of transference in the narcissistic neuroses was explained by libido theory. Freud (1912, p. 102) credited Carl Jung as introducing the term *introversion* to explain the inability of the narcissistic neuroses to externalize or project the neuroses onto the therapist. In narcissistic neuroses, "the portion of libido which is capable of becoming conscious and directed towards reality is diminished" and the portion which is directed *away* from reality and is unconscious, and which, though it may still feed the subject's phantasies, nevertheless belongs to the unconscious, is proportionally increased" (Freud 1912, p. 102, italics original). In contrast, the transference neuroses are seen as building on the possibility of developing a positive transference and mobilizing libido toward the therapist.

It was not until the 1930s that theoretical discussions began to appear in psychoanalytic circles that questioned some premises of Freud's libido theory under the heading of ego psychology (Tyson and Tyson 1990). More recently Greenberg and Mitchell (1983) have made the distinction between drive theories, which remain basically consistent with Freud's tension-reduction model, and relational theories, which to a greater or lesser extent revise Freud's drive model with relational constructs. Freud's original distinction between narcissistic neuroses and transference neuroses can be seen as an early precursor of the difference between drive theories (narcissistic neurosis) and relational theories (transference neurosis).

THE MEDICALIZATION OF TRANSFERENCE

Otto Fenichel's (1938) classical work synthesized the debate between Reik, Glover, Ferenczi, and others over issues of transference. Fenichel's view of transference became the cornerstone on matters of psychoanalytic treatment. He maintained Freud's hierarchical superior-subordinate model of transference as well as the paternalistic role of the therapist as a father figure.

Fenichel formulates a series of prerequisites that he considers necessary for effective therapy. First, he defines the clinical setting as requiring the patient to be in a horizontal position with the analyst out of the patient's eyesight. These arrangements are justified so as to maintain the transference from becoming contaminated. This aseptic view of therapy conjures up the image of the clinical setting as a surgical room. The therapist-surgeon with his knowledge, preparation, and pristine technique coldly and impartially carries out therapeutic interventions leading to a cure. The patient acquiesces to the therapist's expertise in hopes of becoming free from his illness.

Fenichel in effect transforms Freud's surgical metaphors of psychoanalysis into a medical procedure requiring an aseptic clinical setting. The therapist waits passively for the transference to make its appearance before he can act. Analytic work, according to Fenichel, should aspire to a relationship of strict neutrality with the patient. With the medicalization of psychoanalysis the view of the patient becomes extraneous from social reality.

A FUNDAMENTAL KEY: THE PATIENT'S SOCIAL REALITY

Fromm questioned and criticized this view of transference. He pointed out that so-called positive transference,[1] apparently so necessary for the cure, was very unlikely to have a positive effect on the treatment, particularly when it was the result of practical and unavoidable facts. For example, in the Cuernavaca seminars that I attended he commented on his analysis with Hans Sacks. When in one session of analysis he hung his own coat next to Sacks's, the gesture was interpreted as evidence of a "positive transference." In fact, Fromm commented "there was no other place to hang it" (personal communication, 1970a).

In *Escape from Freedom* (1941) Fromm analyzed the many factors that led to stunted development. Among the factors mentioned were individual limitations, experiences of rejection, the types of alliances and bonds that were established, the nature of relationships, sadomasochism, struggles for power, and the war between the sexes. All these schemes that led to dependence on authority figures were analyzed by Fromm from a very different theoretical perspective than Freud's.

In Fromm's analysis fear played a central role, particularly the fear of taking charge of one's life. Dependence on an authority figure with expert knowledge made it easier to believe that some other person could solve the problems of living. This dependence on authority and fear of freedom were played out in the analytic setting as part of a paternal transference. Fromm tried to avoid replicating the experience of oppressive conditions in analysis by creating a less-structured relationship with the patient. He believed analysis should be a process of common apprenticeship for both participants. Fromm's view of analysis emphasized the mutuality of the analytic relationship (Gojman 1983).

This relational model is at the heart of Fromm's concepts of human nature (Fromm 1955, 1968, 1973). Fromm's view of human nature is dialectical and saw human needs as dichotomous. Each human need could be satisfied progressively or regressively, and was rooted in the conditions of human existence, in life itself. By contrast, Freud saw man as predestined, hence incapable of changing in any fundamental way (Freud 1927). Freud's metapsychology was physicalistic and mechanistic, reducing human passions to energy concepts (Freud 1925). Had Fromm completed his work on clinical psychoanalysis, his approach would be more consistent with a more participative and empathic view of the therapeutic relation. Freud's clinical approach unconsciously perpetuates power schemes of hierarchical and bureaucratic society (Funk 1993).[2]

I share with Fromm the belief that the need for human relatedness is the fundamental problem of human growth. The dichotomy of isolation versus relatedness captures the tension of this vital need. Transference is best understood

within the context of this dynamic. For Fromm the fundamental issue in transference reflects the more general need
of humans to adapt to society. According to Fromm (1947)
this adaptation takes place through a process of assimilation—the way in which society affects the individual—and
socialization—the way in which he or she relates to others.
These twin processes are the basis for the development of
character. For Fromm "the subjective function of character
for the normal person is to lead him to act according to
what is necessary for him from a practical standpoint"
(Fromm 1941, p. 283). "The result is a citizenry of individuals wanting to act as they have to act" (Fromm 1955, p.77,
quoted by Greenberg and Mitchell, 1983). It is through the
analysis of these processes we can understand human
adaptation and the human relations that are established as
a result of these processes.

According to Fromm, the basis of hope and what makes
the therapy an adventure is the face to face encounter with
another human being. In this analytic encounter adaptive
processes are studied with the faith that we all have within
us the capacity to grow and change (Millán 1983).

To summarize, Fromm's theory of character (Fromm
1947, Fromm and Maccoby 1970) provides a better understanding of human relations than Freud's theories. The
processes of assimilation and socialization are the means
through which humans become incorporated into society.

Fromm's theory of character originated from the experience with clinical populations and used Freud's clinical
descriptions of character based on psychosexual development—oral, anal, and genital stages—as a starting point
(Freud 1908, Fromm 1970b, Millán 1985). This limitation
has been overcome by recent empirical studies that have
enriched our understanding of social character (Lenkerd
1994, Maccoby 1976, 1988, Tauscher 1993). These new
studies, conducted with participant research methodolo-

gies, have amplified the descriptions of social character by involving the people who are studied as co-participants in the process as described by Lenkerd (1991) and Maccoby (Maccoby and Duckles 1975). Theoretical reflection has expanded from descriptions of character based on clinical settings to the study of normal populations. In other words, the field of study expanded to the process of human integration to society and not just the projection of the father–son relationship onto the figure of the analyst in the consulting room.

These studies observe and assess how people are adapted to their social world by means of an interpretative questionnaire and ethnographic observation (Lenkerd 1994, Millán 1993). Some of these studies have evolved into participative research projects (Barroso 1993, Gojman 1993, Sanchez 1993) based on the theoretical framework of social character—an integration of psychoanalysis and social sciences. These projects powerfully show us the profound contradictions that exist in the human need to adapt to society, and how this adaptation can lead to further isolation and alienation or to the development of stronger communities and human ties.

THE CUERNAVACA SEMINARS

Fromm found it hard to leave a formal legacy concerning psychoanalytic technique. Nonetheless, in his supervision of cases and in his seminars in Cuernavaca he transmitted his ideas about technique to candidates of the Mexican Psychoanalytic Institute (Fromm 1968). In these seminars we find clear principles that allow us to understand his concept of transference and situate it historically in its proper place.

Fromm's point of departure is based on Freud. He emphasized that "transference has to do with the experience of infancy" (Fromm 1968, p. 5), which is repeated in the presence of the therapist. He agrees with Freud "that the interpretation of this transference is the classic method of psychoanalytic technique" (Fromm 1968, p. 2), and that in many ways transference is the repetition of infancy into the present. Yet Fromm thought that "this phenomenon is a limited concept, since it only takes in consideration one irrational aspect" (Fromm 1968, p. 2). However, when other "irrational aspects of the transference are taken into consideration, the definition of transference expands" (p. 2). If, Fromm observes, we look at transference as "an experience in which the patient deposits in the person of the analyst the origins of all of his expectations and fears, these can also not have anything to do with the parents" (Fromm 1968, p. 2). For example:

> If the individual is full of fear, it implies that the other person has more power, which is the same as believing that the analyst and the world are more powerful. . . . In this condition the individual tends to bind himself to other people (neurotically). So if we add fear to the other affects, wishes, or anxieties of the patients (irrational fear), the analyst can understand them more broadly from this perspective, and not just as a repetition of infancy to the present. [pp. 2–3]

This second definition of transference transcends Freud's since it insists that fears go beyond a simple repetition of infantile experience. It is from the broader perspective that Fromm defines the relation with the analyst as "the mirror from which we can observe the whole emotional structure that exists inside the patient, particularly the irrational one" (Fromm 1968, p. 3). In other words, the phenomenon of transference is not just a repetition of experiences from childhood but represents the whole experience of the patient's life.

In still a third definition of transference, Fromm (1968) points out that transference can be "converted into a microscopic observation of the patient's relation with the world, with the advantage that in the analytic session one can observe with greater detail the relationship one has with the world in its entirety" (p. 3). In the seminars Fromm (1968) said that this was the definition which gave him most satisfaction.

Fromm's concepts mark a clear difference from the more orthodox concepts of transference, where the affects projected onto the analyst are not taken as real, but rather are a repetition from childhood and have nothing to do with the analyst as a person. The extreme case of this position is taken by Fenichel and his aseptic technique, which prescribes a strict neutrality for the analyst.

Fromm believed that the concept of neutrality was at best naive and at worst an attempt to hide behind psychoanalytic technique to avoid confronting painful emotional realities for the patient and the analyst. Just as the patient is reacting as a total human being in his relationship with the analyst, so the analyst reacts to the patient as a whole person. The fact that the patient is on a couch or cannot see the analyst does not prevent him or her from being able to seize up and test the personality of the analyst. For Fromm transference is "actually a conglomerate of all relations, including the irrational aspects, that the patient has toward the world" (Fromm 1968, p. 4).

Fromm saw fear as the engine that motivates individuals to bind themselves to another person in a childish and dependent way. Fear of freedom and becoming oneself is the essence of Fromm's thesis. These fears depend on "social factors" (Fromm 1968, p. 12) and force the analyst to understand the transference in "two senses" (p. 9). In one sense the patient in relationship with his analyst is actually projecting something from his infancy and transference has nothing to do with the analyst personally. In another sense, the patient projects all social aspects onto him; that is to say, the person's "projection" is his way of relating.

Faced with these two transferential reactions, Fromm recognized that "the therapist offers a countertransference response that determines the directions he takes and his ability to grasp these two situations" (Fromm 1968, p. 12). The therapist cannot ignore the fact he has to respond to these two different functions of transference "as observer of reactions that are enacted by the patient and have nothing to do with the therapist (per se) and also as an observer of reactions to the analyst as a concrete person." Fromm thought that the analyst should try to find a "functional explanation" for the phenomenon that takes into account the genetic (past) experience as well as an understanding of the forces that sustain the transference in the present.

To sum up, psychoanalysis is the study of transference. However, transference has to be understood broadly as a phenomenon of interdependence that is being enacted within the context of a specific social reality that cannot be ignored.

THE SOCIAL CONTEXT OF TRANSFERENCE

Fromm's contribution compels us to understand character within the context of the social dynamics to which the individual must adapt. In other words, we need to understand social character. As analysts we need not only to pay attention to our countertransference, but also to situate the patient within the context of his social reality in order to gain the knowledge that will help us understand him or her.

We will not be able to detach ourselves from the influence of the predominant ideology and the emotional responses embodied in social character if we do not recognize them. This is a fundamental difference in our approach to transference and countertransference issues from the false ideal represented by the concept of neutrality. The influence exerted by the social context is pervasive as it becomes internalized as social character traits.

As the theory and research of social character demonstrate, one of the main forces that influence the development of social character is the economic factor. Economic forces have powerful repercussions in the members of any given society.

For example, in the so-called First World, we find a high degree of technological advancement, a tendency toward a mechanized automation of society with robotics as a production ideal. Maccoby (1988) has found a series of character-related traits in the children of high-tech managers in transnational companies. These young adults often come from divorced families. These families have had to adapt frequently to new language, customs, and schools. They are usually efficient and competent, can get things done on time and can make decisions quickly. However, this adaptation has exerted a toll. These young adults are distrustful and have many difficulties in developing intimate relations. Maccoby has called this new generation "self developers." From a perspective of human development, this emerging social character is highly adaptable and successful but also narcissistic. It is not surprising that many of these individuals are being described in the writings of contemporary psychoanalytic authors.

Another interesting example comes from social character studies done in the former East and West Germany. These studies are of particular interest given the enormous change that has to take place to integrate East Germany into the larger nation, and they demonstrate clearly that change cannot be imposed by decree. Several character types stand out in this transition process that are of great significance and doubtless are the legacy of forty-year-old socioeconomic structures. These social structures are so different that they cannot erase profound social character differences between individuals from East and West Germany. The contrast between a free market society of the west and an authoritarian state with feudal shadings in the east is much too great to allow for any sudden change of social character types.

The social character studies of West Germans show people with marketing characters and significant narcissistic qualities. Data from East Germany show people with a typical dependence on authority that are adapted to a paternalistic society (Tauscher 1993).

In so-called Third World countries there are certain similarities to the observed contrast between West and East Germany, in the rich–poor divide (Millán 1991). In traditional farming populations facing imminent industrialization, we found that historical and economic forces best explained peasants' receptivity. However in the same population there were individuals with productive hoarding traits (Fromm and Maccoby 1970) who were better able to adapt to changing circumstances. The absence of people with marketing traits was a remarkable finding that can only be explained by the fact that the free market economy has not yet made enough inroads into peasant villages to require this adaptation.

CONCLUSION

While these descriptions of the effects social conditions have on the development of character are sketchy, I hope they illustrate the importance these conditions have in shaping human beings. In pointing them out, my intention is to make us more aware of how attitudes and beliefs shaped by these social forces can make themselves felt in the consulting room as transference and countertransference reactions. By becoming aware of these dimensions of transference and countertransference we can expand the purview of both. The main thesis of my chapter is that transference and countertransference are not separate phenomena from character development, but are synonymous with the process of character development. That is to say, transference is a manifestation of character development as it presents itself to the analyst. The same can be said of countertransference. The analytic setting is a microcosm from which we can see the effects of social adaptation. Seen from this perspective, I believe the analytic dialogue is at once exquisitely private and profoundly social.

ENDNOTES

1. Other examples of trivial details being interpreted as a sign of a "positive transference" are described by Esther Menaker (1989).

2. For Fromm it was fundamental to understand how socio-economic conditions create power structures and lead to the bureaucratization of society. In capitalist systems, social character traits adapted to these structures are a glue that holds society together.

REFERENCES

Barroso, A. M. (1993). The Women's Workshop. Alternatives, encounters and contrasts. In *Cuadernos*, vol. 4, México: Seminario de Sociopsicoanálisis, Instituto Mexicano de Psicoanálisis.

Fenichel, O. (1938). *Problemas de Tecnica Psicoanalitica*. México: Pax, 1960.

Freud, S. (1908). Character and anal erotism. *Standard Edition* 9:167–176.

_____ (1912). The dynamics of transference. *Standard Edition* 12:97–108.

_____ (1913). On beginning the treatment (further recommendations on the technique of psycho-analysis, I). *Standard Edition*. 12:121–144.

_____ (1925). Inhibitions, symptoms and anxiety. *Standard Edition*. 20:75–172.

_____ The future of an illusion. *Standard Edition*. 21:1–56.

Fromm, E. (1941). *Escape from Freedom*. New York: Farrar & Rinehart.

_____ (1947). *Man for Himself: An Inquiry into the Psychology of Ethics*. Greenich, CT: Fawcett.

_____ (1955). *The Sane Society*. Greenich, CT: Fawcett.

_____ (1968). *Siete Lecciones sobre Tecnica Psicoanálisis*. Unpublished text. Seminar, March 11, Cuernavaca. México: Library of the Instituto Mexicano de Psicoanálisis.

_____ (1970a). Communication in the Clinical Seminar in February in Cuernavaca, México.

_____ (1970b). The method and function of an analytic social psychology. In *The Crises of Psychoanalysis*. New York: Holt, Rinehart & Winston.

_____ (1972). Letter to Martin Jay. In *The Dialectical Imagination*, ed. M. Jay. Boston: Little, Brown.

_____ (1973). *Anatomy of Human Destructiveness*. New York: Holt Rinehart & Winston.

Fromm, E., and Maccoby, M. (1970). *Social Character in a Mexican Village: A Sociopsychoanalytic Study*. Englewood Cliffs, NJ: Prentice-Hall.

Funk, R. (1993). Fromm's approach to psychoanalytic theory and its relevance for therapeutic work. In *Cuadernos* vol. 4, México: Seminario de Sociopsicoanálisis del Instituto Mexicano de Psicoanálisis.

Gojman, S. (1983) Vampirismo y Poder. In *Cuatro Neurosis en Busca de Argumento*, ed. A. Aramoni, pp.78–108. México: Siglo XXI.

_____ (1991a). *Revaloracion del cuestionario interpretativo en una comunidad minera despues de tres años de trabajo comunitario* (diseño experimental pre y post-aplicacion a la experiencia de trabajo de grupo). *Report to Consejo Nacional de Ciencias y Technologia*, México.

_____ (1991b). Un camino a la autonomia. In *Cuadernos*, vol. 1. México: Seminario de Sociopsicoanálisis del Instituto Mexicano de Psicoanálisis.

_____ (1993). An overview of the Mexican project of sociopsychoanalytical participative research in a mining community. In *Cuadernos*, vol. 4 México: Seminario de Sociopsicoanálisis del Intituto Mexicano de Psicoanálisis.

Greenberg, J., and Mitchell, A. S. (1983). *Object Relations in Psychoanalytic Theory*. Cambridge, MA: Harvard University Press.

Lenkerd B. (1991). La relacion entre los tipos de caracter social descritos por Erich Fromm y Michael Maccoby. In *Cuadernos*, vol. 2. México: Seminario de Sociopsicoanálisis del Instituto Mexicano de Psicoanálisis A. C.

_____ (1994). *Meanings and Motivations at Work: The Social Char-*

acter of Managers and Staff at the U.S. ACTION Agency. Ann Arbor, MI: UMI.

Maccoby, M. (1976). *The Gamesman.* New York: Simon & Schuster.

_____ (1988). *Why Work: Leading the New Generation.* New York: Simon & Schuster.

Maccoby, M., and Duckles, R. (1975). El proyecto Bolivar: un experimento de reorganizacion del trabajo. *Revista de Psicoanalisis, Psiquiatria, y Psicologia* 7–8:119–140.

Menaker, E. (1989). *Appointment in Vienna.* New York: St. Martin's Press.

Millán, S. (1983). Travestismo, un sustituto Mecanico. In *Cuatro Neurosis en Busca de Argumento,* La Praxis psicoanalitica, ed. A. Aramoni, pp. 160–182. México: Siglo XXI.

_____ (1985). El concepto del sociopsicoanálisis. In *Anuario.* México: Instituto Mexicano de Psicoanálisis.

_____ (1988). El trabajo de sociopsicoanálisis en una comunidad minera. In *Anuario.* México: Instituto Mexicano de Psicoanálisis.

_____ (1991). El tercer mundo y el caracter social. In *Cuadernos,* vol. 2. México: Seminario de Sociopsicoanálisis del Instituto Mexicano de Psicoanálisis.

_____ (1993). Methodology for the evaluation of the interpretative questionnaire used during the sessions of the Mexican Seminar of Sociopsychoanalysis. In *Cuadernos,* vol. 4. México: Seminario de Sociopsicoanálisis del Instituto Mexicano de Psicoanálisis

Sanchez, G. (1993). See, hear, feel and speak: the children's workshop. In *Cuadernos,* vol. 4. México: Seminario de Sociopsicoanálisis del Instituto Mexicano de Psicoanálisis.

Tauscher, P. (1993). Comparative study of the social character of teachers in Eastern and Western Germany. In *Cuadernos,* vol. 4. México: Seminario de Sociopsicoanálisis del Instituto Mexicano de Psicoanálisis.

Tyson, P., and Tyson, R. (1990). *Psychoanalytic Theories of Development: An Integration.* New Haven, CT: Yale University Press.

14

Erich Fromm's Concept of Social Character and Its Relevance for Clinical Practice

Rainer Funk

FROMM'S APPROACH TO PSYCHOANALYSIS

In recent American psychoanalytic thinking, Fromm is usually seen as a representative of object relations theory and of Sullivan's theory of interpersonal relations. As Guntrip (1969) pointed out, the British object relations theory can be seen as paralleling Sullivan's theory of interpersonal relation, for both attempt to replace Freud's libido theory with a theory of objects or interpersonal relations.

There are also key differences. Although Fairbairn developed a "radical" object relation theory (Eagle 1988) and argued that the libido primarily seeks not for pleasure but for the object, still he is mainly interested in the relation to the *internalized* objects and, in this respect, follows Melanie Klein's approach. Fromm, on the other hand, is not so far removed from Fairbairn's understanding of internalized objects. In contrast to Freud, both are convinced that what is experienced as threatening is not a forbidden inner striving or impulse of the id, but rather negative experiences with outer objects that have then been internalized. Thus one seeks to do what the objects, or in Fromm's terms, what society, forces one to do to be socially functional.

Here we come to the point where I think Fromm developed his own unique approach to psychoanalysis, an approach that has not received the attention it deserves. Fromm's interest is not in the outer or the internalized "object" as such; for him, the outer or inner object by itself is the representation of society. To bring society into the discussion may seem far-fetched or irrelevant for clinical problems.

For most psychoanalysts engaged in clinical work the importance of society is secondary; while society may have some influence and should not be neglected, it is felt on the whole to be remote from the therapeutic situation. Society is seen as something over and against the individual; it is other people, an impersonal object, an entity opposed to the individual. Usually our concept of the individual is elicited by emphasizing individuality at the expense of other people. Since this concept is entrenched, any attempt to develop another concept is bound to encounter a good deal of skepticism.

Nevertheless I would suggest considering another concept of the individual, one that Fromm always had in mind but did not make as clear as he might have. To authenticate Fromm's special understanding of society and individual, one has to go back to his earlier career, before he became a member of the Frankfurt school and a representative of the so-called Freudo-Marxist group. One also has to focus on the specific Jewish background in which he grew up and was taught and that never ceased to mold his thinking. This Jewish understanding of the individual and society was lived out in his parents' and religious teachers' Orthodox Judaism in Frankfurt and was greatly influenced by Salman Baruch Rabinkow, a Hasidic teacher in Heidelberg, with whom Fromm studied from 1920 to 1925. This understanding is in Fromm's dissertation, completed in 1922 (Fromm 1989b) and also in his early German writings. It is summarized in a 1937 article, which I found four years ago in the New York Public Library. It is the last article that Fromm wrote in German and the only one he himself translated into English (although the translation was never published). In this paper, Fromm (1992d) explains:

> Society and the individual do not stand "opposite" each other. Society is nothing but living, concrete individuals, and the individual can only live life as a social being. His individual life practice is necessarily determined by the life practice of his society or class and in the last analysis, by the manner of production of his society, that means, by how this society produces, how it is organized to satisfy the needs of its members.
>
> The differences in the manner of production and life of various societies or classes lead to the development of different character structures typical of the particular society. Various societies differ from each other not only in differences in their manner of production and their social and political organization but also in that their people exhibit a typical character structure despite individual differences. We call this the "socially typical character." [pp. 76–77]

Fromm's main interest in looking at the individual is always what he here calls the "socially typical character" and later "social character." The point is that if you look at an individual you are primarily confronted with those psychic strivings and impulses, both conscious and unconscious, that the individual has in common with others living in the same socioeconomic circumstances. What makes this person different from, and unique among, others living in the same circumstances, his or her special and possibly traumatic experiences, is, in this respect, of secondary interest. These character orientations and traits were mediated by parents and other objects to whom the person was and is related. But these object relations are to be understood as representatives of society, molded by social orientations and expectations:

> I do believe that one cannot understand a person, an individual, unless one is critical and understands the forces of society which have molded this person, which have made this person what he or she is. To stop at the story of the family is just not enough. He will also only be fully aware of who he is if he is aware of the whole social situation in which he lives, all the pressures and all the factors which have their impact on him. [Fromm 1991, p. 102]

Doubtless this way of looking at man is plausible if one studies society by analyzing the social character of persons living in similar conditions. But the appeal of Fromm's approach is not diminished by looking at an individual or a patient. Fromm is interested first in the *social character* of a specific person. We are used to thinking just the opposite, namely that one can only understand an individual by looking at the unique conditions and circumstances specific to him. Not so with Fromm:

> Just as in all type forming, in the socially typical character only certain fundamental traits are distinguished

and these are such that, *according to their dynamic nature and their weight, they are of decisive importance* for all individuals of this society. The fruitfulness of this category is proved in the fact that . . . that analysis traces back the individual's character with all his individual traits to the elements of the socially typical character and that an understanding of socially typical character is essential to a full understanding of individual character. [Fromm 1992d, p. 77, my emphasis]

I want to emphasize that for Fromm the orientation and the traits shared with others assume decisive importance according to their dynamic nature and weight. While Fromm considered constitutional factors and unique experiences important, for him the social character was of at least equal significance. This focus on common traits and orientations is just the opposite of our usual way of looking at people. Especially in psychotherapy we prefer the individualistic point of view and thereby overestimate what is most individual. We focus on the highly individualistic conditions and events in the patient's childhood. We are used to looking at the individual as an entity clearly distinguished and separated from society, although perhaps endowed with internalized aspects of society (by the superego or by inner objects); or we see the individual as only secondarily influenced by society, but principally separated from it.

This is not Fromm's way of looking at a person or a patient. In his dissertation about the function of the Jewish law, in an encounter with a patient, or in his analysis of political events, Fromm is always primarily interested in those fundamental traits and orientations that result from a practice of life *common* to many people. This is the meaning of his statement that "the individual can only live life as a social being" (Fromm 1992d, p. 76). This is—as I understand Fromm—the real meaning of his concept of social character.

Before attempting to apply Fromm's psychoanalytic approach to some therapeutic questions, I want to qualify the statement that Fromm is primarily interested in the social character of an individual. Fromm's interest in social character is always an interest in the question whether the orientation of the social character is productive or nonproductive. There are many aspects of productivity versus nonproductivity. One aspect that seems to me decisive for psychotherapy and the relation between the psychoanalyst and analysand is the degree of alienation underlying all nonproductive social character orientations. In the 1950s Fromm described a clinical concept of alienation and self-alienation as an essential part of the marketing orientation. This type of marketing alienation marks the specific form of nonproductive social character orientation that is typical of many diseases confronting us in our therapeutic practice.

ALIENATION AND FROMM'S INTEREST IN A PRODUCTIVE SOCIAL CHARACTER ORIENTATION

To illustrate what Fromm means by alienation let me start with some statements made by a 21-year-old patient I see in practice. Tom is a student who, in the course of three semesters, has twice switched his major and suffers from an inability to form satisfying relationships with others. He says, "I am always forced to blend in with my surroundings; the colors of the world around me rub off on me; I can't help slipping into the character of another person and hearing and feeling as this person does; in any case I must keep up my cover because this is all I have; I am a sponge that soaks up everything." This student is alienated from himself and suffers from the absence of a sense of authenticity. Thus to feel himself at all, to experience any sense of identity, he has to soak up feelings, ideas, and stimuli from others to compensate for his inner emptiness. For some, Tom's manner of living and experiencing himself, while somewhat exaggerated, is on the whole quite normal, but this manner of sensing his or her identity is only "normal" because it is so widespread in industrial societies that it is usually not felt as alienation.

"Literally speaking," says Fromm, in a lecture given in 1953 at the New School for Social Research in New York, alienation "means that we are aliens to us or ourselves, or the world outside is alien to us" (Fromm 1991, p. 59). The process of becoming alien to oneself was first described by the prophets' critique of idolatry in the Old Testament; later Hegel and Marx coined the term *alienation* in the same sense; likewise the phenomenon of transference, as discussed in psychoanalysis, can be understood as a process of alienation (Fromm 1992a).

> The idolator is a person who prays to the product of his own hands. He takes a piece of wood. With one part, he builds himself a fire in order, for example, to bake a cake; with the other part of the wood, he carves a figure in order to pray to it. Yet what he prays to are merely things. [Fromm 1992c, p. 24]

Transference as known in psychoanalysis is a manifestation of idolatry:

> A person transfers his own activities or all of what he experiences—of his power, his love, of his power of thought—onto an object outside himself. . . . As soon as a person has set up this transferential relatedness, he enters

into relation with himself only by submitting to the object
onto which he has transferred his own human functions.
Thus, to love means: I love only when I submit myself to
the idol onto which I have transferred all my capacity for
love. . . . The more powerful an idol becomes—that is the
more I transfer to it—the poorer I become and the more I
am dependent on it, since I am lost if I lose that onto which
I have transferred everything that I have. [Fromm 1992c, p.
24]

Fromm is describing here alienation by symbiosis,
which is typically manifested under authoritarian conditions, and to the extent that psychoanalysis is organized
along dogmatic and authoritarian lines, one can expect
transference to be still understood in the symbiotic-
authoritarian sense sketched above. But Tom, the patient
referred to earlier, is not suffering from a symbiotic
dependency; his problem is that he is able neither to
develop a stable relationship with another person nor to
stabilize his empty self by a constant—even alienating—
symbiosis. What has happened here? How was the phenomenon of alienation managed to shift from relating
symbiotically to being unrelated but dependent on identity-
giving figures?
    To illustrate how this has come about, Fromm refers to
the fairy tale of "The Emperor's New Clothes" by Hans
Christian Andersen.

Modern man's perception of reality is fundamentally
different from that of the people in the fairy tale of "The
Emperor's New Clothes." . . . [There] the emperor still
exists. The issue is only that he is in reality naked,
although people believe that he is wearing clothes. Today,
though, the emperor is no longer present. Today man is
real only insofar as he is standing somewhere outside. He
is constituted only through things, through property,

through his social role, through his "persona"; as a living person, however, he is not real. [Fromm 1992b, p. 26]

People who are self-alienated in the authoritarian mode project their living substance—their love, wisdom, strength, all human potentialities that grow through practice—onto unliving, wooden, golden, or other things, thus making the idols into living things. Submitting to these idols allows one to participate in one's own projected psychic forces. This does not hold for people who are self-alienated because of their marketing orientation. The market is not a concrete superimposition; the market is an anonymous entity that, chameleon-like, changes its color every day. Nevertheless the market forces us to sell our personality on the marketplace, to renounce all human potentialities that are not salable on the market, that is, it obliges us to become commodities.

But, even as commodities, we cannot deny our psychic need for a sense of identity and our need for relatedness to others. These needs are part of our human nature, are inherent in our *conditio humana*. The marketing person who is unable to project his or her own psychic forces onto idols (because the market is an anonymous entity) and is unable to deny needs that are part of human nature, then proceeds to deny his or her own potentialities by expropriating them. The marketing person expects all growing, loving, humanly satisfying attributes of life to flow from consuming and appropriating commodities. The "having" mode of existence now predominates and replaces a productive way of relating the self and giving an authentic sense of identity.

By expropriating their own human faculties and denying what they can produce from themselves, through their own feelings, thoughts, and activities, human beings turn themselves into things, make idols of themselves. At the same time, they hallucinate that things that can be bought, consumed, and appropriated are actually living, human entities that will bring back what they have turned their backs on. To be active and alive is an attribute of human beings who are related by their own reason and love to reality and other human beings. Since denying one's own faculties makes it impossible to feel one's own vital wellsprings, the "solution" is to smoke a cigarette hoping for a surge of energy, to buy jogging shoes hoping this will restore a sense of aliveness, and so on. The marketing person needs this hallucination to compensate a fundamentally terrifying feeling of emptiness, boredom, loss of identity, inability to relate, deadness. And since this hallucination is a socially and economically accepted way of relating to oneself and to others, the individual usually manages to avoid experiencing the lifelessness of this way of being.

With this short sketch of alienation as a socially accepted disease aggravated by the loss of authoritarian structures and the predominance of the market economy, I have sought to illustrate the basic strivings people today suffer from, namely alienation from their own productive forces by turning themselves into things, dead commodities—the upshot being that they seek to enliven themselves by hallucinating acts of appropriation. To repeat once more Fromm's own words: "Today, man is real only insofar as he is standing somewhere outside. He is constituted only through things, through property, through his social role, through his 'persona'; as a living person, however, he is not real" (Fromm 1992b, p. 26).

THE RELEVANCE OF SOCIAL CHARACTER
FOR CLINICAL PRACTICE

Let me now come to some conclusions relevant to therapeutic practice. First, regarding Fromm's primary interest in social character, in contrast to prevailing ways of looking at the individual Fromm sees the individual *a priori* as a representation of society and as a socialized being in the grip of dynamic forces predominantly molded by the necessity to produce and, in highly specific ways, fit into a specific historical situation of society. Not only what is peculiar to a patient but especially what a patient has in common with his social group is, for Fromm, of primary interest.

Second, looking at a patient and primarily concentrating on his or her social character (with its strivings and dynamic forces) means being interested in the productive or nonproductive orientation of the social character, these orientations being understood as alternatives. Fromm developed several concepts to delineate the choice a patient is caught between. The first formulation was the alternative between spontaneous activity and passivity (Fromm 1941), then between productivity and nonproductivity (Fromm 1947), then between biophilia and necrophilia (Fromm 1964) and, finally, between the "having" and the "being" modes of existence (Fromm 1976, 1989a). Although Fromm described several orientations of nonproductive social characters (the authoritarian, the receptive, the exploitative, the hoarding, the marketing, the narcissistic, and the necrophilic social character), his primary concern is never to classify a person according to the list of possible nonproductive character orientations but to establish contact with the productive forces, that is to say, with those sides of the patient that show growth potential and longing to come alive—with the patient's "flowers," to use a metaphor of Michael Maccoby.

Third, if we focus our interest on the therapeutic situation and the relation between psychoanalyst and analysand, therapy for the individual should not be approached independently of the dominant social character traits in the individual and the therapist. The *social char-*

acter as key to the understanding of the individual applies to the analyst as well as to the patient. Both represent specific social character orientations. The less an analyst recognizes his own social character traits, the more likely it is that analyst and patient will both unconsciously suffer from the same nonproductive social character orientations, that they will, accordingly, fall victim to the "pathology of normalcy" (Fromm 1955) and dismiss the disorder by rationalizing it away. The pathology of normalcy is reflected in the fact that what society demands is readily accepted as "what everyone is doing," as "good common sense," as "the most normal thing in the world," as "objective obligation," or as "scientifically proven knowledge." This is how a thoroughly "sick society"—in the sense of Freud's (1930) "communal neurosis"—can come about. The sick society, however, doesn't generally admit to suffering from this "defect," rationalizing it away instead as "normal." Thus, Fromm suggests calling this unconscious suffering a "socially patterned defect" (Fromm 1955) as opposed to the individual neurotic disorder suffered, in more or less isolation, by the patient.

If both analyst and analysand are not aware of being in the grip of the pathology of normalcy, they will not be able to work together to change the basic nonproductive social character orientation and dynamic of the alienation. On the other hand, committing the patient to join in a common struggle against his socially accepted but alienating strivings diminishes the gap between analyst and analysand and reduces the analysand's dependency on the analyst. Both now have the common goal of reducing the self-alienating orientation of being outside oneself; both now strengthen their affirmation to let their intrinsic human powers and faculties achieve expression. This presupposes that becoming aware of one's own social character orientation is a sine qua non for all therapists participating in psychoanalysis, the goal of which is to overcome alienation and alleviate neurotic symptoms by establishing contact with unconscious and repressed aspects of the self.

Fourth, by concentrating on the productive aspects of the social character orientation in both analysand and psychoanalyst one should achieve a clear and distinct concept of the dynamics of alienation. I have tried to describe the differential dynamics of self-alienation in authoritarian socioeconomic structures in contrast to self-alienation in a marketing economy and society. Since the marketing form of alienation is prevalent today, the alternative basic orientation is a nonalienated relation to oneself and to others, as characterized by a basic human striving "to *express* [one's] faculties toward the world, rather than in [one's] need to *use* the world *as a means* for the satisfaction of [one's] physiological necessities" (Fromm 1992b, p. 156).

It follows that if psychoanalysis is practiced with the goal of making the patient function again and enabling him or her to become a better commodity and market success, whether on the job or in the family, it will not succeed in strengthening the productive orientation, because the very opposite aim is being supported. The therapeutic aim should not be that a patient can succeed on the market. Decisive, productive striving is geared to strengthening the patient's own forces, feelings, and ideas, whether they are conscious or repressed and unconscious. The psychoanalytic situation must always be defined by the insight that whatever achieves expression sui generis furthers growth, independently of what is expected by the marketing society and its agents in the workplace or the private sphere or during leisure time.

Fifth, with the dynamics of marketing alienation clearly in mind, love of life, joy, energy, and happiness, as goals of a productive social character orientation, are dependent "on the *degree to which we are related, to which we are concerned*—and that is to say [the degree] to which we are in touch with the reality of our feelings, with the reality of other people, not experiencing them as abstractions like commodities in the market" (Fromm 1991b, pp. 75–76). This holds especially for the relationship between analyst and analysand. The analyst must be genuinely interested in, and related to, the analysand, both his or her conscious and unconscious and repressed aspects. This active interest and ability to relate does not mean giving up the necessary therapeutic abstinence. Indeed the opposite is the case. For the more the analyst is able to be concentrated and enter into contact with the analysand's total personality, the less narcissistic will be the analyst's contact. But to be actively interested in the patient is an activity on the analyst's part (by avoiding the pitfall of activism). Such active interest can also mean just shutting up and listening. But the quality of this silence and listening is an active one where the analyst is authentically relating to the patient. Whenever the analyst relates to the analysand in such an active and productive way, he will experience his developing relation with the analysand as a source of energy and will therefore never feel bored during sessions. Or to put it the other way round, if the analyst feels bored and exhausted, then this indicates an inhibited ability to relate, which may have its origin in the analyst's nonproductive social character orientation, with the result that the analyst avoids with the patient his or her real issues.

Sixth, being related to the patient in an active way demands construing transference and countertransference in such a way as to avoid marketing-oriented alienation. As we have seen, Fromm understands transference in psychoanalysis only as a special form of alienation where "a person transfers his own activities or all of what he experiences—of his power, his love, of his power of thought—onto an object outside himself" (Fromm 1992b, p. 24). By submitting to authority, the person can reestablish contact with his own, albeit projected, human forces. The classical psychoanalytic setting seems to foster this alienation, even though the social character orientation of both analyst and analysand are no longer authoritarian. Maybe the orthodox emphasis on a firm setting—with four hours a week, the infantilizing couch, and a very rigid dogmatism concerning both theory and institutionalization—has the function of artificially strengthening an authoritarian structure to enable this very same authoritarian form of transference.

Today, however, there is a much greater danger: the marketing orientation has also changed our understanding of transference. No longer is there an authority to whom we can transfer our own activities. The situation is rather one where we deny our own capacities and become stimulated by the other person without really establishing a relationship with him. This can apply as much to the analyst as to the analysand. The analyst offers his technical know-how, that is, his willingness to listen and give interpretations. His capacities as therapist are not constituted by his productive social character orientation, that is, by his engagement, empathy, and readiness to relate with love and reason, but instead by his therapeutic role, by the school and the distinguished supervisors he has trained with, by the attractiveness of his office, by his membership in prestigious psychoanalytic societies, and so on. The therapeutic capacity has itself become alienated and a commodity. The same, incidentally, has happened to psychoanalytic theory. If one wishes to succeed in the market of psychoanalytic research, one has to coin new concepts and terms, to produce learned articles and quote what is currently "in" on the psychoanalytic marketplace, to attend congresses, to give a speech here and a presentation there, to publish in respected journals, and so on.

As far as the analysand is concerned, marketing-alienated transference means parading before the analyst all that has happened, whether it is feelings, dreams, associations, memories of childhood, events of daily life, and so on—but without really relating to himself or to the analyst. Many therapies go on for years in this marketing-oriented transference mode, with nothing happening or changing. Both analyst and analysand have become commodities, exchanging information according to their respective roles and paid for by the insurance companies. As long as the analyst does not confront the analysand with this alienating arrangement, which is the only chance of stimulating a real contact with his or her own feelings and ideas, nothing will happen. But confronting the patient presupposes that the analyst has himself first experienced that this sort of therapeutic arrangement is a typical marketing-oriented transference situation.

Therapy invariably entails the concrete discovery of an alternative to the nonproductive social character orientation. If the discovery of this alternative is to occur, it can only be in the context of a directly experienced, loving relationship between therapist and patient. Only by being aware, as therapists, of our own social character orientation and only by strengthening our own productive orientation can we overcome our alienation from our own productive forces. The art of being a good psychoanalyst can only be learned by first acquiring the art of being instead of having. At the end of the posthumously published book, *The Art of Listening*, Fromm (1991) states:

> [The analyst] must be endowed with a capacity for empathy with another person and strong enough to feel

the experience of the other as if it were his own. The condition for such empathy is a crucial facet of the capacity for love. To understand another means to love him – not in the erotic sense but in the sense of reaching out to him and of overcoming the fear of losing oneself. Understanding and loving are inseparable. If they are separate, it is a cerebral process and the door to essential understanding remains closed." [pp. 192–193]

There are other implications of Fromm's psychoanalytic approach in regard to clinical problems. If man is primarily determined by passionate strivings rooted in his social character orientation, this implies focusing therapeutic interest on the present lifestyle of the patient rather than on his childhood. Many neurosis have their origins in childhood and in complications arising during differentiation of psychic structure, when character structure is established. But the pathogenic denials, projections, identifications, internalizations, and repressions that were unavoidable in the patient's childhood very often resulted from the dynamics of social character orientations exemplified by the parents as agents of society. By and large, many pathologies, including many severe ones, that have their origins in early childhood are the result of nonproductive social character orientations still at work; in many cases, they are stronger today than in childhood and reinforce the pathological solutions found then.

If man is primarily determined by passionate strivings rooted in his social character orientation, this means the main pathogenic conflict should be seen as emerging from the patient's conflict between his human needs and the demands of society, which are contradictory. To quote from a lecture Fromm gave in 1956:

Man is not only a member of society. Man is a member of the human race. Man has necessities of his own which exist quite independently of any other society. It is true that man has to live in such a way that he will fulfill the demands of society, but it is also true that society has to be constructed and structuralized in such a way that it will fill the needs of man." [Fromm 1992e, p. 108]

If man is primarily determined by passionate strivings rooted in his social character orientation, this means therapeutic regression is not a favorable aim of psychoanalytic cure. The patient is suffering from human forces (which seek to grow and develop) conflicting with the demands of an alienating society. Therapy has to cope with this conflict by strengthening and making conscious the autonomous human forces in man that continue to be repressed by society. The way to overcome this repression is neither to advise the patient what he has to do to strengthen his productive forces, that is to say, to be related to the patient as if he were only an adult, nor to infantilize the patient by furthering his regression, that is to say, to be related to him as if her were only a child, but rather to confront the patient with the conflict, that he *is* a child of, say, 5 years and that he *is* simultaneously a well-functioning adult, and that he has successfully sought to avoid *feeling* this contradiction and conflict, which he very much needs to *experience*.

If man is primarily determined by passionate strivings rooted in his social character orientation, this means analysts must be trained to understand their own predominant social character orientations and to strive for greater productiveness in their own social character. So-called didactic analysis should lead to a growth of the analyst's own human forces such as will enable him to relate to and take an interest in other human beings and patients. This, and not only possession of a skill or therapeutic technique and know-how, is what qualifies the analyst. Fromm spoke about the analyst in a lecture given in 1959 at the William Alanson White Institute:

> I'm convinced you cannot separate your mode of relatedness to the patient, your realism as far as the patient is concerned, from your mode of relatedness to people in general and from your realism in general. If you are naive and blind to your friends and to the whole world, you will be exactly as naive and blind to your patients." [Fromm 1992f, p. 149]

REFERENCES

Eagle, M. N. (1988). *Recent Developments in Psychoanalysis. A Critical Evaluation*. New York: McGraw-Hill.

Freud, S. (1930). Civilization and its discontents. *Standard Edition* 21:57–145.

Fromm, E. (1941). *Escape from Freedom*. New York: Holt, Rinehart & Winston.

_____ (1947). *Man for Himself. An Inquiry into the Psychology of Ethics*. New York: Holt, Rinehart & Winston.

_____ (1955). *The Sane Society*. New York: Holt, Rinehart & Winston.

_____ (1964). *The Heart of Man: Its Genius for Good and Evil*. New York: Harper & Row.

_____ (1976). *To Have or To Be?* World Perpspectives vol. 50, planned and edited by R. N. Anshen. New York: Harper & Row.

_____ (1989a). *The Art of Being*, ed. R. Funk. New York: Continuum.

_____ (1989b). *Das jusische Gesetz. Zur soziologie des Diaspora-Judentums. Dissertation von 1922*, ed. R. Funk, and B. Sahler. Weinheim and Basel: Beltz.

_____ (1991). *The Art of Listening*, ed. R. Funk. New York: Continuum, 1994.

_____ (1992a). *The Revision of Psychoanalysis*, ed. R. Funk. Boulder, CO: Westview.

_____ (1992b).*Gesellschaft und Seele. Beitrage zur Sozialpsychologie und zur psychoanalytischen Praxis* (Schriften aus dem Nachlaß, vol. 7, ed. by R. Funk). Weinheim and Basel: Beltz.

_____ (1992c). *On Being Human*, ed. R. Funk. New York: Continuum.

_____ (1992d). Die Determiniertheit der psychischen Struktur durch die Gesellschaft. Zur Methode und Aufgabe einer Analytischen Sozialpsychologie. In *Gesellschaft und Seele*, ed. E. Fromm, pp. 23–97. (The page references refer to the German edition; the quotations are taken from the English typescript, which was translated by Erich Fromm.)

_____ (1992e). Psychische Bedurfnisse und Gesellschaft (Psychic needs and society. Lecture given 1956). In *Gesellschaft und Seele*, ed. E. Fromm, pp. 99–109. (The page references refer to the German edition; the quotations are taken from Fromm's English typescript.)

_____ (1992f). Das Unbewubte und die psychoanalytische Praxis. (The unconscious and the psychoanalytic practice. Three lectures given 1959 to the William Alanson White Institute in New York). In *Geselleschaft und Seele*, ed. E. Fromm, pp. 111–167. (The page references refer to the German edition; the quotations are taken from Fromm's English typescript.)

Guntrip, H. (1969). *Schizoid Phenomena, Object Relations and the Self*. New York: International Universities Press.

15

Self Development and Psychotherapy in a Period of Rapid Social Change*

Richard Margolies

What does self development mean to today's patients? How can knowledge of Erich Fromm's work help psycho-analytic therapists assist these patients' aspirations for their own adult development? What can therapists learn about the changing nature of social character and work today that will help them in their clinical work?

Fromm's belief that understanding broad social and historical developments is necessary to achieve a fuller understanding of individuals has been borne out in my clinical work. Fromm provided an approach to understand how the values and drives of large groups of people are shaped by social forces. He described this relationship

---

*I would like to thank Daniel Burston, Mauricio Cortina, Barbara Lenkerd, and Michael Maccoby for their helpful comments on this chapter.

between history, society, and human development with his concept of social character.

In many of his writings on social character Fromm (1941, 1947) described a broad historical shift from the patriarchal-hoarding to the capitalist marketing social character. His description of society and social character, however, is outdated and misleading for work with patients today. His concept of social character needs to be newly employed and developed by analyzing systematically how modern changes in work are affecting people's development.

In this chapter, I describe recent social character research that offers new insights for therapists, and I present an illustrative clinical case vignette. In addition, I discuss how the changing direction that psychoanalytic theory and therapy is taking fits these changes in the nature of work and social character.

Fromm's understanding of society is rooted in his concept of patriarchy. For Fromm (1970), patriarchy is organized around the principles of conditional love, duty, conscience, rationality, abstract thought, and progress. This social form is characterized by the hegemony of males and has been said to exist for seven or eight millennia. Nonetheless, Fromm (1976) in his last years acknowledged the decline of patriarchy: "It is . . . slowly diminishing in the more affluent countries or societies—emancipation of women, children, and adolescents seems to take place when and to the degree that a society's standard of living rises" (p. 71).

It is not the rising standard of living that causes the change of patriarchy, however. This transformation results from new information and computer technology, mass media such as television, increased international competition in a global economy, mass education, the pill and the ease of contraception and abortion, female economic independence and the changing family structure, and the changing nature of work, including the fact that modern work requires fewer physical qualities such as brawn. Prominent among these socioeconomic and technical factors is how telecommunications and computer technology transform work roles and the relationships, skills, and attitudes necessary for work today. These socioeconomic factors are shaping the social character necessary to adapt to and be a contributor to today's work. Fromm, who died in 1980, did not analyze these dynamic social forces. The question is whether people react in rebellious, passive-aggressive, narcissistic, or authoritarian ways, or actively develop themselves through work, as they endeavor to transform their organization and their society toward social and human ideals.

Fromm's character and values are *pre*-capitalist (Maccoby 1982). In his German radio broadcasts toward the end of his life Fromm expressed his social character clearly and consciously:

> Being the only child of two overly anxious parents did not, of course, have an altogether positive effect on my development, but over the years I've done what I could to repair that damage. Something that had a positive influence on me, or a least a decisive one, was my family heritage. I was born into a strictly Orthodox Jewish family with a long line of rabbinical forefathers on both sides. I grew up in the spirit of this old tradition, a tradition that was certainly more medieval than it was modern. And that tradition had greater reality for me than the twentieth-century world I was living in. . . . My sense of the world . . . was not that of a modern man but of a premodern one; and that attitude was reinforced by studying the Talmud, reading the Bible a lot, and hearing a lot of stories about my ancestors, who had all lived in a world that predated the bourgeois world. . . . I found the

modern world strange. . . . It still surprises me. I've remained an alien in the business or bourgeois culture, and that explains why I developed such a harshly critical attitude toward bourgeois society and capitalism. [Fromm 1986, pp. 98–99]

This premodern view contrasts with the experience of many men and women in dual-career families today who are attempting to work out how to share child rearing, income earning, and family responsibilities. People in families working to create new gender roles might ask: Would Fromm have been so "harshly critical" toward modern society and its changing social character, if he had been a father active in child rearing in a dual-career family in the 1990s, or if he had a different social character?

Many men and women today are attempting in their family relationships to go beyond patriarchy and matriarchy. This change is driven by socioeconomic and technological forces that transform work. It does not result from a new messianic or prophetic consciousness, nor from affluence, nor even from the recognition of the greater power of love, equality, and justice, although these ideals do influence people, such as in the desire of women to be independent of men. This radical transformation of patriarchy is being driven mainly by the changing nature of the means of production. This change at the technological and work base of society has profound sociocultural consequences, including the emergence of a new social character and greater freedoms. The change in the means of production and work, and its effects on everyday life, also bring tremendous social disruptions and human costs: spectator escapism, mass addictions and violence especially among the young, alienation between men and women, a confusion about authority, and a dulling of awareness of evil and moral choices.

SOCIAL CHARACTER: FROMM'S CONCEPT
VERSUS HIS 1947 TYPES

Social character is one of Fromm's major contributions to psychoanalysis. Love and work are two major achievements on the lifelong course of development. It is important to recognize the central place of work in patients' development over their life span. Adapting to the significant change in social character and work today expands clinical method. We honor Fromm's theory by bringing it up to date.

Fromm differentiates individual character from social character. Individual character is seen in the ways people differ within the same class and culture. Individual character arises from differences in parents, family dynamics, and in the material and psychological variations of the immediate environment in which the child is raised. There are also somatic, constitutional, and temperamental differences, which are the biological base of inherent talents and gifts.

Individual character is a system within the person. Social character describes the shared patterns of drives, values, and emotional attitudes that characterize large groups of individuals in a given society. The social character-as-system is seen developing, therefore, within a larger, containing social system, which has work at the center. Social character as a dynamic system "has developed as an adaptation to economic, social, and cultural conditions common to that group" (Fromm and Maccoby 1970, p. 16).

We are not human beings in an abstract sense. We are born at a particular moment in a culture and in a class being affected by dynamic historical forces. These historical forces are defining aspects of the larger containing system that shapes character, via the family, and through our work as adults.

"Institutions of schooling, work, and leisure do not differ essentially from the way of life transmitted to the child in his family" (Fromm and Maccoby 1970, p. 22). In stable periods work reinforces adaptations made in early life. That most people's character remains the same from early childhood is "due less to the fact that it is rigid and incapable of modification than to the mutually reinforcing relationship between character and environment" (Fromm and Maccoby 1970, p. 22).

In 1947 Fromm described what he called social character types, divided into four so-called nonproductive orientations, and the so-called productive character, which is a religious and human ideal (Maccoby 1982, 1994) but not a social character type. The three so-called nonproductive types correspond to Freud's pregenital stages (receptive—oral receptive; exploitative—oral biting; hoarding—anal), while the marketing social character is Fromm's own conceptualization. There are several key aspects to consider:

• The 1947 types were based on patients in therapy. He did not, however, describe the particular social conditions that gave rise to the character of these patients. Elsewhere Fromm described the social character of a nonclinical population in his research on the German working class in the early 1930s (Fromm 1984), on the authoritarian character in the 1940s, and his research on social character in a Mexican village in the 1960s (Fromm and Maccoby 1970).

• It is only possible to conceptualize four of the 1947 types as nonproductive if one assumes with Fromm that modern society is not sane and is inherently alienating. Fromm himself tried to modify his initial ideological conceptualization by showing that each of these so-called nonproductive types had productive traits. Since social character describes normal character in society, they are by definition adaptational types. The best conceptual language would therefore give a mental picture of their productive goals, what each type strives for and values in work and life. The best description of each type pictures the dynamic interaction between the productive and unproductive propensities, some of which are conscious, while others are unconscious.

• Fromm's 1947 conceptual language, used to name his types, is either based on a body zone (e.g., receptive), or uses heavy moral language: hoarding, exploitative, or marketing. The 1947 types, nonetheless, came to have a wider acceptance perhaps because they were more generalizable, and not culture-specific. These 1947 conceptualizations are therefore partial social character types, in the meaning defined by the theory, because of their limited etiological and cultural evidence, and the absence of attention given to the person's adaptation through work.

RECENT SOCIAL CHARACTER RESEARCH

In *Why Work: Leading The New Generation* (1988), Maccoby describes five social characters, highlighting their social nature by emphasizing adaptation to work and social structure. (A revised second edition [1995] is titled *Why Work? Motivating The New Workforce*.) This seven-year research surveyed several thousand managers and employees in diverse for-profit and governmental organizations, and followed up about 300 of those surveys with two- to three-hour sociopsychoanalytic interviews. From the study of these interviews emerged five social characters: the expert, the helper, the defender, the innovator, and the self-developer. Maccoby describes how today there is a basic character shift occurring. The old patriarchal expert, usually the male, and the helper, usually the female, are fading as the dominant types. In ascendance is the self-developer, the emerging dominant social character that defines the era.

The *expert* seeks to demonstrate his or her competence, skill, and achievement. Experts value mastery and hard work, and strive to achieve self-esteem through being recognized for their performance. Their motto is "one best way," the way they favor or know. They highly value autonomy and control. They are more interested in measuring up to what is expected of them and pleasing their bosses than in serving customers. Their dreams are often of taking tests or solving problems. On the Rorschach they often see beavers or squirrels, hard-working and hoarding animals. Experts are the majority type in America today because they have been required by industrial hierarchies and bureaucracies. As the majority type their traits tend to become the dominant metaphor for character development. Their positive traits are diligent work, quality of product or service, attention to detail, and doing things well. Their negative traits are inflexibility, nit-picking, rules-driven, control-seeking, and bureaucratic. Experts resist delegating and teamwork (except where they can be in control). Experts are overly individualistic, and do not naturally work interdependently with others.

What situation produces people with these dynamics? Experts' character is formed in the now-fading traditional father-dominated family. The child in such a family tries to gain the approval of the expert-oriented father. The family is a support system for the father's success, his work determines where the family lives, and his success determines the family's standard of living. The child of this family has a dominant drive toward mastery of self and success at school, rewarded by the parents' approval.

The *helper*, a different social character entirely, seeks to help people, and create relationships. In the patriarchal family, now in decline, the father tended to be an expert and the mother a helper, since her work was usually in the home caring for the young children. But our research found that in the general population these types were not gender specific. Male and female helpers like to help and care for people directly, are idealistic, and have a cooperative spirit. The negative tendency of this orientation is that they often overestimate their ability to help, and can make people depend on them.

Helpers often try to help without sufficient knowledge or understanding of people, yet expect appreciation for their efforts. They can be gullible, and think people are good and can immediately get along with each other. They are reluctant to speak out and defend their views. They can get disappointed, burned out, and become hardened because they often overestimate how participation alone will achieve teamwork. They are among the first to welcome new leadership that develops skills and focuses on satisfying customers. But they often don't pay sufficient attention to conflicting views about how to achieve organizational success, and lack courage to try new approaches.

Helpers often grow up in mother-centered families. Our research has found two major patterns in these families. One pattern occurs in a family that is often religious, where the mother or grandmother kept the family together. The other pattern occurs under a strong "liberated" mother, a background of abundance, and an explicit family value on service to others.

Experts and helpers are the majority and dominant adaptive social characters of the fading patriarchy. Experts are usually the male breadwinners who worked in industrial hierarchies. They looked to bosses for recognition and rewards, as they looked up to their fathers when they were boys. The helpers were also a part of this fading social system with the two-parent family and the stay-at-home mother. The defenders and innovators, described below, are minor types in the industrial-bureaucratic system.

The *defender* seeks to defend values and principles against those who they feel would violate them. They become advocates for customers, subordinates, the public, or the excluded. They defend the organization from enemies, cheats, or those who break or bend the rules. They courageously defend values, though they often cause conflict in the process. While it is positive to protect people and principles, they often divide people into loyal friends and potential enemies. They can personalize conflicts and destroy networks.

While they defend their own and others' dignity, they are often touchy and unwilling to hear criticism. They can become paranoid and suspicious if people don't agree with them. Their zeal for justice is a contribution to society and organizations, but they can identify their own ideas with the law or the cause itself. While their protector role is often needed, they can bully others and project hostility, which causes angry responses, confirming their own suspicious tendencies.

People who become defenders grow up in one of two types of families, although these can be blended. In one family situation, the child is picked on because he or she is weak or different, or the family was torn apart. The child reacts with courage and becomes acutely sensitive to humiliation and injustice. In the other family situation, the child comes from an intact family of strong standards in which he or she has had to struggle against adversity, poverty, or prejudice. In each formative situation the defender's childhood involved a struggle for justice, to be treated with respect, and to triumph over humiliation.

The *innovator*, a fourth type, seeks to create something

new and have it implemented. Motivated to create new products or services, innovators redesign organizations to do that. Innovators create new rules, roles, and relationships, whereas other types try to work within the old ones. Innovators are organizers, instigators, and strategists. They like to excite others, "juice up" their motivation, in the process of creating something new and power for themselves and others.

Innovators are playful and inventive, although they can become overly attached to their vision. They have a critical, independent attitude, although this can lead to little patience for those who don't share their vision or grasp it quickly. They are often systems thinkers, grasping the interrelationships of many parts of complex, whole systems. They are strategists, risk takers, and are able to act. They often have a drive for glory, to play in the big leagues, and they like to redesign organizations to create new products and services. They are flexible, enthusiastic, and like to make work fun, although this can become manipulative and hype. Narcissism is a weakness of innovators, especially where they are successful and gain acclaim; this can lead to their undoing.

What is the life story of innovators? What dynamic interaction between their young impressionable psyche as children and their environment produces innovator social character? They generally come from families where they felt valued, supported, and were encouraged to explore their own ideas and paths. These families have a playful attitude and a culture of freedom. They were often involved in entrepreneurial activities at school, and gained financial independence from parents.

The emerging social character type in industrialized countries, especially evident in the United States today as the new American character, is the *self-developer*. The main social character shift of our time is from the expert to the self-developer. Self-developers seek to develop themselves through continual learning and new experience, and strive to achieve a balanced life. But this new sociohistorical human type is not defined by age alone, but by their values and drives. Self-developers approach life and work as a continual process to learn, grow, and develop themselves. At best they strive to be whole people, but at base they want to maintain their marketability in an economy that no longer guarantees tenure in jobs or even that one's expertise will be valued over time. They respond most enthusiastically to the new ideas and organizational forms of the innovators. Work is very important in their view of life.

They seek to balance work with other aspects of life: friends, family, sports, exercise, maintaining their health, and entertainment. They want to develop what they call the "male" and the "female" sides of themselves, and they seek gender balance and equality in their relationships.

People with strong self-developer drives are best adapted to the uncertainty and challenges of today's economy. They want to maintain their marketability, self-esteem, and security by continually upgrading their skills. They see the need to integrate information from the organization, facilitating and working in teams, and understanding customers' needs. Brought up in a world of change, they have learned to adapt to people and situations, and while preserving their independence they can accept their responsibility. They want to stay fit and competitive, seize opportunities, and enjoy life. People with these drives, however, can have a propensity to become detached, reluctant to commit themselves and take on parental-type leadership.

Self-developers are flexible, experimental, and do not like bureaucracy. They want to be businesslike. But these strengths can have emotional costs: self-developers often show little caring for others, little resonance with others as human beings, and their response to people is often shallow. They do not listen well to their own inner voice and to their needs for intimacy and meaning. They fear closeness and are counterdependent.

In their search for balance, self-developers seek to struggle against materialism, and to be content with what they have. Many want to make the world better, but they don't want to create bureaucracies that make people dependent. But these fears often leave them without meaningful projects, or models of maturity or leadership they want to emulate. Self-developers can often be energetic, unfocused, and lonely.

The major immediate factor forming this emerging social character is the breakdown of the traditional, patriarchal family. What is the life story of those who become self-developers as adults? Most come from two-career, divorced, or mobile families. Growing up in these families a child experiences continual change, mobility, and lack of clear norms other than the need for continual learning and adaptation to changing conditions. Where both parents work outside the home the child has limited access to parents, and is often in the hands of other caregivers, even if they are expert and caring. The dual-career family seeks balance between male and female authority, and the lack of paternal dominance, or the unavailability of both parents, frees the child from strong dependent bonds and facilitates peer relationships. Yet frequent parental absence or unavailability can lead to self-protective detachment.

Fromm's description of the nonproductive marketing character takes attention away from understanding the life stories and positive drives of the emerging dominant type of our era. The picture he paints of the marketing character describes the negative side or potential of the self-developer. Marketing, however, is not an adequate description of a whole new class of educated managers and employees who are highly motivated regarding lifelong learning, gender equity, and a balanced life.

Everyone is a blend of social characters. Nonetheless, most individuals, when participating in a survey, will in a matter of minutes easily identify with a dominant and a secondary orientation. The new social characterology that emerged from Maccoby's (1988) research was not developed from a clinical population, nor was it based on Fromm's revision of Freud's libidinal types. The new typology was based on systematic interviewing using open-ended questions, which are interpreted in a group process. These are ideal types, not moral types. In fact, each type has a potential to make a positive, or a negative, contribution to others, society, organizations, work, and family life.

It is possible, however, for a person to have not developed one's human capabilities, to be troubled, alienated, or morally underdeveloped, because of individual etiological factors, or the absence of a supportive social environment. Since each social character has negative and positive potentials, it is part of the therapeutic goal to strengthen their positive potentials to develop fully. Nonetheless, we know that many patients come to treatment with a more immediate and sometimes narrower goal.

The use of a typology is to further understanding, not to "type" or pigeonhole individuals. People are a mix of types, and their unique feelings and experiences are not reducible to a type. Perhaps it is useful to treat the types as a kind of perceptual poetry, to aid insight and emotional connection with the person. In this way, it is better to think of the person's life story, with the types in the background to help them express their life which is in progress.

For the therapist who is concerned, like Fromm, with the larger issues of human and social development, adult human development can be defined as the flowering of each of these positive social character potentialities within the individual, since each person has to some degree all the social character elements. To develop one's expertise, helpfulness, defense of values, and innovativeness means the continual development of oneself and others. And this occurs within the normal range of development. To go further requires the deeper development of the heart, the fuller capacities for love, independence, and creativity. This vision of human growth has been described by Maccoby (1994) as Fromm's "prophetic voice."

Fromm moved too quickly to "wake up" the patient to his own view of the higher developmental meaning of love, independence, and creativity. This led to forcing the patient to rapidly incorporate Fromm as a new superego transferential object (Maccoby 1982). This clinical method was fed by Fromm's contempt for modern society.

THE ROLE OF WORK IN ADULT DEVELOPMENT

Central to the cultural origin of social character is the nature of work in a society. To understand adult development today it is helpful to see how work and social character are changing. Families prepare children for the "real world," the world of work, by developing the traits, emotional attitudes, values, behaviors, and relationships work requires. Social character is a concept useful for understanding this normal character development. It illuminates how character changes dynamically as historical forces transform society and families, which are the psychic factories of character.

Different psychoanalytic schools attempt to understand work from the standpoint of a part of the psychic process, an intrapsychic part-process (Margolies 1981). Freud only focused on work problems as inhibitions of libidinal and aggressive drives and fantasies. The ego psychologists discussed the inherent activeness of the child, and the developmental stages of learning in relation to ego skills and mastery. The ego psychologists writing on work include Lantos (1943, 1952), Hendrick (1943), Erikson (1963, 1964, 1968), Neff (1965), and White (1952, 1959). For Kohut and the self psychologists work provides "the most important outlet for transformed grandiose-exhibitionistic narcissistic tensions through creativity" (Kohut 1977, p. 10).

Social character theory is a form of systems thinking that is broader and of greater explanatory value than partial intrapsychic models. Social character describes the relationship between the social-physical environment and the psyche.

Most clinicians, however, know little if anything about the concept or research on social character. Clinical training, psychotherapy theories, the nature of supervision and professional conferences—in fact the whole therapeutic culture does not recognize the importance of understanding work and social character. This is an aspect of the resistance to the innovative thinking of Erich Fromm.

In the ebb and flow of clinical sessions, work is just one focus. For some patients, emotional issues with spouses, lovers, parents, or siblings predominate. Or issues of their own identity or self-worth are prominent; others are deeply troubled by depression, anxiety, or schizoid or narcissistic states. Others are alexithymic, not knowing the name for their emotions, or are in a state of disaffection from their feelings, fantasies, and wishes.

In my clinical practice with mostly high-functioning adults, their emotional, interpersonal, or intrapsychic issues clearly affect their work. With one exception, all my patients work outside the home. For Freud this was not true. Most of his patients either were too disturbed to work, were wealthy or upper middle class, or were women who did not work outside the home. Today psychotherapy is an aspect of life for millions of people in advanced industrial societies. Psychotherapy is now part of popular culture, unlike during Freud's life or even the years when Erich Fromm practiced.

The better we understand what our patients confront in their work, the more effective we will be as psychotherapists. That is, to be effective in *our* workplace—the psychotherapeutic session—we will benefit from a more systematic understanding of our patients' work, workplace, and social character. In advanced economies, we may see the inclusion of psychotherapy as a guaranteed element of health care for all citizens. This will likely increase the bureaucratization of the private practitioner. Like it or not many therapists will be forced to adapt to the increasing role of organizations in their work. Better understanding of how work effects us and our patients will help us navigate through the turbulence of rapid social change.

The public is growing aware that early experience affects development. However, the public discussion often centers around abuse, addiction, co-dependence, or gender inequities. While important, these issues are often sensationalized. A danger of this politicized phase of cultural development is that if one claims abuse one feels justified in abusing others, or in demanding special treatment from society. People have been freed after committing heinous crimes because they were "temporarily in-sane." With the transformation of patriarchy, the content of the superego of many people changes to a focus on "correctness." This results from a mechanical, reflexive concern for fairness and a push for power by many who have been treated unequally. The concern about correct-ness is a tremor of the shifting plate tectonics of patriarchy and social character.

These social flash points divert attention from the discussion of adult development in these times. Thera-pists and scientists should be active in this public discus-sion, illuminating the central role of work in the sense of dignity, self-worth, and mature development for adults. Fromm's concept of social character and his normative view of human development is essential to this under-standing. Is social character as deep and important a reality in character development as gender or other as-pects of diversity, for example? While diversity is widely discussed, social character differences are rarely men-tioned in public media or forums like schools where one might expect that character development is a shared concern. Feminist researchers like Gilligan champion the matriarchal ideal and assert that women are more rela-tional. Gilligan has not, however, researched male rela-tionships, nor distinguished relationships based on dif-ferent goals or values that people pursue through them.

"Relationships" is an abstract category that needs to be disaggregated. It is more useful diagnostically to describe what values are sought through relationships, since, as Fromm points out, to be sane people must establish a mode of relatedness to others. The different modes of relatedness help definite character. For example, de-fenders seek loyalty through their relationships, while helpers seek caring and support. Under the patriarchal division of labor women were raised to be helpers and relational in terms of nurturance of children and supportive of the men. Today this is changing. Our research shows that only one of the social character types described by Maccoby (1988), the helper, values relationships based on caring, but this social character includes men and women (even though there was a greater percentage of helpers who were women). The emphasis on caring relationships is not a trait, however, for men or women who are dominantly experts, or the other social character types.

THE VALUE OF SOCIAL CHARACTER KNOWLEDGE IN PSYCHOTHERAPY

In psychoanalytic therapy patients work to understand their current challenges, in light of their early experience. They become more conscious as they *un*learn what they had thought and felt they had to do. They work on what they want to do, and discover what they are passionate about. They work on their self development. This is a focus for many patients today.

Knowledge of people's social character life stories helps us understand what they are experiencing during this historical era when traditional patriarchal structures, thinking, and values are being transformed. Patients struggle in their families, their relationships, within themselves, and within their work to dynamically adapt to a world in which for many the values of their expert patriarchal father and helper mother are not the keys to their development.

Clear theory shows the meaning of choices patients face, and the meaning of their conflicts. An important part of Fromm's psychoanalytic theory involved the evolution of social forms that he drew from his study of the nineteenth century writer J. J. Bachofen's ideas about matriarchy and patriarchy. According to Fromm, matriarchy is organized around the principles of unconditional acceptance and love, equality, natural bonds, pleasure. Matriarchy as a dominant, defining social form has not existed in the West for thousands of years. However, patriarchy and matriarchy are each a system of interrelated psychological values. These value systems can be seen, more or less clearly, in some individuals and groups, for example, matriarchy in some hippie communes of the 1960s, and patriarchy in an American professional football team.

When patriarchal and matriarchal values clash, heightened by technological and socioeconomic changes,

the matriarchal principle manifests itself in motherly overindulgence and infantilization of the child, preventing [his or her] full maturity; fatherly authority becomes harsh domination and control, based on the child's fears and feelings of guilt. . . . The purely matriarchal society stands in the way of the full development of the individual, thus preventing technical, rational, artistic progress. The purely patriarchal society cares nothing for love and equality; it is only concerned with man-made laws, the state, abstract principles, obedience. . . . A viable and progressive solution lies only in a new synthesis of the opposites . . . on a higher level. [Fromm 1970, pp. 108–109]

As Mumford (1967) points out, the paradigm of the bureaucratic, hierarchical, overly patriarchal era is the machine. This model is vividly represented in Freud's intrapsychic closed mechanism of id-ego-superego driven by energy. An alternative model by Fromm proposes a synthesis of matriarchal and patriarchal principles as a humanistic definition of emotional development. Social character provides a systems explanation of the interaction between the child-family-society in a historical setting. Fromm's idea of the synthesis of matriarchal and patriarchal principles and his concept of social character provide a better understanding of how new technology and the new forms of organization are molding the emerging social character.

The development toward interactive and systemic thinking can also be seen in the movement of theory away from mechanical psychoanalytic metapsychology, as in the critique of Roy Schafer (1976, 1978). Psychoanalytic clinical method is also moving from an expert/doctor-centered orthodox method to a more dyadic, interactive method, as in the intersubjective approach of Robert Stolorow (Stolorow et al. 1987).

Fromm's analysis of the progressive potentials within modern social character is sketchy at best. When describing the clinical setting he posits a preindustrial patriarchal doctor–patient working relationship, and covertly encourages a rebellious attitude toward modern industrial society. Fromm's model is the analyst as superego psychologist expressing a premodern ego ideal, "liberating" the patient from the mother tie. Today's challenge is to apply Fromm's insights into unconscious drives and values, which are the basis of character, without his view of industrial society and the so-called marketing personality as inherently shallow and dehumanized (Maccoby 1982).

The history of psychoanalysis and psychoanalytic institutes has been one of rivalry over the "true" theory or clinical method, another form of political correctness. With the dawning of a new scientific paradigm and new social values the psychoanalytic community can move beyond this. Today many clinicians recognize the different schools of psychoanalytic thought as alternative ways of looking at human development (Pine 1985). Clinically, we know that finding the appropriate language that connects with the patient's deep feeling at the moment enlivens the therapy. If instead therapists work with only one theory or are too theoretical, they can lose the emotional connection that can make therapy deeply educational, playful, and mutative for patient and therapist.

TODAY'S CHANGING SOCIAL CHARACTER

The research for *Why Work* (Maccoby 1988) showed that about 50 percent of the various samples, drawn from diverse industries, agencies, and organizations, are still dominantly experts. The social character needed today in advanced economies, however, is not the expert. This was the dominant social character type for bureaucratic hierarchies, which are now increasingly seen as socially unproductive, and are in fact, in retreat. Our research, organizational consulting, and psychotherapy work, indicates the emerging social character type is the self-developer.

Marx and Fromm acknowledged that the advance of capitalism brought new freedoms, but they also saw that the emergence of this new socioeconomic system caused the withering of many qualities of life and human values. Today, we can see that the new technology, work and organization, and social changes are also threatening the erosion of valuable human qualities. Among these are the expert's sense of dignity, loyalty, and perseverance. The experts' devotion to perfecting their craft or professional competence, and their commitment to deep, long-standing relationships are less valued in today's world that demands flexibility, continual change, and innovation.

In this time of major social upheaval and rapid change we have not yet seen the emergence of a reinforcing fit between character and environment. In fact, many patients come to therapy because their values, attitudes, and aspirations, as structured in childhood, no longer fit the realities of work today. Many patients today suffer from the painful *lack* of fit.

The emergence of the self-developer has been widely misunderstood and resisted by the media and social commentators. Denounced as a "me generation" or a "culture of narcissists," self-developers are little affirmed or appreciated for their qualities. While escapism is an issue for self-developers, they are interested in learning and teamwork, and they evidence initiative, playful enthusiasm, and an interest in health and a balanced life. There is little discussion of this new social character type in professional meetings or in journals of the therapeutic network.

The self-developer is needed by the new types of work involving information technologies, automation, and flat hierarchies organized around multifunctional and flexible project teams. Self-developers like working in these teams to innovate products and services for customers. This is a tremendous sociocultural shift from the world of work when Fromm was seeing patients and writing books.

Social character means that people come to want to do what they have to do to make the system (the mode of production) function. There is therefore a potential fit between the self-developer and the new forms of work. Many patients today have problems fitting in because they have the social character adapted to the rapidly fading old bureaucratic-hierarchical patriarchy but are facing the daily challenges of the new social system. A character-society dysfunctional fit has been called "character lag" by Fromm and Maccoby (1970).

For a large number of people the new technologies and work organizations can routinize and simplify their jobs, as organizations strive to become more efficient. The modern economy requires the learning of new skills and the development of new attitudes and styles of working. While many are able to learn and adapt, for many others their freedom to change jobs, develop independent work, or develop themselves through their work is limited. The negative possibilities facing many in the modern economy is a challenge to those who share Fromm's critical, humanistic tradition.

What does the potential, and the threat, of the modern global economy imply for working with patients? First of all, it is helpful for therapists to be aware of the rebellious or resistant qualities of some patients to the new work system, and ask: What is their rebelliousness rooted in? Are they motivated to adapt? Some might read Fromm and conclude that rebelliousness itself is a sign of health. But as Maccoby suggests (personal communication) rebelliousness needs to be analyzed to distinguish its various forms. There is a form of healthy rebellion, which is against oppressive conditions, either in interpersonal relations or in society. If this form of rebelliousness does not find a productive outlet or if the person can't change one's situation, it can turn destructive. If people are humiliated or hurt, they can become sadistic or destructive and begin to feel that their only sense of potency or effectiveness is to dominate, hurt, or control. There is also the normal rebelliousness of a child whose saying no to the parents is a way to invite the parents to set limits on the child's own expansive aggressiveness. If the parents don't set limits, the child keeps rebelling and this too leads the child away from healthy development and an understanding of social reality and natural limits.

It is important, therefore, to distinguish the different

forms of rebellion, as well as passive, compliant "accom-modation," to use Piaget's concept, from active transfor-mation. I believe that healthy development involves this activeness in becoming an aware, innovative employee or leader who helps transform today's reality and brings out the best in the productive potentials of people and the new social system. This requires both adapting and trans-forming. Active transformation means working pragmat-ically, based upon human values, to develop organiza-tions, work itself, and its impacts on people, the community, and society.

Fromm said 50 percent of understanding a person's character is seen in their social character, while 25 percent is temperament and 25 percent is their individual experi-ence (personal communication to Michael Maccoby). The following clinical vignette suggests the value of under-standing changing social character and work in therapy. Nine of my patients filled out the survey from *Why Work*. Four of the sample (44 percent) described themselves as primarily expert, while the remaining five scored them-selves as secondarily expert. In other words, being an expert described them to a large degree, which fits our research findings that 50 percent of the population today are primarily experts. Much of the suffering of these patients was rooted in this patriarchal expert character structure.

A CLINICAL VIGNETTE

This 34-year-old, white, Irish-American, Catholic man scored himself on the survey as dominantly a self-developer, the emerging social character type, and secondarily as an expert. This is both clinically and historically interesting. He contains within himself, or we might say within his self-system, dynamic changes in his containing social system, the United States in the late twentieth century. The treatment was twice weekly, 50 minute sessions, face-to-face psychoanalytic psychotherapy lasting 2 years 3 months, or approximately 200 sessions. Involving him in a real person to person dialogue about his self development was important to his changing in treatment.

Born in a working class–lower middle class, ethnically mixed neighborhood of a large industrial city he was the oldest of four boys, the only one to move away from the close family network. His mother worked as a nurse in an old people's home, and was the most steady earner of income. Though I did not survey or interview either the father or the mother, she was probably an expert, and the tougher of the two parents. His father was probably primarily a helper and secondarily an expert as a senior manager in a relatively small local business. The father had had a number of middle management jobs, largely as an accountant, often losing those jobs after several years. The father held his last job for many years until the firm disbanded. About this time, when he was in his forties, the father, a close friend of their parish priest, created and ran a drug rehabilitation program.

The patient did well at a local, Jesuit-run college majoring in English, liberal arts, and film. He went to Washington to work for several members of Congress. Eventually, with his talents and interests, he became the campaign manager for a congressional candidate. To have the position as campaign manager attests to the capabilities of this young man.

When he came to treatment he was running a service business that he started, supplying computer and temporary help to firms. He expanded the business by taking on more projects and employing more people. He started to rent computer hardware and software to his clients, including designing data management systems for them.

He entered treatment because he was not happy, would get depressed, and did not feel he was progressing in his life. He knew his anger at his workers was anger at himself. He was afraid of his own ambitions in the fields of writing and film. He was a gourmet cook, but felt he had to control his love of eating good food. He feared becoming like his father, yet he felt "diminished" because his father didn't show sufficient interest in him. He stated he wanted a dialogue with me, that he liked that I was attentive in listening, but felt vulnerable not knowing about me. He asked numerous questions about me. He had been in therapy twice before.

He had a wonderful literary sensibility in describing people, events, and the phenomena of daily life. Yet he couldn't figure out his own unhappiness or gain the deeper knowledge of himself he wanted or how to really conquer his depression. A recovered alcoholic, he regularly attended Alcoholics Anonymous meetings, and had many AA friends.

While he had amassed several hundred thousand dollars from his business, he was living the life of an impoverished student; renting a house with a roommate, he had no car, little furniture, and spent most of his spare time reading. He loved books and literature and often cited stories or characters from world literature to illuminate an experience or person. Although a businessman, with an active interest in politics, his real talent and enlivening interest was literary. I started to think of him as an Irish writer. He also had a rebelliousness, often seen in the Irish. He disdained money and commerce, as well as the ordinariness of daily work.

He had two romantic relationships, socializing, traveling, and sleeping with both women. Each knew of the other. He could not choose between them. Later in treatment he revealed that he had frequent homosexual fantasies, though he had never had homosexual experiences and didn't want to, as he was enjoying his two heterosexual relationships. His two relationships kept him from a deeper involvement with either of them.

The major change in family structure causing the emergence of the self-developer is the dual-career family. The dominant family structure of the fading bureaucratic-industrial system is the patriarchal family with the father as the income earner and the mother as the at-home care-provider. In the dual-career family children learn early to be independent and care for themselves, as they realize their parents aren't there for them much of the time. This can lead to a pseudo-independence, which can compromise development. On the other hand, these children grow up with a strong sense of responsibility to develop themselves.

The patient, who described himself as a self-developer–expert, feared that he would be like his father, a helper-expert who didn't succeed well in the old patriarchal business system. But he also wanted his father to show more interest in him — the wish for patriarchal recognition. This inhibited his emotional independence and drive for development. His addiction also suggests an oral longing for nourishment and happiness in the maternal orbit.

As is characteristic of self-developers, he was peer-oriented, as seen in his work, but had an underlying parental longing. Because of these unresolved parental ties, he was not able to enjoy or consolidate his success at running the entrepreneurial business he created and thereby becoming more independent. He inhibited his intellectual, aesthetic, and artistic creative impulses. He made a partial transition from his parents' life and work in organizations, but not a full, zestful use of his own talents and interests.

From a social character standpoint, he had one foot in the world of his extended family, and one foot in the world of being a self-developer from a dual-career family. But he had not made a full emotional separation from either parent, and this compromised his life solution and brought him to treatment. Looking closer we can see how these dynamics play out through his life story and work.

He started a service business that used computer technology and employed educated young people paid on a project, not a salary, basis. He organized his company in an informal, low-bureaucracy, high-teamwork structure. He often worked on projects along with his employees. His firm combined parts of matriarchal egalitarianism, and patriarchal focus. From organizational consulting I have seen the challenges of managing this new kind of firm. The leader's thinking, character, and ability to motivate make the difference.

Important to his work were the intense, direct, demanding

interpersonal relationships with both men and women in his firm, and in developing new projects with clients. He tried to transcend the patriarchal hierarchy by creating a more matriarchal firm that helped others, but he couldn't make a full transition. These work problems were a recurring focus throughout the treatment. He tried to solve these character and interpersonal issues by, not surprisingly, involving a brother and his father in helping him, but over time this did not work. Eventually, the patient realized that his compromise work solution was holding him back from his real passion: literature and film. He applied to film schools, and was admitted to a summer film program in a distant state. He let his business diminish, and turned the firm over to his employees. His future success as a filmmaker will require his developing the ability to work with others, since films are the product of many differing disciplines of technicians, artists, and business people. This will further push him beyond the limits of the independent expert.

During treatment the work focus alternated with love issues. Again we can look, at least in part, at these from a social character standpoint. As we analyzed his love choices we saw that one woman was from a well-to-do family, ran her own business, and wanted the patient to socialize with her country-club group. He liked her maturity, sense of style, and her class, but did not feel a part of it or want to live that way. The other woman was more informal, spontaneous, and committed to developing herself intellectually. The daughter of a professor, she was interested in becoming an architect, and was making plans for graduate school. He felt more an equal with her seriousness, her art, and enjoyed being with her.

It emerged later in treatment that his father had had an affair with a wealthy woman, which indicated the father's conflicted relationship with the patient's mother. The analysis of this allowed the patient to dissolve the relationship with the well-to-do woman, as he became conscious of reenacting his father's conflicts and social aspirations. He committed himself seriously to the woman who wanted to develop an architecture career. They discussed marriage. They planned how to stay together though heading to different parts of the country for education. They bought a house together, each signing the ownership papers, though they were not married.

The patient's father had given up going to graduate school to marry the patient's mother. Instead of investing in his self development, the father had bought a house and married. It was a lifelong disappointment to the father that he hadn't gone further with his education. The father's jobs and business activities were never fully successful. His son, however, decided through his psychotherapy that his own education and development was most important for his happiness. The patient and his girlfriend decided to delay marriage. Their sexual life became more zestful and satisfying. The homosexual fantasies almost completely died out. Without the full perspective on his life offered by understanding his social character, a therapist might overemphasize the sexual identity issue of this patient and miss the importance of his self development work drive. The delay of marriage and the commitment to continual development is a pattern that many therapists have probably seen in patients today. This is often an aspect of the self-developer social character. Recall that at this age the patient's father had given up his education, married, and had several children.

Any case presentation is a selection from a rich tapestry of feelings, experiences, interpretations, genetic reconstructions, confrontations, special language and interactions between two individuals engaged in an intimate, structured dialogue. This case vignette was selected to illustrate the value of social character knowledge in creating the working alliance, diagnosing, understanding, and working through with patients in this period of rapid social system and value change.

While some sessions focused more on the genetic

reconstruction of the patient's history, and his emotional development, others focused on a path of inquiry about his adult development choices. The perspective of the inquiry for the therapist is not between focusing on early development and the patient's present life choices, but rather for the therapist to have a full life cycle model of development. For example, when the pattern of the patient's work or love relationships became evident over many sessions, questions such as these might be asked: "Is this a reenactment, or parallel of what your parent(s) did?" "Is this what you want for yourself, or what your parent(s) want for you?" "How does this pattern fit your goals for your development?" It is this kind of active working alliance focused on issues of their development that people with the emerging modern character especially value.

Self-developers often come from dual-career families where both parents work outside the home. Children see little of their parents' work and often know little about what they actually do. Basic attitudes toward authority and responsibility within self-developer families are changing toward equal gender roles, with the children treated as equals in the family. Necessity drives these families to encourage their children's independence and responsibility at an earlier age, and gives them many choices so that they learn the natural consequences of becoming self-managing. This can leave a yearning for a nurturing mother, and for a father who is respected for his authority. Many women today find it difficult to manage the conflict between achieving career goals and being nurturant mothers. Many men today are searching to redefine their authority in a culture that devalues their traditional role, or maligns them as culpable for society's ills. Longings for these emotional parental relationships can often lead self-developer children in later life to have problems with establishing strong relationships whether in love or work, and to maintain coherent, sustained commitments to their own goals. Therefore, transference/ resistance analysis, and self development–focused dialogue are both important in working with many of these patients.

This patient's transference had several elements in which I was, at times, the longed-for father while at other times I was the longed-for mother. He wanted me to help him develop his business by drawing on my knowledge, in that he could tell by my office that I also worked as a consultant to organizations and leaders. Another aspect of his transference was wanting me to arrange for medication when he felt his depression intensifying and felt himself "being pulled out to sea, and I'm afraid I won't be able to stop it." We analyzed his fears and his wish that I have him medicated. I finally asked him to make the choice since I thought he should try to see if he could do without it, and that we could monitor together how he was doing. He chose to forgo the medication and work to understand his fears without it, although he understood that taking the medication would not foreclose the analytic work.

When the depressive mood abated he felt a significant sense of new self-mastery, confidence, and strength. His fear of helplessness, and his wish that I protect him, as the longed-for mother, with magical medicinal nourishment, was analyzed and dealt with in a direct, person-to-person manner from which he drew insight and strength in the face of his fears. Following Fromm we see a mother transference in his wish to be nourished and his actions to overcome the fears and "break the mother-tie" as he confronts his regressive impulses.

There was also a self-developer aspect intertwined with

the father transference. The patient was very interested in Buddhism, and he would often bring into the sessions Buddhist stories or concepts. He wanted me to be like a Buddhist master and point out his path of development. This meant more than a career path, although as a self-developer his work was an important element, with his love relationship being the other important aspect he wanted to bring into a balanced life. He was persistent in trying to get me to tell him what he should do. Over many sessions we analyzed this transferential wish. In one of the later sessions he said, citing a Buddhist story: "I realize now that you are like a gardener, you prepare the soil, you add compost [a comment on what he thought of some of the sessions], and you water the ground, but I must plant the seed and make it grow." Transference interpretations were important in the treatment, as was the real relationship to define and strengthen his self-development drive.

Neither parents nor his religious school had supported the patient's real talents and developmental aspirations. Treatment strengthened his resolve to develop his passionate interests, his self-developer social character, and showed him he could overcome his depression, without medication, and master his emotions.

THE CHANGING WORK OF PSYCHOTHERAPY

We live in a period of transformation of patriarchy. Therapy itself, as a form of specialized work, is also changing. The patriarchal model with the therapist as supposedly neutral, blank screen is changing, as it must, to an interactive model in which there is more active, direct engagement and dialogue, and the therapist as a "real person" is present. Fromm advocated this years ago. It seems now that practice is catching up. Milton Viederman (1991) states:

> Change occurs not only by analysis of the transference or by analysis of conflict . . . but also in the context of transactions between analyst and patient as they pertain to dialogue about the patient's life. . . . Successful outcomes in analysis may occur with . . . the internalization of the dialogue between analyst and patient. . . . The nature of the analyst's interventions, his timing, what he chooses to select for scrutiny and what he ignores, act as social referencing that powerfully influences the patients, even though their intent may be to focus on areas for examination and are experienced by the analyst as neutral. . . . One must take seriously the powerful effect of the real person of the analyst, the intensity of his emotional involvement with the patient over many years . . . and the use of noninterpretive interventions. [pp. 486–487]

Knowledge of social character, combined with the presence of the analyst as a real person in dialogue with the patient can have these powerful developmental influences. They are not, however, a substitute for the analysis of transference and resistance. Nor is being fully present as another human being interacting with the patient intended to give a "corrective emotional experience." Psychoanalytic psychotherapy is a structured dialogue that follows rules of inquiry. It is based upon a theory of human development and unconscious character structure that is expressed through the unfolding interpersonal, clinical relationship. Through this relationship emerges the transference and resistance. Social character knowledge is useful in structuring the inquiry to reveal the values and aspirations of the patient.

When this knowledge is used by the involved, active therapist it can help create a collegial, almost partner-like working alliance with a patient. How is this facilitated? The therapist, with knowledge of changing social character and changing conditions of work, can bring out the lack of fit between the patient's character, aspirations, and work, as well as any inhibitions or fears that block the patient's active responsibility for his or her own development.

Everyone has a theory of character and its formation, whether it is conscious or not. How worked out and informed by the current social process is it? How do therapists and scientists connect their (social) character theory to the various schools or theories of psychoanalytic thinking? Therapists and theoreticians may be attracted to a particular school because it resonates with their own character. This highlights the need to integrate these various partial theories into a more comprehensive, systemic theory. Pine (1985) speaks about the four intrapsychic languages of psychoanalysis as drive theory, internalized object relations, self experience, and ego functioning.

> I believe all of [these languages] are relevant to every treatment because experiences organized around drive, ego, object relations, self, and reality are inevitably part of the life of every developing person. . . . The several intrapsychic psychologies become interrelated in such a way that all psychic acts eventually come to have multiple functions. [Pine 1985, p. 179]

Social character is a systems understanding of the patient's life story shaped by a specific historical social process. It is not articulated in the language of the intrapsychic psychologies, but as a general psychology of psychoanalysis. Social character is psychoanalytic because it describes how a system of largely unconscious values and emotions develops in individuals living in a particular historical social process. Social character contributes to the general psychology of psychoanalysis because it shows how outer demands become internalized.

Social character knowledge becomes a natural language of the self when it is articulated in nontechnical language of adult aspirations, not in an expert's special language describing only an intrapsychic part of the person. Psychoanalytic psychotherapy, when employing social character knowledge as discussed here, helps make conscious the unconscious elements and etiology of the patient's aspirations. This empowers them to become more active and creative in the real world of constraints and possibilities they have before them. Analysis alone only takes an object of study apart into its component parts. Synthesis (Ackoff 1981) develops knowledge of how the parts are defined by their function within the whole, and looks at the whole in terms of its role in the larger system of which it is a part. Social character knowledge, a form of systems thinking, can help the whole person understand and develop in their world of aspirations and work.

Social character could be articulated in the multiple functions of the four intrapsychic languages. Fromm and Maccoby (1970) largely employ drive and ego languages in describing motives, adaptation, and energy as a metaphor for level of activity or passion. For example, they state: "Character can be defined as the (relatively permanent) form in which human energy is structuralized in the process of assimilation and socialization" (p. 69). I believe that the language of action, or the "life narrative" (Schafer 1976, 1978), is the natural language for social character. Schafer (1978) states: "[The] critique of structural concepts shows that the concept of structure, as proposed by Freud, describes or names consistencies of action; it does not explain them. These consistencies remain basic reference points for psychoanalytic interpretation" (p. 134). Social character knowledge helps understand and explain these "consistencies of action" of the adults who become more conscious of what their self development requires of them in today's realities. Each social character has a life story, or life narrative that explains these consistencies of action.

Funk (Chapter 14 in this volume) observes the rise of narcissistic, depressive, addictive, and codependent problems. I would add sexual identity, marital, and child-rearing problems to this list. While Funk attributes these to a nonproductive society (1992), I attribute these problems to the disintegration of traditional patriarchal authority, the lack today of a developed alternative, and the emergence of new productive forces including people. I believe there are signs of hope in the changing social character, and in the evolving nature of the family, work, and organization. Patients bring these problems to clinical sessions.

I agree with Funk (in this volume) that we should analyze our own social character as clinicians. This often means becoming conscious of the expert's drive to follow the analytic rules closely, or the helper's overriding wish to help the patient, and how these lead away from the enlivening, real person dialogue. Much of the analytic community is still enmeshed in the hierarchical thinking of experts trying to display their professional competence in arcane expert language. The trend toward intersubjectivity (Stolorow) and interactiveness in psychoanalytic clinical dialogue are signs of hope that the work of clinicians is also changing with the social dynamics. Method is moving in the direction of Fromm's concept of psychoanalysis as a "participatory, humanistic encounter" (see Maccoby, Chapter 2 in this volume).

The definition of healthy development itself is affected by the socio-historical process. Without knowledge of social character, theoreticians and clinicians tend to define health in terms of the dominant social character of their times. In the history of psychoanalysis we see this unfolding today. Earlier in the century and until recently, the dominant definition of health emphasized independence, defined as autonomy and self-reliance. Autonomy is a central value of experts and fits a world of independent professionals and large bureaucratic organizations. In addition to these values from the work culture, the United States is a country of immigrants who had to uproot themselves to adapt to a new culture. Fromm's emphasis on breaking the mother tie and Mahler's separation-individuation model of development are examples of this powerful bias in these two European immigrants (Kirshner 1988; also see Cortina, Chapter 3 in this volume).

The recent trend within psychoanalytic theory is toward defining healthy development as *relational*, emphasizing the interpersonal nature of our work and of healthy development. This is a shift away from the role of the therapist as being a detached expert and toward a more participative and interactive role. This new emphasis comes at a time when interdependence and teamwork have become essential for the workplace. The relational emphasis can be seen as a balance to the patriarchal expert's definition of healthy development in psychoanalysis.

The paradigm of our age is evolving away from mechanistic and fragmented thinking that looks at parts of systems as if they were separate or separable from their containing whole. Mechanistic thinking conceptualizes the mind as a machine composed of parts that affect each other. Or the mind is conceived as a pneumatic-hydraulic system of energy coursing through channels. These mind-as-machine concepts fit the industrial machine era.

Today's value system and social structure is moving away from the industrial era's patriarchy and hierarchy. The emerging scientific paradigm is complex systems, emphasizing interactive, multidisciplinary thinking. The emerging social value system and structure is the development of interactive cooperative teams that are competitive in their external environment. The ideal of this team culture is the development of the organization and its members for mutual success, based on principles of continual learning and adaptation.

Social character methodology can facilitate understanding a person, not as an isolated individual with a mind-as-machine, but as part of this larger, containing social system in which the person dynamically works and interacts in an evolving historical process.

We are moving into the second century of psychoanalysis as a theory, a therapy, and an art. As we approach the twenty-first century it is appropriate to learn social character methodology and knowledge as a useful tool for systems thinkers, researchers, consultants, and therapists.

REFERENCES

Ackoff, R. (1981). *Creating the Corporate Future*. New York: Wiley.

Erikson, E. H. (1963). *Childhood and Society*, 2nd ed. New York: Norton.

_____ (1964). *Insight and Responsibility: Lectures on the Ethical Implications of Psychoanalytic Insight*. New York: Norton.

_____ (1968). *Identity, Youth and Crisis*. New York: Norton.

Freud, S. (1926). *Inhibitions, Symptoms, and Anxiety*. New York: Norton, 1959.

Fromm, E. (1941). *Escape from Freedom*. New York: Rinehart.

_____ (1947). *Man for Himself: An Inquiry into the Psychology of Ethics*. Greenwich, CT: Fawcett.

_____ (1955). *The Sane Society*. Greenwich, CT: Fawcett.

_____ (1970). *The Crisis of Psychoanalysis: Essays on Freud, Marx, and Social Psychology*. Greenwich, CT: Fawcett.

_____ (1976). *To Have or To Be?* New York: Harper & Row.

_____ (1981). *On Disobedience and Other Essays*. New York: Seabury.

_____ (1984). *The Working Class in Weimar Germany*. Cambridge, MA: Harvard University Press.

_____ (1986). *For the Love of Life*. New York: Free Press.

Fromm, E., and Maccoby, M. (1970). *Social Character in a Mexican Village*. New York: Prentice-Hall.

Funk, R. (1992). *Fromm's approach to psychoanalytic theory and its relevance for therapeutic work*. Paper presented at the Seminar on Socio-psychoanalytic Field Research, Instituto Mexicano de Psicoanálisis, October 15.

Hendrick, I. (1943). Work and the pleasure principle. *Psychoanalytic Quarterly* 12:311–329.

Kirshner, R. S. (1988). The assenting echo: Anglo-American values in contemporary psychoanalytic development. *Social Research* 57:821–857.

Kohut, H. (1977). *The Restoration of the Self*. New York: International Universities Press.

Lantos, B. (1943). Work and the instincts. *International Journal of Psycho-Analysis* 24:114–119.

_____ (1952). Metapsychological considerations on the concept of work. *International Journal of Psycho-Analysis* 33:439–443.

Maccoby, M. (1976). *The Gamesman: The New Corporate Leaders in America*. New York: Simon & Schuster.

_____ (1982). Social character vs. the productive ideal: the contribution and contradiction in Fromm's view of man. *Praxis International* 2:70–83.

_____ (1988). *Why Work: Leading the New Generation*. New York: Simon & Schuster. (Revised second edition: *Why Work?*

Motivating the New Workforce. Alexandria, VA: Miles River Press, 1995.)

_____ (1994). *The two voices of Erich Fromm: the prophetic and the analytic*. Paper presented at the Erich Fromm International Symposium, Washington, DC, May 5–8.

Margolies, R. (1981). *The Psychoanalytic Meaning of Work*. Doctoral dissertation, Yeshiva University, New York.

Mumford, L. (1967). *The Myth of the Machine: Technics and Human Development*. New York: Harcourt Brace Jovanovich.

Neff, W. S. (1965). Psychoanalytic conceptions of the meaning of work. *Psychiatry* 28:324–333.

Pine, F. (1985). *Developmental Theory and Clinical Process*. New Haven, CT: Yale University Press.

Schafer, R. (1976). *A New Language for Psychoanalysis*. New Haven, CT: Yale University Press.

_____ (1978). *Language and Insight*. New Haven, CT: Yale University Press.

Stolorow, R., Brandschaff, B., and Atwood, G. (1987). *Psychoanalytic Treatment: An Intersubjective Approach*. Hillsdale, NJ: Analytic Press.

Viederman, M. (1991). The real person of the analyst and his role in the process of psychoanalytic cure. *Journal of the American Psychoanalytic Association* 39:451–481.

Waelder, R. (1936). The principle of multiple function: observations on Overdetermination. *Psychoanalytic Quarterly* 5:45–62.

White, R. W. (1952). *Lives in Progress*, 3rd ed. New York: Holt, Rinehart & Winston, 1975.

_____ (1959). Motivation reconsidered: the concept of competence. *Psychological Review* 66:297–333.

_____ (1960). Competence and the psychosexual stages of development. In *Nebraska Symposium on Motivation*, ed. M. Jones, 97–141. Lincoln: University of Nebraska Press.

_____ (1963). Ego and reality in psychoanalytic theory: a proposal regarding independent ego energies. *Psychological Issues* 3(3), monograph 11.

A Commentary

Sandra Buechler

At the end of his poem, "Two Tramps in Mud Time," Robert Frost gave us his sense of how we should relate to work:

> But yield who will to their separation,
> My object in living is to unite
> My avocation and my vocation
> As my two eyes make one in sight.
> Only where love and need are one,
> And the work is play for mortal stakes,
> Is the deed ever really done
> For Heaven and the future's sakes.

This commentary explores the idea that it is possible to identify aspects of a healthy relationship to work, and healthy relationships at work, that are timeless and transcend the mores of any particular culture, or social character type. Regardless of the specific situation, what is it *human* to want at work? Culture, time, place, and individual resources affect work situations, but not essential human emotions, not strivings toward wholeness and life affirmation. I will argue that human beings have certain work-related needs, and that it is consonant with the spirit of Fromm's writings to judge the degree to which a society facilitates meeting these needs.

I will begin by sketching a portrait of a disturbed work relationship, and draw some implications from it about what a healthy relationship would look like. I will then, very briefly, comment on each of these elements of health at work.

Now in his forties, the patient chose a profession in his youth for reasons that are no longer vivid to him. He gives work the attention it requires, and is considered successful. He isn't looking for great meaning in his work, and isn't bothered by its absence. An accomplishment sometimes gives him pleasure, but not joy. An obstacle frustrates or irritates him, but does not mobilize any passionate opposition. He is hoping to get through to retirement, which is, for now, a vaguely conceived release from pressures and demands, without any content of its own. Retirement will be the absence of what bothers him in the present. If asked what he feels about his work, he says, "It's OK," and he would be very anxious if his position were threatened, not because of the loss of his job, but because he would have to go through the effort of finding a new one. A favorite pastime is veiled humor with other employees about the highest level of management, or about the absurdity of aspects of the system. But these criticisms hold no real rage, or hope of change. They have the feel of resentments, more like aches than pains. Occasionally, some work-related problem may punctuate his usual dutifulness, and he will, for a moment, become passionately involved, intensely curious, truly devoted. But when this particular problem is solved he goes back to his usual demeanor, and may look at this moment of intensity almost as though it had been a temporary illness of some sort, an aberration that is utterly engrossing at the time, but outside of real life.

What is wrong with this picture? Because of time, I can only mention the grave shortcomings in his ability to use work for self-expression, self-integration, active, creative engagement with the world, the development of genuine, alive interests, and a sense of personal meaningfulness.

Regarding the first aspect of a healthy relationship to work, the importance of work as an outlet for self-expression, Fromm (1968) tells us how important it is for us to have the opportunity to use each of our faculties. Whatever we were born with, yearns for expression:

> The dynamism of human nature inasmuch as it is human is primarily rooted in this need of man *to express his faculties in relation to the world rather than in his need to use the world as a means for the satisfaction of his physiological necessities.* This means: because I have eyes, I have the need to see; because I have ears, I have the need to hear; because I have a mind, I have the need to think; and because I have a heart, I have the need to feel. In short, because I am a man, I am in need of man and of the world. [p. 72]

We need the chance to make use of our whole selves, including, I will argue, the whole range of our emotional selves, and work can provide an important medium for such expression.

Dr. Margolies's case vignette might be looked at from this point of view. Here is a man for whom love and need had to become one, a man trying to exist in a political and entrepreneurial life, with unlived literary and aesthetic passions. Fortunately his treatment helped him live more of himself. However, what I would like to suggest, is that in emphasizing the patient's adaptation to changing cultural values, Dr. Margolies did not sufficiently address pathological aspects of this man's functioning. This emphasis on adaptation also left out the importance of maintaining a critical eye toward our society, to judge the degree to which it does and does not promote human growth.

Dr. Margolies asks, early in his chapter, what therapists can learn about the changing nature of social character and work today that will help them in their clinical work. I would reframe his question into two parts:

1. How do theories about current changes in social character and work environments *focus us differently*, as we listen to clinical material? What of the patient's material do we hear differently because of our interest in, and knowledge of, social character theory?

2. How can we integrate this societal focus with our understanding of the patient's predominant pathology so that, together, the two frames of reference enhance our clinical understanding and help us work as advocates of human growth, opposing individual and societal forces that thwart it?

Using the case example furnished by Dr. Margolies, I will briefly address these questions. I believe that the social character frame of reference makes a tremendous difference in what the clinician hears, focuses on, responds to, considers pathological, and chooses to address in the treatment. If Dr. Margolies's patient had walked into my office, for example, I probably would have seen his character as predominantly narcissistic. Some of his behavior, which can be defined as evidence of the "self-developer" mode, such as his career dissatisfactions and difficulties, would probably look to me like the narcissist's unwillingness to accept the limits of *one* self-definition, *one* career, *one* life. The patient's inability to settle into a single relationship, yearning for the positive aspects of both, would seem similarly narcissistic. His depression would, for me, fit the typical picture of the narcissist's reaction to life's limitations, the depression many clinicians see as the underside of grandiosity.

Obviously, given the rich clinical material, there is much else that would look different to me given my orientation to the material. The patient's need for an interactive therapist would sound, to me, like a cry for the "mirroring" he never got from his absent parents. I would see their psychological inability to provide him with an adequate, clear sense of self and self-definition as paramount. I would view this as a pathogenic situation, rather than seeing their dual career family structure as fostering adaptive "self development" tendencies. In short, what looks to Dr. Margolies like self development might look to me like a lack of clear, defined sense of self, along with a narcissistic unwillingness to accept life's limitations. I would also need to explore further the patient's sadism, as evidenced in some of the fantasy material.

I think these differences are profound, not simply linguistic. We would focus on different aspects of the material, would define the pathology differently, and might well have different treatment goals in mind. I believe we wouldn't be hearing the same patient. Although I would hope that I would take cultural and societal pressures into account in my view of the patient's real life situation, I would want to pay a great deal of attention to his individual pathology.

Can we integrate these frames of reference? To some degree, of course, we have to, since we must see the patient in his individuality, as well as in the context of his culture/society/historical period. But I will argue that one frame of reference needs to predominate, that we can't see through too many prisms at once. For me, the knowledge of broad cultural shifts, affecting us all, including the patient and myself, is like the frame of a painting, an important delimiting piece of reality that in the consulting room should be noted, but not my main focus. For me the fundamental, essential human strivings for work and love, the ever-repeated defensive patterns, the central forms of pathology are core. They are framed differently in different cultures. But it is to them that I must pay most attention, for it is our expertise in understanding their interplay that gives us the ability to help patients become freer to use their resources more productively, to express themselves more fully. If our society is also delimiting the patient's use of his resources it is, I think, in the spirit of Fromm for us to become critics of that society, and not its agents helping patients merely adapt to it, at the expense of the full use of their human potential. Our focus on society should be as advocates for the fullest expression of human talents and resources. When individual pathology and/or societal ills block the full realization of human potential, we should be opposing these forces.

Whole-self expression means, to me, that work must discourage compartmentalization. In *The Sane Society* (1955) Fromm makes this point eloquently:

> One cannot separate work activity from political activity, from the use of leisure time and from personal life. If work were to become interesting without the other spheres of life becoming human, no real change would occur. In

fact, it could not become interesting. It is the very evil of present-day culture that it separates and compartmentalizes the various spheres of living. The way to sanity lies in overcoming this split and in arriving at a new unification and integration within society and within the individual human being. [p. 326]

The Dickensian industrial era sweatshop might be the quintessential compartmentalizing workplace. Such a setting would have to evoke a deep and chronic despair. Most of one's self must have been irrelevant, unrecognized. To survive, one would probably become furtive, stealing morsels of pleasure, in secret moments of escape from duty. One would define one's real self, one's real life, as taking place outside work. Thus, there would be two selves—a passive, masked lifeless work-self, and a pressured, intense "real" self. But how much has the average worker really escaped from this alienating nightmare? Has technology really freed us, or, as the popular writer Barbara Garson (1994) suggests, "The computer permitted a form of electronic supervision that exceeded anything conceivable in the old-fashioned factory. So twenty-first century technology was used to introduce nineteenth century labor discipline" (p. 221). I wonder, further, what Fromm would feel about the increasing encroachment of insurance company surveillance on the *analyst's* experience of his professional work, and on the human relationship in treatment.

Garson, surveying work in factories, industrial offices, and insurance companies, goes on to describe how some innovations, in the name of increased efficiency, reduce work to meaningless routine. Initiative, imagination, creativity have no place.

In "For the Love of Life," Fromm (1986) addresses the human need to do creative work:

People have other interests that go beyond the practical, the functional, the object as tool or utensil. They want to be active in a creative way; they want to give shape to things, to develop powers latent in themselves. [p. 16]

Fromm warns that "depression is what results from an incorrect way of life," (p. 146). There is a price to pay if the human need for the joy and power of creating is ignored. Fromm (1955) put the matter succinctly when he said, in *The Sane Society*:

Creation and destruction, love and hate, are not two instincts which exist independently. They are both answers to the same need for transcendence, and the will to destroy must rise when the will to create cannot be satisfied. [p. 42]

Thus, the deadening or disuse of an aspect of our humanness, our creativity, results not merely in the loss of a potential, but in the development of a destructive trend.

The last three elements—activity, interest, and meaningfulness—have something in common, for they all ask of the workplace that it promote aliveness. Consider Schachtel's (1959) description of some essential human motives:

Curiosity, the desire for knowledge, the wish to orient oneself in the world one lives in—and finally the posing of man's eternal questions, "Who am I?" "What can I hope for?" "What shall I do?"—all these do not develop under the pressure of relentless need or of fear for one's life. They develop when man can pause to think, when the child is free to wonder and to explore. . . . They represent man's distinctive capacity to develop *interest*—the autonomous interest which alone permits the full encounter with the object. [p. 274]

Schachtel's understanding of the interest, active exploration, and effort to find meaning that are inherent in
being human suggests to me that these are qualities we
bring to the workplace. If they are encouraged, if our
intense emotions find a place to spread out, if assertion is
welcomed, interest is deepened, and the capacity for
surprise is not deadened, then we are fortunate.

From this perspective Dr. Margolies's stimulating paper
raises questions on many important issues:

1. The adaptation to society as a treatment goal. Current societal definitions of progress and the meaning of
work cannot be accepted as givens in treatment. How do
we help patients develop, not as rebels, not as conforming
adapters, but as whole persons?

2. The role of the expert today: Although Dr. Margolies
suggests that all social character types can contribute, the
expert here seems portrayed as a primary problematic
holdover.

3. How can we have analytic identities, truly believe in
a way of working, embrace some truths without, as Dr.
Margolies warns the potential expert in all of us, rigidly
advancing a particular theory?

4. How can we maintain a critical eye on societal
changes and pressures, defining our role as advocates for
the full use of human potential, and working to modify
both individual and societal pathology that thwarts
human development?

To summarize, I come to Dr. Margolies's paper under
the sway of the belief that there are universal, timeless
human emotions that seek expression in all of our relationships, including our relationships at, and with, work.
If we are human, we not only bleed, but also feel fear,

anger, love, and hate, and we deeply desire expression of our curiosity and striving to affirm life. Every aspect of our emotional equipment for living that is taboo at the workplace splits and deadens us, and leads to a chronic, schizoid despair. I believe it is consonant with Fromm's spirit that we keep a watchful eye on the changes in our current work climate, careful of any assumption that so-called progress is always for the good. A team may be no more life-enhancing than a patriarchal employer, if the individual's true voice is still unwelcome. In fact, I wonder if an illusion of team cooperation, company concern, and openness to difference might be especially spirit-shattering. The employee must then act as though he can freely speak, hiding wariness in his heart.

I would like to end on a more personal note. I have long wondered why I find reading Fromm not merely enlightening, but also therapeutic. I experience his words as a challenge to work, and generally live more fully and honestly. He demands that I recognize how precious is time and the opportunity to participate in life. In his presence, I have to face what I waste. I am more aware of what in myself I don't live. The poet Rilke (1934) once said,

> If we think of this existence of the individual as a larger or smaller room, it appears evident that most people learn to know only a corner of their room, a place by the window, a strip of floor on which they walk up and down. Thus they have a certain security. [p. 68]

Fromm demands, for the love of life, that we dare to expand.

REFERENCES

Fromm, E. (1955). *The Sane Society*. Greenwich, CT: Fawcett.
_____ (1968). *The Revolution of Hope*. New York: Harper & Row.

_____ (1986). *For the Love of Life*. New York: Free Press.

Frost, R. (1934). Two Tramps in Mud Time. In *The Poetry of Robert Frost*, ed. Edward Connery Lathem. New York: Holt, Rinehart & Winston, 1969.

Garson, B. (1994). *All the Livelong Day*. New York: Penguin.

Rilke, R. M. (1934). *Letters to a Young Poet*. New York: Norton.

Schachtel, E. (1959). *Metamorphosis*. New York: Basic Books.

IV

ERICH FROMM'S PLACE IN THE PSYCHOANALYTIC MOVEMENT

16

Erich Fromm: A Brief Biography

Daniel Burston

Erich Pinchas Fromm was born on March 23, 1900. His father Naphtali was a small wine merchant, and the head of a local chapter of the Hermann Cohen Society, which was devoted to the ideas of the great neo-Kantian ethical philosopher. Naphtali wanted young Erich to be a rabbi. His mother Rosa, on the other hand, had musical aspirations, and hoped her son would be the next Arthur Rubinstein (Funk 1983). Erich Fromm disappointed both parents, however, and became the most popular and prolific psychoanalytic author of the 1950s and 1960s.

Though widely admired for his lively and accessible writing style, which is readily intelligible to people from all backgrounds and walks of life, it is impossible to understand Fromm personally without appreciating his Jewish roots. During his adolescent years, he studied with some of the leading religious scholars of his day, including

Rabbi Nehemia Nobel and Rabbi Zalman Baruch Rabinkow. Nobel and Rabinkow left a deep impression on
Fromm. They both combined traditionalism in religious
observance with deep openness to others' traditions and
ideas—Nobel being steeped in Goethe, the German Enlightenment, and psychoanalysis, and Rabinkow being
steeped in socialism, Hasidism, and kabbalah (Funk 1983).
The two traits his teachers shared, namely rootedness in
tradition, combined with openness, originality, and syn-
cretism, shaped Fromm's attitude toward socialism and
psychoanalysis in later life.

Fromm's interest in social psychology was kindled by
the events surrounding World War I. As Germany prepared for war, Fromm noted with dismay that many of his
friends and teachers were swept up in the prevailing war
hysteria. As the war wore on, as he later recalled, Fromm
felt a deepening sense of doubt and betrayal at the official
lies and propaganda churned out by the German newspa-
pers. When the war ended, Germany was in ruins, and
Fromm, now 18, was desperate to understand more about
the roots of human destructiveness—a preoccupation that
would stay with him for the remainder of his life (Fromm
1962). As a result, during the 1960s and 1970s Fromm
would write extensively on human destructiveness, challenging the rival orthodoxies of Freud and B. F. Skinner in
provocative and illuminating ways.

Four years later, at the age of 22, Fromm received his
doctorate in sociology under Alfred Weber at Heidelberg.
The subject of his dissertation was the function of Talmudic law in three Jewish communities: Orthodox Jewry,
Reform Jewry, and the Karaites. At 24, he met his first
analyst, and later his first wife, Frieda Reichmann, a
progressive Jewish psychiatrist trained by Kurt Goldstein
and Hans Sachs. A formidable person in her own right,

Fromm's first wife would go on to achieve considerable recognition in the United States under her married name of Frieda Fromm-Reichmann. With her assistance, Fromm's training analysis with Wilhelm Wittenberg commenced at age 25 in Munich, and was followed by a year under Karl Landauer back in Frankfurt. He finished his training with two more years under Sachs and Theodor Reik in Berlin, returning to Frankfurt shortly thereafter (Funk 1983).

Although Fromm trained during his Berlin years with steadfast Freud loyalists, his real sympathies lay with Freud's loyal opposition, or those independent-minded analysts who tried to reconcile their fidelity to Freud with other influences and ideas, but who attempted to remain within the analytic mainstream. When Fromm began writing in the late 1920s, Freud's loyal opposition could be divided into two camps—the Marxists and the non-Marxists. The non-Marxists were somewhat dispersed geographically, and were so strikingly individual, in many ways, that one hesitates to call them a "group." But their number included analysts like Sandor Ferenczi, Georg Groddeck, Karen Horney, Ludwig Binswanger, and Paul Schilder, among others.

By contrast, the left-leaning analysts included Wilhelm Reich and his followers, other participants in Otto Fenichel's Kinderseminar, and a sprinkling of Viennese and Hungarian analysts like Bruno Bettelheim and Paul Gero, who were peripheral players in Fenichel's circle (Jacoby 1983). During the late 1920s and early 1930s, the intellectual center of gravity for this group was Berlin. Here again, however, characterizing Freud's left-wing loyal opposition as a "group" is problematic, because despite various collaborative efforts, they fought bitterly, and expressed their differences with a cold and furious pedantry rooted as much in left-wing sectarianism as it was in the jealous, fratricidal atmosphere Freud cultivated among his less independent followers (Burston 1991).

In retrospect, it is interesting to note that Fromm was the only one among them with an academic, rather than a medical, background. In 1927, at the invitation of Max Horkheimer, he became the director of social psychology at the Frankfurt Institute of Social Research, a left-leaning scholarly enclave that would later have an enormous impact on postwar intellectual life in the United States and Europe. Fromm was the only psychoanalyst at the institute and in the course of his duties there conducted a (posthumously published) empirical study of pro-fascist tendencies of German workers (Fromm 1984)—the forerunner, in fact, for *The Authoritarian Personality* by Theodor Adorno and colleagues (Burston 1991).

Although Fromm was a follower of Reich's for about a year, Reich and he quarreled prior to his appointment to the Frankfurt School (Burston 1991, Eros 1992), and Fromm had no respect for Fenichel whatsoever. One of the differences between Reich and Fromm was Reich's involvement with the Communist Party, which Fromm and his associates—notably Horkheimer and Marcuse—viewed with deep suspicion (Eros 1992, Jay 1973). Another divisive issue was Freud's libido theory, which Reich retained (in modified form), but which Fromm soon abandoned.

Freud's left-opposition, such as it was, was fragmented and dispersed by the events preceding World War II, and the flight of European émigrés to America. Fromm arrived in 1933. Though he avoided the sterile controversies between Reich and Fenichel, in 1938 Fromm left the Frankfurt School for Social Research, now in exile at Columbia University, arguing, among other things, about the issue of fidelity to Freud. As Fromm later recalled,

Horkheimer was deeply displeased with his recent criti-cisms of Freud. After Fromm's departure, Adorno joined the institute (Jay 1973).

Shortly after his arrival, Fromm set up practice in New York, where he became a regular member of Harry Stack Sullivan's Zodiac Club, socializing with Sullivan, Karen Horney, Clara Thompson, Ruth Benedict, Ralph Linton, Margaret Mead, and Abram Kardiner, among others. In the war's immediate aftermath, innovative and indepen-dently minded analysts were increasingly enveloped by (and answerable to) a resurgent orthodoxy that swept psychoanalysis in the United States, when McCarthyism ran rampant, and pressures for mindless conformity in America were prevalent and intense. In this new political climate, Reich, a former Stalinist, became a staunch anti-communist, and a great admirer or Dwight D. Eisen-hower, while Otto Fenichel managed to conceal his Marxist past (Jacoby 1983) and aligned himself with the orthodox analytic establishment. Fromm, undeterred, made no secret of his socialism, but was angrily attacked by Fenichel for his "revisionist" views on psychoanalytic theory.

Other attacks from the left came from Adorno, who was about to embark on *The Authoritarian Personality* (Jay 1973), and from another Frankfurt School alumnus, Herbert Marcuse. Marcuse discovered Freud after the Second World War, and had evidently hoped to find in him a "revolutionary" philosopher. As far as I know, Fromm never bothered to respond to Fenichel or Adorno publicly. But the debate between Fromm and Marcuse, which began in 1955, was a long and bitter one, indicating that Fromm attributed much more importance to Marcuse's attack than the ones that preceded it (Burston 1991). And indeed, in retrospect, it *was* more important, as most of the New Left intelligentsia sided with Marcuse after 1968, dismissing Fromm as an idle conformist—an assessment that has contributed to the comparative neglect of Fromm ever since.

After his ejection from the International Psychoanalytic Association, Fromm was made clinical director of the William Alanson White Institute in New York City. He held this position from 1946 to 1950, although in the fall of 1949 Fromm and his second wife, Henny Gurland, moved to México in hopes of arresting or reversing Gurland's rheumatoid arthritis. As it turned out, however, they were not successful, and she died early in 1952. Fromm was devastated by her death, but at the invitation of leading Mexican psychiatrists, decided to stay on, and to found the Mexican Institute of Psychoanalysis, which he directed until 1967, when a heart attack prompted a retreat to Locarno, Switzerland, to recuperate for several months (Burston 1991).

In the intervening decade and a half, from 1952 to 1967, Fromm led a varied and active life. In December 1953 Fromm married his third wife, Annis Freeman, an American woman, who was his constant companion, and who helped design their tasteful home in Cuernavaca. Erich and Annis solicited help in planting and landscaping their lovely garden from the noted Zen scholar D. T. Suzuki, who, together with his lovely young secretary, lived in a small hut on their property throughout much of 1959, and taught Fromm about Buddhism and meditation.

While deepening his familiarity with Asian art and ideas, Fromm was also immersing himself in the culture of his newly adopted home. In 1955 and 1956, Fromm, who had taught anthropology with Ralph Linton in 1947, joined Dr. Lorette Cenourne for an intensive postgraduate seminar on the religion, economics, and history of pre-Columbian cultures in Central America. With this new knowledge now firmly in his grasp, from 1957 to 1963,

Fromm and his associates conducted a comprehensive study of a peasant village, Chiconcuac, in which they gathered all the available historical and anthropological data on the 162 households, and did detailed psychological testing, face-to-face interviews, and naturalistic observation on a day-to-day basis. The findings, published as *Social Character in a Mexican Village* (Fromm and Maccoby 1970), is a much neglected classic in the history of social psychology.[1]

During his immersion in Mexican culture, Fromm continued to live and teach for three months a year in the United States. For most of this time, he stayed in New York, but he also spoke and taught for brief periods all around the country. This was the time of Fromm's greatest fame and popularity, and he used his reputation to further the causes of nuclear disarmament, civil rights, and, in due course, the anti–Vietnam War movement.

In 1967, after a hectic odyssey of public speaking engagements in the United States, Fromm succumbed to a heart attack, and began to withdraw from public life. In 1968, his popularity slowly began to wane, as the rise of the counterculture and the New Left brought many new ideologues into the limelight—among them, his old adversary Marcuse. Nevertheless, in 1969, he began work on his *The Anatomy of Human Destructiveness* (1973), a massive and engrossing study that wove his clinical, sociological, and philosophical erudition together with recent findings in genetics, ethology, and neurophysiology. And at around this time, Fromm began to study Theravada Buddhism, and to cultivate a correspondence with one of its greatest living exponents, Nyanaponika Mahathera.

To Have or To Be?, published in 1976, was Fromm's last effort to synthesize the psychoanalytic and spiritual traditions that informed his work with the kind of humanistic social criticism that characterized *The Sane Society* (1955).

Greatness and Limitations of Freud's Thought, published in
1980, shortly before his death in Locarno, is a testament to
Fromm's creative ambivalence toward Freud. On the one
hand, Fromm is unsparing in his criticism of Freud's
mechanistic materialism, his muddled metapsychology
and theory of the instincts, his incorrigible sexism, and his
authoritarian tendency to turn psychoanalysis into a set of
dogmatic precepts, rather than an open and evolving field
of inquiry.

On the other hand, his veneration for Freud is also plain
throughout, and evidenced, among other things, in his
lifelong project of distilling and expanding the essential
core of Freud's thought, which he regarded as humanistic,
while discarding those elements that are reductionistic,
parochial, or outdated. This attitude of Fromm's, which I
call "Freud piety," not only estranged him from many
anti-Freudian thinkers and theorists, it also created fric-
tion in his relations with Sullivan and Horney. As a result,
to the end of his life Fromm was deeply displeased with
the "neo-Freudian" or "cultural school" labels that were
used to group him and his former associates together, and
took every opportunity of reminding readers that he felt
much closer to Freud than they did.

Fromm's attitude toward Karl Marx was more forgiving,
and less realistic than his relationship to Freud. While his
basic attitude toward Freud never wavered, despite shifts
in emphasis over the years, his attitude toward Marx
became decidedly *less* critical with the passage of time. In
The Sane Society (1955), for example, where Fromm introduced the concept of alienation as a major social problem
in the industrialized world, Fromm drew up an illuminating catalogue of Marx's errors and oversights, and
drew attention to authoritarian features of Marx's personality and leadership style that fostered the emergence of
Leninism and Stalinism later on. His assessment here was

quite sound. However, in *Marx's Concept of Man* (1961), Fromm shifted the blame for subsequent developments entirely off of Marx's shoulders, and like Trotsky, faulted others for the alleged distortions and deviations from Marx's original message.

Still, *Marx's Concept of Man* was a timely and important book, which fostered a revival of socialist humanism in North America and around the world. It contributed enormously to the burgeoning literature on alienation—an idea first thematized in Hegel's *The Phenomenology of Spirit*, and developed systematically by Feuerbach and by Marx in the *Economic and Philosophic Manuscripts of 1844*. Borrowing from the early, humanistic Marx, Fromm noted that the way in which we are constrained to fulfill our material needs and aspirations in a competitive, materialistic, and technologically dominated society is often profoundly at odds with our *existential needs* for self-actualization and solidarity with other human beings. This socially patterned discrepancy, which is seldom fully conscious, gives rise to the frequent violation and eventual constriction of our "humanistic conscience," resulting in many varieties of anguish and self-estrangement.

Because of Fromm's vast and varied readership, his deep and extensive erudition in philosophy and sociology, and his curious reticence on clinical matters, it is frequently forgotten that he was a dedicated and capable analytic clinician with a compelling theoretical vision. Accordingly, the authors in this volume are committed to demonstrating the applicability of his ideas to a wide range of clinical syndromes and problems, and getting dialogue and debate on Fromm's contributions started again. This may not be easy, of course. Many of Fromm's ideas have been assimilated into the analytic mainstream without due acknowledgment, chief among them being the realization that narcissism generally betokens an absence of genuine self-love, and that real self-love and the love of others are conjunctive, and not opposed, as Freud supposed on the basis of his libido theory (Fromm 1947). Indeed, many clinicians use or make reference to Frommian themes and ideas without being the least bit aware of that fact!

An old adage has it that imitation is the sincerest form of flattery. And while this may be taken as an indirect measure of success, this strange development also fosters a deeper tendency to neglect, since few of those who fall into this category are motivated enough to study Fromm's work with the effort and seriousness he deserves. Fromm was not a benign optimist or a Pollyanna, as many of his critics allege. On the contrary, he was always alert to the tragic dimension of human life—to the inevitability of death, and the fact that no one, however fortunate or favored, ever realizes his or her full human potential. Nevertheless, despite his diminished energy and hopefulness as the end drew near, he always lived and worked in the name of Life, and would wish to be remembered that way.

ENDNOTE

1. Editor's Note: *Social Character in a Mexican Village*, presently out-of-print, will be re-issued in 1996 by Transaction in Rutgers, NJ.

REFERENCES

Burston, D. (1991). *The Legacy of Erich Fromm*. Cambridge, MA: Harvard University Press.
Eros, F. (1992). Wilhelm Reich, Erich Fromm, and the analytical psychology of the Frankfurt School. In *Erich Fromm und die*

Frankfurter Schule, ed. M. Kessler, and R. Funk. Tubingen, Germany: Francke Verlag.

Fromm, E. (1947). *Man for Himself*. Greenwich, CT: Fawcett Premier.

——— (1955). *The Sane Society*. Greenwich, CT: Fawcett Premier.

——— (1961). *Marx's Concept of Man*. New York: Frederick Ungar.

——— (1962). *Beyond the Chains of Illusion*. New York: Simon & Schuster.

——— (1973). *The Anatomy of Human Destructiveness*. Greenwich, CT: Fawcett Premier.

——— (1976). *To Have or To Be?* New York: Harper & Row.

——— (1980). *Greatness and Limitations of Freud's Thought*. New York: Harper & Row.

——— (1984). *The Working Class in Weimar Germany*. Cambridge, MA: Harvard University Press.

Fromm, E., and Maccoby, M. (1970). *Social Character in a Mexican Village*. Englewood Cliffs, NJ: Prentice-Hall.

Funk, R. (1983). *Erich Fromm*. Hamburg: Rowohlt Taschenbuch Verlag.

Jacoby, R. (1983). *The Repression of Psychoanalysis*. New York: Basic Books.

Jay, M. (1973). *The Dialectical Imagination*. Boston: Beacon.

17

Erich Fromm's Courage

Paul Roazen

The duty of an intellectual, as I understand it, entails a commitment to resisting power. This principle amounts to the proposition that it behooves freethinkers to oppose, as a matter of principle, whatever current fashions might dictate. It has always appalled me how, both in academic life as well as in the outside world, most people seem so apt to worship blindly that which is currently established. This sort of enslavement may make some sort of sense for those who stand to gain, in terms of self-interest, by following the dominant trends in society. But for individuals who are supposed to be devoted to the life of the mind, endorsing any aspects of the status quo amounts to a special sort of degradation. Intellectual life, as I see it, is a secularized priestly calling. And therefore I treasure such programmatic statements as can be found in books like Julien Benda's *The Betrayal of the Intellectuals*, or

Raymond Aron's *The Opium of the Intellectuals*. And while I think that Fromm would doubtless have been unhappy, on political grounds, for me to link him with Aron's work, since Aron directed his polemic at the way Marxism could attract so many otherwise highly cultivated French thinkers, what I have to say would seem to me in keeping with the dominant thrust of what I take to be the essential spirit of Fromm's teachings.

Although many of my writings have been about Freud and those thinkers who considered themselves loyal to the movement he started, I have also been especially concerned with the fate of the analysts who were stigmatized as so-called deviants. Freud made no bones about calling both Alfred Adler and Carl Jung, for example, "heretics." In light-hearted moments Freud found no difficulty, despite all his proclamations as a scientist, in likening himself to the Pope, even if he surely knew that his was a new Church, one that was explicitly opposed to traditional religions. Fromm makes an interesting exception to most generalizations connected with alleged dissidents from the mainstream of psychoanalysis. For on the one hand, like others who have caused trouble for the prevailing powers-that-be in psychoanalysis, Fromm insisted that he was singularly faithful to the true meaning of Freud's message; Fromm thought he was genuinely psychoanalytic while he believed those who invoked Freud's legacy, within the International Psychoanalytic Association and its affiliates, for example, were actually false to the truest implications of Freud's heritage. At the same time Fromm took some pains to distance himself, for example, from Jung, Freud's most notorious enemy, who founded a dissident school of analysis. And yet Fromm became, in his own lifetime, one of those underdogs whom I think it should be the job of intellectuals to accord special credit for the kind of accomplishments he was able to achieve.

In my own adulthood Fromm's reputation has under-
gone a dramatic change. It was while I was taking a
government department honors tutorial at Harvard College in my sophomore year, 1955–56, that I first read
Fromm's *Escape from Freedom*. At that time nobody could
be considered well educated in the social sciences without
having absorbed Fromm's argument in that text and I
think that *Escape from Freedom* remains a momentous
contribution in twentieth century intellectual life. The
commercial success the book had must have done much, I
suppose, to have offended some of Fromm's former allies
at the Frankfurt school of critical sociology, which had
moved to New York City temporarily during World War
II, since they were less successful than Fromm in being
able to articulate an argument that could appeal to the
broad reading public.

Like others, such as today's most resolutely systematic
popularizing defender of Freudian orthodoxy, Peter Gay,
I was initially attracted to psychoanalysis by Fromm's
writings. As far as I can recall, I was reading Fromm's
many books long before I studiously set out to read Freud
himself, although I had been assigned Freud's *Civilization
and Its Discontents* (1930) in my first year as an undergrad-
uate in an introduction course to political philosophy. At
one time I could be certain that I had read everything by
Fromm, at least all that had been translated into English.
I whisked through his book *Sigmund Freud's Mission* when
it first came out in 1959, although I am afraid at the time I
did not believe some of his critique of Freud. My skepticism about Fromm's argument, I hope, can be traced to the
way in which, as the years passed, Fromm was increasingly tempted to make Marx into a hero (Fromm 1961),
while I had always been dubious about Marx's standing in
Western thought. Max Weber, and in particular his *Protestant Ethic and the Spirit of Capitalism*, had an early appeal

to me because of his insistence on the independent force of religious ideas, and in general the power of the mind to affect the course of history. Marx's insistence on the inevitability of class struggle seemed to me alien to the world as I had experienced it, and then Fromm appeared bent on humanizing some of Marxism's most revolutionary features.

Although I was dubious about parts of the thesis in *Sigmund Freud's Mission*, it was not long before I began reading for myself Ernest Jones's three volume biography of Freud. At the time, the early 1960s, Jones's detailed account of Freud's life and ideas seemed enormously seductive, and hard to challenge. Jones constructed an edifice that has attracted many besides myself, and Jones, an expert in power-seeking, knew the force that historical legend could exert. I later found out that some famous orthodox analysts, in New York City for instance, were grateful to the successful political act that Jones had accomplished through his biography.

It took me some time to appreciate the central weaknesses in Jones's approach. An orthodox analyst like Robert Waelder (1963) had known enough to wade in and write an article against Fromm's *Sigmund Freud's Mission*. Jones's saga, in the meantime, appeared incontrovertible. It was only when I undertook to do my own interviewing, in the mid-1960s, of those people still living who had had personal contact with Freud, that the blinders I had once had started to dissipate, and I could absorb the full merits of Fromm's position about Freud. By the time Fromm sent me a personally inscribed copy of *Sigmund Freud's Mission*, with an acknowledgement of what I had accomplished with my 1969 *Brother Animal: The Story of Freud and Tausk* (Roazen 1990a), I understood how successful Fromm had been so early on in pulling the rug out from under Jones's version of Freud.

When I met Fromm in 1966, he was a relatively isolated figure within the world of psychoanalysis. It was paradoxical that it was in the radical days of the late 1960s that Fromm's reputation among North American intellectuals began its serious slump. The more successful Fromm became in running rings around official psychoanalysis and the better he was able to appeal to general readers, the easier it became to write him off as a popular preacher, a psychoanalytic Norman Vincent Peale.

In the hindsight appropriate to the history of ideas, Fromm deserves full acknowledgment for being one of the earliest to have raised some of the key, even if elementary-seeming, questions about Freud's work. Fromm undertook a psychoanalytic exploration of Freud's life, in the course of his short text on Freud's "mission"; Jones, with all his invaluable documentary material, had been able to evade an objective appraisal of Freud's psyche. Fromm, for example, asked some deep questions about Freud's relation to his mother, a subject that has still received an inadequate amount of attention in the vast literature about the creator of psychoanalysis. I doubt that Fromm knew some of the minutiae about Freud's life, for example that he had failed to attend his mother's funeral in Vienna and had stayed home that day writing letters; Freud sent his daughter Anna to the ceremony as his "representative," just as she had gone to Frankfurt to accept the Goethe Prize in Freud's behalf. Freud was also late for his father's funeral, another detail I suspect Fromm may have ignored; but Fromm had the brains to detect that Freud's complex tie to his mother was something that Jones neglected to explore, even though that key relationship necessarily had to be an essential constituent of Freud's whole psychology.

Fromm's courage seems to me the most obvious attribute of his contribution. The large number of Fromm's

works that are in print around the world indicates that
Fromm's courage has paid off. In contrast, Erik H. Erikson, an analyst who was terribly fearful of being excom-
municated from the movement and temperamentally
given to having only the most elusive confrontations with
Freud, has not fared nearly as well with the general
population. Erikson was enormously talented as a psychologist (Roazen 1975, 1976a,b, 1980, 1992c). And yet the
cautious way Erikson expressed himself, with the ex-
quisite care he took in distinguishing his own work from
Freud's, meant that Erikson has been in a slump of his
own in recent times. Erikson was determined not to have
his own work associated with that of Fromm, despite the
similarities in their using social science as a corrective to
Freud's framework, and Erikson would have been unhappy to have been mentioned in association with
Fromm. But Fromm's outspokenness, and the courage he
showed in constructing his own theoretical system, has
meant that his writings are today accessible, in Spanish,
Italian, German, and French, as well as in English, in a
way that Erikson's books are not.

By the time I met Fromm in 1966 he was seemingly
detached from the outside world. When I traveled to see
him, he was not even available in México City, and I went
to visit him in Cuernavaca. Yet millions of people are still
reading his works today; no other psychoanalyst's writings, around the world, are still as accessible to airport
bookstore browsers. And yet these books are studied not
as class assignments in schools or training institutes; nor
does Fromm's audience depend on whatever prestige may
be associated with lining office bookshelves with "official"
authors—that explains why so many psychoanalytic texts
are bought even if they remain unread. Furthermore,
Fromm's capacity to achieve his success, such that it has
been outside of most official psychoanalytic circles, is all

the more remarkable in that he was for the most part not writing in his native language.

At the time I met Fromm, vicious stories were circulating about him in North America. One famous neo-Freudian analyst in New York City said that Fromm was then inhabiting a palace carved out of stone outside México City. In fact Fromm lived in circumstances that were modest, certainly as compared with the lavish Park Avenue apartment my informant enjoyed. One relatively emancipated Toronto analyst, who at the time was probably earning about 300,000 Canadian dollars a year thanks to a lavish provincial insurance system that subsidized analysis for an unlimited amount of time, not only thought of Fromm as immensely rich, but also maintained that Fromm was "quietly going mad" in México.

Today psychoanalysis in North America has long since been eclipsed by the many advances that have taken place in so-called biological psychiatry. If I were a young man now, instead of being as concerned about the abuses of power within psychoanalysis as I was then, I would probably be making a study of contemporary psychiatrists, for, with a naive commitment to the possibility of making exact-sounding diagnoses, they are capable of perpetrating the kinds of misuse of scientistic authority that took place around the turn of the century before Freud's revolution in ideas got under way.

Fromm's interest in asking the most fundamental questions, and his conviction that Freud had not been radical enough, meant that Fromm was able, starting in the 1930s, to tease out some of the central moral and philosophic bases of Freud's outlook. Fromm was shrewd as a Marxist in spotting the middle class liberal premises Freud took for granted. At the same time Fromm shared Freud's belief, especially as expressed in Freud's post-1923 cancer-ridden phase, that psychoanalysis had succeeded in attaining the status of being a neutral scientific body of knowledge. We now know that despite Freud's protests about being compared with traditional philosophers, even as a young man he was far better acquainted with philosophy, and more sophisticated, than one might have imagined. I am told that in Freud's library in London there is a book of Kant's with Freud's marginalia in it, despite the fact that there is scarcely even now, with all that has been written about Freud, anything to speak of about his links with someone like Kant.

Fromm's special contribution as a psychologist was to be concerned with understanding the social forces that both stabilize as well as undermine society. Freud had looked on society chiefly as the individual's enemy. But Fromm was interested in the problem of social change, and how such sociological issues can be understood in the light of depth psychology. Fromm's concern here was not just a theoretical one, although his abstract contributions as a thinker were remarkable. For in his last years he helped coauthor a fascinating study of Mexican peasantry, *Social Character in A Mexican Village* (Fromm and Maccoby 1970), which shows how Fromm was able to think through concrete problems afresh. His posthumously published *The Working Class in Weimar Germany*, which only appeared in English in 1984, illustrates how he had always possessed an empirical dimension to his thinking, even though he has so often been accused of merely being a moralist. Freud too had a rabbi's voice in him, but had a way of camouflaging it so that at least for a time in North America the intelligentsia swallowed the line that he was primarily a scientist.

Fromm naturally had his predecessors within psychoanalysis, and Wilhelm Reich may be perhaps the most notable among those who tried to unite Marxist and Freudian thinking. Reich has, however, because of his unfortunate last years, tended to be almost eliminated from the orthodox history of the development of Freudian thinking. As in Stalinist historiography, which rewrote the past to exclude the contributions of someone like Trotsky, so Reich's key role within the Vienna Psychoanalytic Society has been obscured by simply omitting to mention his work or even his name (Roazen 1990b). Reich's attack on the role of patriarchal family structure in mobilizing oedipal reactions, and his yearnings for a utopian society in which the worst constraints of middle class family life would be lifted, so that a new and nonneurotic humanity might arise, seemed serious enough for Freud to have sat down to write *Civilization and Its Discontents* as a warning against Reich's sort of thinking.

Fromm's reputation has suffered from different sources than those that have undermined Reich's contributions, which include notable work by Reich on negative transferences, the role of nonverbal communications, and the problem of so-called technique in psychoanalytic therapy. Orthodox Freudians not only succeeded in wiping Reich off the map of the history of modern psychology, but they nearly managed to efface Fromm's work as well. Once Fromm was dead, it no longer seemed necessary to carry on diatribes against him; but I was amazed, for instance, when my collection *Sigmund Freud* (Roazen 1987) first appeared in 1973, containing an article by Fromm, how much of the review in the *International Journal of Psycho-Analysis* was taken up with an assault on Fromm.

After Fromm's death in 1980 he necessarily became less menacing to orthodoxy. Certain psychoanalytic journals, which have been known to reject advertisements for books by "deviants," now began to accept money from publishers of Fromm's books. Thanks to the feminist movement, and a reconsideration of Freud's alleged ideas about female psychology, Karen Horney's works crept back into the bibliographies of papers that appear in official psychoanalytic quarterlies. It may still be the case that it would be unwise, if one is to get a paper accepted by an orthodox psychoanalytic journal, to list too many citations to the works of someone like Jacques Lacan, but then he is a current-day danger, and his followers still a threat to the International Psychoanalytic Association, whereas Horney is no longer deemed such a terrible problem.

Fromm's standing has suffered not just from the most fanatical Freudians, but there are other modern Ayatollahs as well in Fromm's case, die-hard Marxist hardliners have been determined to dismiss Fromm as a so-called social democrat. In certain circles such a designation is as damning as it would be for someone to be called a Jungian in the New York Psychoanalytic Society, or to acknowledge an indebtedness to Franz Alexander in Chicago. The school of self psychology, initiated by Heinz Kohut, came to be deemed by Anna Freud as antipsychoanalytic; but Kohut, one of the leaders in trying to thaw out the rigidities of classical analysis, would have shied away from being linked with the dissidence of either Jung or Alexander. Fromm had to deal with the same sort of sectarianism not only within psychoanalysis, but from embattled Marxists as well. It is still true in Canada, for example, that the standing of Theodor Adorno, who disapproved of his former ally Fromm, rides high; and Adorno's friend Herbert Marcuse published a famous critique of Fromm. Despite Fromm's (1958) telling response to Marcuse's failure to understand the therapeutic side of Freudian thinking, Fromm's rebuttal of Marcuse's indictment has still not attained the currency it deserves (Howe 1958, Roazen 1987).

Fromm, when I saw him, acknowledged that at one

point he had himself been an orthodox Freudian, although his withdrawal from that sort of thinking was unclouded by any problems with Freud personally, since Fromm had had no contact with Freud. Nonetheless it is hard to believe that Fromm could easily forget how his *Escape from Freedom* had once been denounced as a betrayal—all hell broke loose over his innovating ideas. Karl Menninger, who wrote a blistering review of the book, tried to maintain in his last years that he could not remember what could have separated him from neo-Freudians like Horney, and Menninger even tried to cover his tracks by writing flatteringly to Thomas Szasz. (The kind of hatred Szasz could inspire took even Marcuse's breath away.) But Menninger had, on the appearance of *Escape from Freedom*, done his best to discredit Fromm publicly. Horney, along with Fromm, Harry Stack Sullivan, and Clara Thompson, formed the psychoanalytic Left; people like Abram Kardiner, Sandor Rado, and Alexander were on the identical side of the antiestablishmentarian fence.

But left-wingers are notoriously difficult to hold together organizationally, and each of these people tended unnecessarily to differentiate their own publications from those of others. I suppose it is the fate of brave pioneers to have special difficulty in hanging together. Still, it is appalling in retrospect to find Alexander criticizing Horney; and Fromm himself, who may well have later regretted tarring Otto Rank's use of "will" with fascism, looks from a Rankian perspective now as someone who did not hesitate on occasion to stoop to conquer.

Had Fromm ever functioned as part of a prestigious research university, his work would never have been as underrated as it is now; this attractive hypothesis has been advanced by as acute an observer as David Riesman.

Yet although Fromm was outside the mainstream, and in her lifetime Helene Deutsch was very much a part of it, both of them were capable of taking the identical view of the writings of Otto Fenichel. Deutsch told me she thought Fenichel's famous textbook was the "cancer" of psychoanalysis, and Fromm too thought that Fenichel, one of his opponents over *Escape from Freedom*, engaged in a kind of obsessive theorizing that meant the end of psychoanalysis.

Fromm in his lifetime was notable for his not being afraid to be alone, even in the face of the worst threats of heresy-hunting. And he generalized about how difficult it was for most people to risk his own kind of solitude. Fromm told me that he had had a "brief" orthodox phase, from about 1926 until 1935; yet if one examines some of his papers in the early 1930s the seeds of later ideological trouble are already discernible. When I talked with Fromm, I tried to press him to elucidate in writing what the implications of his ideas were for practical issues connected with the conduct of psychoanalytic therapy. Fromm said he was going to do a book-length work on the matter, but never fulfilled that objective.

Freud, too, had not wanted to write much about technique, and I think only got into the subject in order to differentiate his approach from that of Adler and Jung (Roazen 1975, 1992a). Students have an excessive need for certainty and leap at every chance to be given rules and guidelines. Freud had not initiated the idea of training analyses; that represents a contribution of Jung, who doubtless thought that Freud's lack of being personally analyzed helped account for the kinds of troubles Jung had had with him. Only after Freud was already sick did didactic analysis become standard training for future analysts, even if in Paris today there are prominent analysts who want to do away with the practice of training analyses. Lacan's seemingly arbitrary ways of proceeding in certifying people as analysts is not really so different from

Freud's own habit of personally anointing those to be sanctioned within the profession as qualified to treat patients. (For all the Lacanian interest in experimenting with time, little seems to be remembered about what Alexander had to say on the subject; nor was Alexander aware of how much he owed to Jung, although heresy-hunters would have been delighted to associate Alexander with the Jungian "deviation.")

Before almost anyone else, Jung had gone to some lengths to show why the use of the couch had authoritarian implications; yet few in Paris today, for example, seem aware of the possible drawbacks to its therapeutic use. Fromm told me that he simply thought that the couch was not "helpful," and he preferred having the patient sit in a chair. The problem with the couch, according to Fromm, is that "nothing happens" therapeutically, and here Fromm turned to discuss his own "unsuccessful" analysis with Hans Sachs. Fromm never mentioned to me any other analysis that he underwent except that one with Sachs, although one researcher has now concluded that Fromm had something of a record in having had some four other analysts (Haynal and Falzeder 1994).

Fromm thought that Sachs had excelled in making "ludicrous" interpretations. (Helene Deutsch told me she thought Sachs was a poor therapist; she readily acknowledged how many of his analysands seemed to appreciate him, but she felt it was apt to be at the expense of their relationship toward Freud.) Fromm said he was obliged by the injunction to free associate to be "conscientious," and expressed from the couch just what sort of animal (a pig) Sachs reminded him of. Actually, Fromm said, Sachs bore more exact resemblance to an owl. But Sachs had responded to Fromm's observation by insisting that Fromm's hanging his coat on a peg right beside Sachs's coat belied Fromm's own negative-sounding words. But

Fromm insisted to me that such an interpretation made no sense, since realistically there was nowhere else in the room to put his coat.

Fromm had met Sachs in later years when Sachs was established as the first training analyst in Boston. At that point Sachs had both a servant and a butler, the first butler Fromm had ever seen, or Sachs either according to Fromm. In those days, Sachs had an abundance of Wasp upper-class patients, and Helene Deutsch told me how when she had moved to Boston, becoming the second training analyst there, Sachs had moaned about the difficulty of trying to conduct analysis without using rabbi stories. After about a year, Deutsch ran into him again and asked how he was doing without the rabbi tales; fine, Sachs said, he changed the rabbi into a minister, thereby "baptizing" the jokes. Humor was an essential aspect of Freud's and Fromm's own therapeutic practice, although little is written about this aspect of their therapeutic approaches.

Since I had been trained as a political scientist, and Fromm understood what sort of field work I was then conducting, he encouraged me to try and find out "where the power lay" within the psychoanalytic movement. (Although much has been written about the so-called secret committee around Freud, I do not think he ever yielded the mantle of the authority of psychoanalytic leadership.) Fromm's wife, who sat in on our interviews (and I seem to remember cats wandering around), wondered aloud where on earth the New York analysts had gotten their technique from, since the aim of neutrality and distance seemed so foreign to how Freud himself had proceeded. Her question was an excellent one, which I have thought about a lot. I concluded later that the Americans had come to Vienna in Freud's sick phase, and identified with the relatively distant, detached, dying

Freud. But there was also hypocritical disguising of what Freud had actually been like (Roazen 1990c), and this shared secret became a powerful bond among Freud's loyal disciples.

Fromm, when I saw him, was astonished to hear about the change that had taken place in Anna Freud. He recalled her as a modest, shy, and retiring person, and Fromm seemed to have little idea about the political power she was capable of wielding. He knew that London had been responsible for himself being dropped as a direct member of the International Psychoanalytic Association, but somehow he did not link this expulsion with Anna Freud herself. He correctly perceived that there had been a "court" around Freud, and Fromm wanted to be sure that I found out who were the most important figures there. (Although I have not examined the letters at the Library of Congress between Waelder and Anna Freud, it is a safe bet that his attack on Fromm got directly sent to her.)

Fromm mentioned Freud's mother's dream, which was reported by Lancelot Whyte, about the death of her famous son Sigmund. When I contacted Whyte, he was not certain whether it had been a "dream" of the old woman's or a waking vision; in any event Fromm made the shrewd point that when Freud's mother described how she had visualized the major heads of state of the European countries standing around her eldest son's casket, she was revealing a curious conception of him, and of herself. For how many mothers, and Jewish ones at that, if they had had such a fantasy, would have allowed that calamity to cross their lips? Freud's mother obviously had an image of Freud as a powerful warrior, one that he himself shared; so that when he took the night train to London in 1938, old and sick, still he dreamt that he was arriving at the same place in England as William the

Conqueror in 1066. Fromm had his own prophetic streak, which may have helped sensitize him to this side of Freud. And Fromm also had a special interest in exploring the primal tie to mothers, and how it can be coped with.

From Fromm's point of view, Freud's strongest point had been his "honesty," but I think this is rather harder to discuss than Fromm might have thought. Fromm was after all a representative of old German culture, whereas Freud remained a Viennese to his fingertips. For Viennese, I am convinced, truth-telling was a complex matter, and Austrians rather sneakier than Germans. I am reminded of a story told me by a bookseller in pre–World War II Vienna when in 1938, after the Anschluss, he found that the concierge was flying a Nazi-party flag. This seemed a surprising partisan affiliation, so the concierge then took the Viennese bookseller up to his apartment; he opened a closet that was full of the party flags of every possible political group, from the monarchists to all the left-wing organizations. Whoever had come out on top would have been celebrated with an appropriate flag. One cannot exactly see that as old Viennese dishonesty, since none of them were, by North American standards, straight shooters. Freud could talk out of both sides of his mouth, sending praise to an author while simultaneously asking a disciple to tear the author's book to pieces (Roazen 1992a). Freud's subtle capacities for artistic inventiveness turn up in the way he fashioned his case histories, which is likely to seem to many contemporaries now as falseness and an unscientific example of rhetorical partisanship.

Freud, as Felix Deutsch admitted privately, was a great "fighter," and I think he had a complicated set of weapons at his disposal. Freud's disappointment with Jung meant that he never got over the loss of that most talented of all his students, and as one of Freud's pupils once remarked to me, all Freud's writings have to be understood in the light of the opponents he was trying to rebut. Kurt R. Eissler, like Freud before him, collected a set of his own stated "war plans." And Fromm himself could be embattled. He told me how Jung had been a "destructive" force, and Fromm knew all about the most unfortunate sides of Jung's politics in the 1930s (Roazen 1991).

But as knowledgeable as Fromm could be, he seemed to have little precise information about Jung's private life, or any of the involvements with his patients that we have subsequently learned so much about. Fromm did know exactly who in Switzerland had immediately denounced Jung's collaboration with the Nazis in Germany. One of Jung's enduring contributions, despite his politics, was his interest in being more explicit in linking psychology and philosophy. Here Fromm aimed to be himself more systematic, and Jung, rather similarly to Erikson, was temperamentally, and perhaps culturally, incapable of the kind of theoretical clarity that Fromm was so good at.

I think that what Freud had going for him, and helped him prevail against all his opponents, was not just that he was such a masterful writer, but that he succeeded in getting his own version of events, without contradiction, into the history books. Only years later, for example, long after their historic falling out, did Jung mention in a seminar in the 1920s what had happened between himself and Freud, and that text did not subsequently come into print until 1989 (Jung 1989). Freud had a powerful sense of history, a sense that Fromm also shared, which is what prompted him bravely to contradict Jones's version of Freud. (At that time, when Jones's books were widely being hailed as definitive, only Bettelheim was willing to state publicly that Jones had failed to be properly psycho-

analytic [Roazen 1992b].) Fromm also published a Fore-
word to Helen Puner's 1947 *Sigmund Freud*, a strikingly
prescient early biography (Puner 1992).

My historical work can be seen as fleshing out some
points that Fromm had early on understood on the basis of
his theoretical convictions. As courageous as Fromm had
been in challenging Jones, Fromm was unaware of the
degree of hanky-panky that has afflicted Freud's texts. It
turns out that not only had Freud's letters been tampered
with, at least up until the time I published the unedited
version of Freud's comments to Lou Andreas-Salome after
Tausk's suicide, but even the published versions of
Freud's writings have also been altered, when it suited his
students to do so. It is not only the case that most of
Freud's correspondence has to be republished someday,
but texts now in the Library of Congress indicate that
passages have been cut from papers of Freud's that are
treated as canonical in the professional literature. Readers
should be alerted that unless something appeared in
Freud's lifetime, it is likely that changes have been introduced by his heirs after his death. Freud's letters are now
appearing uncut, starting with the Freud–Jung correspondence in 1974. But we are only now learning about how
his other texts have been tampered with (Grubrich-Simitis
1993). Freud's "Project" for a scientific psychology, his
"Outline of Psychoanalysis," as well as a posthumous
paper on the occult and telepathy all show signs of
dubious editorial practices.

The aim of retranslating all Freud in English, however,
seems to me a hopelessly misguided undertaking; the
French translations of Freud, which are still not complete,
have dragged into his works all sorts of words that have
not been used for centuries. Worse still, purism about
translations, which are inevitably an act of interpretation,
is apt to reinforce the idea that what we have with Freud

is a new gospel. Instead of treating what Freud said as holy writ, it seems to me better to acknowledge that on central points he could be wrong. Here Fromm was one of the most important of Freud's critics, and fixing up translations, and reediting Freud's writings, is not capable of correcting some more central problems — just where Freud could be mistaken.

Fromm stoutly maintained that he himself did not believe in "kowtowing" to free associations. He reported how in Berlin, during the time Fromm was active there, it was commonly discussed how important it could be, from the therapists' point of view, to analyze dreams that analysts had when they fell asleep during sessions with patients. Fromm implied not only that analysts could get bored, but that such nonsense of trying to find the psychological significance in the content of the dreams of delinquent analysts reflected the early conviction that the truth about the patients was already known. Fromm was impressed enough by our encounter for him to tell me that he was eager to hear from me in the future, and over the years we exchanged a number of letters about what I had been finding out.

Unfortunately, it seems that Fromm's own correspondence has by and large disappeared, at least what he kept in his files. Fromm's conviction about preserving his own privacy may deter others from appreciating the stature he genuinely deserves in the full-scale account of the history of psychoanalysis. Kohut and Donald Winnicott, for example, have both had volumes of their letters appear. And Freud himself seems to have had somewhere between 20,000 and 35,000 letters that survived the upheavals of both world wars. Such documents are ready fodder for scholars, and to the extent that we have lost such material in connection with Fromm it is going to be harder to reconstruct his proper role. In Freud's case, for example, it has recently been discovered that there was an early draft of his paper on war and death, in the form of a lecture he gave to B'nai B'rith in Vienna under the title of "Death and Us" (Meghnagi 1993). It is going to take a long time until scholars come anywhere near exhausting the Freud primary sources, and only in the next century is the sealed Freud Archives at the Library of Congress going to be made available for the inspection of neutral scholars. It might be better if scholarship devoted more of its energy to verifying the merits of what someone like Fromm had to say, rather than continuing to track down the intricacies, interesting though they may be, of what we can learn about Freud.

I am convinced that part of Fromm's strength came from a genuine identification that he made with Freud. For Fromm everything in psychology was supposed to be open to question, even if on some points even he may have been too credulous about what Freud had to say. It is one of the critical aspects of the history of psychoanalysis that to be genuinely like Freud means that one has to be independent. But this means that there are penalties to be paid, in that the crossing of trade-union boundaries entails that there are bound to be organizational squabbles. I have found, in some of my recent travels among psychoanalytic groups, that one dividing line has to do with those who read and those who do not; it is imposible to defend oneself against those who do not examine texts, not to mention against people who make no pretense of trying to be fair-minded. If one already holds the key to genuine knowledge, the ideal of toleration makes no sense. Fromm was, I think, being true to the best spirit of Freud as an investigator to the extent that Fromm tried to give expression to what he himself had experienced. That sort of outspokenness should be more important than any allegiance to organizational bodies. But Fromm's kind of independence is bound to come at a price, and not everyone is willing to pay the kind of price he did.

Too many in psychoanalysis have been willing to have twisted thoughts, and unclarified positions, in order to avoid the dangers of heresy. Both Paul Federn and Sandor Ferenczi were so intimidated by the risks of deviancy that their work suffered as a consequence; I wonder how widespread this phenomenon has been. The problem is that each of the many sects that have grown up within psychoanalysis has been relatively unaware of what others have been doing; and therefore it has been hard to establish all the continuities in the history of ideas that the historiography of psychoanalysis should be aware of. It is no genuine tribute to Fromm, however, to try to assimilate his original ideas in the work of subsequent analysts, like the object relations school for instance, since these later people have been able to proceed with the mutual support of one another, running little ideological danger. That ideas might be in style now should not be taken by itself to enhance Fromm's pioneering, since that amounts to insulting him by looking through the wrong end of a telescope.

In my own experience, once I published *Brother Animal* (1990a) there was a special series of attacks on me. This war was felt necessary because my first book, *Freud: Political and Social Thought* (Roazen 1986), had been welcomed by powerful orthodox analysts. When I was interviewing Freud's pupils and patients, I think it was assumed by those I saw that somehow I would ultimately be controllable. Analysts are after all dependent on colleagues for referrals, and the unconscious ways people can be intimidated into conformity ought never to be underestimated. As a student of the history of ideas, with no clinical practice of my own to defend, there were no conceivable practical sanctions, aside from the possibility of hostile reviews, that could be exerted against me. Silence in the face of publications is always an effective device. Although it looked to orthodox Freudians like I had betrayed the "cause" from inside, which helps account for the anger of Eissler and Anna Freud (Roazen 1993), I always felt secure in my own independent course.

Implicit in my approach, as in the work of Fromm, was an ideal of objectivity; although the truth may be impossible to discover, I believe it is essential in all scholarship to proceed as if the standard of truthfulness is the ultimate recourse. Although it is unfashionable in many academic circles today to say this, still I would insist that putting a premium on our own subjective responses can endanger not just the pursuit of research but democracy itself. How I interacted with Fromm personally, and my own educational background, had a profound impact on what I happened to learn from him. I would not doubt that someone else, with a different set of concerns, would have come up with an impression of both him and his work that would be unlike my own. I am also not sure that I can prove that my own version of Fromm is in any sense definitive, and I would certainly be eager to agree that many others, far more knowledgeable about Fromm, are in a better position than I to write about his contribution. Simplistic scientism, the belief among some analysts that causes can be directly linked to effects, needs to yield to a less-linear outlook that concedes the inevitability, and desirability, of allowing more leeway to legitimizing interpretations that are unverifiable.

But I would insist that my own hesitancies, and awareness of how illusory objectivity can be, does not in any way imply that there does not in principle have to be such a thing as truth. A permanent danger of fascism exists in the modern world, and perspectivism or moral relativism, no matter how attractive tolerance for diversity may seem, can be an invitation to the idea that might makes right. Giving up the standard of objective truth, which Fromm refused to do, can lead to deferring to whatever happens to be dominant at any time. Fromm, like other émigrés from Germany, was centrally concerned with the rise of fascism; I would argue that the success of Hitler in overcoming the Weimar republic is the single most important political event in twentieth century history. The Nazi revolution did not take place violently, but Hitler's success occurred within the confines of the preexisting republican political system. The fact that Weimar Germany could self-destruct is an essential part of why Nazism continues to be so troubling a turn of events.

Fascism, however, has many possible sources, some of them stemming from the way intellectuals think. I gather that in later years, long after Fromm wrote that paper against Rank, Fromm had his doubts about reprinting the piece. Anyone like Fromm who witnessed the triumph of the Nazis is perhaps entitled to be supersensitive to ideas that might sound congenial to a Hitlerian point of view. Fromm was right to denounce Jung's collaboration with the Nazis, although Jung's unfortunate antidemocratic politics, not to mention his anti-Semitism and opportunism, does not mean that his psychological thinking cannot still have something vital to teach us. Dostoyevsky was a defender of the Czar and the Orthodox Russian Church, and also anti-Semitic, but that cannot refute his being one of the greatest psychological understanders of all time. The relationship between psychology and politics is a complicated one, and just because a thinker is sound politically, or that we find a figure attractive democratically and socially, does not mean that a profound psychology is necessarily embedded in a theorist's work. Fromm's own critique of American policies at the height of the Cold War (which I did not happen to share) helped

damage his standing among the typically hard-nosed
political scientists who on policy grounds grew to suspect
the author of *Escape from Freedom*. (The extensive FBI
dossier on Fromm is a tribute to how nonsensical J. Edgar
Hoover could be.)

Even though I would have disagreed with Fromm
politically, he has something to teach us about the dangers
of all sorts of collaboration. He was highly critical of
Erikson's ego psychology, on the grounds that it embodied an implicit sort of conformism; and to some extent
Fromm was right about Erikson, although I learned a lot
myself from contact with him. In university life right now
in North America we are, I think, being swept up by a
dangerous form of righteousness, called political correct-
ness, which is a movement I consider seriously at odds
with the ideals of the objective search for truth. Hannah
Arendt and Karl Jaspers wrote to each other about what
they considered the collapse of German universities at the
beginning of the Nazi regime (Arendt and Jaspers 1992). I
only wish it were easier to be brave within today's
university pressures, and to insist on the significance of
merit alone as opposed to all the nonacademic criteria that
are being imposed on us. It is one thing to have courage
within psychoanalysis, when I remain an outsider to the
field; but I concede it is a lot harder, as a member of
academic life, to assert the priorities of merit that are so
precious to the life of the mind.

Although these observations about contemporary academic life may seem a digression, I admit that courage is
harder to come by than may seem to be the case, and that
Fromm is to be commended for the risks he took, which
after all involved not just his livelihood but the conge-
niality and support of traditional colleagues. I hope he
found sources of sustenance in México. It still seems to me
remarkable how he was willing to stand up for what he

believed in, as he could tolerate a kind of isolation that surely was not always easy to bear. He should be a model of independence and autonomy for us all.

One can hope that intolerance among the Left in psychoanalysis can be minimized; for it is those people, not the mainstream, who have had all the new ideas, although it is hard to detect which currently fashionable ideas are to be attributed to identifiable earlier thinkers. How many Kohutians, for example, would feel comfortable with considering what Jung wrote about the self and processes of individuation, and yet why should that lineage cause so much concern? Donald Winnicott happily went about distinguishing the "true" self from the "false" one, even though any such philosophical-sounding talk would doubtless have offended Freud. Originality should not require a certified pedigree within psychoanalysis; some of the most interesting new thoughts have come from people whose names are apt to be anathema to orthodox analysts. I would be in favor of doing the best work one can, and claim Fromm's example even where he might have disagreed with the specific conclusions.

In the history of psychoanalysis, it is too often the case that earlier figures get forgotten. Whenever I have been on a Ph.D. board and met Marxists, I have always tried to ask some questions about Marx's enemy Mikkel Bakunin. Because Marx won and Bakunin lost, within the struggles of the First International, says nothing about the merits of the points that each of them had to make. I was originally attracted to psychoanalysis because of the way in which its respect for failure was at odds with political science's tendency to glorify success. Whatever Freud's personal snobberies might have been, his system of thought paid the greatest respect to those parts of us that malfunction. In keeping with Freud's original standing as an outsider, it is striking how much of an uphill struggle it has been to establish the legitimate role that Fromm has played in the history of psychoanalysis; but that only makes me think that rectifying the situation, and paying him his due honor, is especially incumbent on us. Whatever legitimate disagreements there ought to be about what Fromm's legacy adds up to, I think few can deny that his responsible outspokenness, which I have called courage, should be a special beacon for us all.

REFERENCES

Arendt, H., and Jaspers, K. (1992). *Correspondence 1926-1969*. ed. L. Kohler, and H. Saner, trans. R. Kimber and R. Kimber. New York: Harcourt Brace.
Aron, R. (1957). *The Opium of the Intellectuals*. London: Secxer & Warburg.
Benda, J. (1955). *The Betrayal of the Intellectuals*. Boston: Beacon.
Frend, S. (1930). Civilization and its discontents. *Standard Edition* 21:59-195.
Fromm, E. (1941). *Escape from Freedom*. New York: Farrar & Rinehart.
_____ (1958). The human implications of instinctivistic "radicalism." In *Voices of Dissent*, ed. I. Howe, pp. 313-320. New York: Grove.
_____ (1959). *Sigmund Freud's Mission*. New York: Harper Colophon Books.
_____ (1961). *Marx's Concept of Man*. New York: Frederick Ungar.
_____ (1984). *The Working Class in Weimar Germany: A Psychological and Sociological Study*, ed. W. Bonss, trans. B. Weinberger. Cambridge, MA: Harvard University Press.
Fromm, E., and Maccoby, M. (1970). *Social Character in a Mexican Village*. Englewood Cliffs, NJ: Prentice-Hall.
Grubrich-Simitis, I. (1993). *Zuruck zu Freuds Texten*. Frankfurt: Fischer.
Haynal, A., and Falzeder, E. eds. (1994). *One Hundred Years of Psychoanalysis*. London: Karnac.

Howe, I. (1958). *Voices of Dissent*. New York: Grove.

Jung, C. G. (1989). *Analytical Psychology*, ed. W. McGuire. Princeton, NJ: Princeton University Press.

Meghnagi, D., ed. (1993). *Freud and Judaism*. London: Karnac.

Puner, H. W. (1992). *Sigmund Freud: His Life and Mind*, 2nd ed. New Brunswick, NJ: Transaction.

Roazen, P. (1975). Psychology and politics: the case of Erik H. Erikson. *The Human Context* 7:579–584.

———— (1976a). Psychohistorian as mythologist. *Reviews in European History*, September, pp. 457–465.

———— (1976b). *Erik H. Erikson: The Power and Limits of a Vision*. New York: Free Press.

———— (1980). Erik H. Erikson's America: the political implications of ego psychology. *Journal of the History of the Behavioral Sciences* 16:333–341.

———— (1986). *Freud: Political and Social Thought*, 2nd ed. New York: Da Capo.

————, ed. (1987). *Sigmund Freud*, 2nd ed. New York: Da Capo.

———— (1990a). *Brother Animal: The Story of Freud and Tausk*, 2nd ed. New Brunswick, NJ: Transaction.

———— (1990b). Book review of Peter Gay's *Freud: A Life for Our Time*. *Psychoanalytic Books*, January, pp. 10–17.

———— (1990c). *Encountering Freud: The Politics and Histories of Psychoanalysis*. New Brunswick, NJ: Transaction.

———— (1991). Jung and anti-Semitism. In *Lingering Shadows: Jungians, Freudians, and Anti-Semitism*, ed. A. Maidenbaum, and S. A. Martin, pp. 211–221. Boston: Shambhala.

———— (1992a). *Freud and His Followers*, 2nd ed. New York: Da Capo.

———— (1992b). The rise and fall of Bruno Bettelheim. *Psychohistory Review* Spring:221–250.

———— (1992c). Erik H. Erikson as a teacher. *Michigan Quarterly Review* Winter:19–33.

———— (1993). *Meeting Freud's Family*. Amherst: University of Massachusetts Press.

Waelder, R. (1963). Historical Fiction. *Journal of the American Psychoanalytic Association* 11:628–51.

Index